Portraits with
PROCREATE

A Beginner's Guide to Drawing and Painting Faces

Written, illustrated, and designed by Melissa de Nobrega

Portraits with Procreate
A Beginner's Guide to Drawing and Painting Faces
Melissa de Nobrega
www.makebetter.art

Project editor: Maggie Yates
Project manager: Lisa Brazieal
Marketing coordinator: Katie Walker
Copyeditor: Maggie Yates
Layout: Melissa de Nobrega
Cover design: Melissa de Nobrega

ISBN: 979-8-88814-037-6
1st Edition (1st printing, May 2024)
© 2024 Melissa de Nobrega
Images © Melissa de Nobrega, with additional imagery and icons used under license from shutterstock.com, istockphoto.com, reference.pictures, pexels.com, unsplash.com, and thenounproject.com

Rocky Nook Inc.
1010 B Street, Suite 350
San Rafael, CA 94901
USA

www.rockynook.com

Distributed in the UK and Europe by Publishers Group UK
Distributed in the U.S. and all other territories by Publishers Group West

Library of Congress Control Number: 2023934961

Printed in China

Dear Artist,

It's been my pleasure to create this book for you.

I hope that what I've shared in these pages helps you on your journey to art-making mastery.

If you ever get stuck or frustrated, just remember that it's all part of the process. Take frequent breaks and be kind to yourself.

—Melissa

CONTENTS

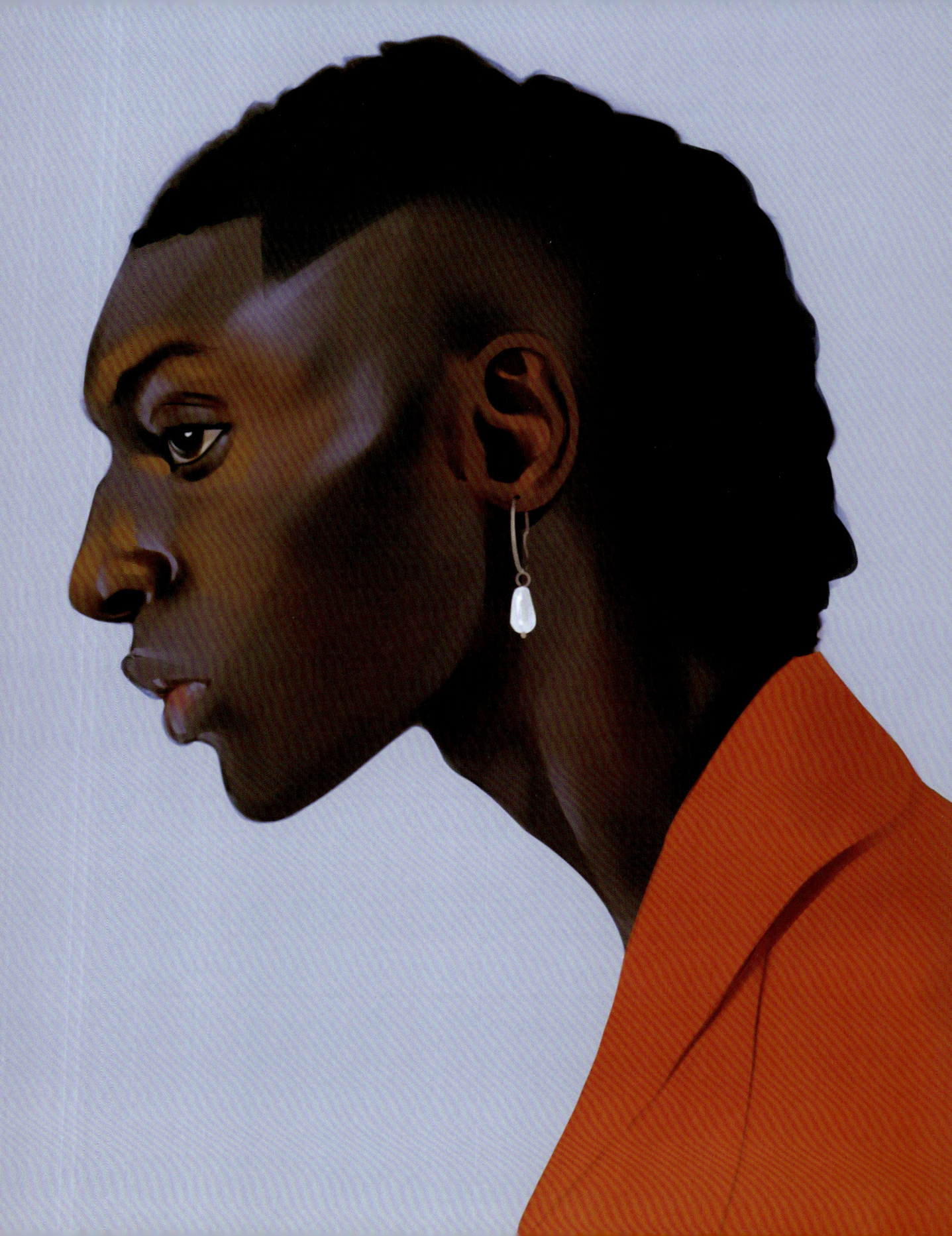

HOW TO USE THIS BOOK

This book is organized into different sections for your convenience. Read through it linearly or skip ahead to the chapters of your choice.

The first part of this book contains a walkthrough of the basics of Procreate. If you have some familiarity with its gesture controls and interface, then it's perfectly reasonable for you to skip ahead to the juicy bits (simply use this section as reference instead). If, however, you're completely new to Procreate, then I recommend reading through the full introduction to get the basics of the program. It'll help you follow the tutorials in the later chapters much more easily.

When it comes to the subject of portraiture, I find that it's best to have at least a basic understanding of the anatomy of the human head when painting. Once you understand the underlying forms of the human body, you'll be able to more accurately render them in your paintings. Therefore, your next stop after the Procreate walkthrough is dedicated to anatomy.

In the anatomy chapter, I'll give you individual rundowns of the anatomy of the eyes, nose, mouth, and ears.

Finally, the later chapters will cover sketching and painting in the Procreate app, step-by-step. I'll include my own personal tips, tricks, and preferences for you to learn along the way.

To get the most out of this book, I would recommend reading through it in a linear fashion. I've organized it in a way that allows you to pick up the fundamentals and then move on to making artwork.

When it comes to getting better at art, practice is the number one thing that increases skill—so don't just read through the book, grab your Apple Pencil and Procreate, and start sketching along! Copying is a fantastic way to solidify newfound knowledge.

WHAT IS PROCREATE?

Procreate is a powerful iOS app that allows artists to make digital artwork using their iPad and Apple Pencil.

Not only s Procreate extremely travel-friendly, but it offers a different, more tactile experience than that of a traditional tablet and desktop combination. Procreate supports a variety of gestures, allowing artists to pinch, scrub, and interact with the canvas using their fingers—you can even finger paint instead of using a stylus!

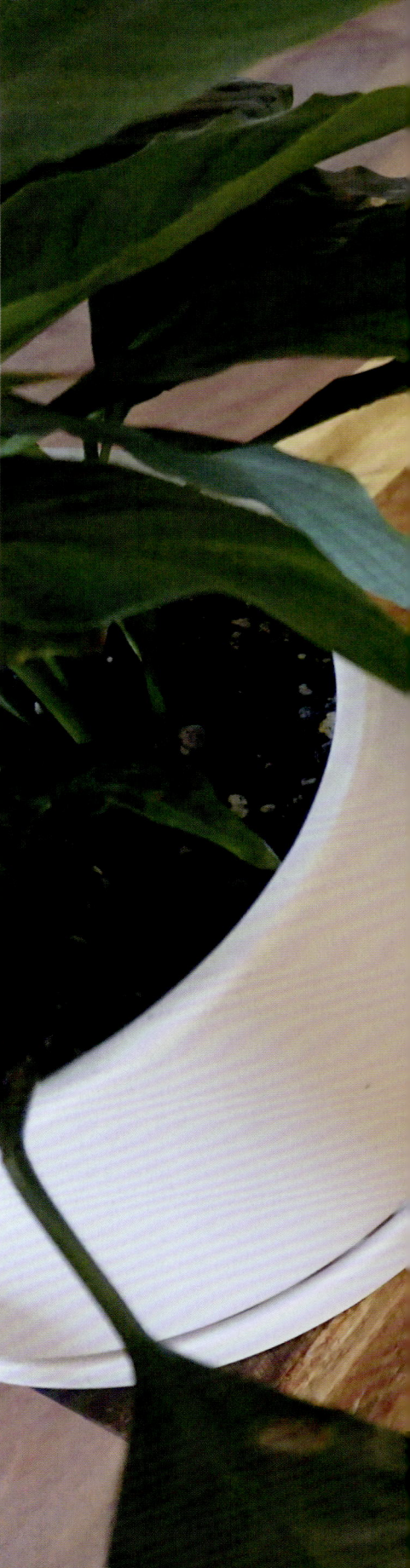

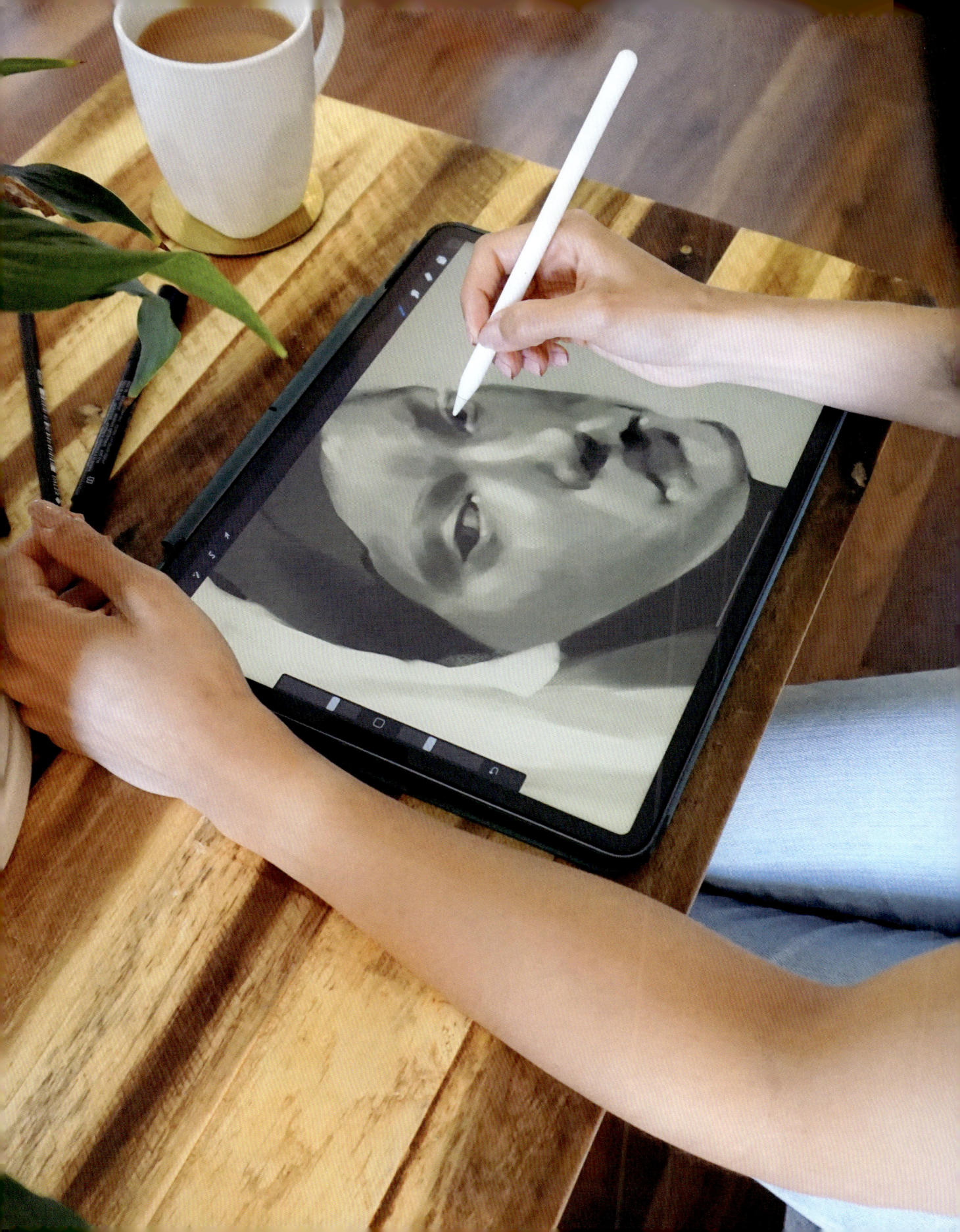

DIGITAL VERSUS TRADITIONAL MEDIUM

It was years ago that I started my digital art-making journey. Coming from a traditional background (using mediums like conte, pencils, and oil paint), it took me a long time to create digital work I was actually proud to share.

The learning curve from traditional to digital is quite steep—and I believe one of the main reasons is because artists don't start their digital art journey with the right mindset.

Digital tends to mimic traditional mediums. Even within Procreate, you'll find "acrylic" brushes, "charcoal" brushes, and even a "Derwent" pencil. This leads people to believe that they can use these tools to paint and draw the same way they do in real life and get the same results. When things don't turn out, it's easy to get frustrated, lose patience, and even feel a bit hopeless—that's what it was like for me.

Upon reflection, the times that I most enjoyed, and excelled, at digital painting was when I left behind the notion that I was using digital versions of traditional tools. In other words, I viewed digital as its own standalone medium. Charcoal is a different medium than markers, watercolors are different than oil paints, and digital is different from them all.

To put it into perspective, a watercolor artist might struggle to use oil paints at first simply because water-based paints do not behave, mix, or even dry in the same way as oil-based paints do. That artist would need to practice with oils, discover new workflows, and experiment before getting great results. I'd say that the same goes for the digital medium. You'll have an insane amount of new and foreign tools at your disposal and workflows to experiment with and discover. It'll take time, patience, and practice to gain confidence in your new chosen medium. So don't get discouraged if you make a mess on the screen for a while—it's all just part of the journey!

Now, if you're already familiar with digital painting (say you've worked in Photoshop or Clip Studio Paint), then getting familiar with Procreate will be a breeze. You'll find some of the same tools and blend modes, and even similar interface options.

If you're completely new to digital painting, then welcome! I'm absolutely honored to help kick-start your journey. Procreate is a great program to start with because the interface is minimalistic and the program offers plenty of gesture controls—which make digital painting feel a bit more tactile. I encourage you to try many of the tools out and be patient with yourself as you learn this new medium.

TOOLS REQUIRED

You don't need a bunch of things to get started, and you certainly don't need the latest and greatest of the Apple lineup to make beautiful artwork. All you'll need is your iPad, an Apple Pencil, and the Procreate app (downloaded and installed).

In case you're curious, here are the details for my setup:

- iPad Pro 13"
- Apple Pencil (2nd Generation)
- Procreate (Version 5.2.7)

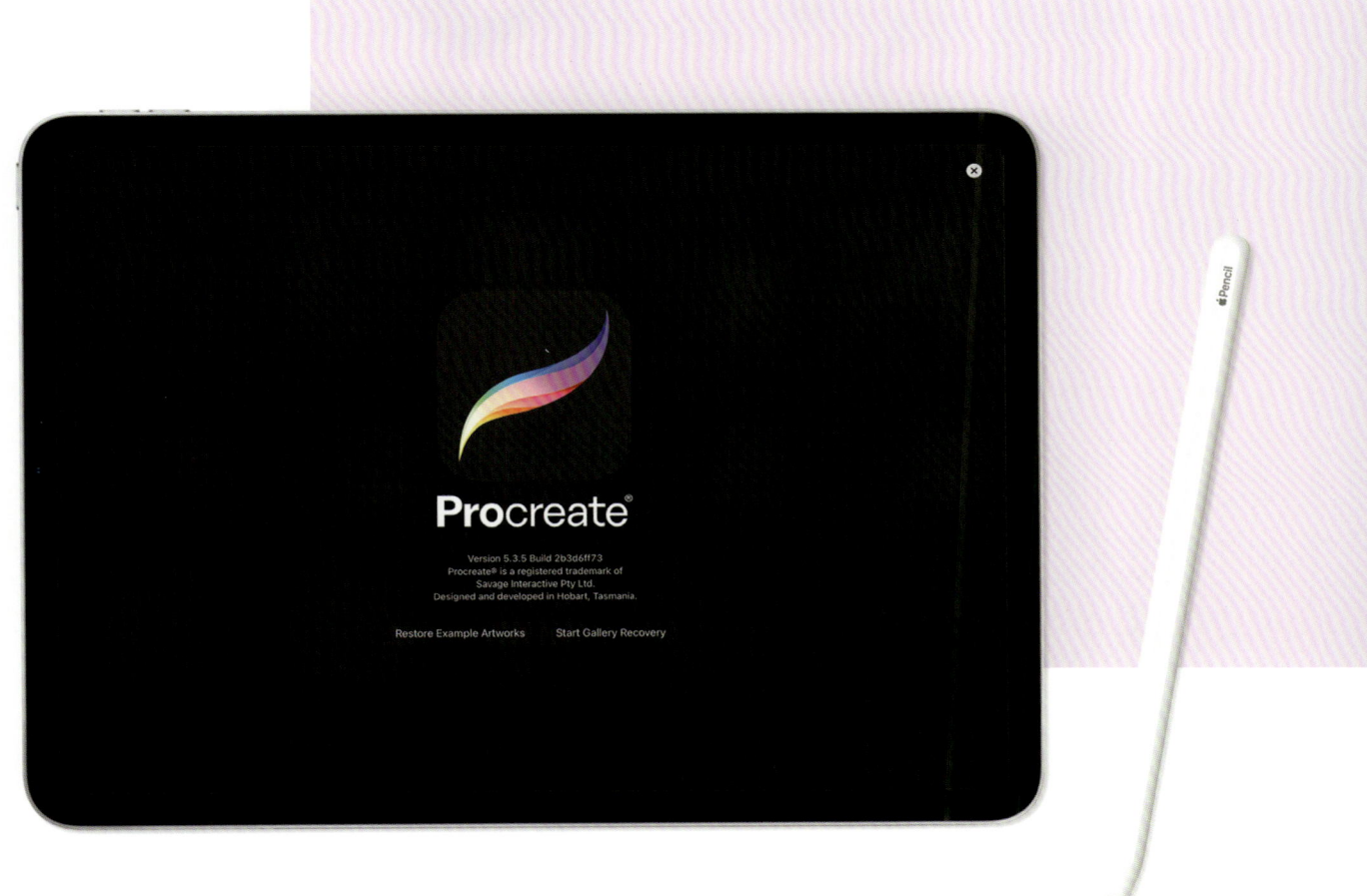

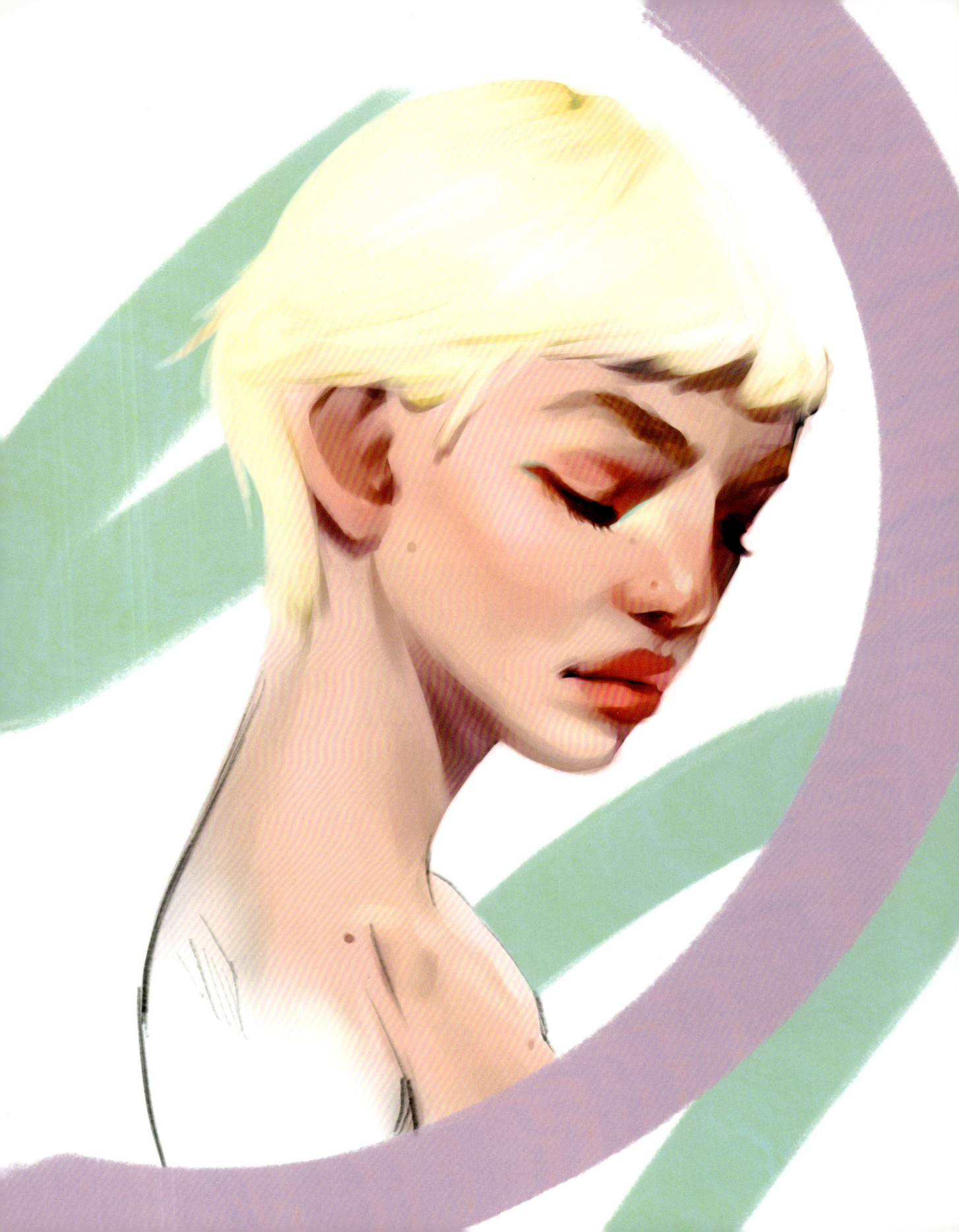

The basics of
PROCREATE

This chapter is your introduction to Procreate's gestures, tools, and features.

I know that interface walkthroughs can be a little dry and it can be tempting to skip ahead. However, I really do recommend that you spend time reviewing the contents of this chapter if you're new to Procreate.

If you already have familiarity with the program, then feel free to skim the contents and use this section as reference when needed instead.

Before we get on with it, here's a teeny-tiny disclaimer:

There's often more than one way to accomplish the exact same task within Procreate. Since there are multiple ways to do the same thing, I've tried to outline only the most beginner-friendly method for all tools and actions in this chapter.

Now, it's pretty safe to say that you'll be using gesture controls nearly as much as you do your Apple Pencil. For this reason, before we dive into Procreate's interface, let's first have an overview of the different types of gestures.

UNDERSTANDING GESTURES

Procreate supports an incredible variety of gestures that you'll use to activate shortcuts to your favorite tools, navigate the program, and perform various actions.

Using gestures while painting will streamline your workflow, and once you get the hang of them, they'll become indispensable!

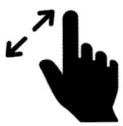

Pinch

Pinch with two fingers to zoom in or out.

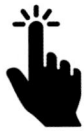

Tap

Tap with either a single finger or the Apple Pencil.

Double/Triple Tap

Double tap with a single finger or the Apple Pencil.

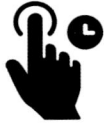

Long Press

Tap + hold with a single finger or the Apple Pencil.

Multi-Finger Tap

Two-, three-, or four-finger tap.

Rotate

Using two fingers, rotate clockwise or counterclockwise.

Scrub

Scrub your fingers back and forth on the screen.

Swipe

Swipe your finger(s) in the direction indicated.

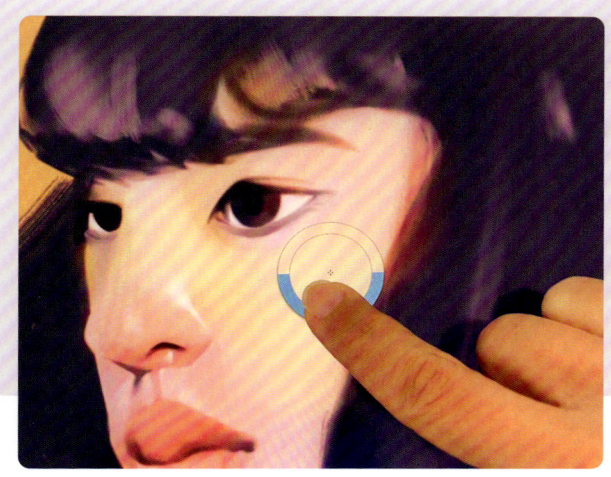

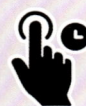

The same gesture can activate multiple actions. For example, a **long press** can initiate the eyedropper tool, but it's also used to move layers around in your layer panel (more on that later).

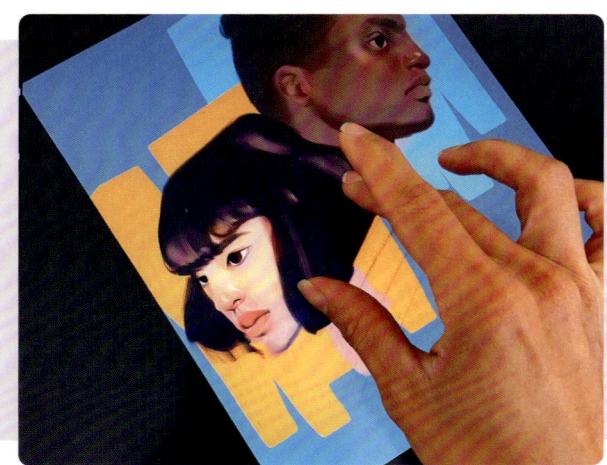

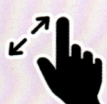

You'll be **pinching** *a lot*. Since the iPad screen isn't very large, you'll need to pinch your canvas constantly to zoom in and out of your paintings. I find it most comfortable to pinch with my thumb and middle finger, especially while holding the Apple Pencil.

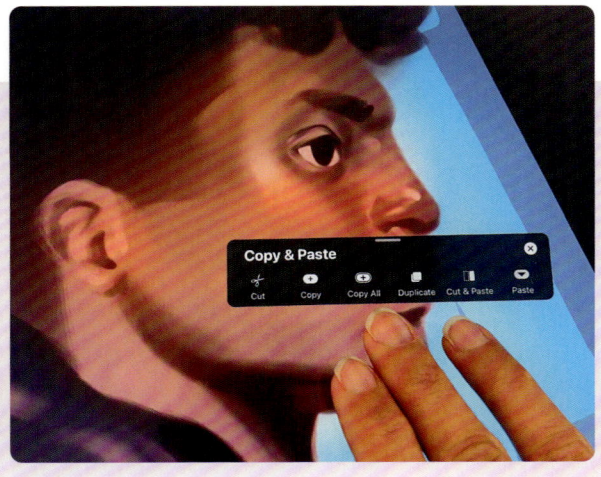

Some gestures are easy to forget like the **three-finger swipe** (upward). This maneuver pops up a hidden menu with actions like cut, copy, and paste.

As a beginner, you're still getting used to the program, so don't feel bad if you forget which gestures to use

PROCREATE'S INTERFACE

Here's an overview of Procreate's interface. It can be divided into three separate sections—editing tools, painting tools, and the sidebar.

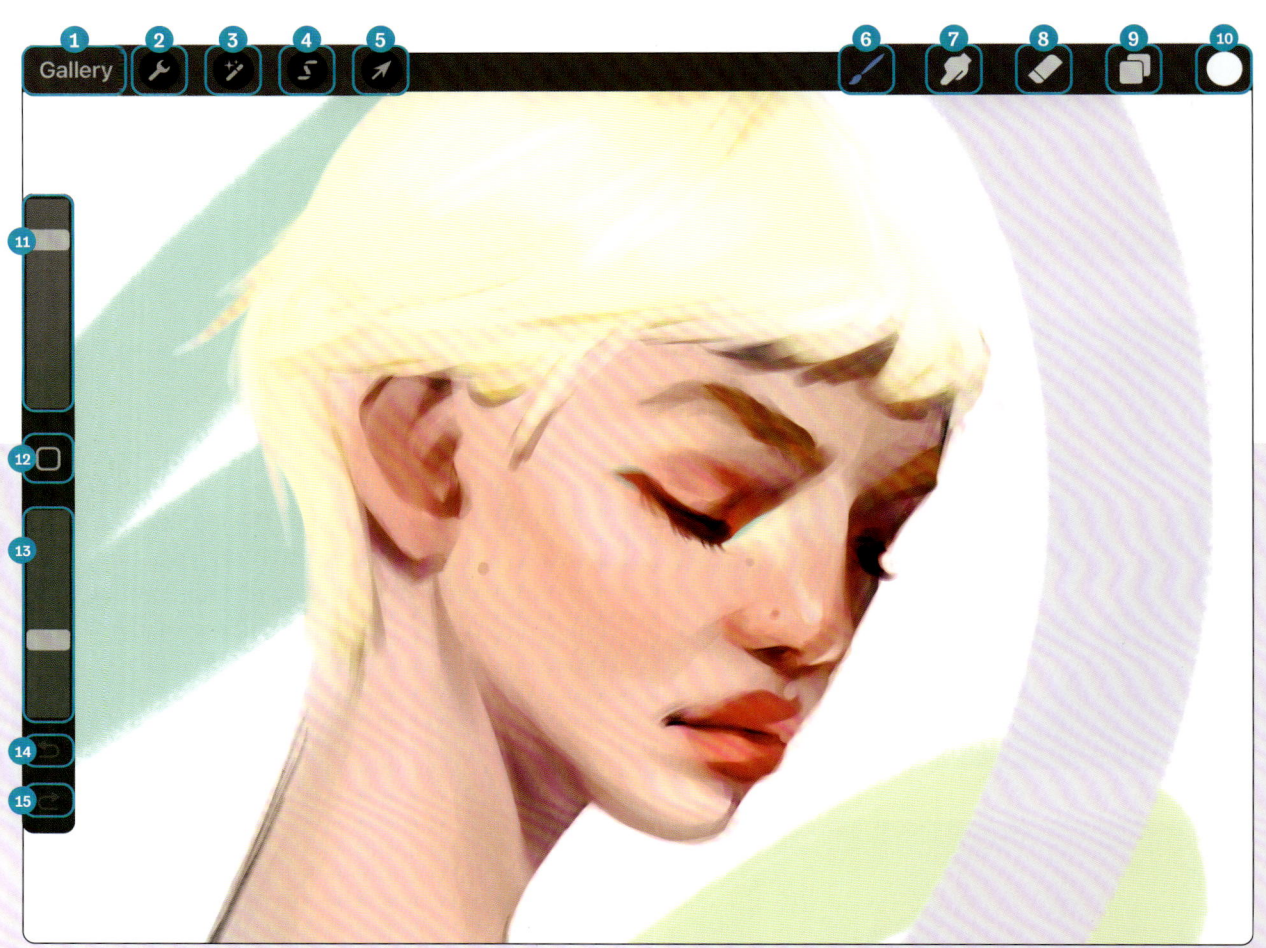

Editing tools

1. Gallery
2. Actions
3. Adjustments
4. Selection
5. Transform

Painting tools

6. Paint
7. Smudge
8. Erase
9. Layers
10. Color

Sidebar

11. Brush size slider
12. Modify button
13. Brush opacity slider
14. Undo
15. Redo

NAVIGATING THE GALLERY

Typically when you open Procreate for the first time, you'll automatically land on the Gallery. If you've never used Procreate before, your Gallery will be loaded with sample artwork made by amazing artists.

I like to think of the gallery as a hub for artwork. It displays all of the paintings ever made in one interface and allows artists to do things like:

1 **Organize artwork into stacks**

2 **Share, preview, or duplicate artwork**

3 **Create new artwork**

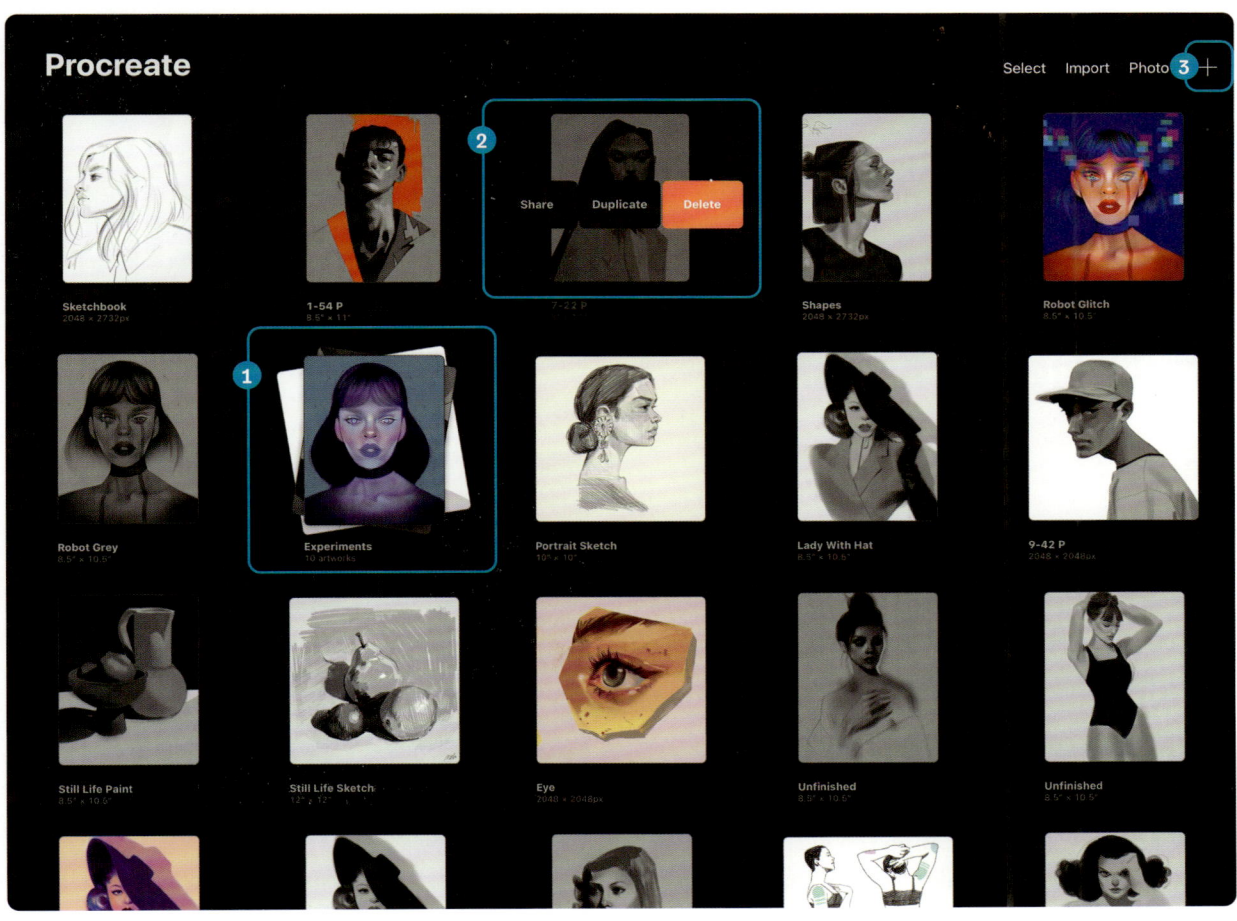

Artwork Actions

Each piece of artwork can be managed individually. Simply swipe your finger to the left on any of the thumbnails to bring up these three options:

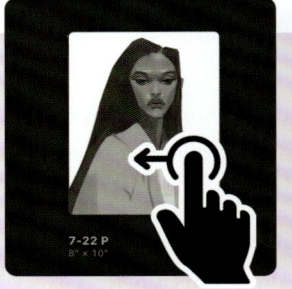
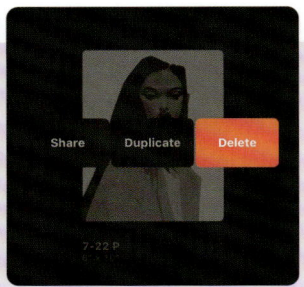

Share
Export your artwork as a PNG, JPEG, PSD, and so on.

Duplicate
Make a copy of the entire canvas.

Delete
Remove the artwork from the gallery for good.

Preview

To quickly preview a piece at a larger size, use the pinching gesture to expand the thumbnail. Use the pinching gesture again to collapse it.

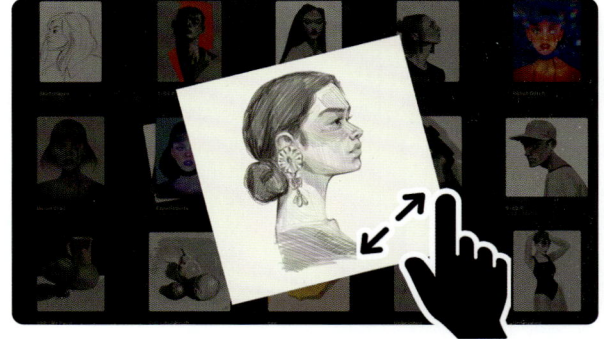

Organizing Your Artwork

Create a Stack

Procreate enables you to organize your work into stacks (think folders). The easiest way to do this is by tapping Select in the top right menu > choosing your pieces > and then tapping on Stack.

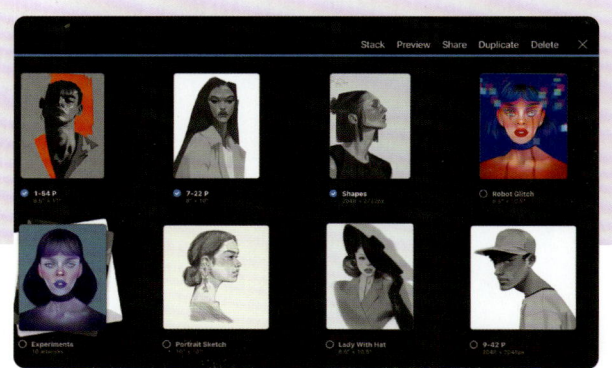

After tapping *Select*, your menu will change and the option to *Stack* will appear. Blue check marks beside a thumbnail's name indicate the ones you've selected.

Remove Artwork from a Stack

Long press on the thumbnail you want to remove from the stack, then drag it on top of the stack name (in the top left). The name will flash blue, then bring you back to the Gallery. Drop the piece wherever you desire.

Arranging Artwork

You can arrange your artwork by long pressing on any artwork thumbnail and dragging and dropping it into its new position. If you drag a piece of artwork over another one, you'll trigger the Gallery's stacking capability, and the two will be grouped together.

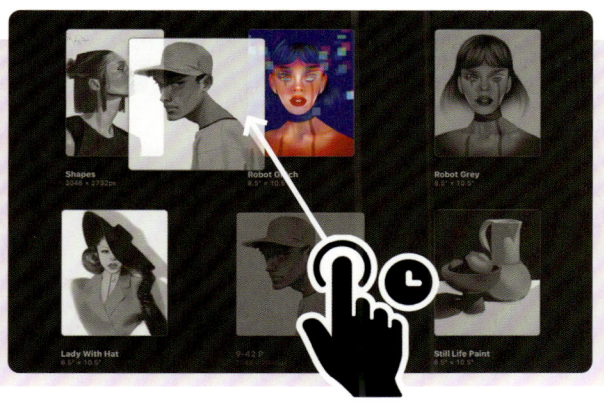

Renaming Artwork and Stacks

By default, anything you create is called "Untitled Artwork." You can rename artwork by tapping on its name, which is located underneath the thumbnail. You can also rename any stack in the same way.

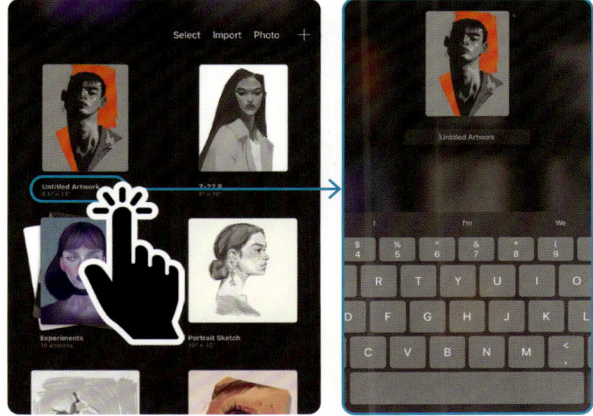

Bulk Actions

If you want to manage more than one piece of artwork at a time, you can do so by tapping *Select*. When you tap on *Select*, your top-right menu will change. You may choose multiple thumbnails and then perform bulk actions such as:

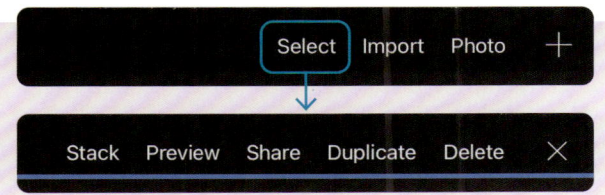

Stack
Group artwork together in a stack (just like a folder). This option is deactivated until you select two or more thumbnails.

Preview
You can select multiple thumbnails and preview only those selected. This is great for presenting artwork. Swipe left or right to move between pieces.

Share
This is the bulk export option. You can share artwork in various file formats such as .procreate, GIF, PNG, and so on.

Duplicate
Make carbon copies of your canvases.

Delete
Permanently remove artworks from the gallery.

WORKING WITH CANVASES

Creating a new canvas is simple. From the Gallery, tap the + icon in the top-right corner of your screen. You'll be able to do the following:

1. **Create a canvas by importing existing files or photos**
2. **Create a canvas and new preset with custom dimensions**
3. **Create a canvas using an already established preset**

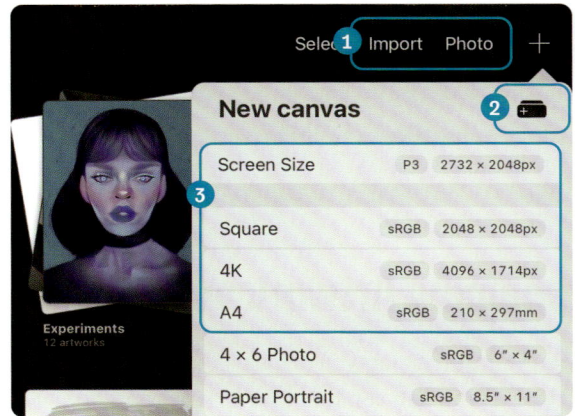

The method you choose to set up a new canvas will depend on your workflow. If you're just doodling, then you'll likely choose "Screen Size" as that option is good enough. If however, you're creating artwork for a particular project, then you'll want to set up a custom canvas or use a preset.

Using Presets

Procreate comes with a short list of canvas presets for you to choose from. Simply tap on the one you want to use and Procreate will create a new canvas with the outlined specs. Knowing the intended use of your artwork will help you determine the size you need. For example, if you're making artwork to post on Instagram, then "Square" may be ideal.

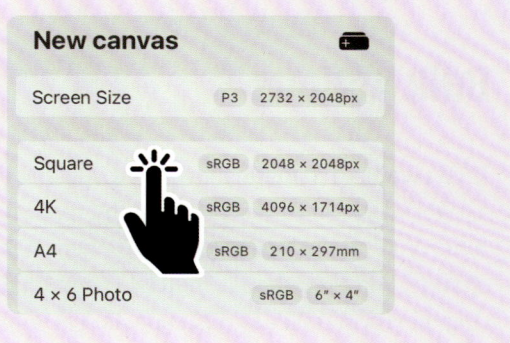

Editing/Deleting Presets

Swipe left on any of the presets to bring up options such as *Edit* or *Delete*. *Edit* will allow you to do things like change the dimensions, the color profile, or the background color of that preset. *Delete* will permanently remove it from the preset list.

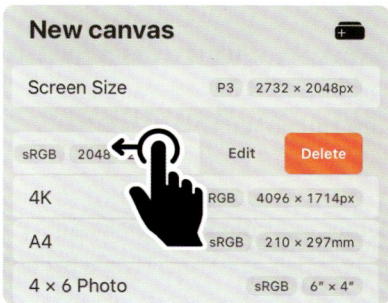

Creating a Custom Canvas

Tap on the icon to the right of "New Canvas." This will bring up a separate interface, shown below.

Anytime you create a new canvas, it will be added to your preset list. Keep your list organized by deleting the ones you don't use.

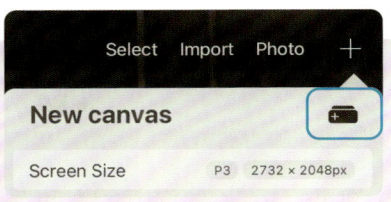

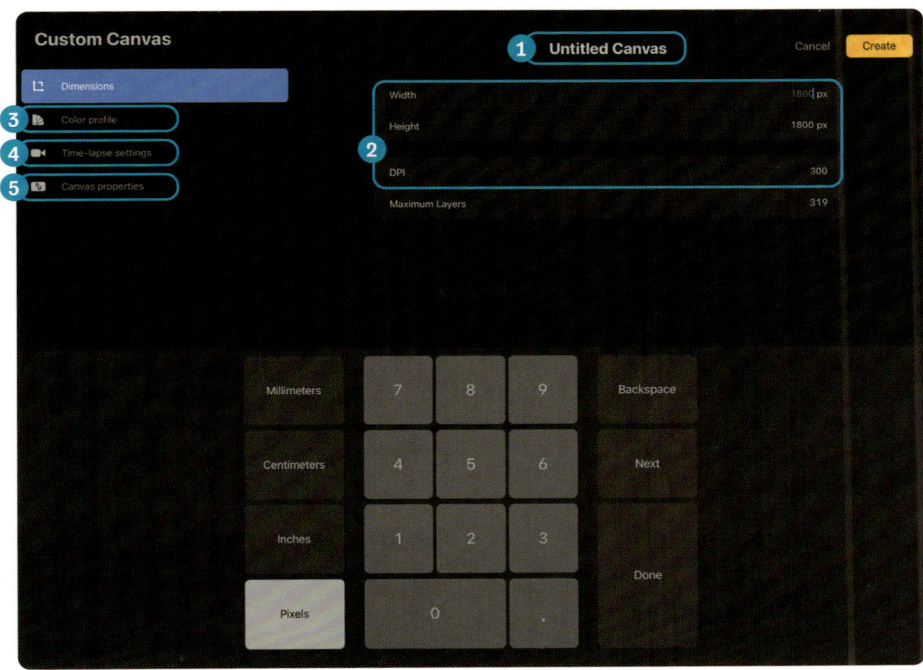

1 Name

Tap "Untitled Canvas" to add a name. This name will be displayed on your preset list.

2 Size and DPI

Set the width and height of your canvas. You can do this in mm, cm, inches, or pixels. Then set the DPI, which will be a single number value.

3 Color profile

Knowing what your artwork will be used for will help you determine the appropriate color profile to choose. If you're not sure, then it's best to stick with a generic RGB profile.

RGB: Stands for Red, Green, and Blue. It's ideal for artwork that will be displayed on screens.

CMYK: Stands for Cyan, Magenta, Yellow, and Black. This color profile is ideal for printed artwork. Most commercial printers ask for files in CMYK.

4 Time-lapse settings

Procreate records every brush stroke you make on screen and then composes a short speed painting video for you. Here you can define the video's settings if necessary.

5 Background color

Under *Canvas Properties* you have the option to set your background color (you can change this later) or set the background as transparent by hiding it.

Understanding DPI

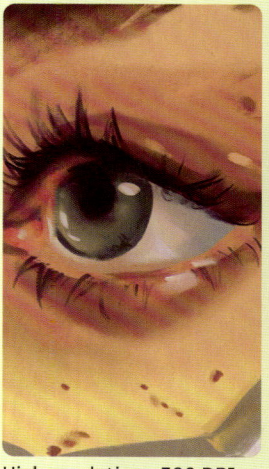
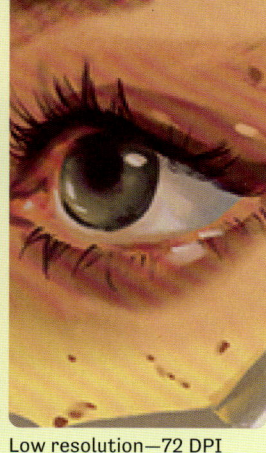

High resolution—300 DPI   Low resolution—72 DPI

DPI stands for "Dots Per Inch," and it's a very important consideration when printing or resizing your artwork.

300 DPI is the standard for high-resolution printing. But having a high DPI will not guarantee good printing results if you upscale your work. For example, a 5"x5" piece with 300 DPI will print beautifully at that size. However, if you double its dimensions to 10"x10" and print it out, your artwork will become pixelated. This is because your new 10"x10" piece actually has a DPI of 150.

Edit an Existing Canvas

You have limited options that you can edit once a canvas has been created.

Crop and Resize

You can change the dimensions or DPI of an existing canvas by going to:

Actions > Canvas > Crop & Resize

To be extra precise, tap on *Settings* to enter the numeric value of your new width and height.

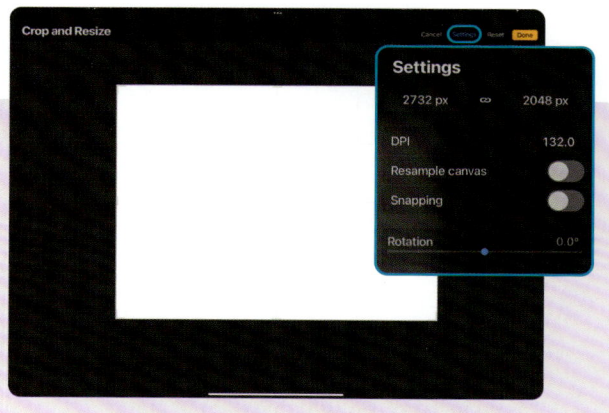

Change Color Profile

Update the color profile of your artwork by going to:

Actions > Canvas > Canvas information > Color profile

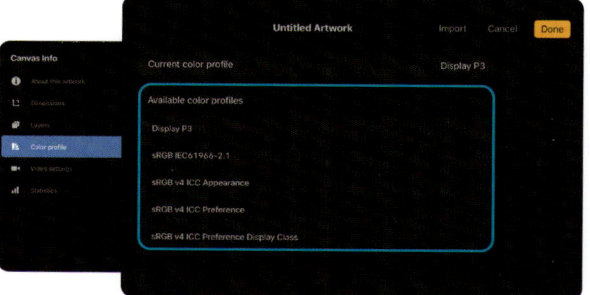

The current color profile is displayed at the top. To change it, tap on the one you wish to use from "Available color profiles."

BRUSHES

Brushes are crucial in Procreate. Whether you're sketching, painting, smudging, or erasing, you will be using a brush. The *Brush Library* comes pre-loaded with a *ton* of different types of brushes for you to use.

Aside from choosing a brush to use from the library, you can also edit existing brushes, organize them into folders, import new ones, and even export your own brush to share with others.

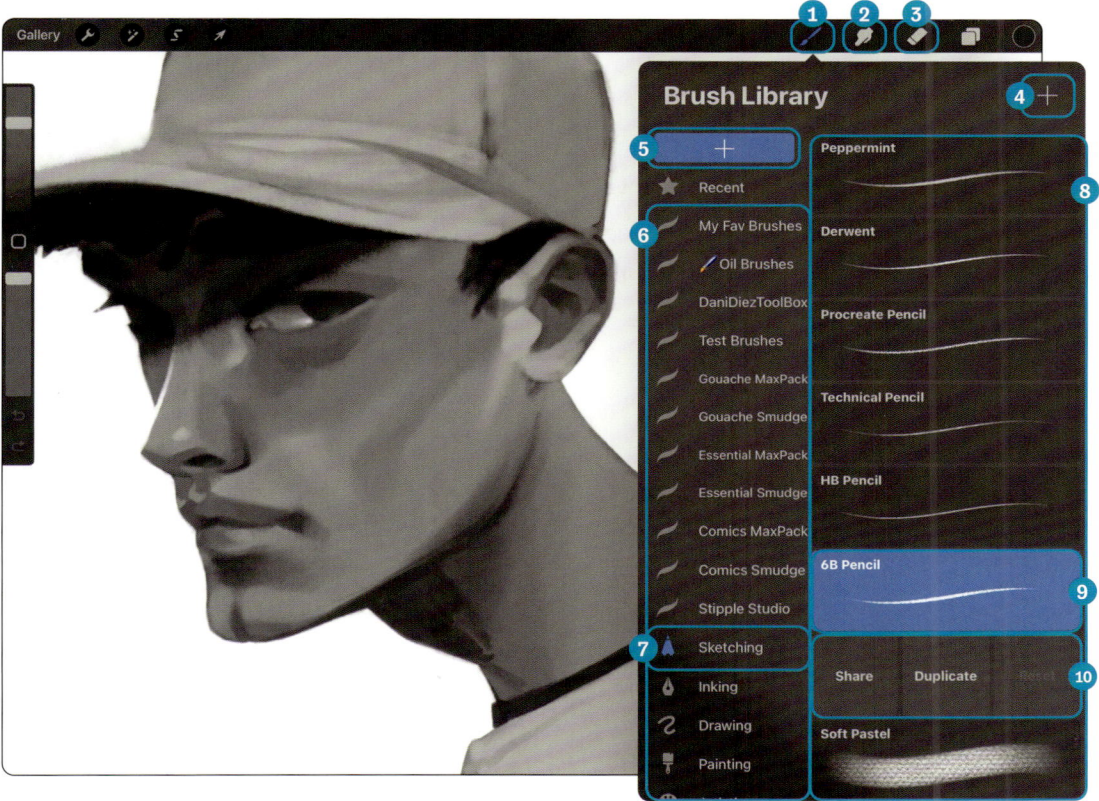

1. **Paint**

2. **Smudge**

3. **Erase**

4. **Create new brush in Brush Studio**

5. **Create new brush set**

6. **Existing brush sets**

7. **Active brush set**
   Highlighted in blue

8. **Brushes in the active brush set**

9. **Active brush**
   Highlighted in blue

10. **Additional brush options**
    Share, duplicate, delete/reset

Paint

Whether you're using the paintbrush to sketch, ink, or paint, this tool will always add to your canvas. You will use it to draw, shade, and color portraits.

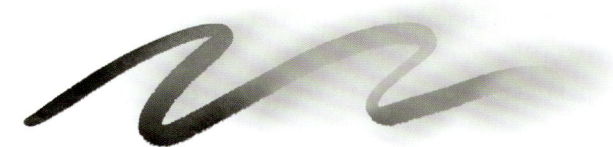

Smudge

This tool will always smear what you've painted onto your canvas. You will use it to blend colors together and soften harsh lines.

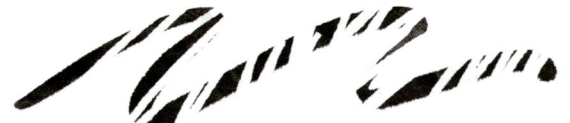

Erase

The eraser will always subtract from what's already on your canvas. Whatever pigment you've got on there will be removed when using this tool.

 Here's a tip!

Although paint, smudge, and erase all use the same brushes, they can be assigned different brushes simultaneously. For example, you can use a watercolor brush to paint and a charcoal brush to erase.

Using the Sidebar

The sidebar is attached to the edge of the screen and contains two sliders.

The top slider controls the size of a brush. Move the notch up to increase the size and down to decrease the size.

The bottom slider controls opacity when painting or erasing and strength when smudging (smudge a lot or a little).

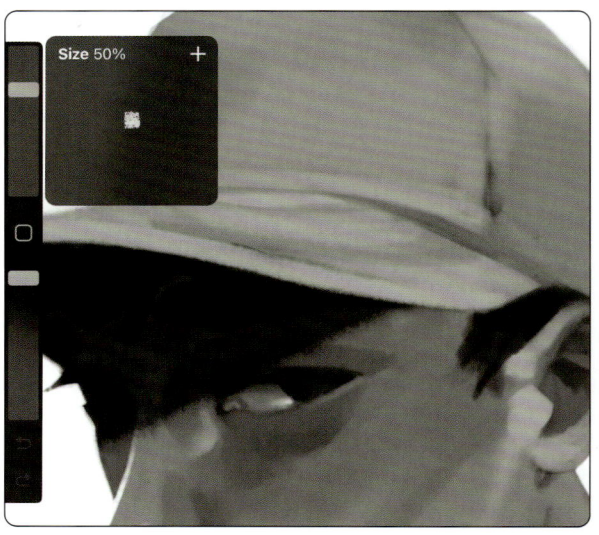

Brush Sets

Create/Import a Brush

In the *Brush Library* panel, tap the + icon in the top-right corner to enter Brush Studio. Create your own brush from scratch by playing around with all the options here (there are many!). If you want to load a brush set that you've downloaded, tap on import, shown on the top right-hand side.

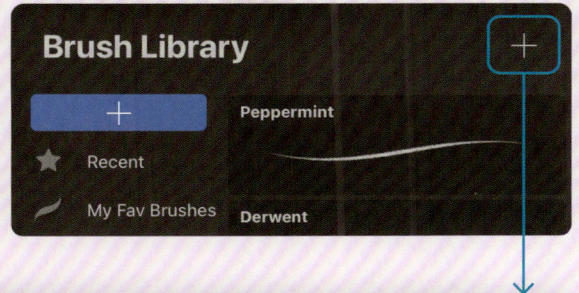

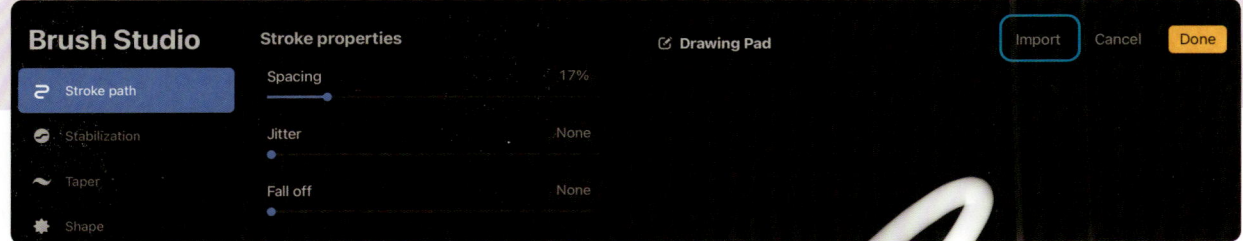

Move Brushes

Move a brush by long pressing it and then dragging it to your desired location. This is how you rearrange brushes within a set or move them to new sets. To create a new brush set, drag down on the existing brush set menu until the + icon appears.

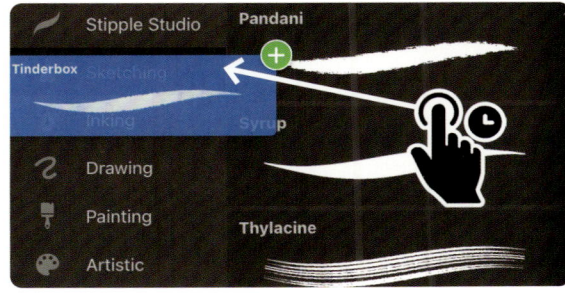

Additional Brush Options

Swipe left on a brush to bring up additional options, such as:

Share
Export your brush to share with other artists.

Duplicate
Make an exact copy of the brush. I recommend using this if you want to play around with a brush's settings but you don't want to lose the original.

Delete
Permanently remove the brush from Procreate.

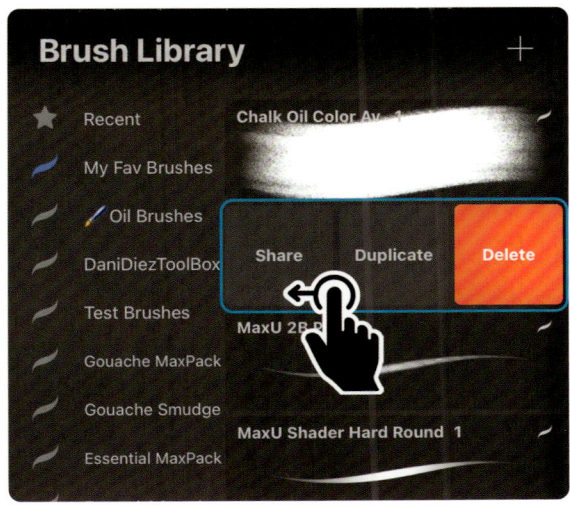

Reset

This option is only available if a brush was a Procreate default—Procreate won't let you delete its pre-loaded brushes. If you've changed the settings of a default brush, then the option to reset it will become available. This will restore the brush's original settings.

Find

Only available in "Recent" set. Procreate will jump you over to the set that the brush is actually in.

Pin/Unpin

Only available in "Recent" set. The recent set is constartly updating to reflect your brush history. Pinning a brush will save it at the top of your history so that it doesn't get lost.

Clear

Only available in "Recent" set. Remove the brush from your recent history.

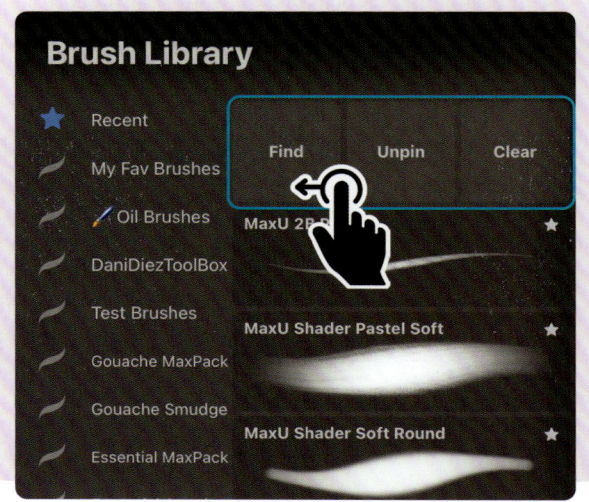

LAYERS

What Are Layers?

When creating digital artwork, instead of drawing or painting directly on the canvas, you do so on layers. For example, you can use one layer to sketch, another to paint, and another to add special effects. **There's no correct number of layers to use.** As you continue to paint digitally, you'll become familiar with your own personal workflow, which will dictate when to add layers and when to reduce the amount you already have.

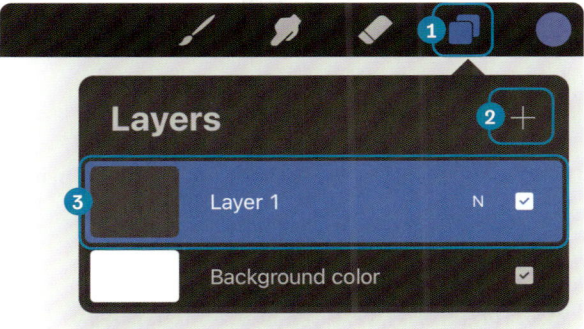

The Layers Panel

Tap the icon with the two squares to pull up the *Layers* panel. By default, every canvas will have a "Background color" and a "Layer 1." Your panel can be broken down like this:

1 **Open/close Layers panel**

2 **Add a new layer**

3 **Active Layer (bright blue)**

4 **Name**
Tap to rename

5 **Blend mode and opacity**
Tap to open options

6 **Layer Visibility**
Tap to turn on/off

7 **Layer thumbnail**
Tap to open additional layer options

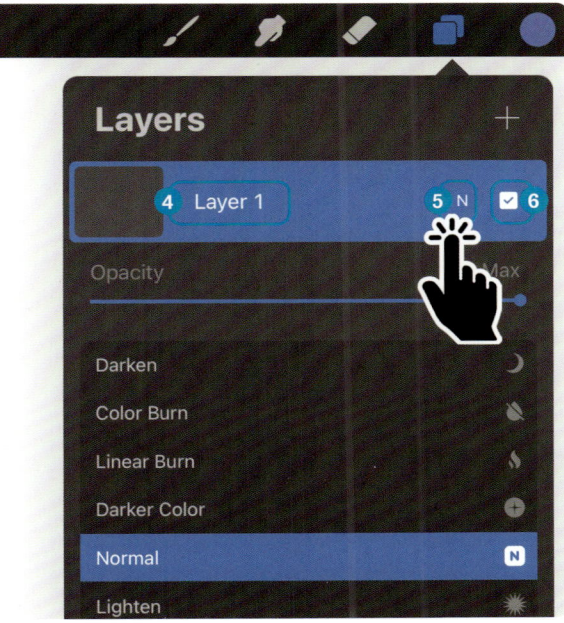

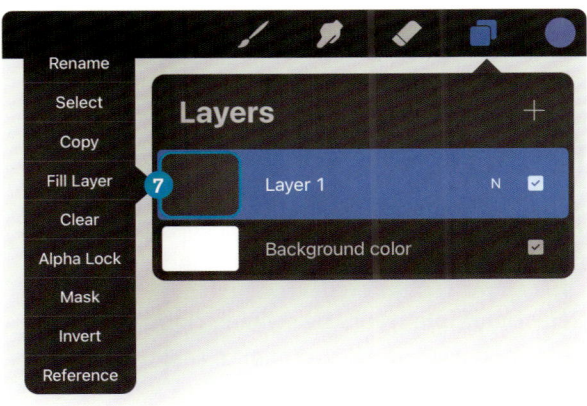

Create a New Layer

Add a new layer to the canvas by tapping the + icon. Procreate will automatically name your layers by number. Tap on its name to rename it.

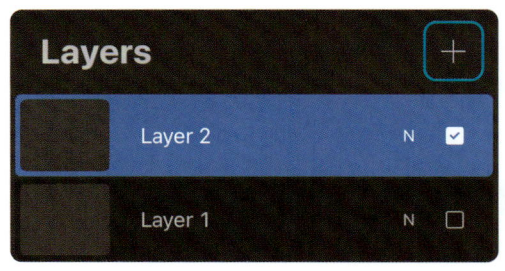

Hidden Options

Using a finger, swipe to the left on a layer to bring up these options:

Lock
Locking a layer prevents you from drawing on it and from accidentally deleting or merging it. Essentially, as long as a layer is locked, it's safe from any mishaps.

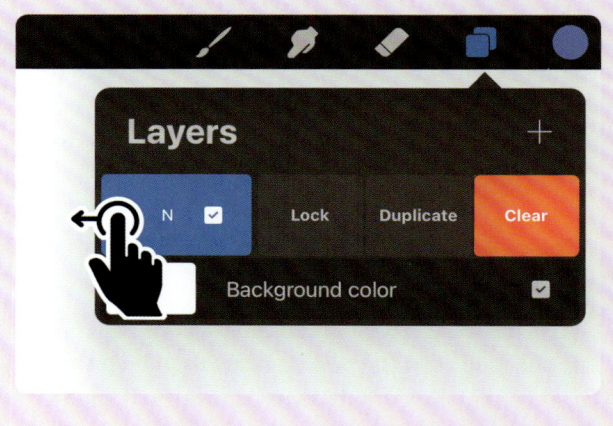

Duplicate
Make an exact copy of the current layer.

Delete/Clear
Permanently delete a layer. If you only have one layer, the option changes to *Clear,* which will clear the contents.

Select Multiple Layers

Swipe your finger to the right on a layer to select it. Selected layers will have a dark blue background.

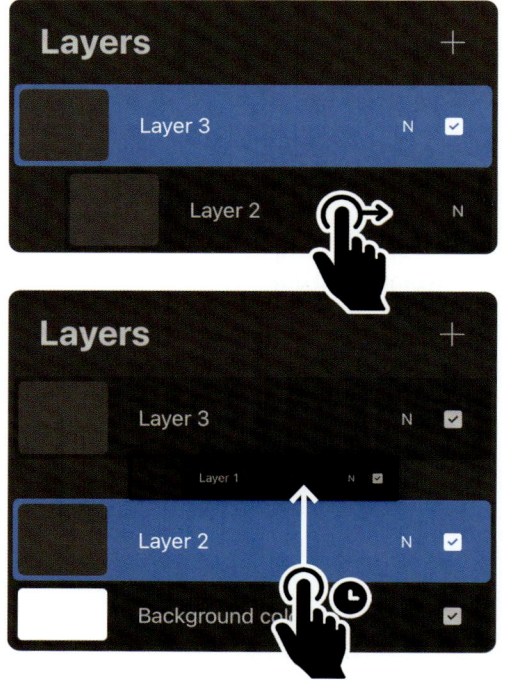

Move Layers

To move a single layer, long press on it and drag it up or down. Release to drop it in place.

Select multiple layers by swiping right, then long press and drag and drop them to their new spot.

Combine Layers

You have two options to combine your layers:

Merge

Combine layers into one by pinching them together. Keep in mind that merged layers "fuse" together and can no longer be edited separately.

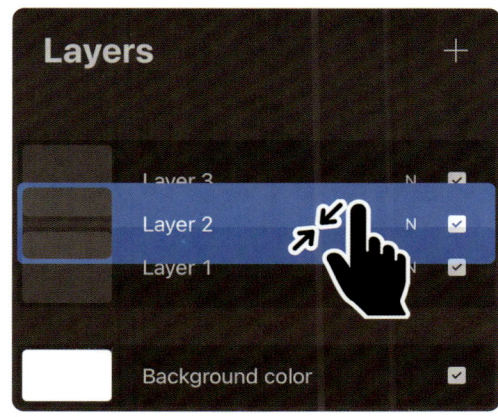

Group

When you select more than one layer, the + icon at the top of the panel is replaced with two options. You can either *Delete* the selected layers or *Group* them together. Grouping layers helps keep your panel organized.

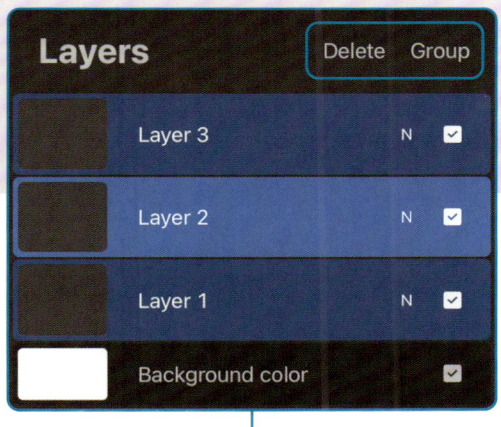

Add an existing layer to a group by dragging it into the folder. Remove a layer from the group by dragging it out.

Groups also have the same "hidden options" mentioned on the previous page; swipe left on the group to access them.

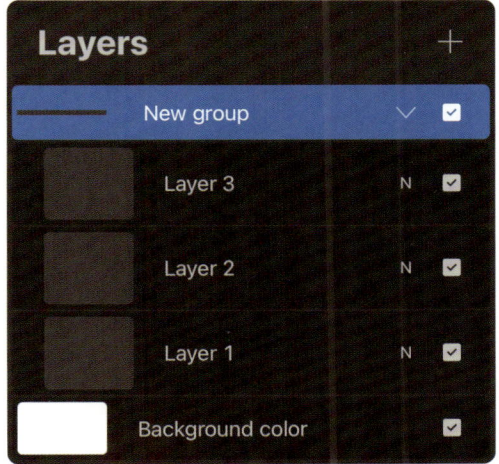

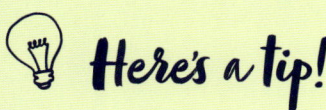
Here's a tip!

Merging layers is what's known as a **hard edit** and is difficult (sometimes impossible) to undo later in the painting process. In contrast, grouping layers is a **soft edit** because your individual layers are still intact and you can also undo a group easily at any point. The way you work comes down to personal preference. I tend to merge my layers, but that's because I prefer to work with few layers over many (even if they're well organized).

Layer Visibility

Hide/View

Tap the checkmark box to hide or view a layer. The same can be done with groups.

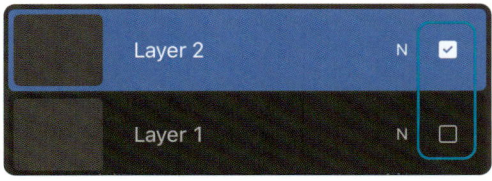

Opacity

Tap on *N* to bring up the opacity slider. Use this slider to adjust the transparency of your layer anywhere from 0 to 100%.

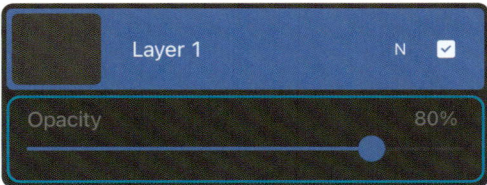

Layer Options

Tap on a layer's thumbnail to open layer options.

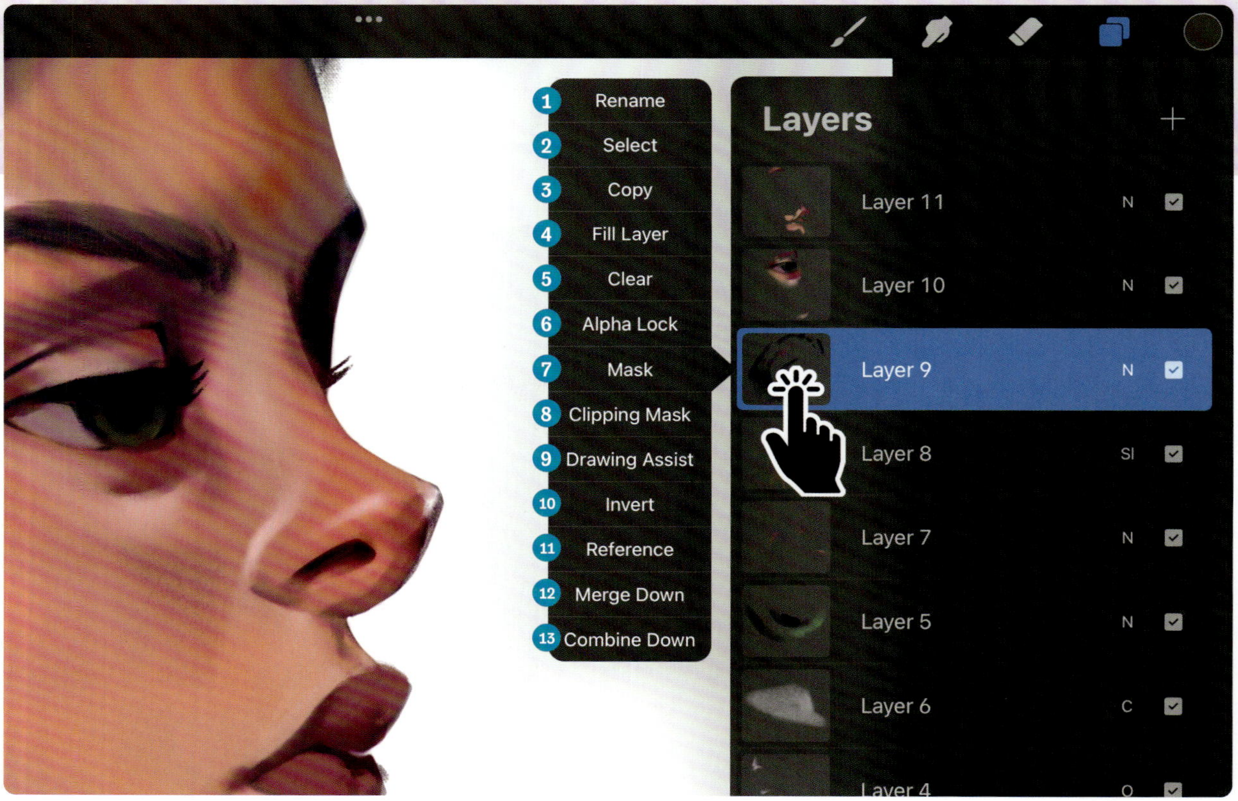

1. Rename
2. Select
3. Copy
4. Fill Layer
5. Clear
6. Alpha Lock
7. Mask
8. Clipping Mask
9. Drawing Assist
10. Invert
11. Reference
12. Merge Down
13. Combine Down

Layers

Layer 11   N ☑
Layer 10   N ☑
Layer 9   N ☑
Layer 8   SI ☑
Layer 7   N ☑
Layer 5   N ☑
Layer 6   C ☑
Layer 4   O ☑

1 Rename

Change the name of your layer.

2 Select

Select the contents of the layer. *Select* will only select the non-transparent parts of your artwork (wherever you've drawn or painted).

3 Copy

Copy the layer's contents to the clipboard. You can paste the content on another layer or canvas, or even within another app.

4 Fill Layer

Fill the entire layer with your active color.

5 Clear

Erase the contents of the layer and reset the opacity to 100%.

6 Alpha Lock

Lock the transparent pixels on your layer so that you can't draw on them anymore. This means you can only paint on existing artwork on this layer. It's a great option for repainting or recoloring certain areas.

7 Mask

Apply a mask to any layer to hide or reveal its contents. A mask must always have a parent layer. Painting with white on the mask will reveal the parent layer's artwork, while painting with black will conceal it. This is a fantastic way of "erasing" content on a layer without actually deleting anything. Masks can have their visibility turned on/off, and they can also be deleted (deleting a mask will not destroy the artwork on the parent layer).

8 Clipping Mask

Clipping masks are great for adding texture or gradients to existing layers. A clipping mask is a layer all on its own. When "Clipped" to another layer, it works the same way as Alpha Lock, except you aren't painting directly on the layer you've clipped it to, so the changes aren't permanent.

9 Drawing Assist

Turn on Drawing Assist on/off for this layer. Drawing Assist works with Drawing Guide:

Actions > Canvas > Drawing Guide

The drawing guide is an assistive tool and automates the way you draw using grids and symmetry.

10 Invert

Swap your current colors with their complementary versions.

11 Reference

This option works best with linework. Assigning a layer as *Reference* allows you to use color drop, on a separate layer, to fill in the image. This keeps your linework and color fills separate.

12 Merge Down

Flatten the layer with the one below it.

13 Combine Down

Group the layer with the one below it.

LAYER BLEND MODES

Blend modes apply mathematical equations to layers to create unique visual results. You need at least two layers in order for blend modes to work.

The best way to familiarize yourself with blend modes is to experiment with them. Some of them prove useful time and time again, while others create really wacky and sometimes jarring effects. You'll find that after a while you'll have your "go-tos" and you might also have a few blend modes you prefer to avoid altogether.

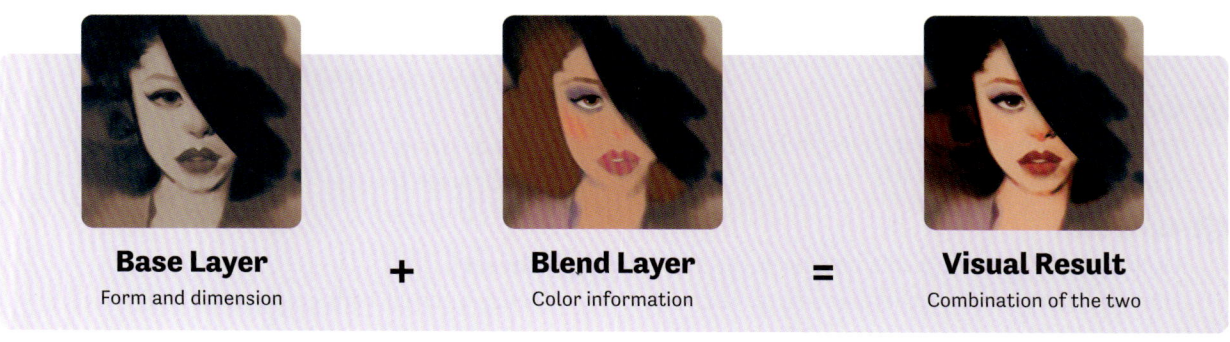

Base Layer
Form and dimension

+

Blend Layer
Color information

=

Visual Result
Combination of the two

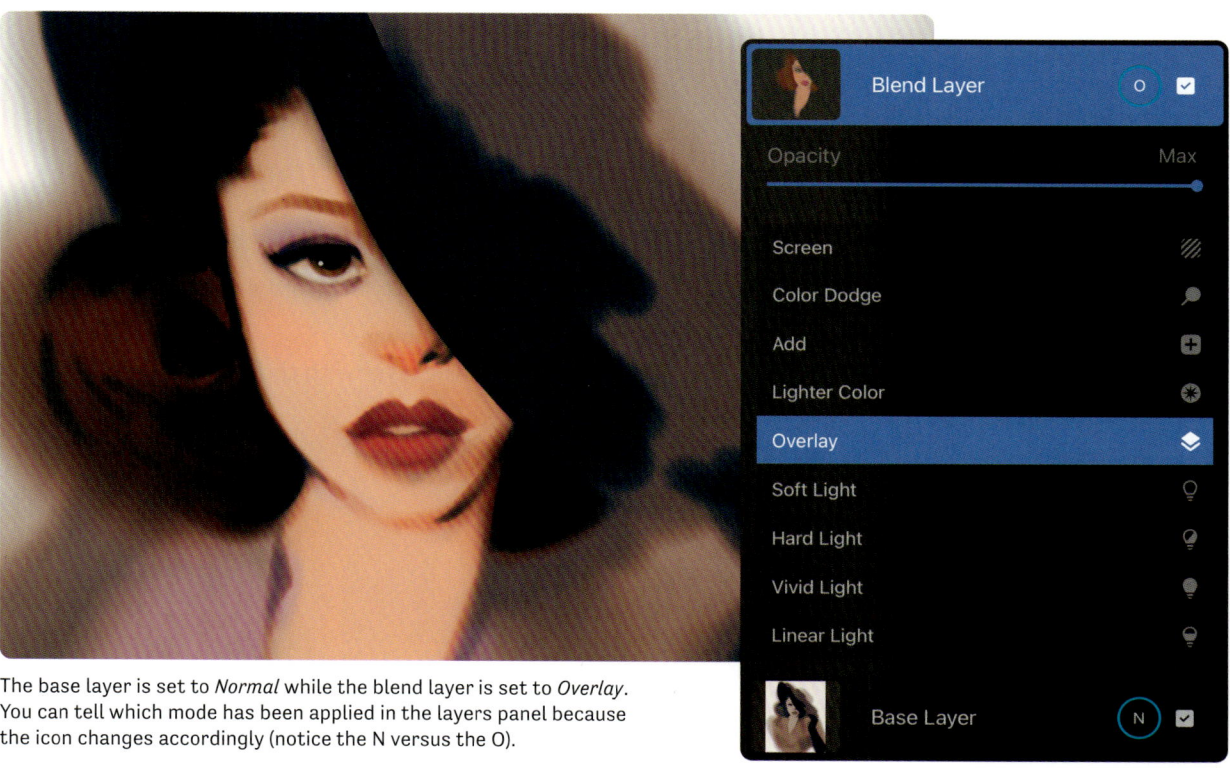

The base layer is set to *Normal* while the blend layer is set to *Overlay*. You can tell which mode has been applied in the layers panel because the icon changes accordingly (notice the N versus the O).

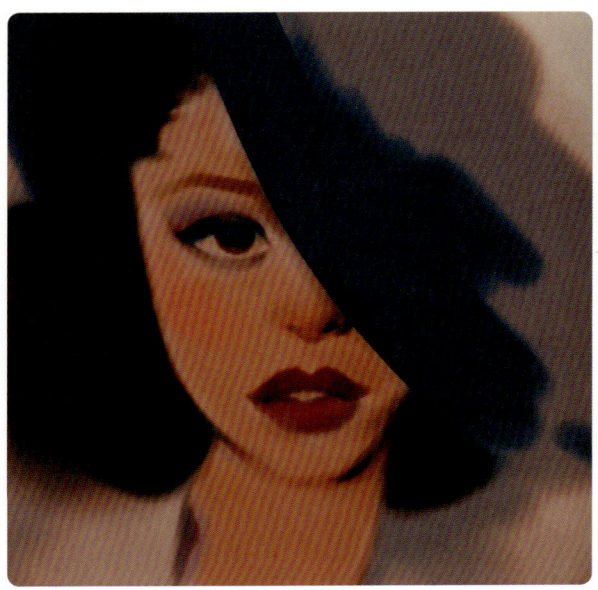

Blend layer set to *Multiply*

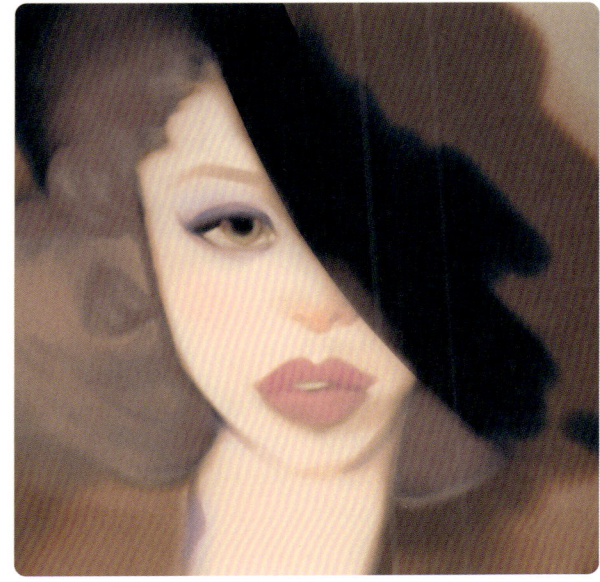

Blend layer set to *Screen*

Darkening Modes

All of the blend modes in this category alter the look of your layers by darkening them in some way.

Multiply

Multiplies the luminosity of the base layer with the blend layer, which always results in an overall darkening effect.

Darken

Compares the colors on the two layers and keeps the darker one.

Color Burn

Mimics the burn tool in traditional photography. It increases contrast between the two layers and typically bumps up saturation as well.

Linear Burn

Decreases the brightness of the base layer according to the colors on the blend layer.

Darker Color

Works like *Darken* but with more nuance.

Lightening Modes

The opposite of darkening modes. Blend modes in this category will always lighten your image.

Lighten

Compares the colors on the two layers and keeps the lighter one.

Screen

Brightens the base layer according to the luminosity of the blend layer. Ideal for highlights.

Color Dodge

Mimics the dodge tool in traditional photography. It decreases the contrast between the two layers, which actually results in highly saturated colors and blown out highlights.

Add

Brightens the base layer, which increases the brightness of the blend layer.

Lighter Color

Works like *Lighten* but with more nuance.

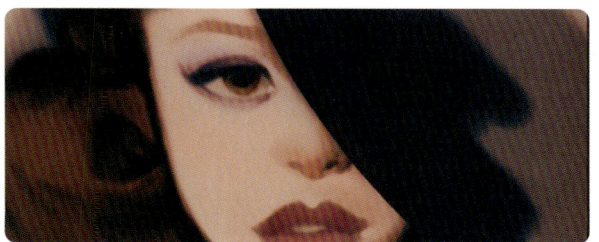

Blend layer set to *Soft Light*

Contrast Modes

This family of blend modes is a mixture between darkering and lightening modes—making some parts of your image darker while bumping up the brightness of other parts.

Overlay
Makes dark colors darker and light colors lighter; creates high contrast.

Soft Light
Like *Overlay* but not as intense.

Hard Light
Combination of *Multiply* and *Screen*.

Vivid Light
A more intense version of *Overlay*.

Linear Light
A combination of traditional photography tools, dodge and burn. Light colors are dodged, dark colors are burned. Results are high in contrast.

Pin Light
Combination of *Darken* and *Lighten*.

Hard Mix
Opposite of high contrast, it flattens colors out.

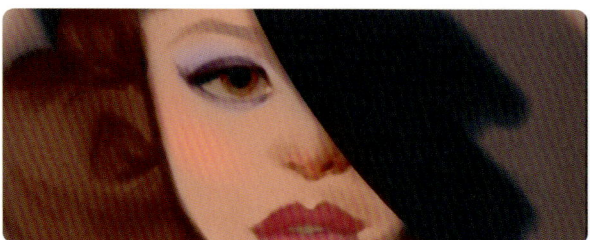

Blend layer set to *Color*

Other Modes

Modes in this category create interesting results; however, they can be quite jarring.

Difference
Looks for the difference between colors on the two layers and creates a blend based off that.

Exclusion
Works like *Difference* but doesn't darken certain tones.

Subtract
Subtracts brightness from light colors but doesn't do much to the dark colors.

Divide
Opposite of *Subtract*—dark colors are brightened and light colors are mostly left alone.

Hue
Keeps the hue of your blend layer and the luminosity and saturation of your base layer.

Saturation
Keeps the luminosity and hue of the base layer while applying the blend layer's saturation.

Color
Keeps the luminosity of the base layer while applying the hue and saturation of the blend layer. It's ideal for coloring greyscale images.

Luminosity
Keeps the hue and saturation of the base layer while applying the luminosity of the blend layer.

COLOR TOOLS

Tap the *Active Color*, located at the top right of the screen, to open up the color panel.

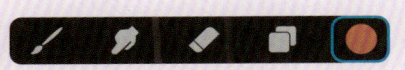

1 **Active color**

This is the color your brush is currently loaded with.

2 **Primary and secondary colors**

The *Primary Color* is to the left while the *Secondary Color* is to the right. If you're familiar with Photoshop, this is like your foreground and background color. You can switch between them by tapping on one. You'll notice that your *Active Color* switches to the one that you tap.

3 **Color picker**

You have a few pickers to choose from. By default, *Color Disc* will be active. Use the picker to fine-tune your color selection. We'll go into more detail later.

4 **History**

A running log of swatches that showcase your most recently used colors. Tap on one to make it your *Active Color*.

5 **Default palette**

Whichever palette you have set to default will show up here, at the bottom of the panel.

6 **Additional color pickers**

The icons at the bottom of the panel represent different pickers that you can use, but essentially they all do the same thing—allow you to choose a color you'd like to paint with. You don't have to use them all. In fact, you'll most likely gravitate toward a picker that feels most intuitive for you to use and stick to it.

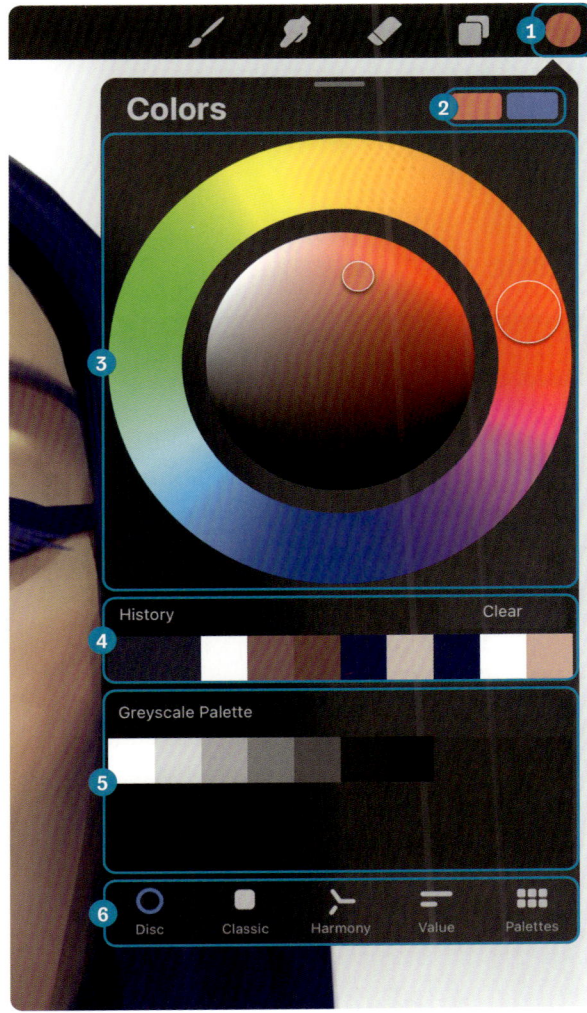

Color Pickers

Disc (Default)

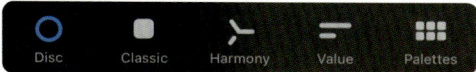

This view is most representative of the color wheel and should prove easiest to use by those with a traditional background.

1 **Use the outer ring to select your hue**

2 **Use the inner circle to change that hue's saturation**

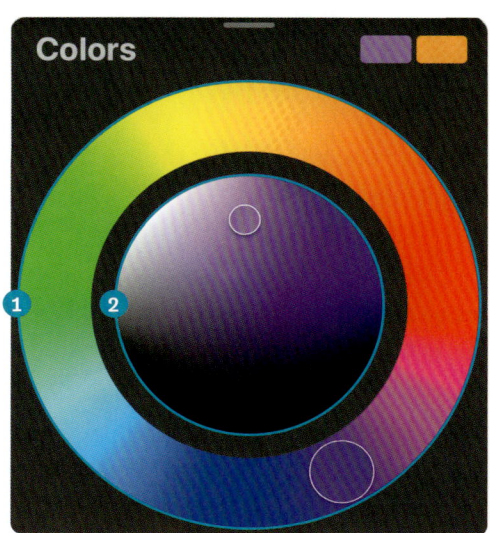

Classic

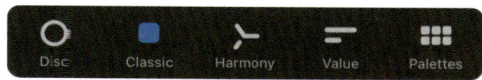

This view is reminiscent of other digital painting software like Photoshop. Move the reticle around the square to change your *Active Color*, or use the sliders at the bottom instead.

1 **Hue slider:** Change your color

2 **Saturation slider:** Adjust the intensity of that color

3 **Brightness slider:** Make the color lighter or darker

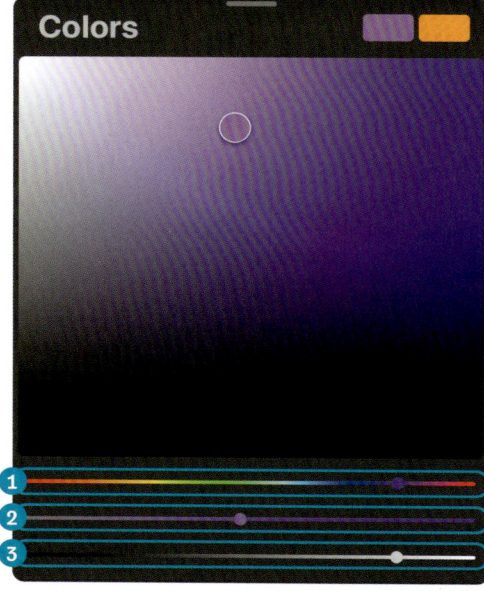

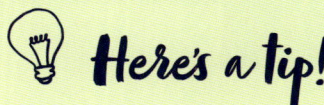 **Here's a tip!**

Tap + hold the white bar on the top of the color panel and drag it elsewhere on the screen. This will pull the panel out so you have permanent access to it while you paint.

Harmony

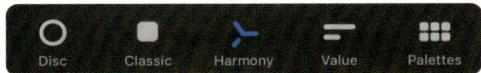

This picker will suggest colors that go along beautifully with your *Active Color*. It's a wonderful way to easily build your own color schemes.

In the top-left corner, underneath "Color" you'll see the mode that's selected (ex. Complementary). The mode tells you which color theory Procreate is using to suggest new colors. Tap on the mode to change it.

1 **Primary reticle:** Move it around the color wheel to select a hue.

2 **Secondary reticle(s):** Depending on the mode selected, there may be be more than one secondary reticle on the color wheel.

3 **Brightness slider**

The harmony picker works well with the next picker, called *Palette*. Use them together to create and save color schemes.

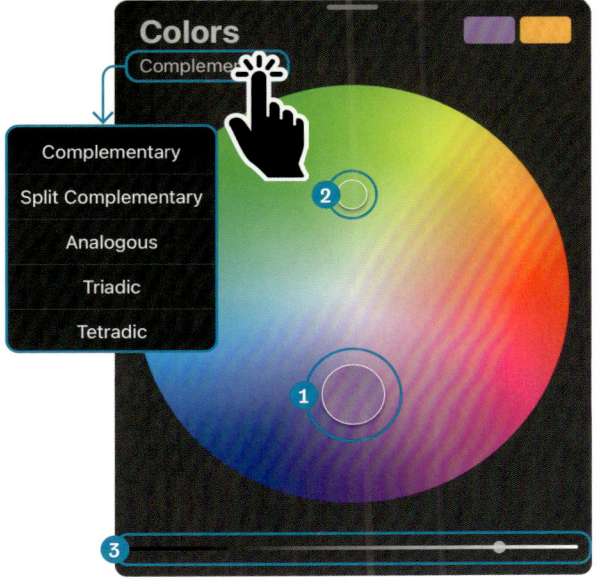

Value

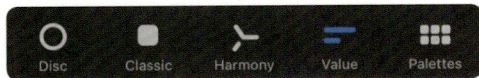

This picker is a bit more technical but very precise.

If you have a specific color you need to use in a project, this picker ensures you can access it. Create a color by using one of these options:

1 **HSB:** Use the sliders or punch in the numerical value of your hue, saturation, and brightness.

2 **RGB sliders:** Use the sliders or punch in the numerical value of red, green, and blue.

3 **Hex code:** Type in the hexadecimal code of your color if you know it.

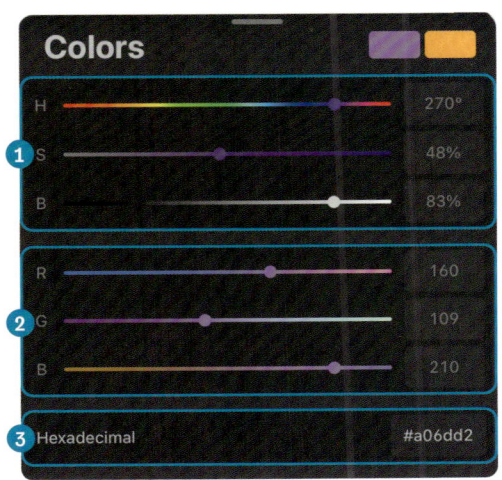

Palettes

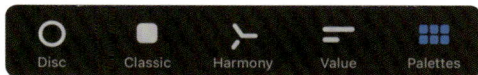

Use *Palettes* to save your favorite colors for use on future projects.

Create New

Tap the + icon in the top right to create a new palette. The first option will allow you to manually create your own palette, while the others will autogenerate a palette based off your image. Tap on the name of your palette to rename it.

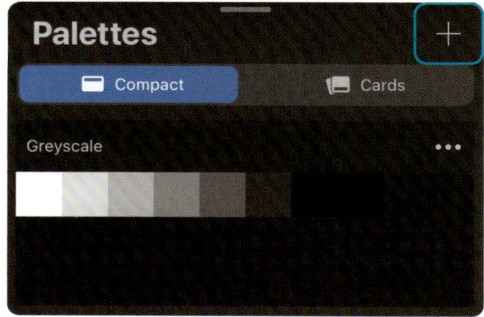

Set as Default

The palette with the blue checkmark is your "default palette," and it's the one that will show up at the bottom of the color panel when using different pickers. Set a different palette as your default by tapping:

• • • > Set as default

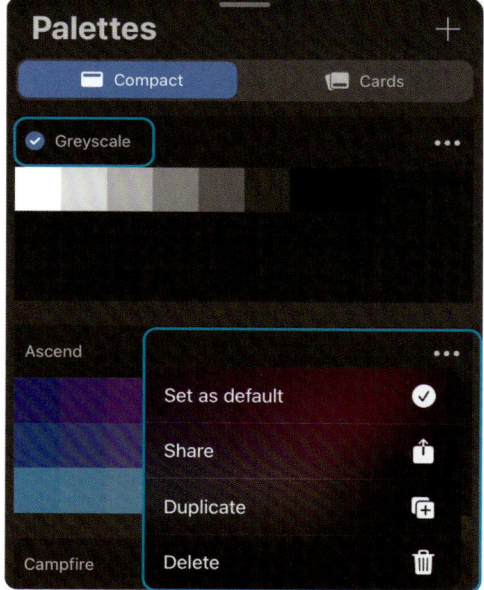

Add or Delete a Swatch

Use another picker, such as *Disc*, to generate a color. Tap an empty square in the default palette area to save the active color to your palette.

Long press on a color to access the option to delete it.

Reorder Swatches

Long press and then drag to move a swatch to a different place.

Set a Swatch as Your Active Color

Tap a swatch to set it as your active color.

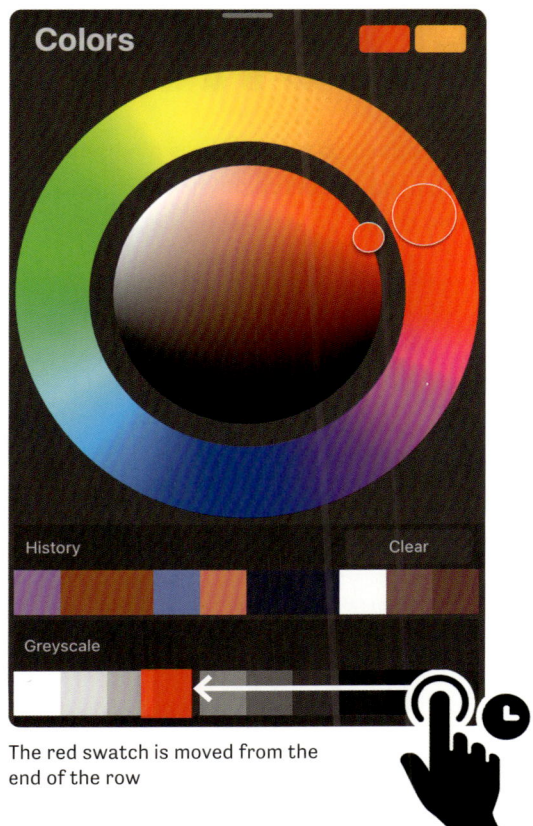

The red swatch is moved from the end of the row

Eye Dropper

While you're painting, you may want to sample a color that already exists on the canvas. To do so, tap + hold with a finger until the eyedropper ring appears. The top of the ring showcases the color you're sampling while the bottom of the ring showcases your *Active Color*.

Move your finger across the canvas until you find your desired color, then lift your finger. Your *Active Color* will change to the one you just sampled.

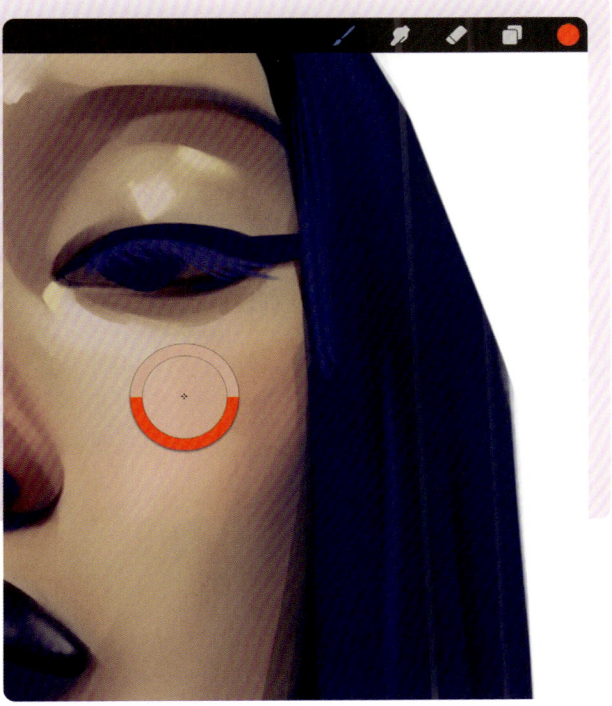

SELECTION

Selection is used to isolate parts of artwork. It's the ideal tool to use when you need to edit your work in some way (like repainting, resizing, or moving things around). It works like this:

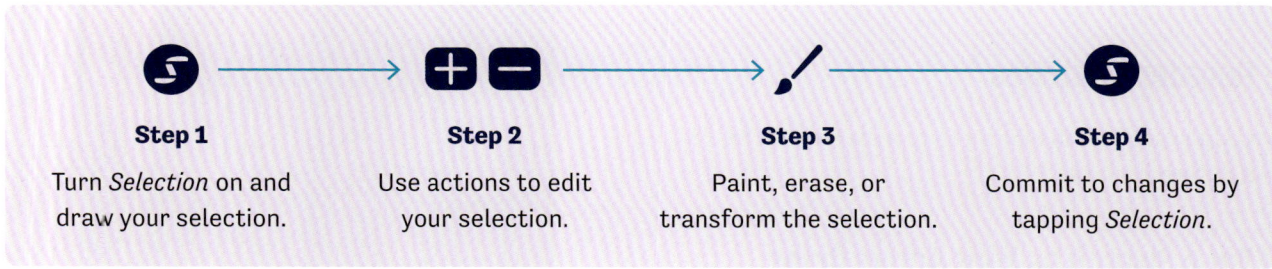

Step 1
Turn *Selection* on and draw your selection.

Step 2
Use actions to edit your selection.

Step 3
Paint, erase, or transform the selection.

Step 4
Commit to changes by tapping *Selection*.

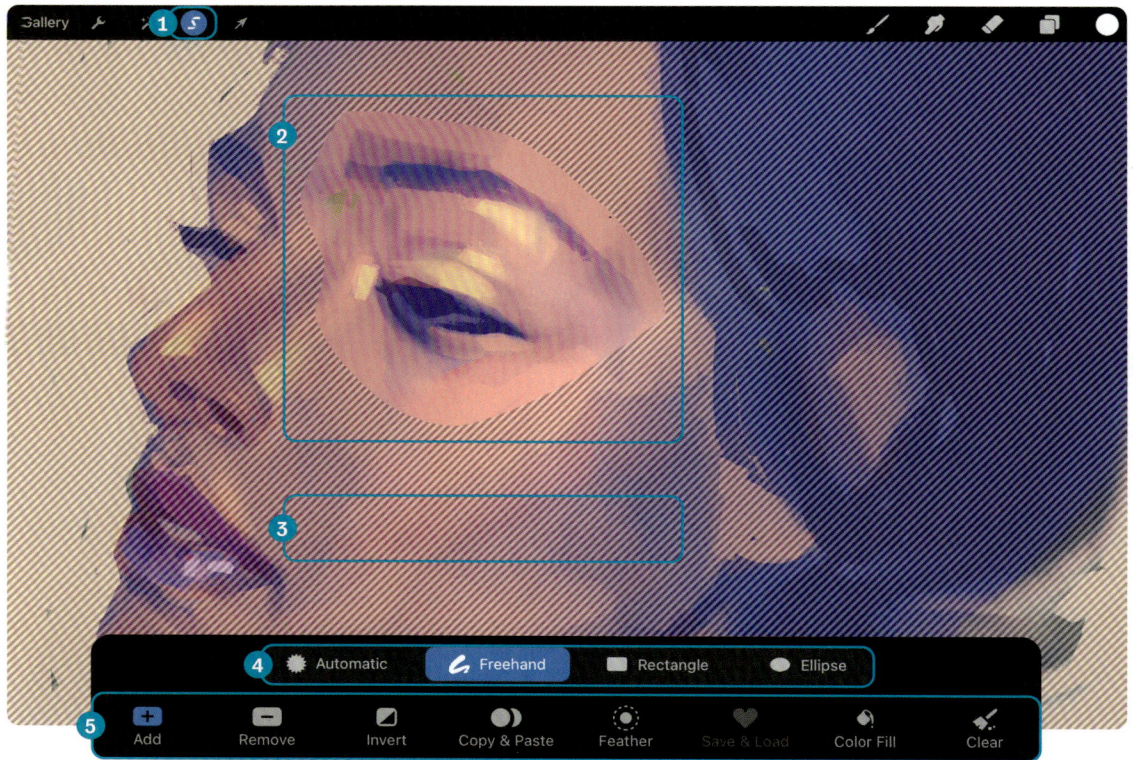

1 **Selection tool**

2 **Selected area of artwork**

3 **Unselected area**
Represented by moving diagonal lines

4 **Selection method**
Automatic, Freehand, Rectangle, and Ellipse

5 **Actions**
Add/Remove, Invert, Copy & Paste, Feather, Save & Load, Color Fill, Clear

Automatic Selection

When you use *Automatic,* Procreate will select an area shown by inverted colors. Adjust the selection by using the threshold slider (at the top of the screen). Move your finger to the left or right to take in less or more of an area.

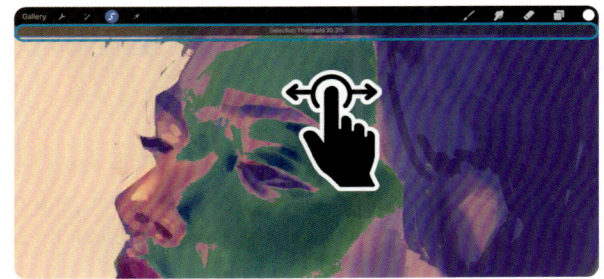

Freehand Selection

Unlike *Automatic,* freehand allows you to draw over a specific area you want to select. Out of the four, I typically use this option because I find it to be the most precise.

The point at which you begin to draw your selection will be marked by a grey dot. To close your selection, tap the grey dot.

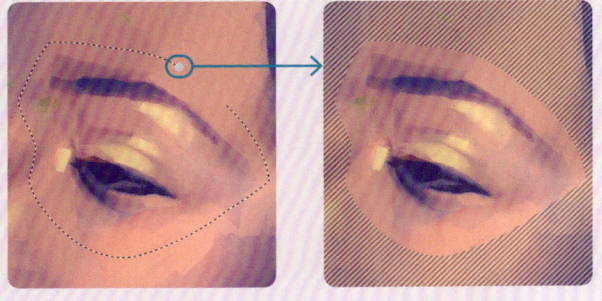

Once you tap the grey dot, your selection will close. The area that you haven't selected will be marked by diagonal lines.

Actions

Add/Remove
Add and *Remove* allow you to be really precise with your selection. For example, if you make a mistake and select too much of your artwork, just redraw over the area you want to remove and tap *Remove.*

Invert
Reverse what you've selected with what you have not.

Copy + Paste
Procreate will copy and paste (as a new layer) the area of your artwork that you selected.

Feather
Soften the edges of your selection. At 0% your edges will remain crisp. Use the slider to dial up the amount of softness you want.

Here's a tip!

You can lift your pencil and zoom in and out while drawing a selection.

Save & Load
Save a selection that you'll use time and time again by tapping Save & Load > + icon. To load it, tap *Save & Load* and select it from the menu. This is a great way to make stamps.

Color Fill
Use this action to lay down large areas of color at once. Tap *Color Fill* then use *Add* and *Remove* to color sections with ease.

Clear
Clear your entire selection and start over.

TRANSFORM

Transform is used to manipulate artwork in various ways—move objects around the canvas and resize, rotate, distort, and flip them. Transform is an excellent tool for making edits to your work on the fly.

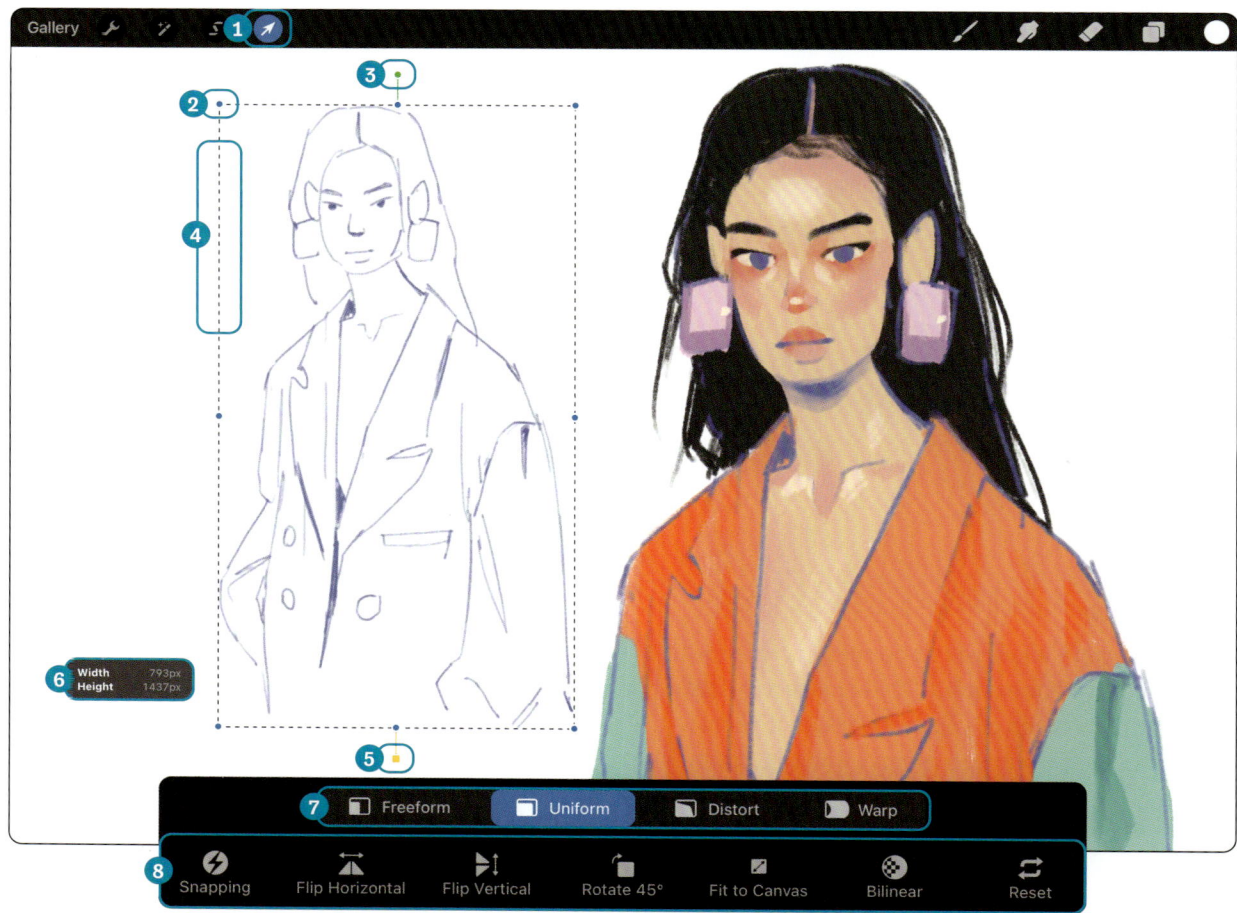

1 **Transform tool**

2 **Transformation node (blue)**

3 **Rotation node (green)**

4 **Bounding box**
Indicated by moving dashed line

5 **Bounding box node (yellow)**

6 **Scale read-out**
A read-out, in pixels, of your transformation's width and height

7 **Transformation mode**
Freeform, Uniform, Distort, and Warp

8 **Actions**
Assistive snap, Flip, Rotate, Fit to Canvas, Interpolation, Reset

The Bounding Box and Nodes

The bounding box and nodes will automatically appear around the object you've selected. The bounding box surrounds the object that you're about to transform and is represented by a moving dashed line (sometimes called "marching ants"). Drag the object on your canvas to move it, or use the nodes to change the shape, size, and rotation.

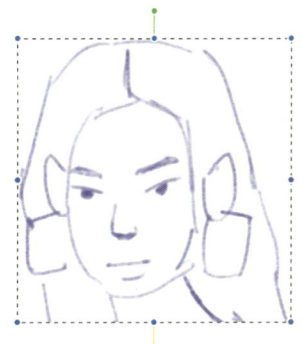

Freeform and Uniform

Freeform allows you to stretch and squish the object within the bounding box. In contrast, selecting *Uniform* will allow you to scale the object evenly. *Uniform* locks the aspect ratio so that you don't accidentally distort your object.

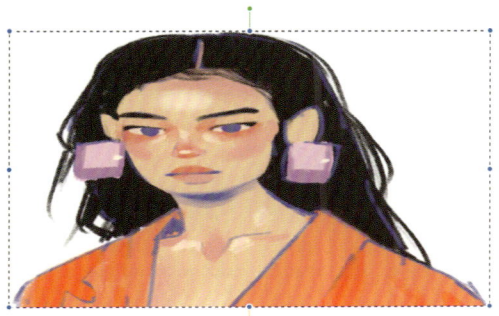

Distort

Use *Distort* to alter the perspective of an object. When *Distort* is selected, the corner nodes of the bounding box will change the perspective instead of scaling an object.

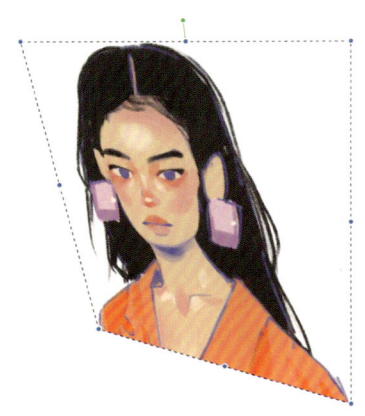

Warp

Warp, like *Distort*, is a great choice if you want to manipulate perspective. Choosing *Warp* will pull up a mesh grid over your object. You can drag the nodes, or the horizontal and vertical lines of the mesh, to create trippy effects (like a fishbowl effect).

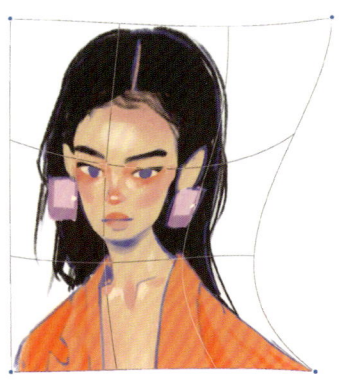

Snapping

Snapping is an assistive tool. Toggle it on to aid you as you move objects around the canvas. You'll literally feel an object "snap" into place.

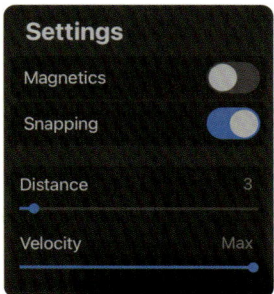

Magnetics

Guidelines appear on screen to help you as you move objects around. This is very handy if you're trying to move an object vertically or horizontally on the canvas.

Right: It may be difficult to see, but notice that there's a blue guideline that has appeared to assist with horizontal placement.

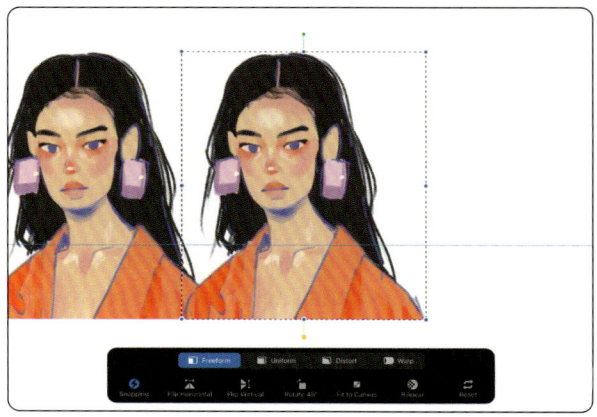

Flip and Rotate

Use the buttons to quickly flip or rotate objects on the canvas. Alternatively, you can use the transformation nodes to perform the same actions.

You can also use gestures when rotating. With two fingers, twist the object to rotate it to the desired degree.

First object is untransformed, second object uses *Flip Horizontal*, third object uses *Rotate 45°*

Reset

Hit *Reset* to undo your transformations and start from scratch.

Apply Your Transformation

Leave transformation mode by choosing another tool. When you do this, your changes will be applied.

ADJUSTMENTS

The magic wand icon will open up color adjustments and filters. We won't need to use the majority of these, but there are a few that will be important for portrait painting.

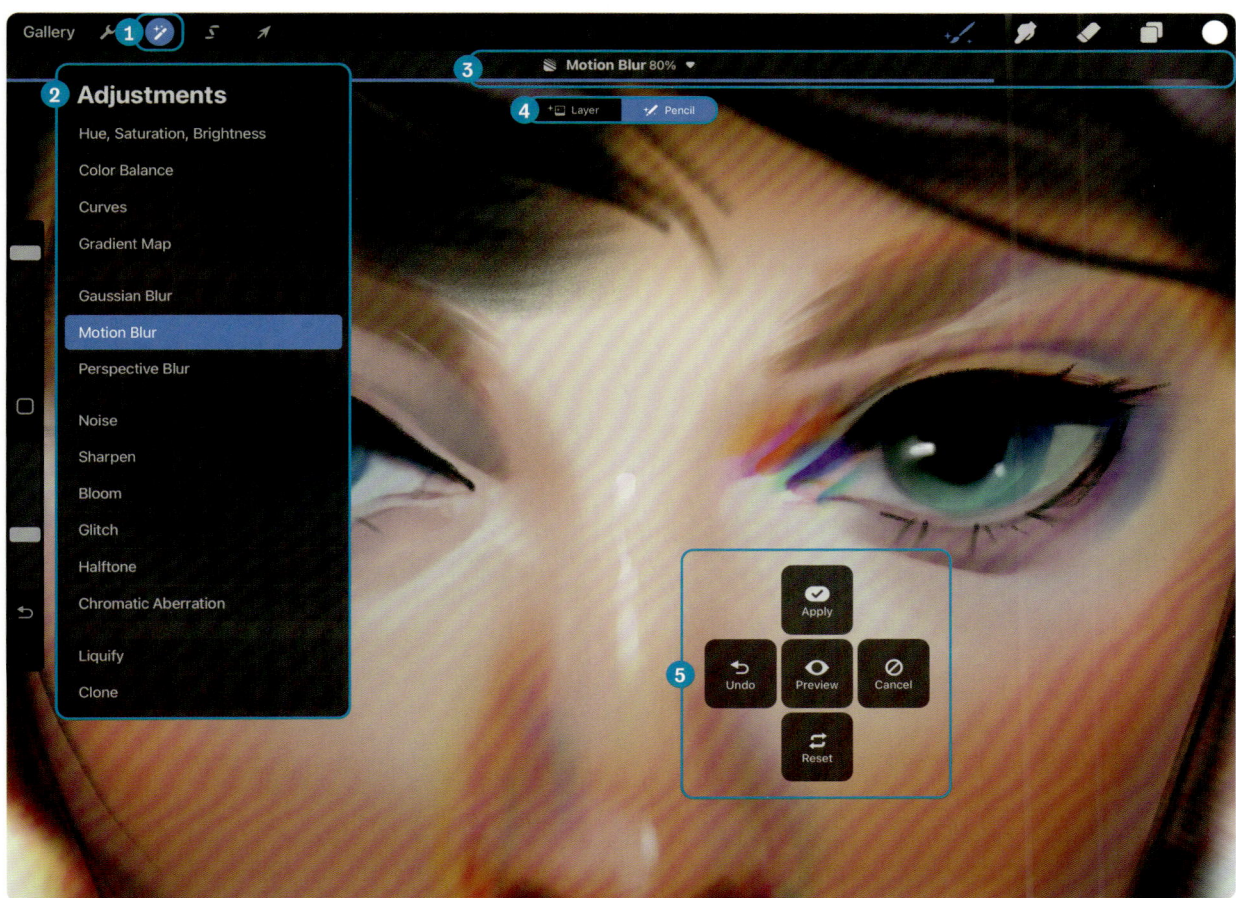

Controlling Adjustments

Adjustments and filters use sliders to fine-tune the effects being applied.

Typically the slider at the top of the screen is used to alter the strength of the adjustment. Some adjustments will have multiple sliders and buttons located at both the top and bottom of the screen.

① **Adjustments tool**

② **List of adjustments and filters**

③ **Strength of adjustment slider**

④ **Application**
Apply to entire layer or use Apple Pencil to paint the adjustment on parts of the layer

⑤ **Adjustment actions**
Preview, Apply, Cancel, Reset, Undo

Color Adjustments

Hue, Saturation, Brightness

Use the three different sliders to adjust the overall hue, saturation, or brightness of a layer. This is especially handy when you want to tweak the colors or boost the vibrancy of your artwork.

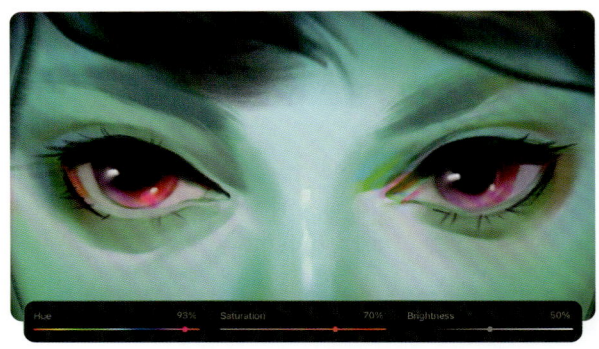

Color Balance

This adjustment allows you to tweak, or completely change, the color scheme of your artwork. You can adjust the shadows, midtones, and highlights separately, which really lets you fine-tune your image.

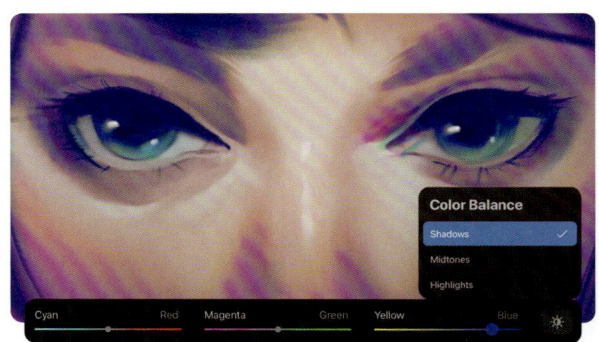

Curves

A powerful adjustment for balancing the colors of your image. The graph is a visual representation of the amount of red, green, and blue (RGB) in your artwork. You'll be able to see which colors are most dominant. Adjust color levels individually (using the individual channels) or altogether (*Gamma*) by adding points on the diagonal line and moving them up or down.

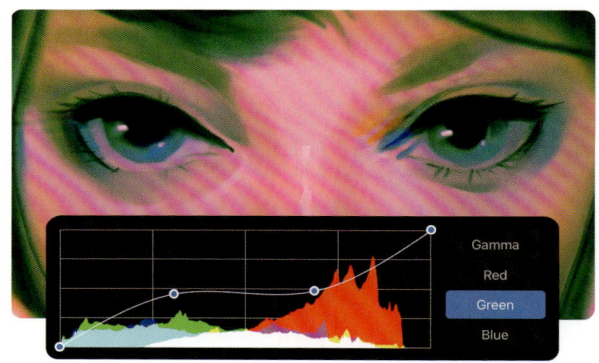

Gradient Map

Replace the shadows, midtones, and highlights of your artwork by mapping them to a gradient. *Gradient Map* comes with presets but also the ability to customize your own gradient.

Flip ahead to pages 142–144 for an in-depth walkthrough of *Gradient Map*.

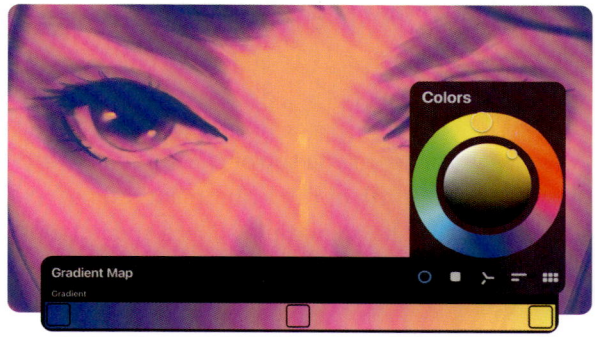

Filters

Applying filters to your work is another way of making an adjustment. In general, when painting portraits, you won't really need to use too many filters. A few good ones are:

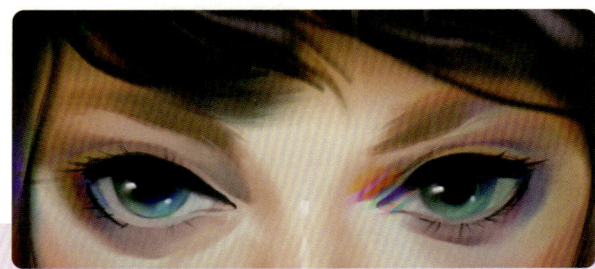

Sharpen and Blur

Use these two filters together to enhance your image. A good technique in portraiture is to keep the focal point sharp and high in detail while allowing the rest of the image to be somewhat out of focus or impressionistic. This contrast brings and keeps the attention of the viewer on the focal point.

Top right: Sharpened
Bottom right: Blurred

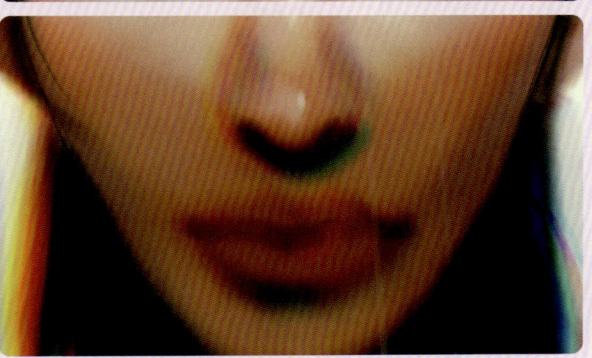

Glitch and Chromatic Aberration

These filters are some of my favorites, and I just find them a ton of fun to use! They quickly create wacky and cool effects that would be very difficult and time-consuming to paint.

Top right: Glitch
Bottom right: Chromatic aberration

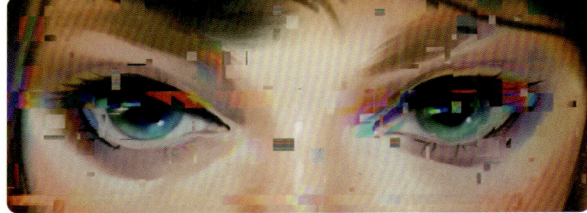

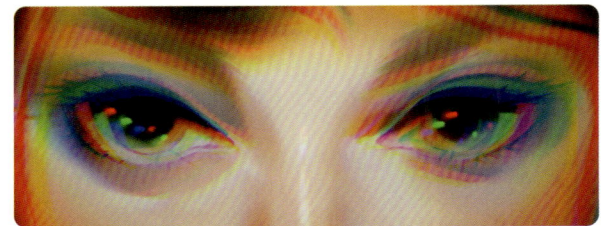

Liquify

This is a really great filter for experimentation!

Use *Liquify* to push, pull, shrink, and grow parts of your artwork. You can use it to help you stylize a portrait, or you can use it to make quick fixes—for example, if an eye is too small, use *Liquify* to expand it as it's much faster than repainting.

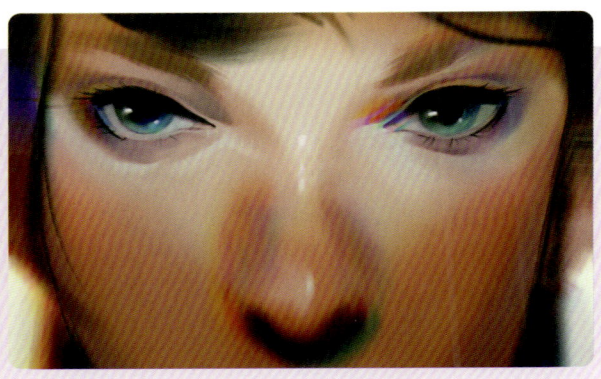

PERSONALIZATION SETTINGS

Procreate offers some great personalization options. These range from changing the interface to altering the way Procreate behaves. I've listed a few settings I think are worth checking out.

Dark/Light Interface

Depending on the situation, you may want to change Procreate's interface from dark mode to light mode. Dark mode is easier on the eyes and allows you to focus on your artwork. Light mode, on the other hand, may be ideal if you're working in a very bright environment.

Actions > Prefs > Toggle Light Interface on/off

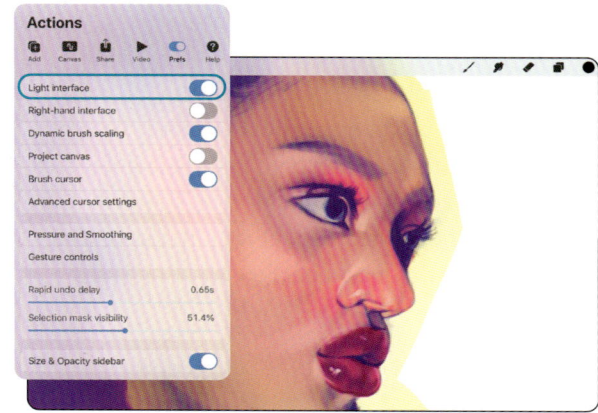

Move the Sidebar

For Lefties

If you're left-handed, then you'd probably prefer to have the sidebar located on the right side of the screen for easier access. Switch sides by going to:

Actions > Prefs > Toggle Right-hand interface on/off

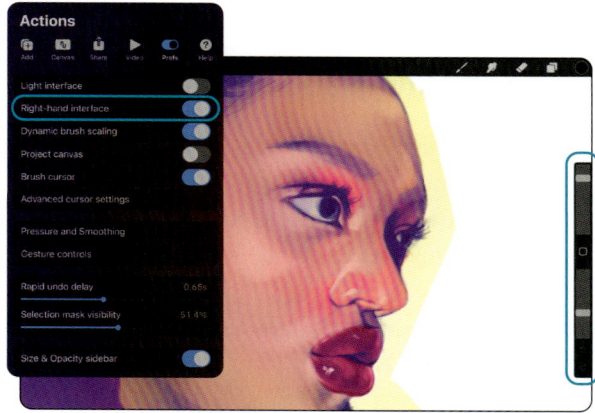

Move the Sidebar

You can do more than just switch the side that the sidebar docks on. To move it up or down, swipe a finger from the edge of the screen over the modify button until the sidebar pops out. Drag it up or down and drop it to place it in position.

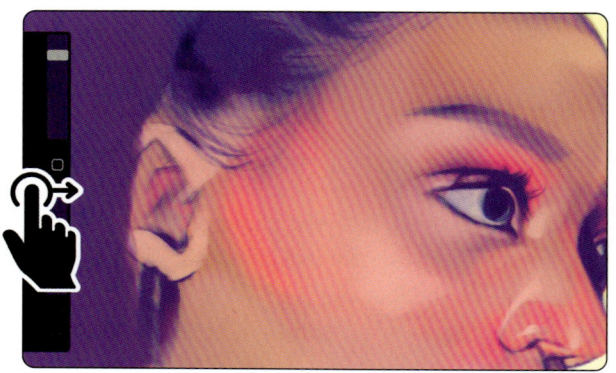

Gesture Controls

Open up *Gesture Controls* to set up your gesture preferences. Go down the list and see if there are any you'd like to change/replace. You don't have to do this immediately, as you may realize that these settings could be optimized for your workflow over time. For example, here you can set up whether you'd like to be able to smudge using your finger, the apple pencil, or neither.

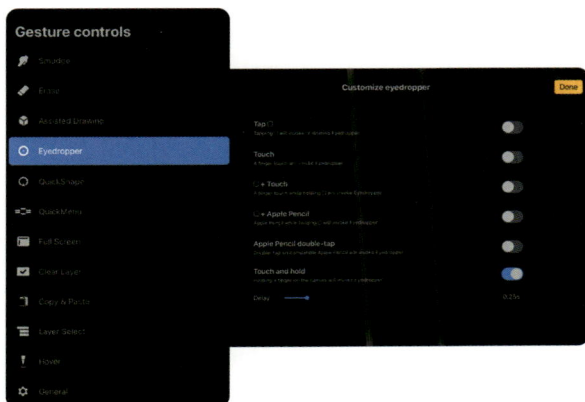

Modify Button

By default, tapping the modify button will invoke the eyedropper. You can set the modify button to trigger other tools. For example, I've got mine set to smudge when I hold the modify button down.

Actions > Gesture controls > Set to tap ☐, ☐ + touch or ☐ + Apple Pencil

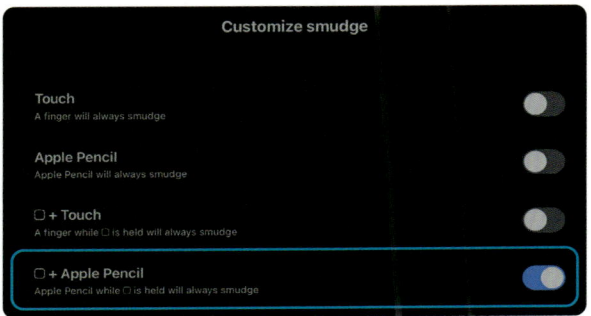

Stroke Stabilization

This is a great accessibility option found under:

Actions > Prefs > Pressure & Smoothing

Turn the stabilization slider up. The higher the percentage, the smoother your lines will get as you draw.

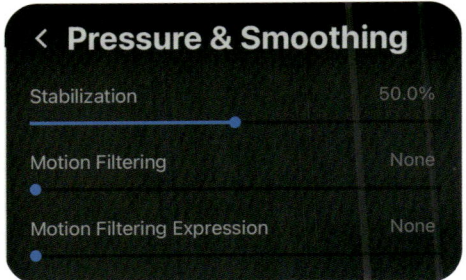

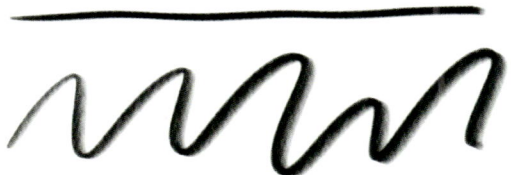

No stabilization

Stabilization at 50%

App Pressure Sensitivity

Change how Procreate responds to the way that you draw. This is especially important to set up if you have a light touch. Locate the graph under:

Actions > Prefs > Pressure & Smoothing

By default, there will be a straight diagonal line on the graph. To make the app more sensitive to light strokes of the Apple Pencil, place a node on the line and move the node up (this will make the line arch upward).

If instead you have a habit of pressing really hard when you draw and you want Procreate to be less sensitive to your strokes, then move the node down. You can have up to six nodes on the line to get really nuanced.

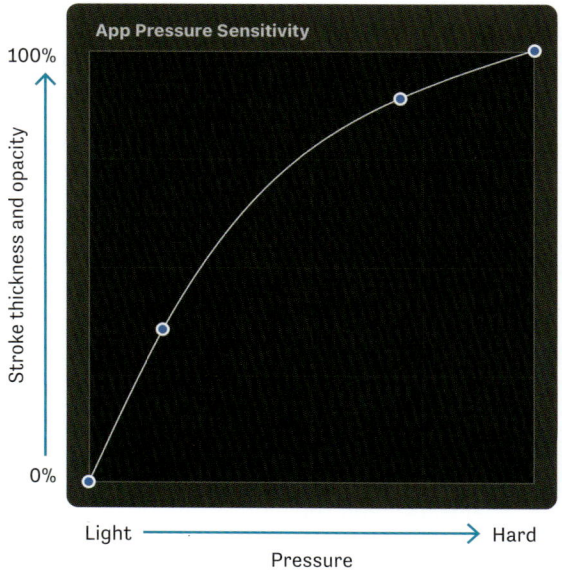

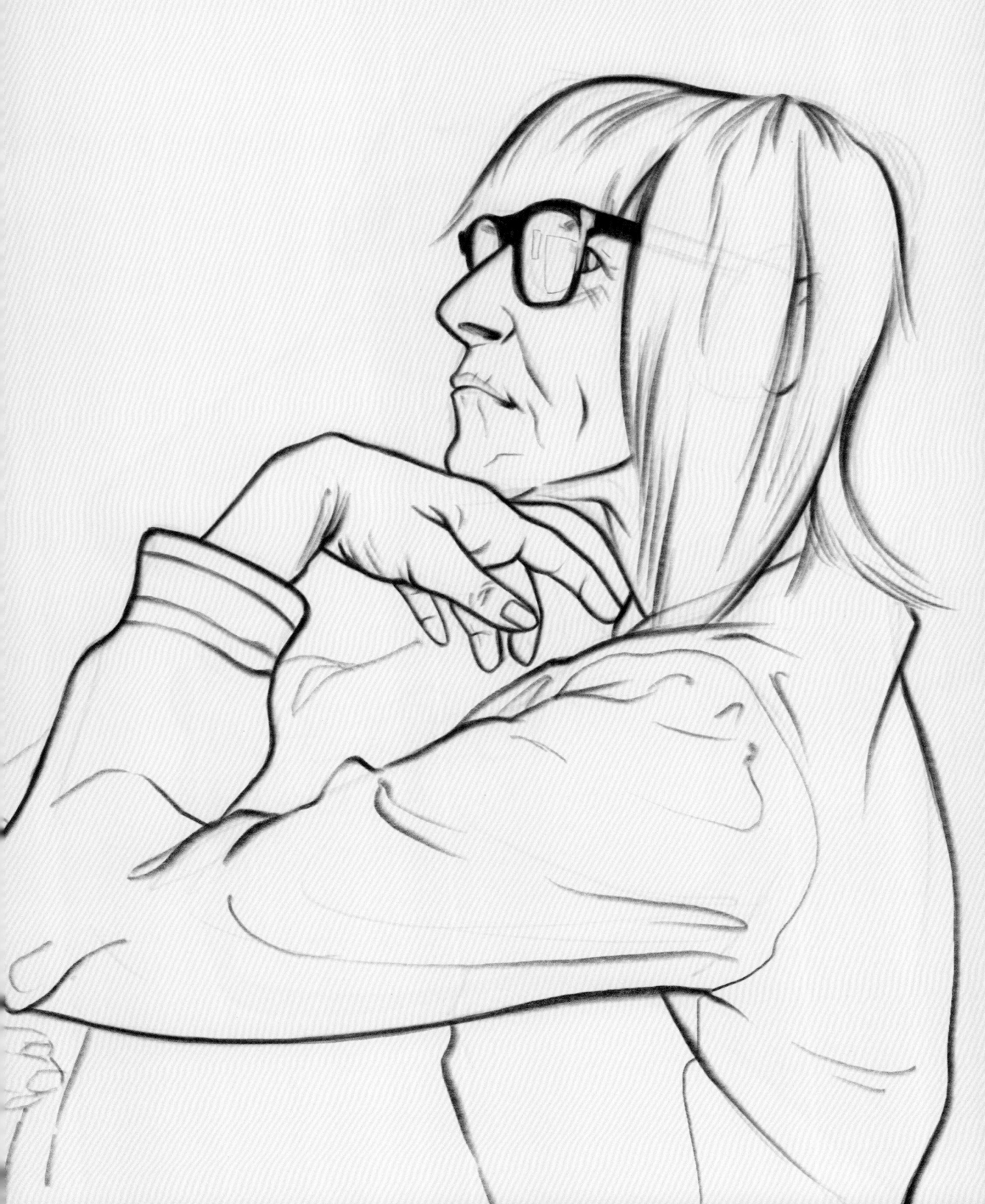

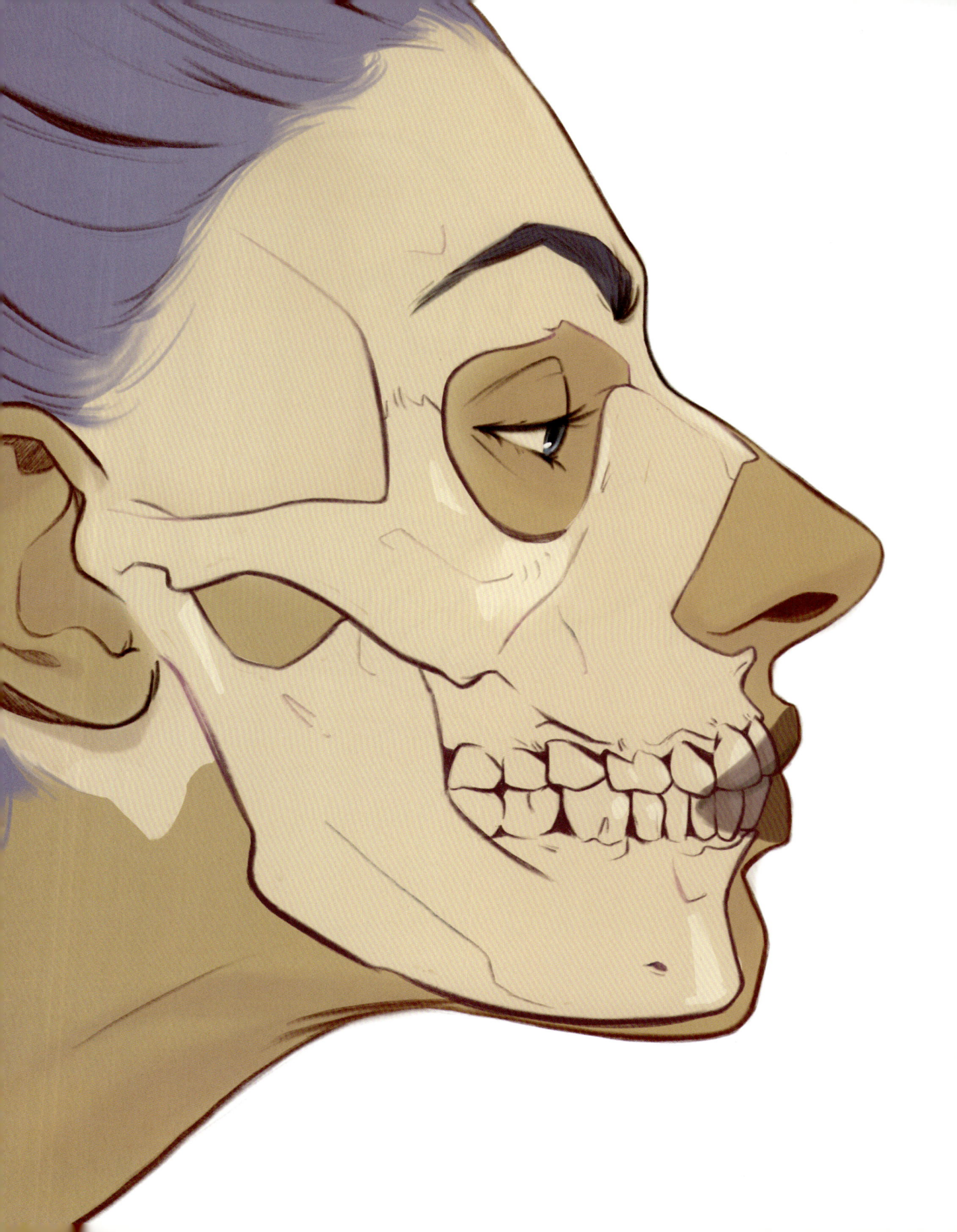

Learning ANATOMY

Learning anatomy provides a solid foundation for understanding the structure and proportions of the human face. It will help you draw portraits that are more accurate and realistic.

By learning anatomy you'll be more confident, especially when drawing with little to no reference. And please don't be intimidated—you don't have to become a master of anatomy or memorize all the names of the muscles and bones! Even learning a little bit will vastly improve your drawings.

STRUCTURE OF THE SKULL

The structure of the skull determines what a person will look like in real life. Muscle, skin, and even clothing conform to its shape.

Using the diagram, we'll cover some of the skull's key landmarks. These key landmarks can be seen in real life and can help an artist with proper placement of the facial features. Even though we're just looking at bones now, when we move into reference imagery, you'll be able to spot some of the parts mentioned here.

Brow Ridge

This is the arch-shaped ridge that sits above the orbital. It's easy to spot from a ¾ view because it sticks out a little bit. The brow ridge is more pronounced in males than in females.

Zygomatic Arch (a.k.a. Your Cheekbone)

These are the widest parts of the face (but not the entire skull). The zygomatic arch borders the bottom of the orbital. It's another easy-to-spot landmark, and it's quite easy to feel in real life as well. The bottom of the arch lines up with the bottom of the nasal aperture and cranium.

Superior Temporal Line

This is an arching ridge that clearly defines the "front" versus the "side" planes of the head. It can clearly be seen on a model depending on lighting.

Orbital (a.k.a. Eye Sockets)

Your eyeballs slot right into these lovely sockets. Musculature and skin will cover up the majority of the orbital, so all you end up seeing is a little almond-shaped slit for the eye. The eyebrows rest on the top portion of the orbital (not quite on the brow ridge as some may assume).

Nasal Bone and Nasal Aperture

No human skull actually has a nose. Instead, our nose (primarily made up of cartilage) is attached to the nasal bone. The cartilage of the nose will cover up the nasal aperture. The size of the nasal aperture can vary according to race.

Mandible and Angle of Jaw

The mandible is also known as our jawbone. It's V-shaped, with a point at the chin. This point is more prominent in females than males.

The angle of our jaw is that almost-right-angle point shown in the image. On certain folks this landmark is especially prominent—when it is, they're typically described as having a strong jaw or jawline. If someone is a bit heavier, this landmark may be harder to see because it will be covered with fat, which would soften the angle and give the appearance of a rounded shape.

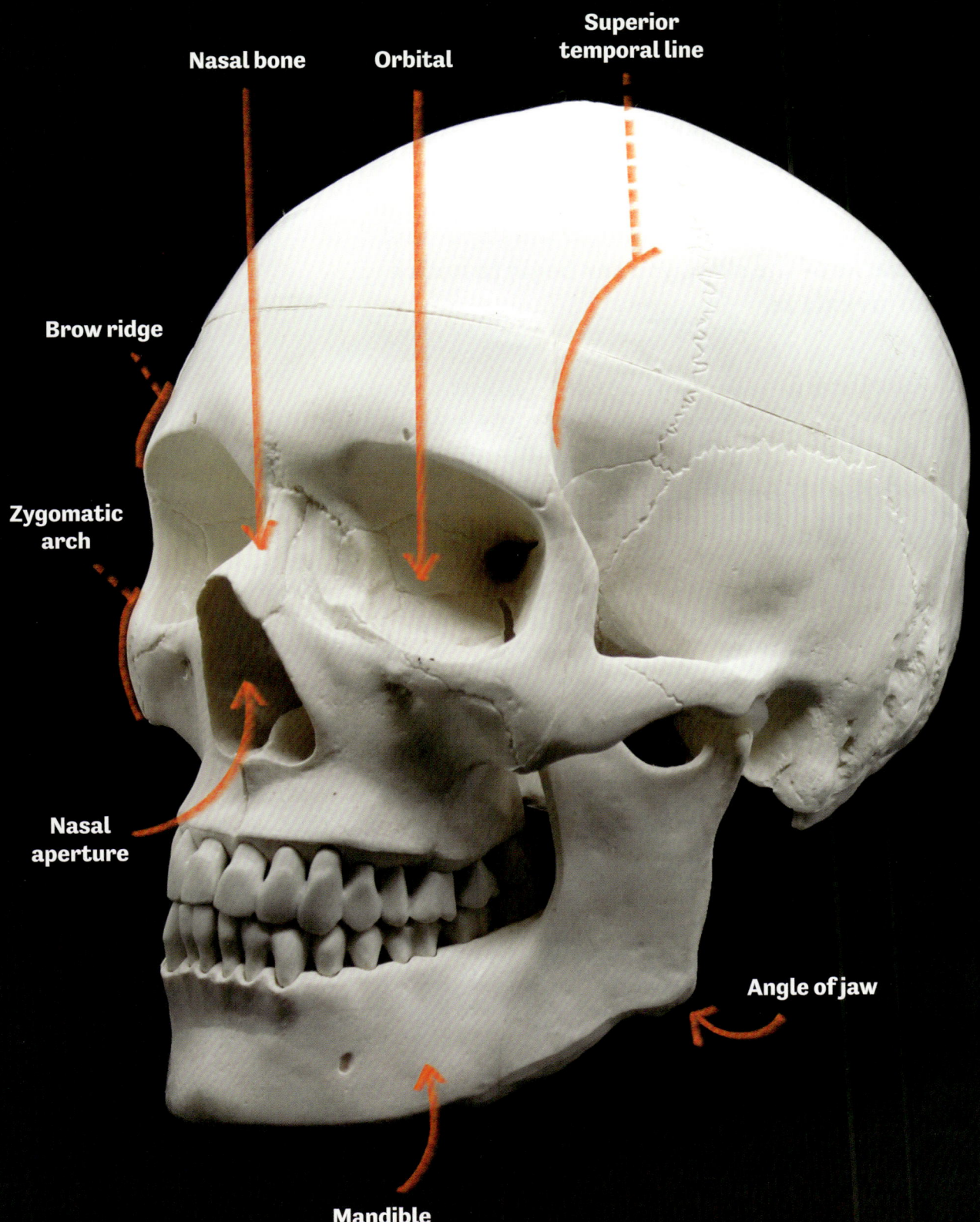

Nasal bone

Orbital

Superior
temporal line

Brow ridge

Zygomatic
arch

Nasal
aperture

Angle of jaw

Mandible

USING LANDMARKS TO DRAW

Now that you've learned some of the important landmarks of the skull, you can begin to notice them in real life.

Being able to spot the key landmarks will help you establish the form of the skull underneath. This will in turn allow you to place features more accurately when drawing or painting.

Remember that there's a ton of muscle, connective tissue, cartilage, and fat hiding underneath the skin. All of these will ultimately affect what you're able to see.

It's also worth bearing in mind that the lighting of a reference image can really help or hinder you. That's because, depending on lighting, some landmarks may be difficult or outright impossible to see.

When visualizing the skull, the brow ridge and zygomatic arch, as well as the angle of the jaw, are the best landmarks to look out for. They're usually pretty easy to spot and they give a great indication of the angle of the skull in space.

Remember that you don't have to get it perfectly right each time. The landmarks are there to guide you. You don't have to spend hours trying to suss out the actual form of an individual's skull—just give it your best guess!

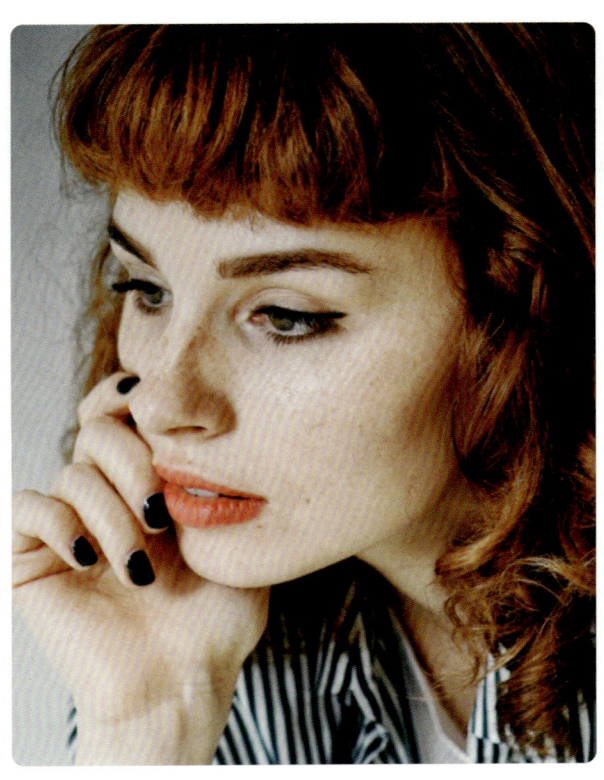
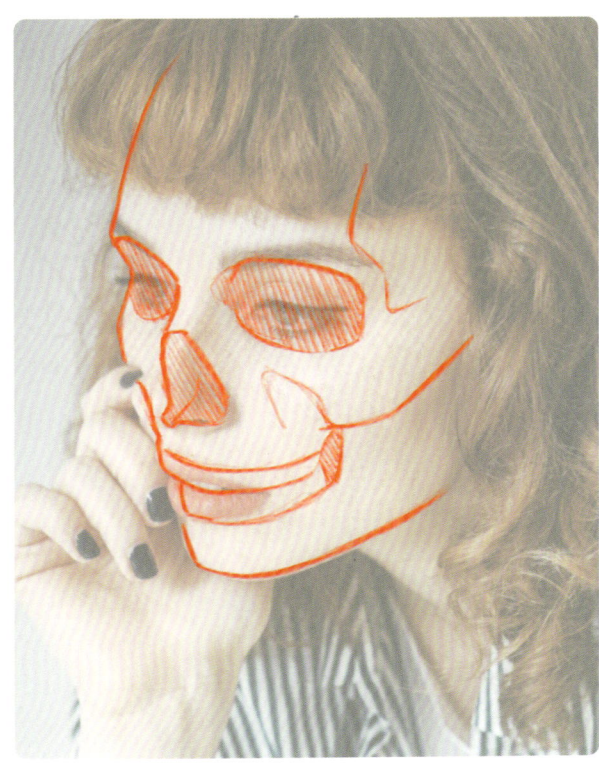
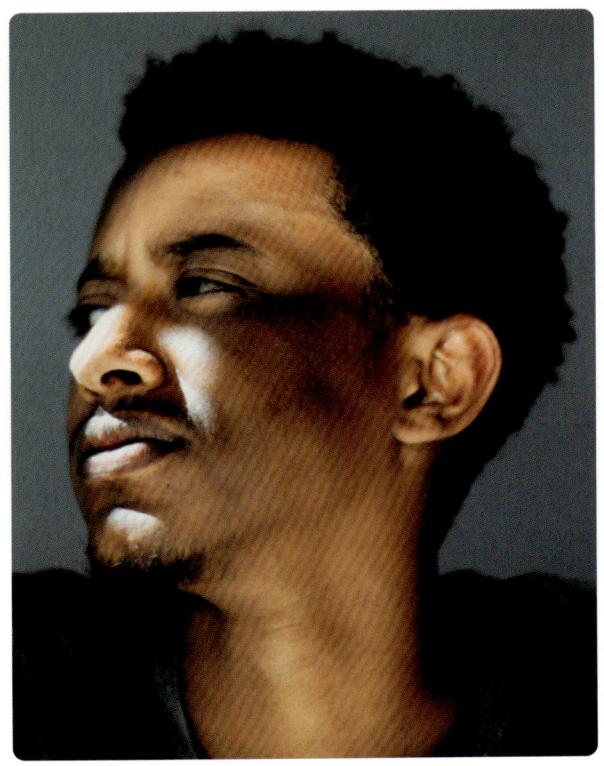
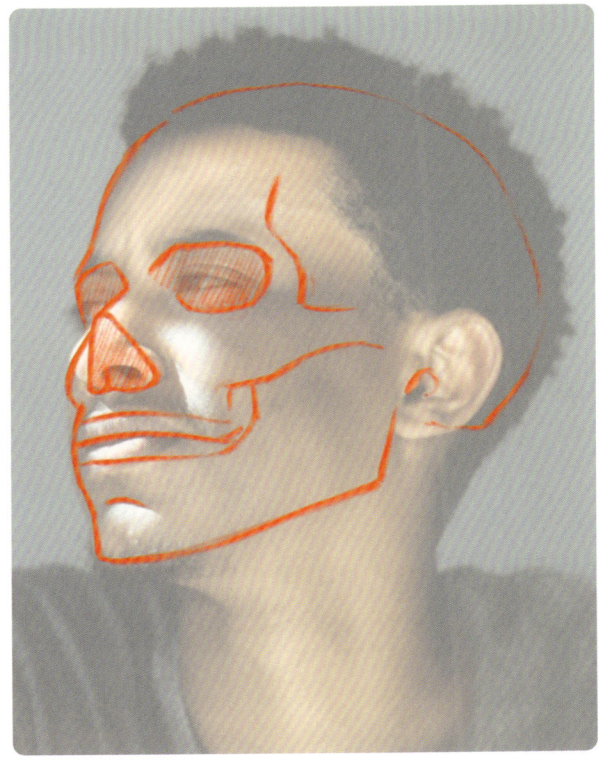

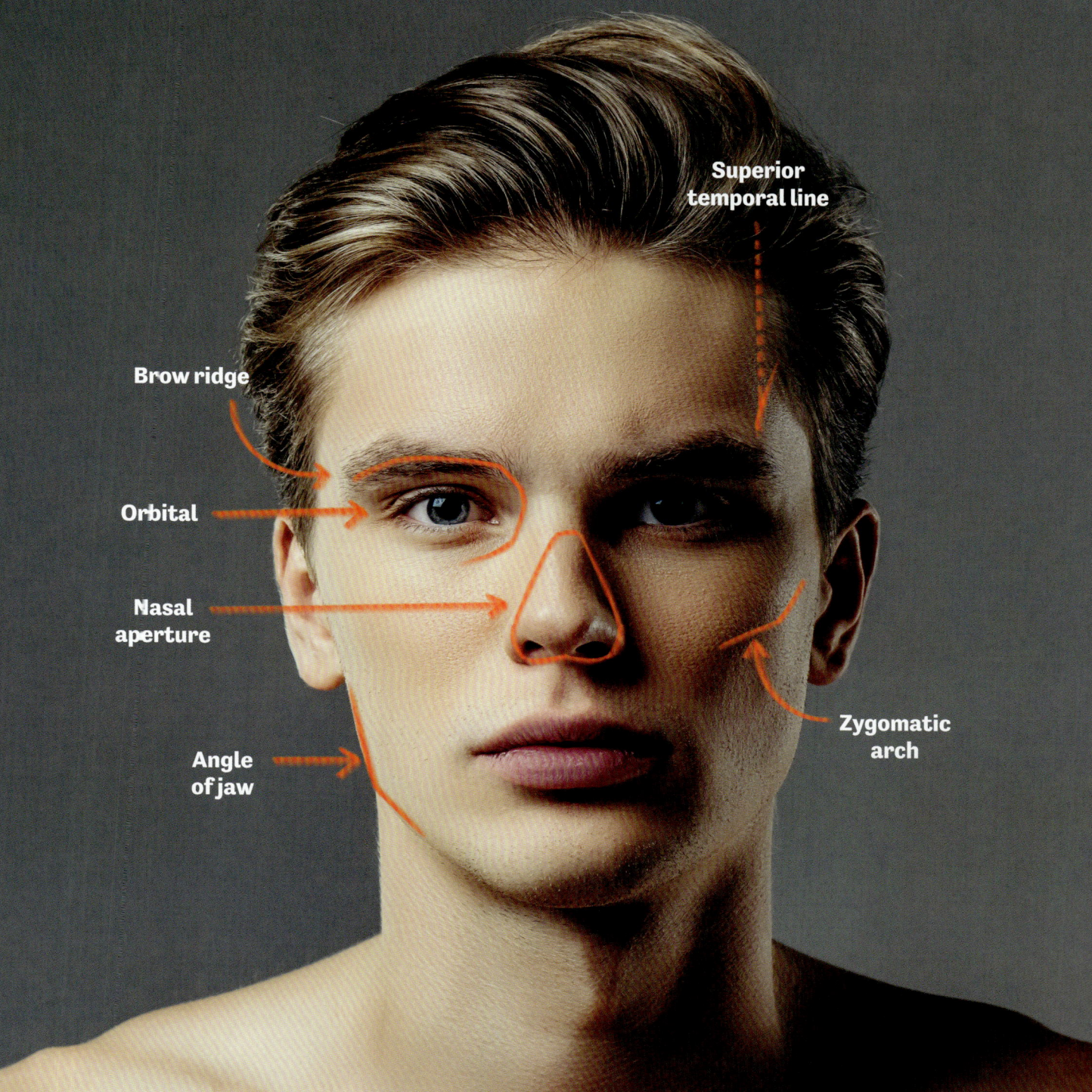

Superior
temporal line

Brow ridge

Orbital

Nasal
aperture

Angle
of jaw

Zygomatic
arch

FRONT VIEW

or Full Face

The front view is often regarded as one of the most static, boring views in portraiture. That's because it's perfectly symmetrical and doesn't offer the brain many points of interest to dwell on.

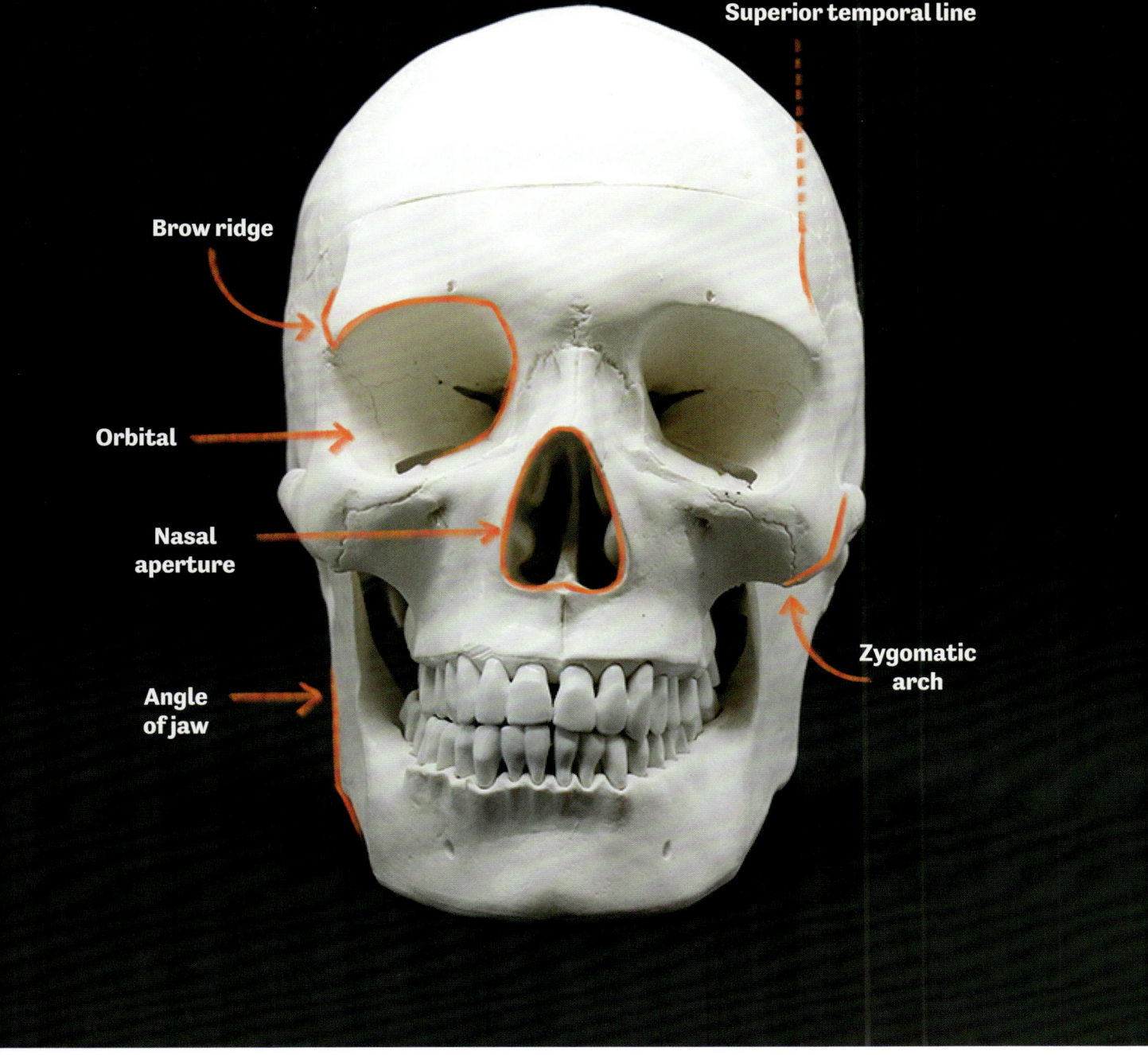

Superior temporal line

Brow ridge

Orbital

Nasal aperture

Zygomatic arch

Angle of jaw

From this view, it's likely that you'll be able to see the zygomatic arch, the angle of the jaw, and, depending on lighting, the brow ridge and superior temporal line.

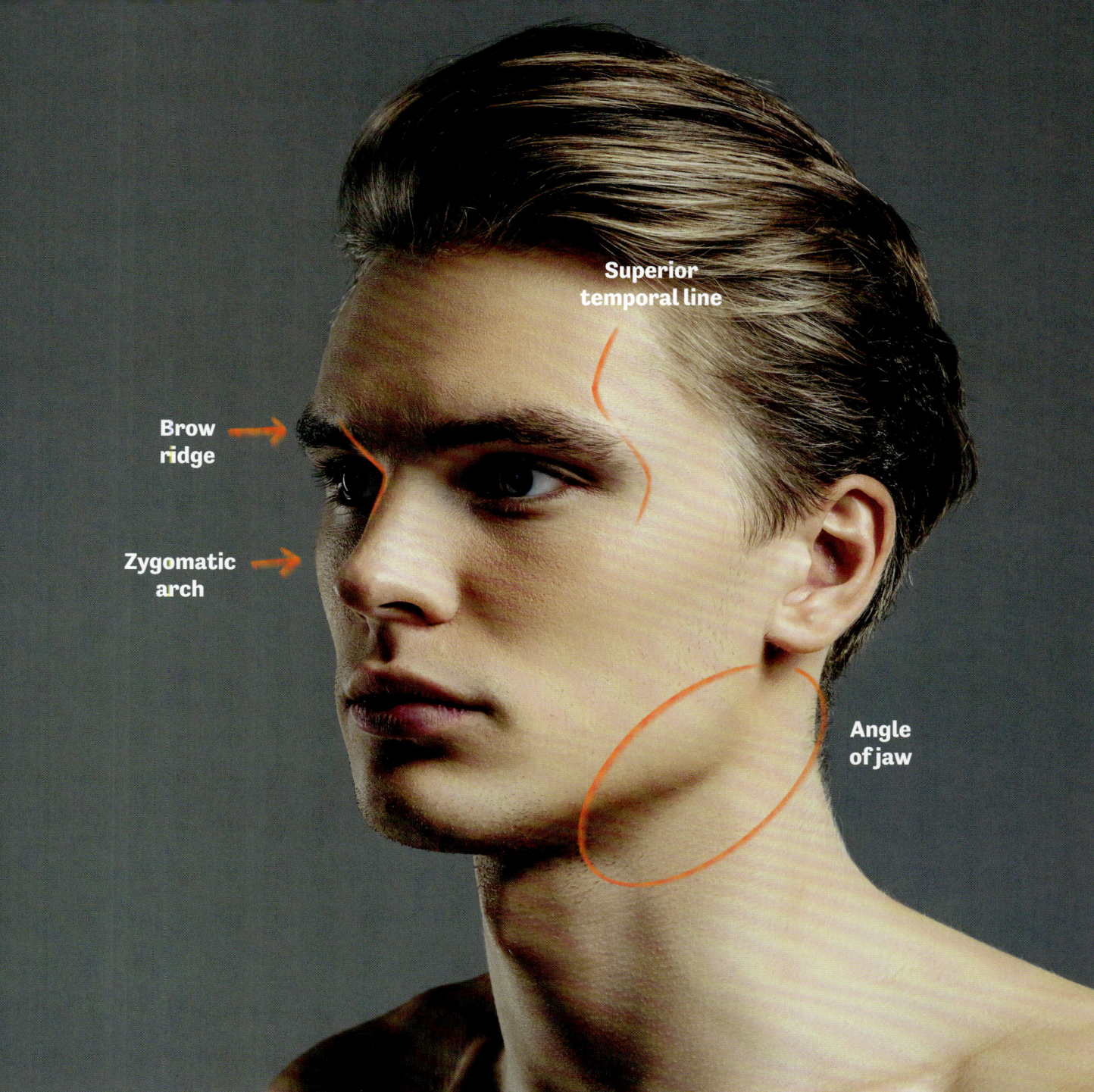

Superior
temporal line

Brow
ridge

Zygomatic
arch

Angle
of jaw

¾ VIEW

This view might be the most challenging of the three, only because you must be able to handle a bit of perspective.

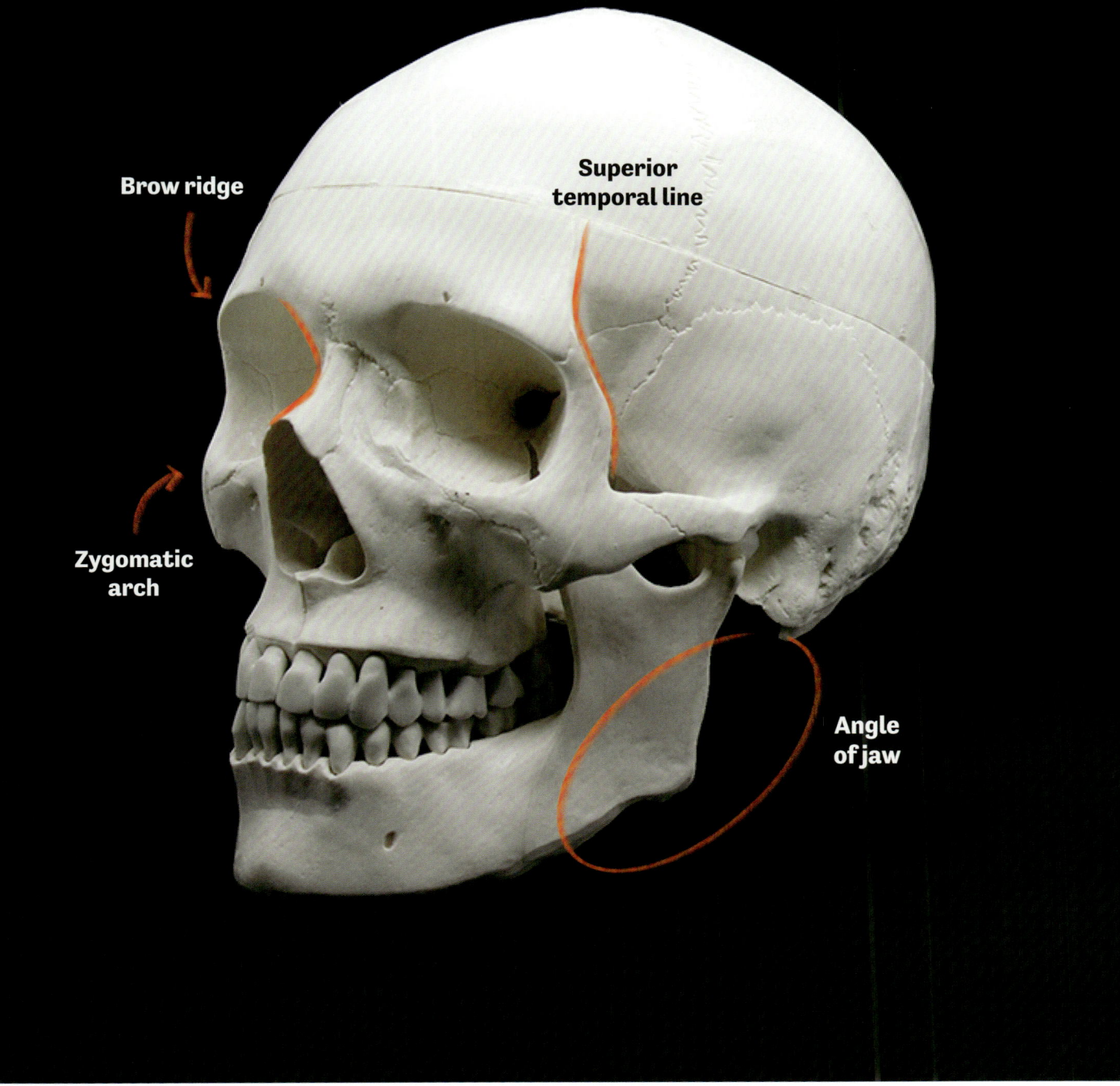

Brow ridge

Superior temporal line

Zygomatic arch

Angle of jaw

From this view, the outline of the brow ridge and zygomatic arch are clear against the background. The angle of the jaw is also clear, and the orbitals and nose bridge will aid in the proper placement of the nose and the eyes.

The superior temporal line is just visible as a highlight on the model's forehead.

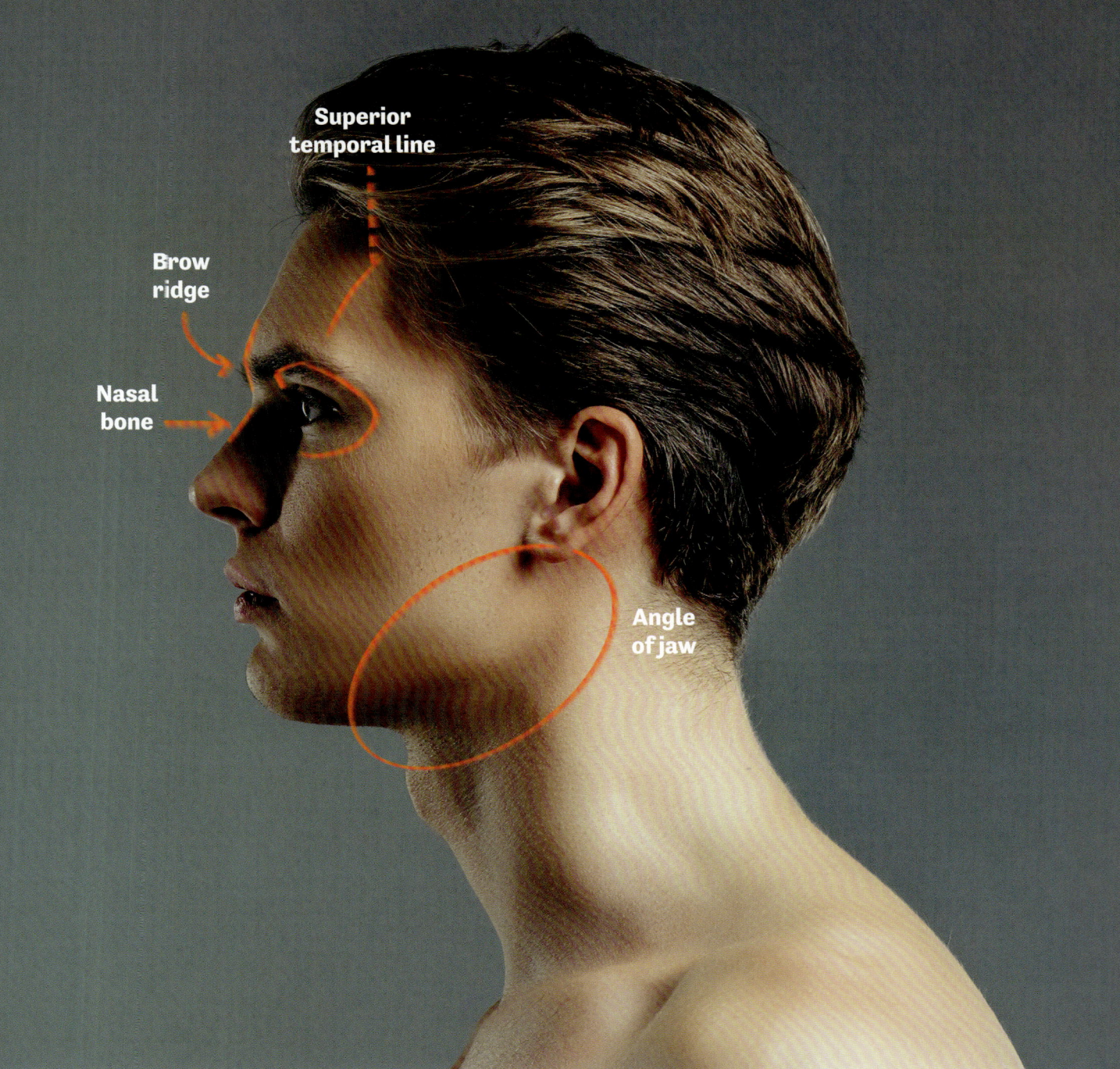

Superior temporal line

Brow ridge

Nasal bone

Angle of jaw

SIDE VIEW

or Profile

This is the easiest view to draw because you don't have to draw with perfect symmetry (only a single eye is ever in view) or deal with the full three-dimensionality of the nose and lips.

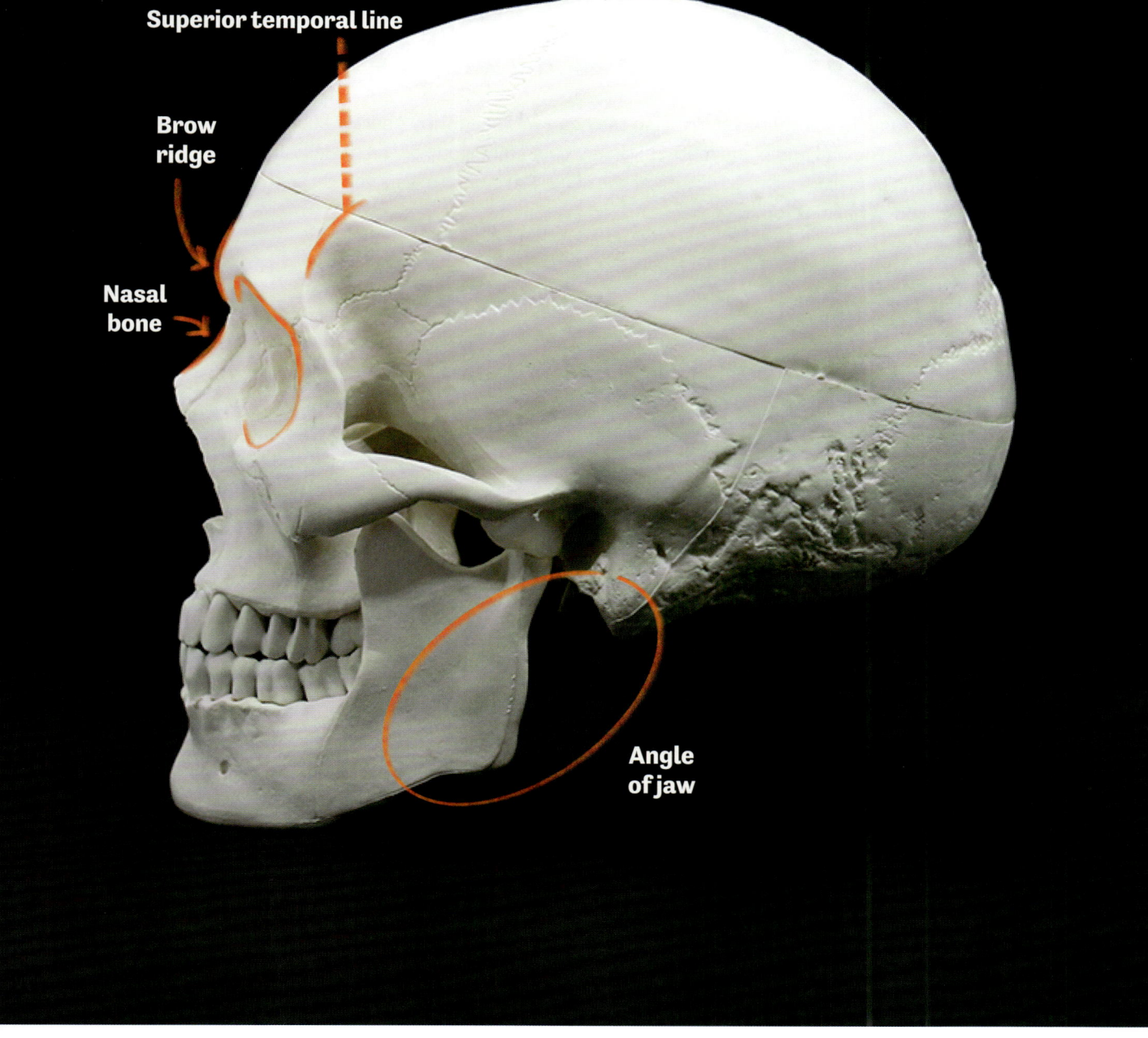

Superior temporal line

Brow ridge

Nasal bone

Angle of jaw

The most notable landmarks in this view include the brow ridge, nasal bone, and angle of the jaw.

It's a common mistake to place the eye too far back on the head—knowing the shape of the orbital from the side view (as seen on the skull) can really help you avoid making this mistake.

The angle of the jaw can be used to give a good idea of the placement of the ear.

Also note that the superior temporal line indicates the side plane of the model's face. In fact, from the side view, the vast majority of what you're looking at is actually the side plane of the head.

DRAWING THE HEAD

One of the most popular methods for drawing the head was taught by Andrew Loomis (the Loomis method or the ball and plane method). In my opinion, it's one of the easiest and clearest methods of creating the structure of the skull. I'm going to walk you through a simplified version of his method.

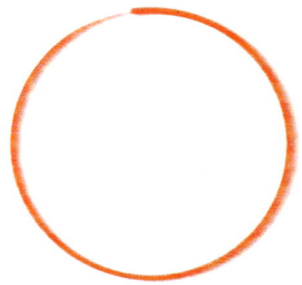

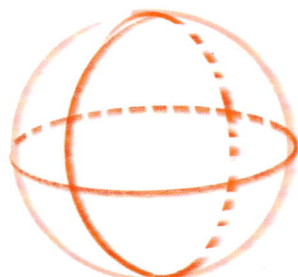

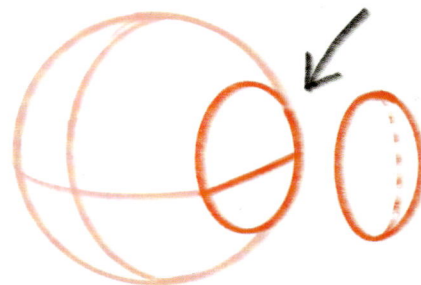

1

Start by drawing a sphere. This will represent the cranium.

2

Add a vertical axis for the middle of the face. Add a horizontal axis for the brow line. These lines must follow the shape of the sphere. It helps to draw through the form to ensure your lines are rounded.

3

Slice off the sides of the sphere to create the sides of the head. This gives a flattened ball shape, which is much more ideal for the skull than a perfectly rounded ball.

Getting Better over Time

I recommend sticking to these measurements for beginners learning to draw the skull for the first time. After a while, and with enough practice, you'll be able to eyeball the spaces, or you may even choose to elongate the spaces between the nose or the chin. The Loomis method gives us a structured formula, which helps us wrap our brains around complex subjects like the head—but no formula is perfect. Individuals are unique, and the size of their heads and the placement of their features will not always (and certainly don't have to) fit into any formula.

4

Using your vertical axis as a guide, drop a line straight down.

Mark off the hairline, brow line, nose, and chin. To find the distances between these measurements, you'll mark halfway from the brow line to the top of the head. That space between the brow line and top of head will be repeated down the midline twice—giving you the nose and then the chin.

5

Draw the V-shape of the mandible underneath the sphere of the cranium. The angle of the jaw will roughly line up with the marker for the nose.

Once you understand this method of drawing the head, you'll be able to use it to create actual characters. See here how a simple skull transforms into an actual face. You'll also be able to turn the head in space confidently by changing the tilt of the axis.

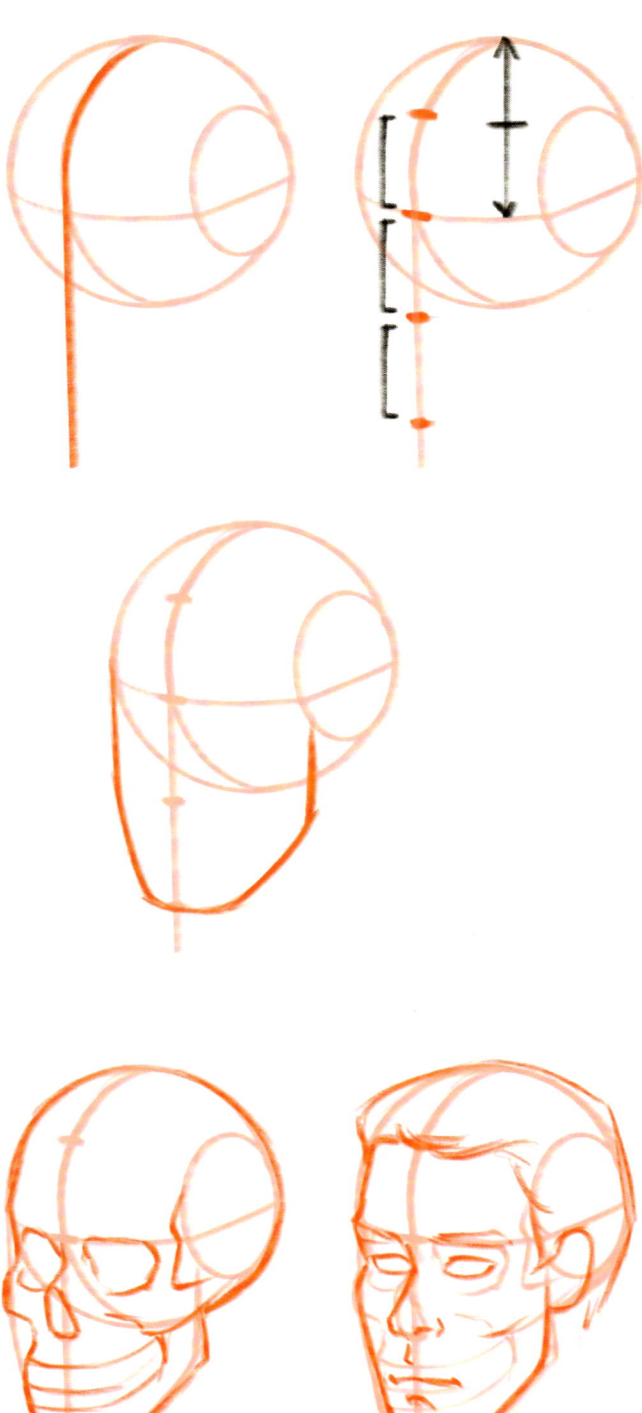

INTRO TO THE EYES

The eyeball itself sits neatly within the skull's orbit. It doesn't take up the entirety of the socket because there are tendons, muscles, fatty tissue, and more that reside in this small space as well.

The primary muscle that we see, covering up the orbit and all its contents, is the orbicularis oculi. This is the muscle that makes up the eyelid and is responsible for squinting.

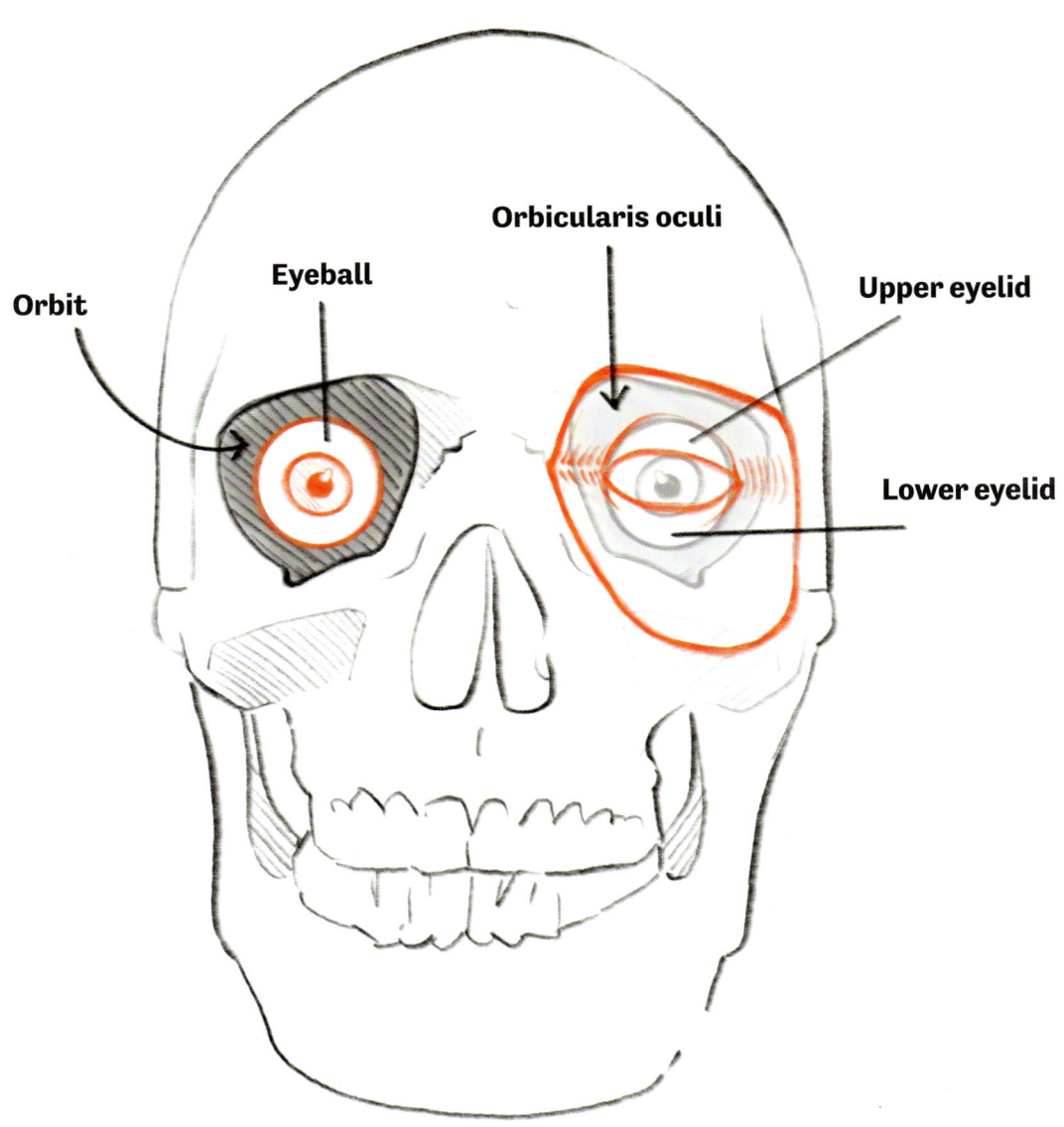

Orbit

Eyeball

Orbicularis oculi

Upper eyelid

Lower eyelid

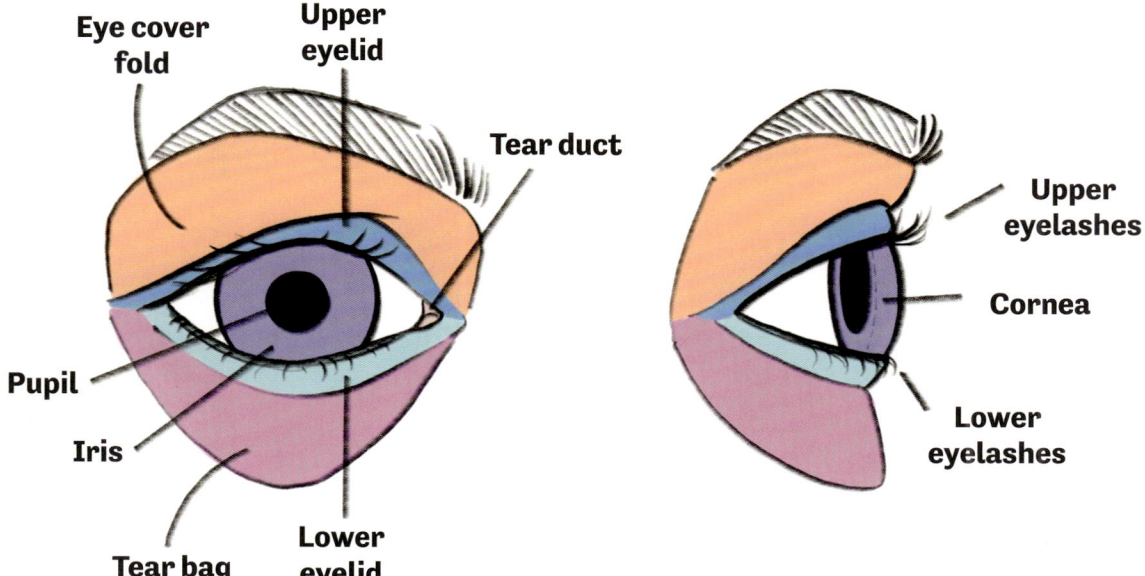

Labels on diagram:
- Eye cover fold
- Upper eyelid
- Tear duct
- Pupil
- Iris
- Tear bag
- Lower eyelid
- Upper eyelashes
- Cornea
- Lower eyelashes

Eye Cover Fold

A flap of skin that partially covers the upper eyelid. As people age and their skin loses elasticity, the eye cover fold may droop, causing eyes to look smaller.

Upper and Lower Eyelid

The eyelids are formed by the orbicularis oculi. The portion of this muscle that makes up the upper lid is called the palpebral portion. This muscle raises and pulls the upper lid down.

Upper and Lower Eyelashes

The eyelashes stem from the edge of the eyelid and are naturally straight or curled. When drawing lashes, it's important to keep perspective in mind as this will determine how much of the lash is visible to the viewer.

Tear Duct

Located on the inside corners of the eyes, these tiny, flesh-colored ducts are often not visible on people with monolid eyes (a.k.a. epicanthal folds).

Pupil and Iris

The pupil is located in the center of the iris and controls how much light can pass through the eye. As a result, the pupil can change in size. The iris is the colored ring around the pupil—colors include green, blue, brown, and hazel.

Cornea

The cornea is completely transparent and covers both the iris and pupil. When working on a side portrait, you may be tempted to draw the pupil and iris right up against the edge of the eyeball, but this wouldn't be accurate. As demonstrated above, the actual edge of the eyeball is represented by the dotted line, but due to the existence of the cornea, the edge of the eyeball looks like it's farther out than it actually is.

Tear Bag

Considered to be part of the lower eyelid, the tear bag can sometimes be subtly seen on subjects. In aging subjects, it tends to be more prominent.

DRAWING EYES

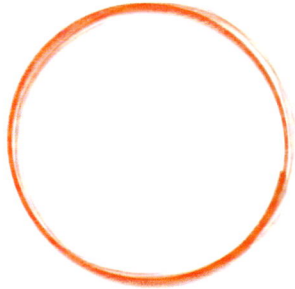 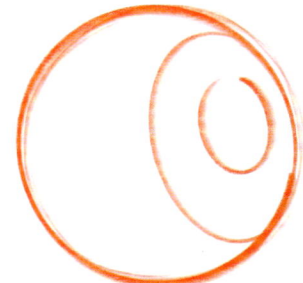 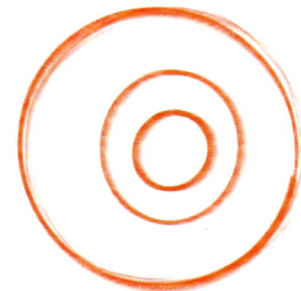

1

Start by drawing a sphere. This will represent the eyeball itself.

2

Place the iris and the pupil within the sphere. The two examples showcase one from a side view and another from the front view.

3

Outline your upper and lower eyelid shapes. Make sure that these wrap around the shape of the sphere.

To make these more interesting (and more realistic), incorporate asymmetry into the design of the lids.

Eyelids wrap around the eyeball shape

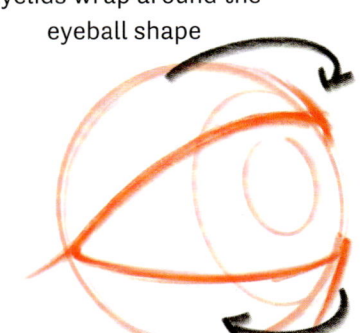

Asymmetrical points of the lids

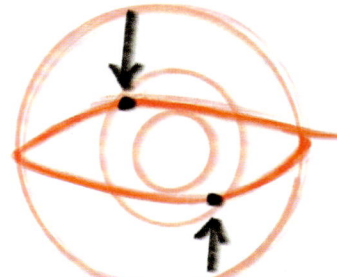

Different Eye Shapes

Monolids, or epicanthal folds, are a type of eye shape that has less definition and is more common (not exclusive) among people of Asian descent. In this type of eye, the upper eyelid crease is absent and the eyelid itself can fold over to hide the tear duct. When drawing monolids, it's best to practice minimalism with your linework.

4

Add the tear duct and creases for the upper and lower eyelids. These are optional additions.

The eye on the left has creases and a bit of the tear duct showing (obstructed due to perspective). The left eye is a monolid, and I've added only the bottom crease for interest.

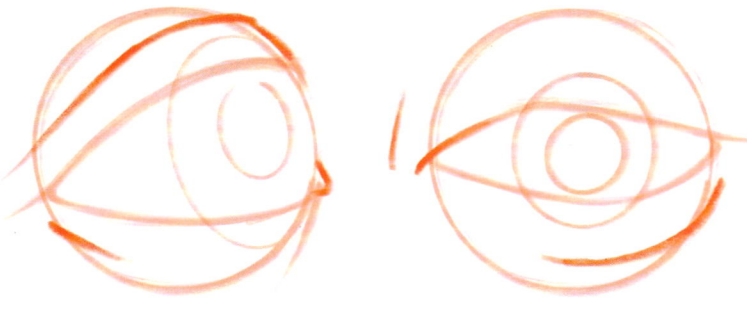

5

Add the eyelashes. Due to perspective, the eyelashes in the middle would be pointing directly at the viewer. Hairs this small would hardly be visible unless curled upward. A thicker line can be used to indicate the presence of lashes without drawing them strand by strand. Also note that the lower lashes tend to be softer and more sparse when compared to the upper lashes.

Thicker line to represent lashes

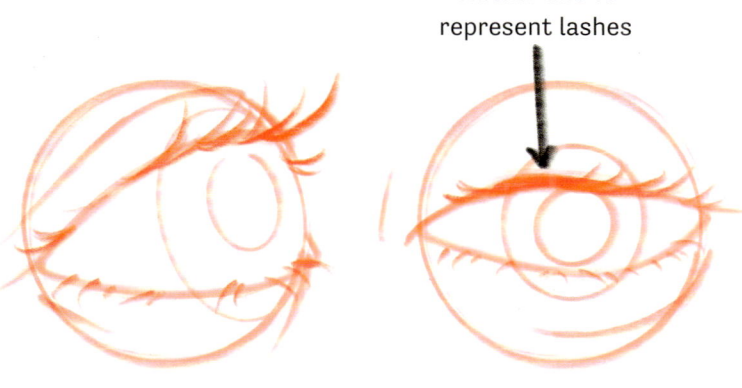

6

Finish your drawing by removing unnecessary linework. Color the pupil in to help viewers immediately recognize the eye.

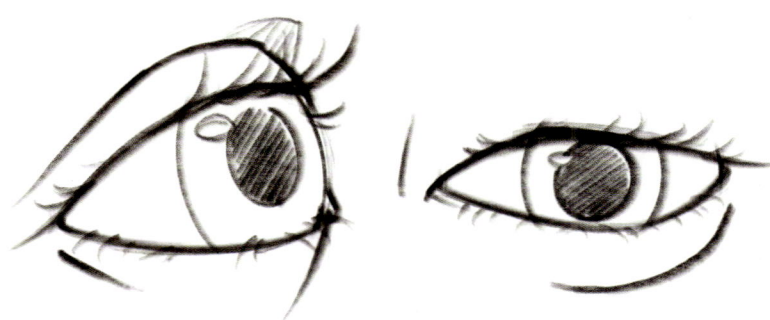

INTRO TO THE NOSE

When looking at the skull, the nose isn't present. That's because it's not strictly made up of bone. Cartilage is the primary material the body uses to make a nose (which is why noses are so flexible), and it connects to the nasal bone to cover the nasal aperture.

Overall, the nose is made up of a combination of bone, cartilage, a tiny bit of muscle, and fat. Noses can vary drastically in shape and size. The cartilage that forms the foundation of the nose can be pointy or rounded, which influences the shape of the final form.

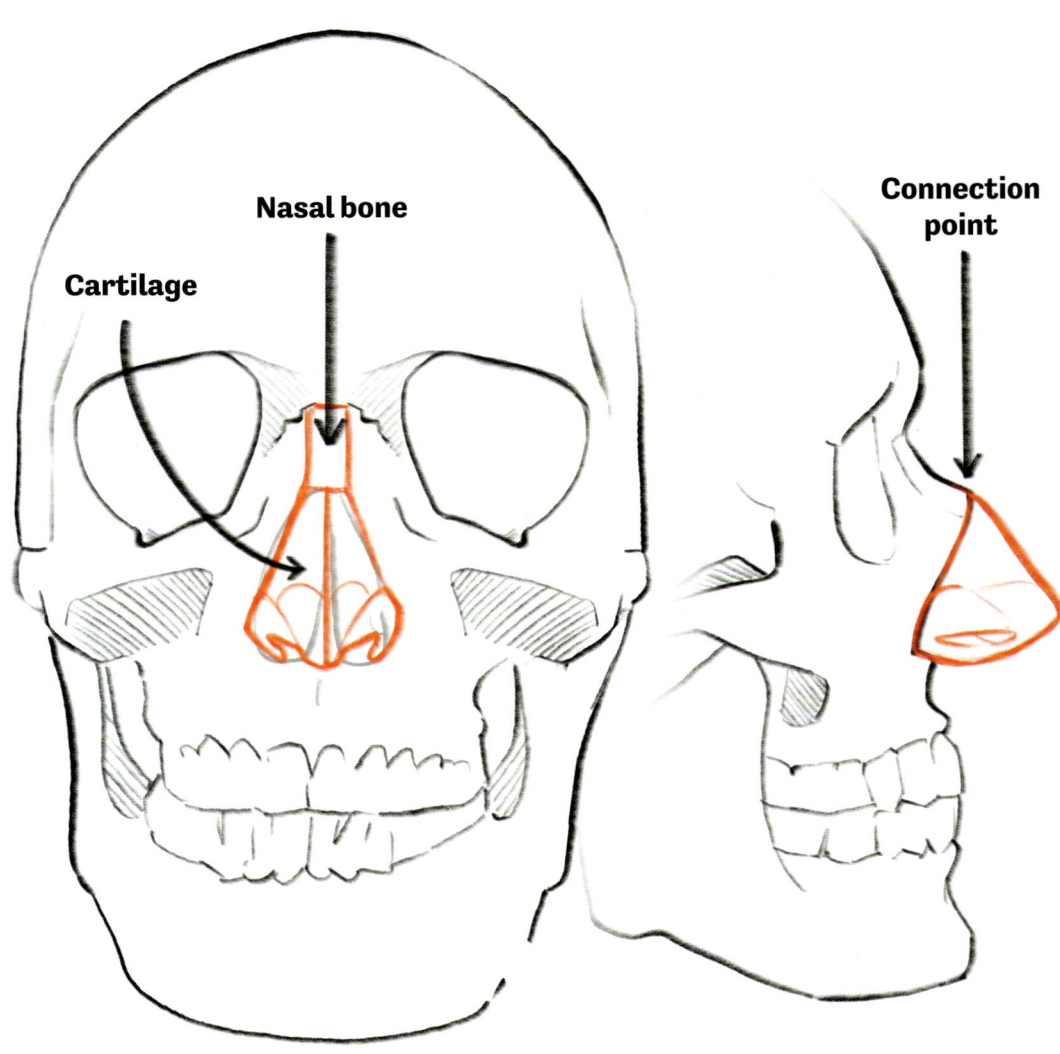

Cartilage

Nasal bone

Connection point

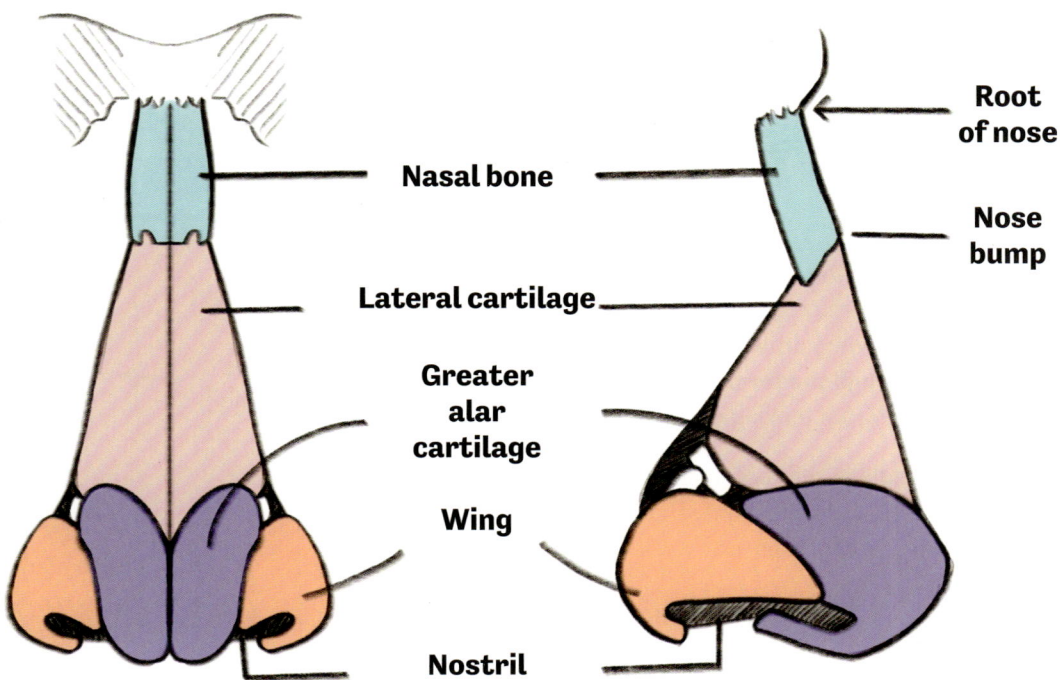

Root of Nose

This is the place where the nasal bone meets the rest of the skull.

Nasal Bone

Part of the bridge of the nose. The nasal bone is made up of two bones that connect to the skull. These small bones vary in size and shape per individual.

Connection Point (a.k.a. Nose Bump)

This is the point at which the lateral cartilage connects to the nasal bone. It does so at an angle, which causes, on some individuals, an apparent bump.

Lateral Cartilage

These are the two large, triangular-shaped cartilages that make up the rest of the bridge of the nose.

Greater Alar Cartilage

These symmetrical cartilages form the tip of the nose. They can vary in size and shape (pointiness) per individual. They may also blend seamlessly into the rest of the nose, or they may be very clearly defined. On some folks, you may be able to see a little notch at the center of the bottom of the nose where the two greater alar cartilages meet.

Wing

The wings of the nose are not made of cartilage, but of dense connective tissue.

Nostril

These are the two openings that allow us to breath. It might seem as though the plane of our nostrils is parallel to the ground, but in reality, the nostrils are tilted slightly. This allows us to see them from a side view.

DRAWING NOSES

1

Use a right triangle for the side view of the nose and a triangular prism for views that require perspective. When drawing the prism, it helps to draw **through the form** to ensure your prism doesn't end up looking wonky.

The top of the triangle is the root of the nose. In the ¾ perspective, the side, front, and base planes of the nose are represented.

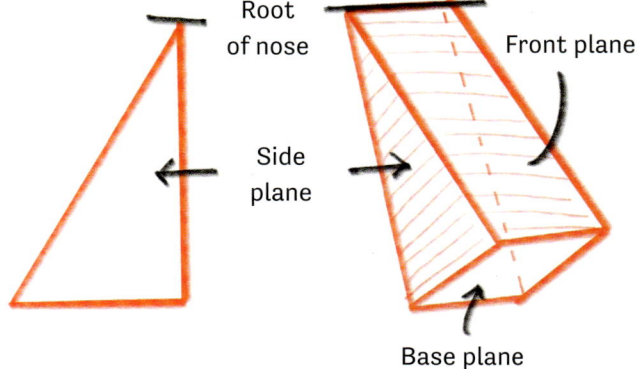

Root of nose

Front plane

Side plane

Base plane

2

Next, you'll set up some guides to help with nostril placement.

For the side view, add another triangle to the bottom of your right triangle. The size and shape here don't matter (this is where nose variety comes into play). Add a straight vertical line just behind the tip of the new triangle to define where the nostril will be—how far back you place this line doesn't matter.

For the ¾ view, draw two lines from the corners to the middle of the base. The shaded areas are the spots where the nostrils will go.

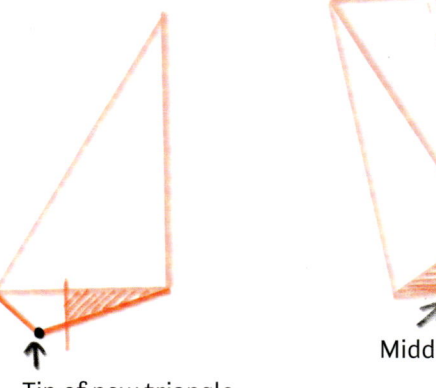

Tip of new triangle

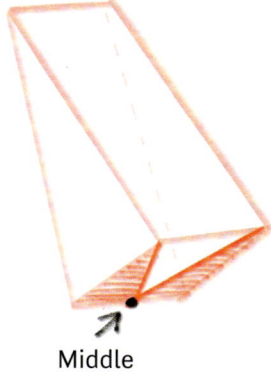

Middle

3

Draw in your nostrils. You can make these simple ovals for now and refine them later.

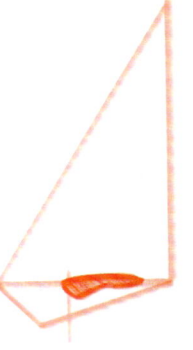

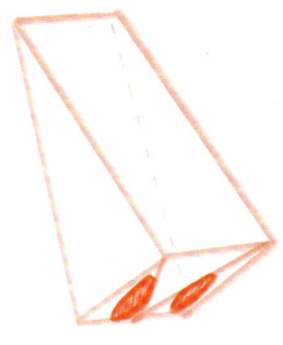

4

Sketch in the greater alar cartilage and the wings. These will help you when it comes to final linework and shading. You can also indicate the bump of the nose and the root of the nose.

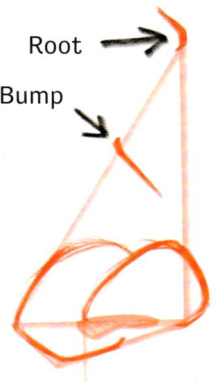

Root
Bump

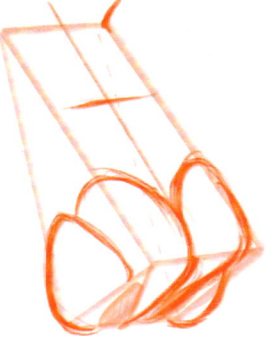

5

Begin your final sketch. Everything we've done up until this point has just been for reference. Don't feel like you have to stick to the red lines. You can emphasize the bump of the nose here, refine the shape of the nostrils, and even round out the tip of the nose (like I've done in the ¾ view).

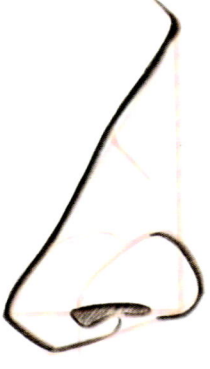

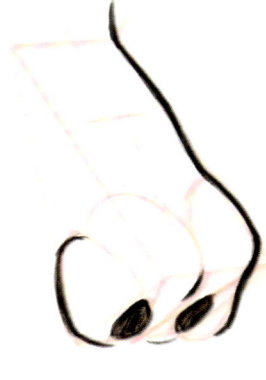

6

Because of the guides you can easily add shading, which will help showcase the plane changes of the nose.

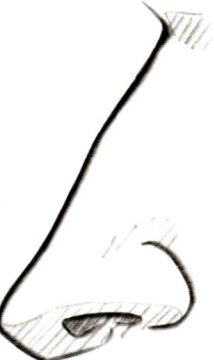

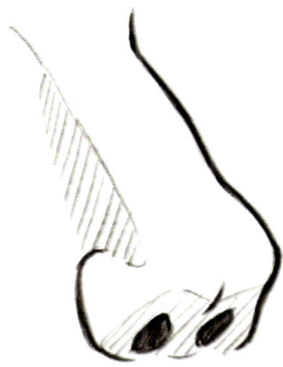

Creating Unique Noses

Not all noses are pointy or have a visible nose bump. To add variety to the types of noses you draw, you can play with the shape and size of the greater alar cartilage and the wings. You can also manipulate your prism—make the top of it thin and the bottom wide. Remember, too, that nostrils come in many shapes and sizes, so try beans or triangles instead of ovals.

INTRO TO THE MOUTH

The mouth region is very fleshy, muscular, and complex. Of all the facial features, it's composed of the largest number of muscles. It extends from the base of the nose to the top of the chin and is bordered by the cheeks on either side.

The main muscle of the mouth is called the orbicularis *oris*, not to be confused with the orbicularis *oculi* (the muscle of the eye). It covers up a good chunk of the mouth region, has a horizontal opening in the middle, a node on either end, and is divided into four parts. Our lips are not independent but are made up of this muscle.

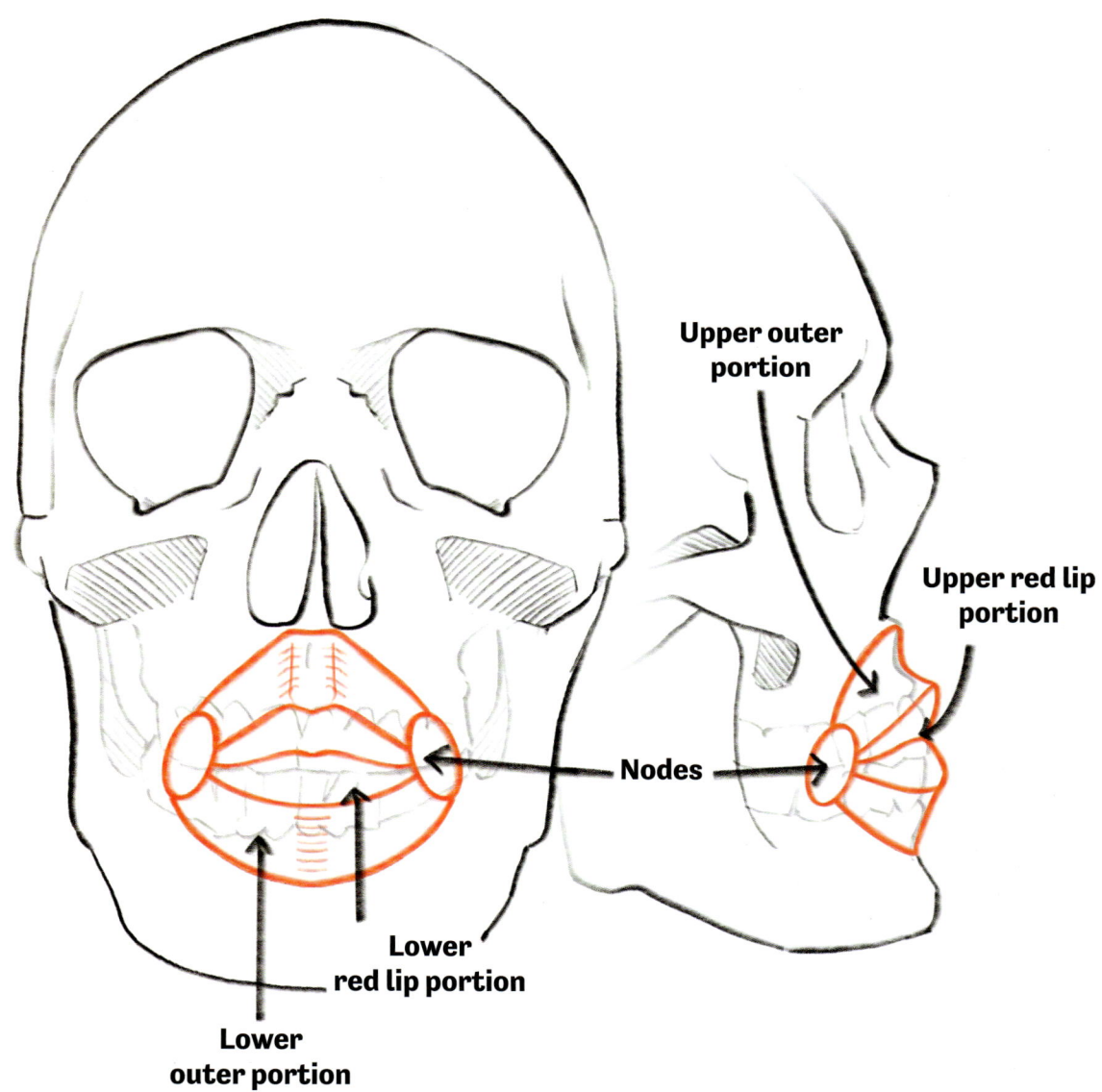

Upper outer portion

Upper red lip portion

Nodes

Lower red lip portion

Lower outer portion

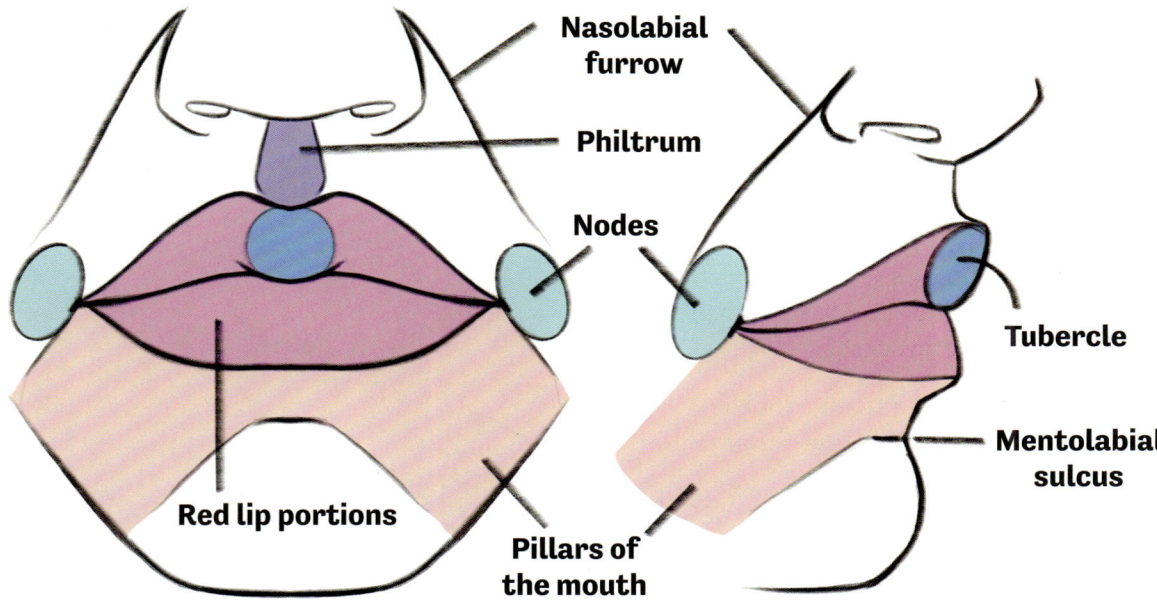

Orbicularis Oris
A thick muscle that covers a large area. It makes up the upper and lower lip, but it also extends beyond the lips. It's divided into four portions: upper outer portion, upper red lip portion, lower outer portion, and lower red lip portion.

Red Lip Portion (Top and Bottom Lips)
Lips have thinner skin than the rest of the face. Capillaries lying close to the surface of the skin give lips their reddish color. However, depending on a person's ethnicity, the color can range from red to pink to brown—the melanin in a person's skin can make it harder to see the blood vessels.

Outer Portion (Top and Bottom)
The outer portions are larger than the lip portions. The top outer portion extends to the base of the nose, while the bottom portion extends to the top of the chin.

Nodes
Think of these as the corners of your mouth. They are the insertion point, or the convergence, of many different muscles of the mouth. Nodes can be slightly visible and can look a bit pudgy depending on the individual and lighting.

Philtrum
The dent, or groove, that's present right above the upper lip. Its wideness varies per individual.

Tubercle
A non-muscular bump right in the middle of the upper lip. It's not a part of the orbicularis oris.

Nasolabial Furrow
Technically this is what separates the mouth region from the cheeks. It is very prominent in older folks and appears as a wrinkle that stretches from the wings of the nose down to the corners of the mouth.

Pillars of the Mouth
This is a grouping of a couple different muscles. They can appear as two large fleshy columns that diagonally stretch from the bottom of the lower lip and around the chin. Depending on the angle of lighting, they may be more visible than normal.

Mentolabial Sulcus
Just like the nasolabial furrow, the mentolabial sulcus is a skin fold. It's a horizontal line that separates the mouth region from the top of the chin.

DRAWING MOUTHS

1

Start by setting up guides for your upper and lower lips. To do this, draw a trapezoid, then add another one upside down.

The two trapezoids don't have to be the same size. Play around with their heights to create interest.

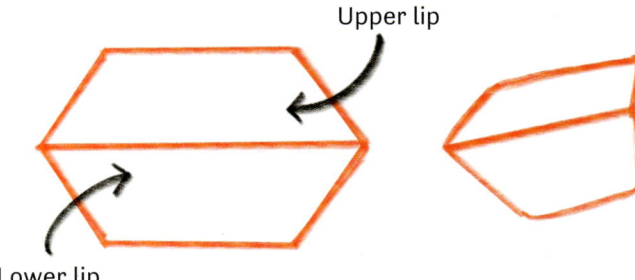

Upper lip

Lower lip

2

Draw a circle in the middle of the top trapezoid. This is the tubercle.

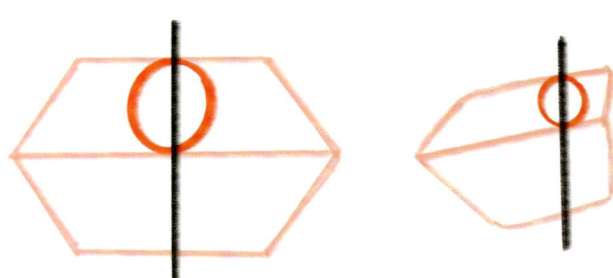

3

Add teardrop shapes on either side of the tubercle. Don't worry if your shapes overlap slightly or go outside the guidelines.

Do the same for the lower lip, with the edges of the teardrops touching in the middle.

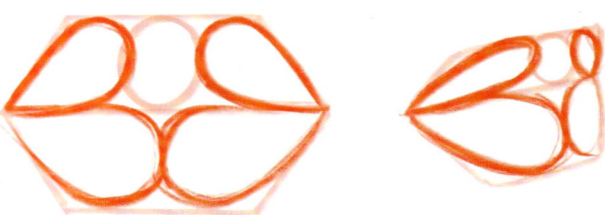

4

Use your guides to define the corners of the mouth and the mouthline.

To find your mouthline, follow the forms of the tubercle on the upper lip and the teardrops of the lower lip.

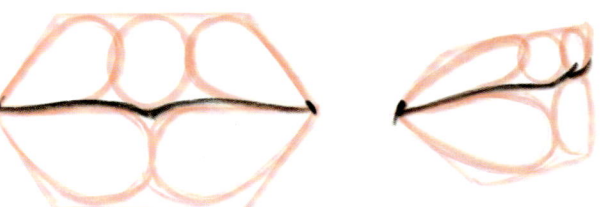

5

Next, add definition to the philtrum and the lips.

Realistically, the lips themselves are defined by a change in color. Therefore, it's recommended that you indicate the lips with minimal linework. Outlining the entire lip will result in a harsh look that flattens your drawing.

Philtrum

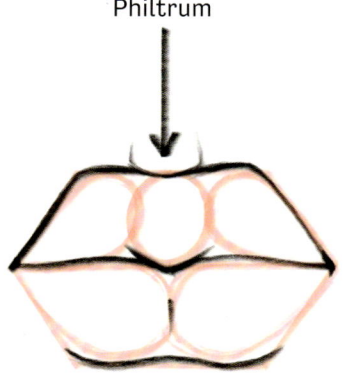

Philtrum seen from an angle

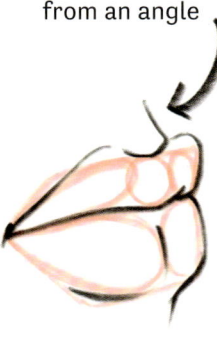

6

You may choose to indicate the nasolabial furrow (which means adding in a nose) and the mentolabial sulcus. Adding in the furrow will age your subject or give them the hint of an expression.

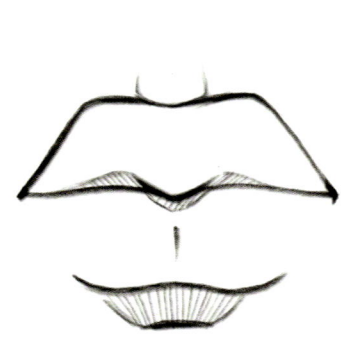

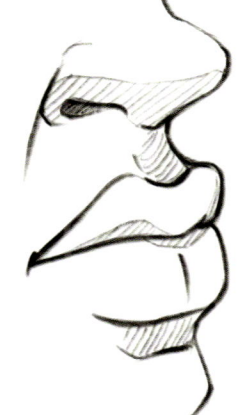

Masculine or Feminine?

Facial features like lips are completely genderless. However, in Western society, thick lips are often associated with a more feminine look (which is interesting because according to a study* the average male has thicker lips than the average female).

Regardless, when you're drawing a portrait, it's important to take our societal views on masculinity versus femininity into consideration. For example, if your goal is to create an easily distinguishable male character, then you'll likely want to emphasize masculine qualities, like a thicker brow, while downplaying feminine qualities, like voluminous lips.

* Sharma, V., Ingle, N. A., Kaur, N., & Yadav, P. (2014). Identification of sex using lip prints : A clinical study. Journal of International Society of Preventive & Community Dentistry, 4(Suppl 3), S173–S177. https://doi.org/10.4103/2231-0762.149030

INTRO TO THE EARS

The ear is an organ and can be divided into three main parts. Of the three, we're only drawing one part. The part we can see and that we typically know to be the ear is called the outer ear. The parts of the organ that we can't see are the middle ear and the inner ear.

The outer ear is made up of cartilage and skin. Its placement is at the side of our head, and it acts

as a kind of funnel to help direct sound into the middle ear via the ear hole.

Although there are proportional guidelines for the typical size of an ear (see *Putting It All Together*, page 76), realistically they can come in many different shapes and sizes. Ears truly do vary per individual, which makes them a boon for beginner artists—they're hard to mess up!

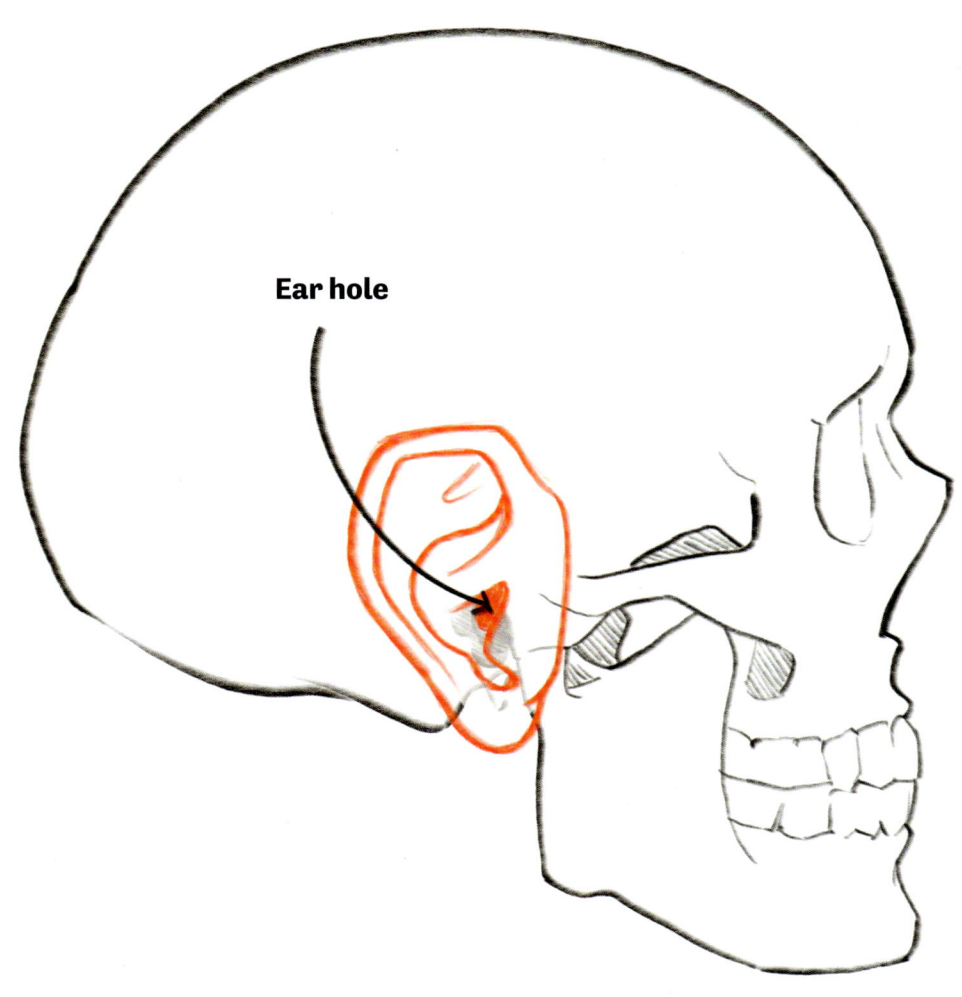

Ear hole

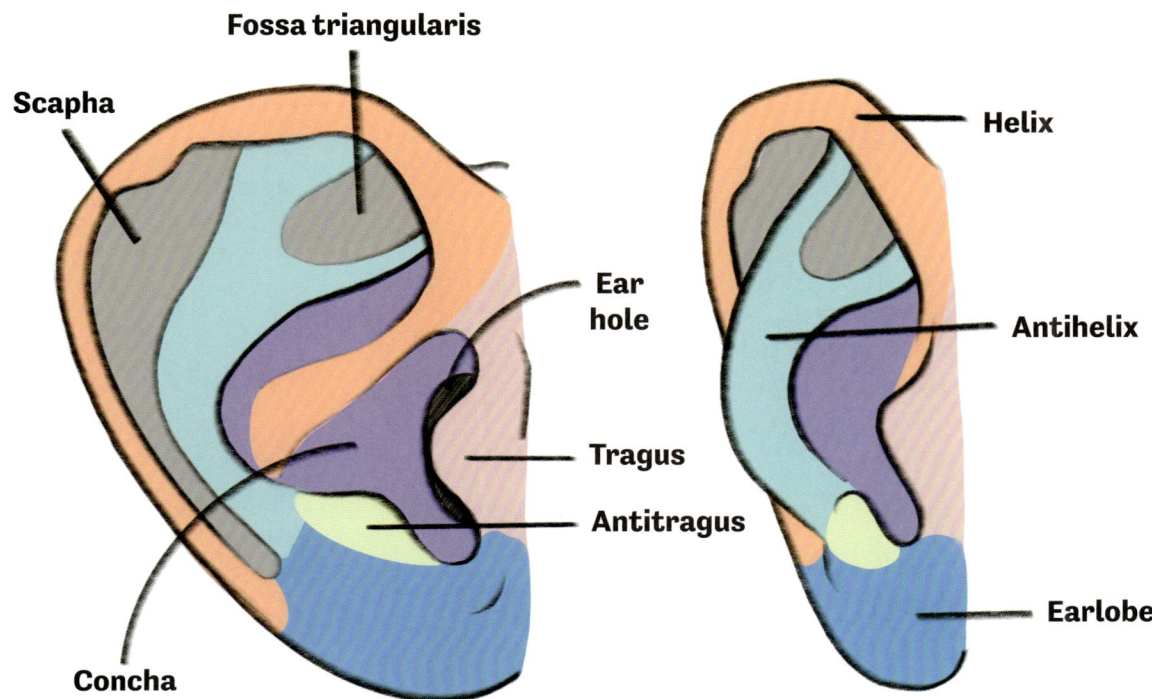

Ear Hole

This hole allows sound to travel into the middle and inner ear for processing. It's partially covered by the tragus.

Tragus

A pointy piece of cartilage that covers the ear hole.

Antitragus

Like the tragus, the antitragus is a pointy piece of cartilage, but it covers up some of the concha instead of the earhole. The antitragus can be found opposite the tragus.

Helix

Starting midway in the concha, the helix spirals around the exterior form of the ear and transitions into the earlobe. For some, this can be a thick piece of cartilage and skin, while for others it can be quite thin and malleable.

Antihelix

A spiral that loosely resembles the helix. The antihelix borders the concha and also transitions into the earlobe. There are two depressions found in the antihelix, the **fossa triangularis** and the **scapha**.

Concha

The deep bowl shape that connects the ear to the head. It's divided in half by the helix.

Earlobe

This is soft, fleshy skin that hangs on the bottom of the ear. The earlobe can vary in size, and it may or may not be connected to the side of the head.

DRAWING EARS

1

Using an oval as a guideline can sometimes create overly rounded ears. Instead, I recommend using shapes that have corners. Start by drawing a rectangle with a slanted bottom. Alternatively, you could try a diamond shape as well.

 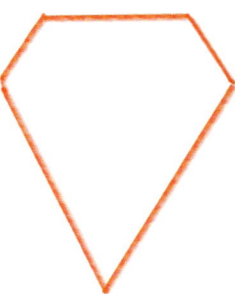

Rectangle with slanted bottom   Rough diamond shape

Thicker helix cartilage

2

Start outlining your tragus, helix, and earlobe. These will give you the main shapes of the ear. Remember that all these components of the ear are highly variable between individuals, so don't be afraid of playing around with the shapes.

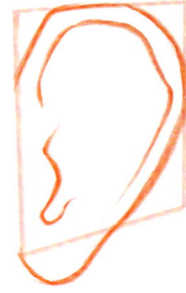 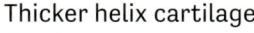

Variation of the tragus

Indication of depression

3

Add the antitragus in—doing so will automatically give you the concha. You may also choose to indicate the depressions of the antihelix.

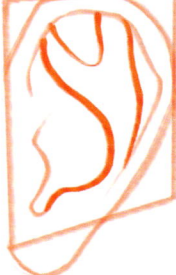 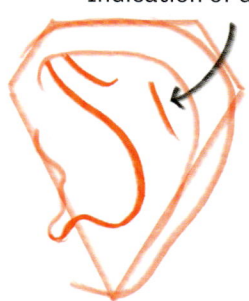

4

Add in any details like ear piercings or jewelry. Add shading to the areas of the ear that are most debossed, like the concha.

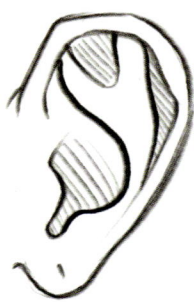 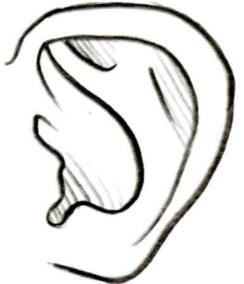

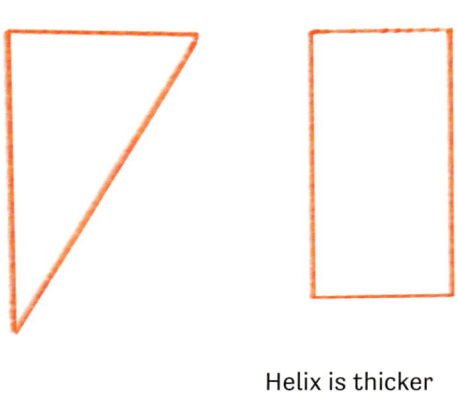

1

The ear looks quite different from the front view, and not all components are visible from this angle. To start, draw a right triangle or slim rectangle as a guide.

Helix is thicker

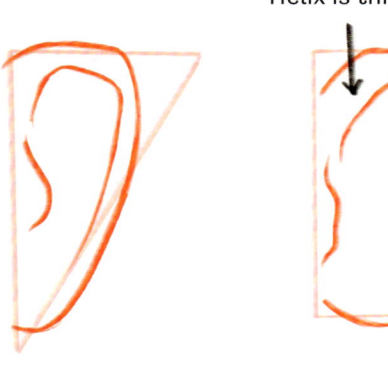

2

Add the tragus, helix, and lobe. Due to perspective, the tragus may not be as prominent, and the spiral of the helix will look thicker on the top where it connects to the head.

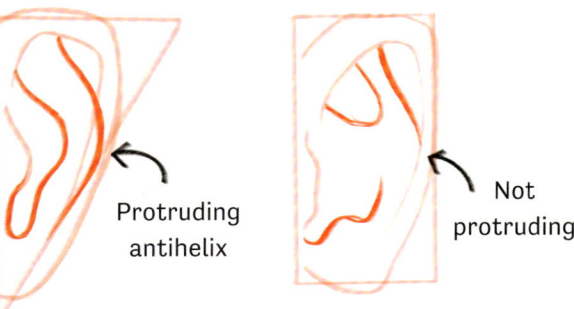

Protruding antihelix

Not protruding

3

The antihelix could project outward and cover a bit of the helix behind it. Use an arch to describe its form. You may want to indicate depressions of the fossa triangularis and/or the concha.

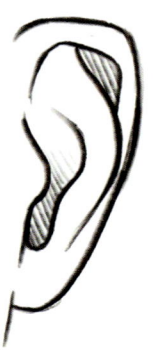

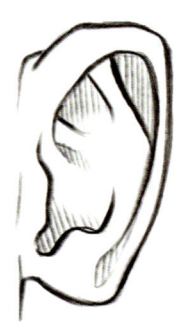

Keep It Simple

When drawing the ear as part of a larger portrait, bear in mind that the more detailed you make it, the more it can distract from your focal point. Sometimes it's best to keep the ear overly simple, even if it means leaving out anatomical components like the fossa triangularis or the scapha.

PUTTING IT ALL TOGETHER

Every face has its own unique features and proportions, but there are general guidelines based on the average human head that artists can lean on to achieve an accurate likeness of their model.

Think of these guidelines as a starting point. From there, you can observe and adapt your drawings according to what you see (or prefer).

As you practice and study reference imagery or people in real life, you'll become better at feature placement, perspective, and proportions. As you become more proficient in these areas, don't be afraid to experiment with proportions. Often, this leads to stylization, which is how people recognize the work of their favorite artist.

Dividing the Head

You learned how to draw the human head using the Loomis method on pages 58–59. Using that method, you already know to divide the head into a couple of sections, reiterated here:

First, draw the cranium using a ball shape. Divide the cranium in half using a vertical line. Since humans are symmetrical, what you draw on one side of the head will reflect on the other side.

Next, mark the hairline, brow line, nose, and chin by following the steps on the next page.

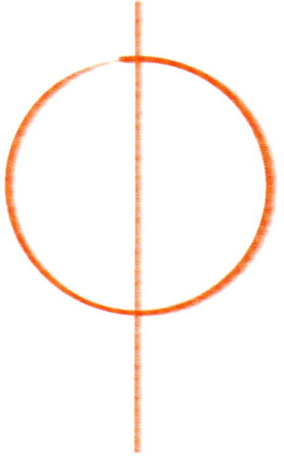

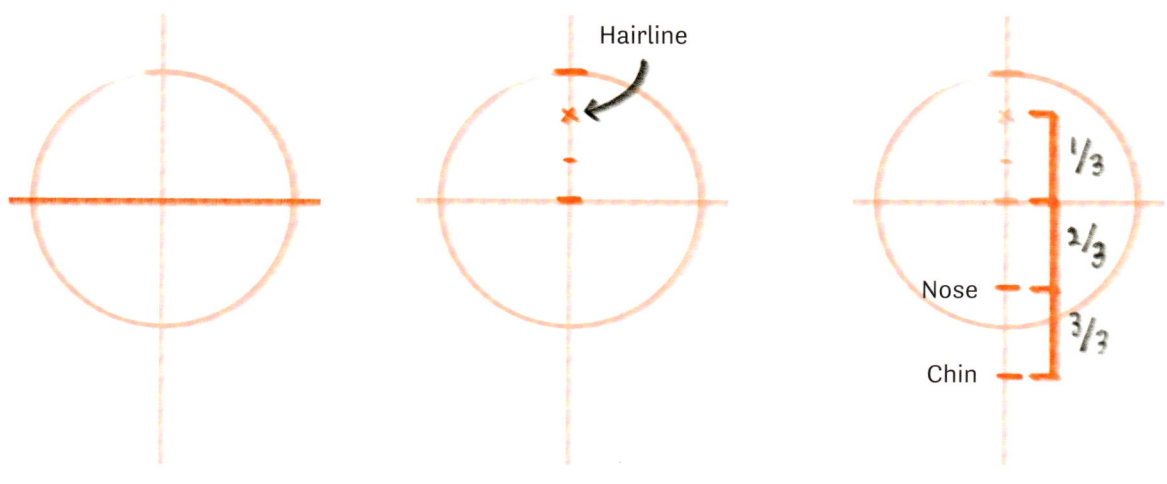

Hairline

1/3

Nose

2/3

Chin

3/3

1

The brow line lies in the middle of the cranium.

2

From this perspective, you'll find the hairline by dividing the space between the brow line and the top of the cranium into thirds.

3

Take the measurement between the hairline and the brow line. Use this amount of space to find the nose and chin.

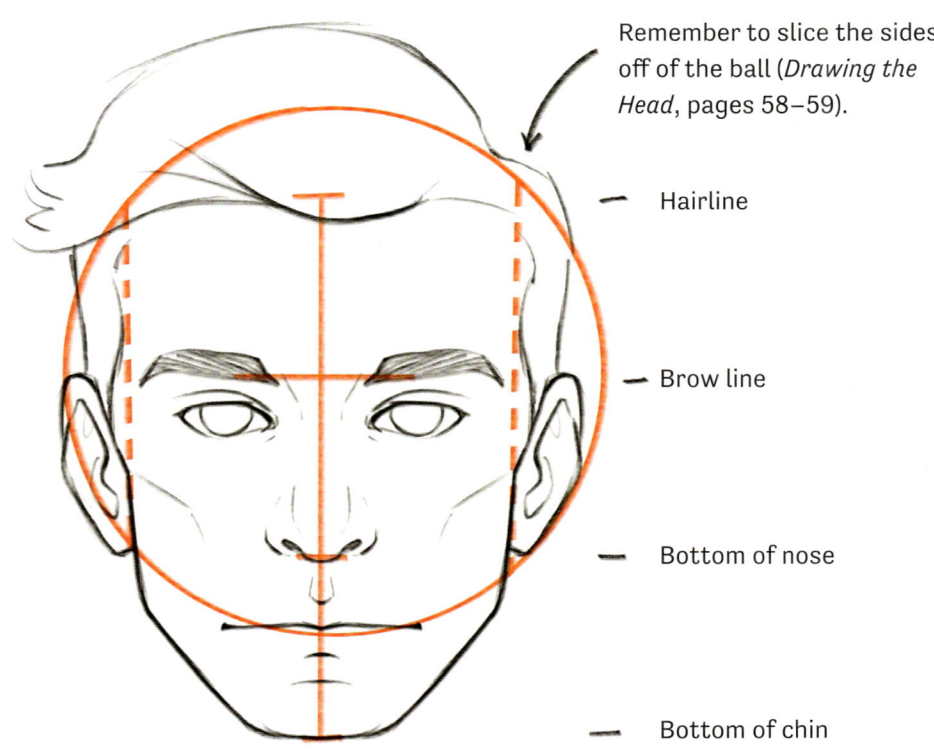

Remember to slice the sides off of the ball (*Drawing the Head*, pages 58–59).

Hairline

Brow line

Bottom of nose

Bottom of chin

Additional Measurements

Now, when looking at the **whole head (and not just at the cranium)**, we can add additional guides. This method of measurement still lines up with Loomis's ball and plane method.

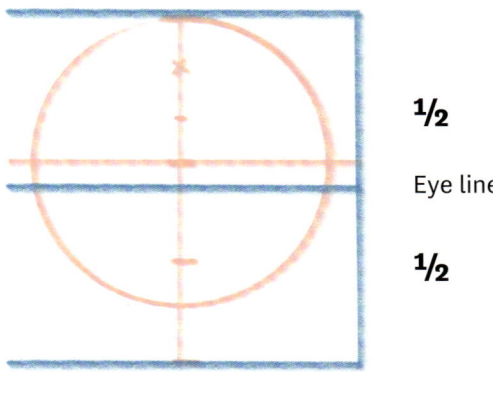

I

Halfway between the top of the head and the chin, you will find the eye line.

½

Eye line

½

2

Split the space between the bottom of the nose and the chin, and you've got a marker for the bottom of the lip.

The length of the ears stretch from the brow line to the bottom of the nose.

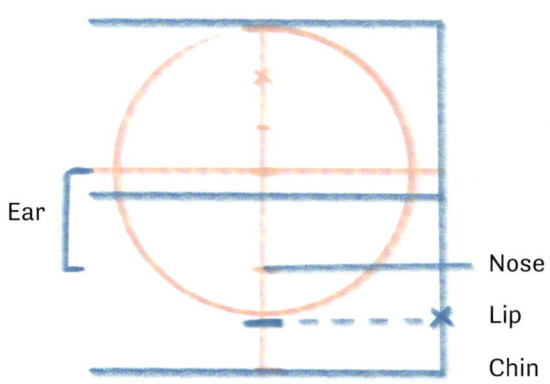

Ear

Nose

Lip

Chin

Remember That It's Not Math

There are lots of proportional methods out there aside from Loomis's. Sometimes these methods can seem like strict rules or formulas that must be adhered to and that define the "ideal human form"—blech.

I think it's most important to **remember that all of these methods are mere guidelines**.

Keeping this in mind is key to building people who are real, because proportions vary, beauty is highly subjective, and it's a hell of a lot more fun experimenting than drawing out a grid and making sure your measurements are perfect every time you pick up your pencil.

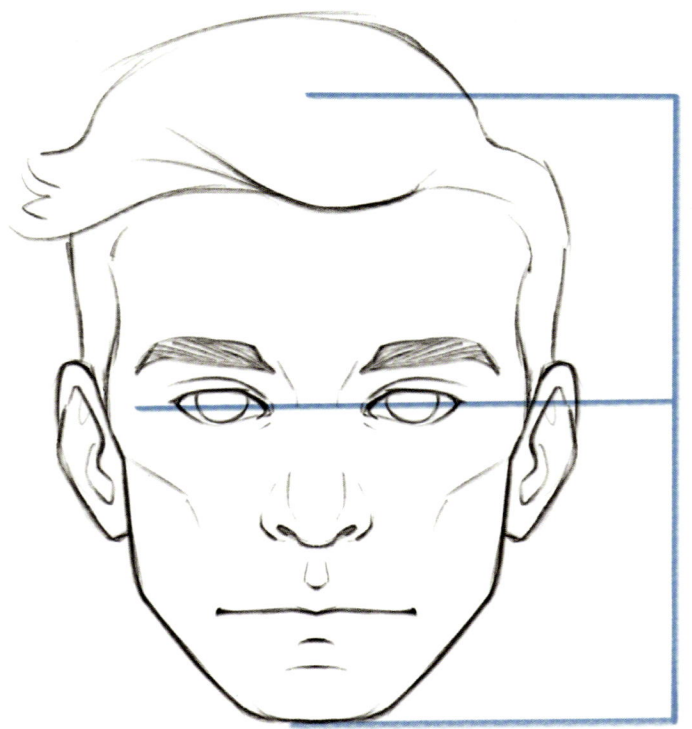

Top of head

Halfway between top of head and bottom of chin is the eye line

Bottom of chin

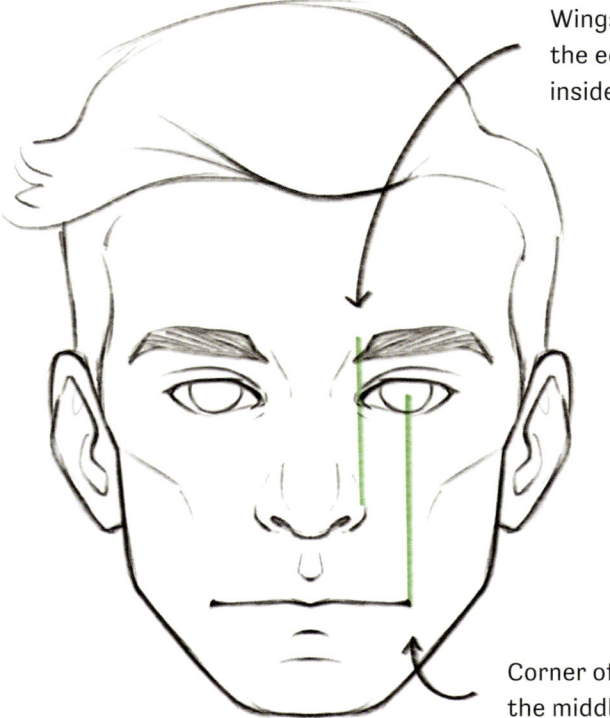

Wings of nose tend to align with the edge of the eyebrow and the inside corner of the eye

Corner of the mouth aligns with the middle of the eye

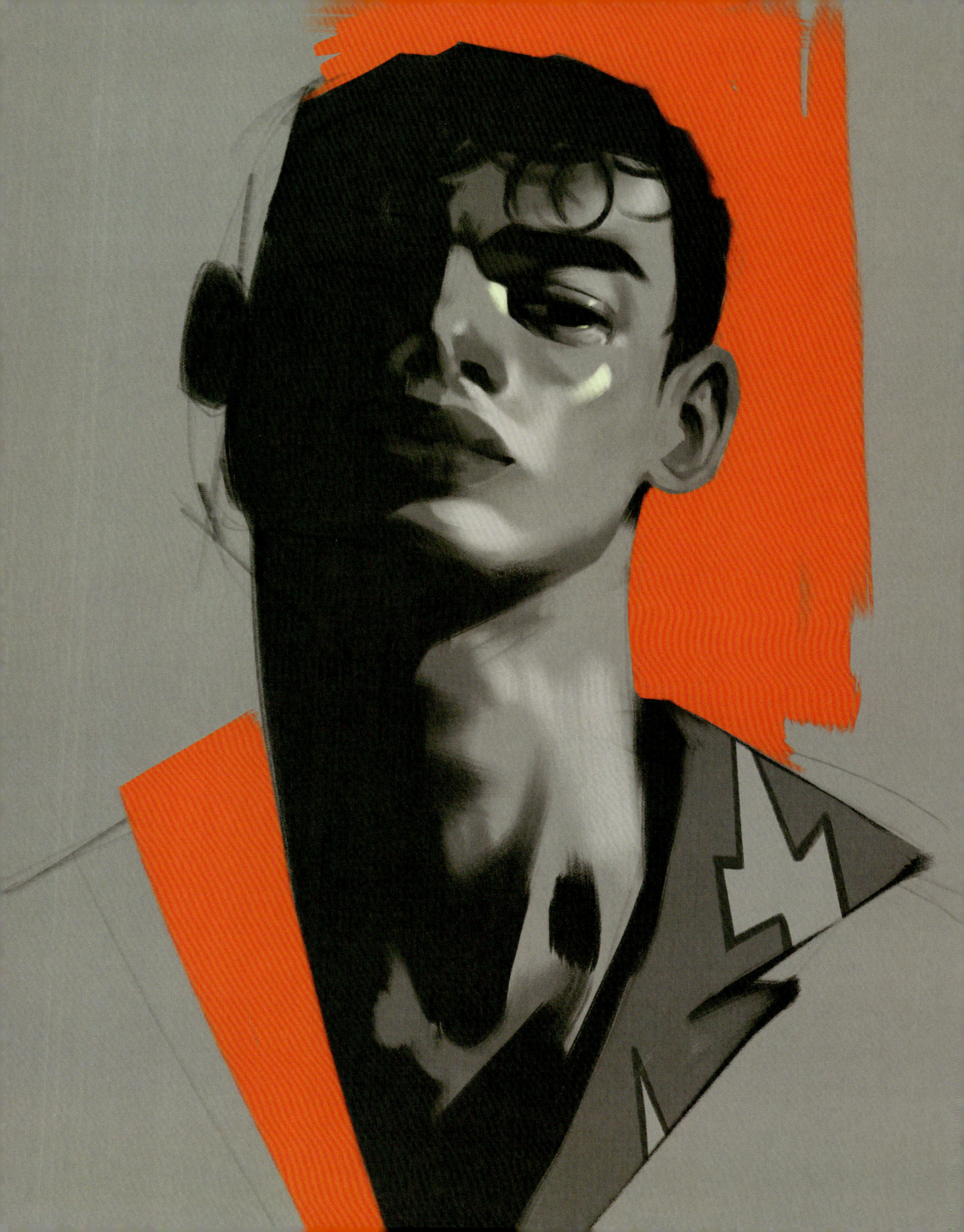

Getting
SET UP

Relying solely on your memory to create artwork can be tricky and easily lead to mistakes. To avoid this frustrating experience, it's crucial that artists use visual aids.

A reference image serves as a guide that allows an artist to study different elements of an image—like proportions, light and shadow, or colors—without getting lost or bogged down.

Using reference is *not* cheating and it doesn't mean that you *must* stick to replicating only what you see.

Think of reference imagery as a starting point—it's up to you, the artist, to interpret what you see and create your own unique vision.

SHOULD YOU DRAW FROM LIFE OR FROM PHOTOS?

There are pros and cons to using real life or photography as your reference.

When I went to art school, I was taught to draw from life and highly encouraged to stay away from using photo references. Life drawing was (and still is) a highly valued method of learning. It has many benefits, but it's also challenging and not as easily accessible as photography.

When you draw or paint using a photograph, that photo has already passed through the filter of the camera. In many instances, the image is enhanced; colors are richer, parts of the image are intentionally sharpened or blurred, or there are other effects that have been applied that alter your subject in ways you may not even know.

In contrast, drawing from life really allows an artist to connect with their subject. It allows an artist to see, and interpret what they see, without obstruction.

I assume that a lot of folks learning to paint digitally using Procreate are going to start their journey using photos for reference. It's natural since you're already using a computer and you'll have access to the internet and the crazy amount of imagery on there. If this is the case, then make sure you read through the next couple of pages. While it's not a crime to use photo reference, you must have a good idea of the kinds of pictures you should seek out and the ones you should avoid. Good reference will allow for a much smoother art-making experience. Bad reference can cause frustration and self-doubt.

Coming out of art school and for quite some time afterward, I felt bad for using reference photography. It took me a while to ditch the opinion I had adopted in school. I certainly don't want you to feel like it's a bad thing if you draw from photos. You should use what you have access to while keeping in mind that there are other methods of learning (I'm talking about life drawing) that could benefit you greatly.

WHAT MAKES A GOOD REFERENCE PHOTO?

If you're using photography as reference and not drawing from real life, then it's important to have an understanding of the kind of images that will serve you best and which ones you should avoid.

Soft Versus Hard Details

Cameras and filters can make every part of a photo razor-sharp in detail. This isn't how our eyes naturally work, and the abundance of information can confuse many artists.

Compare the photos to the right. The one of the man is extremely sharp—individual hairs, stubble, and even the pores of his skin are visible. The way the light catches on his cheekbone and around his nose is confusing since the light is broken up, making it difficult to understand the forms underneath. In contrast, the photo of the woman is soft, and the light around her eyes and lips feels simplified by comparison.

When looking for good reference, try to find a balance between the two and avoid photos that are overly soft or sharp.

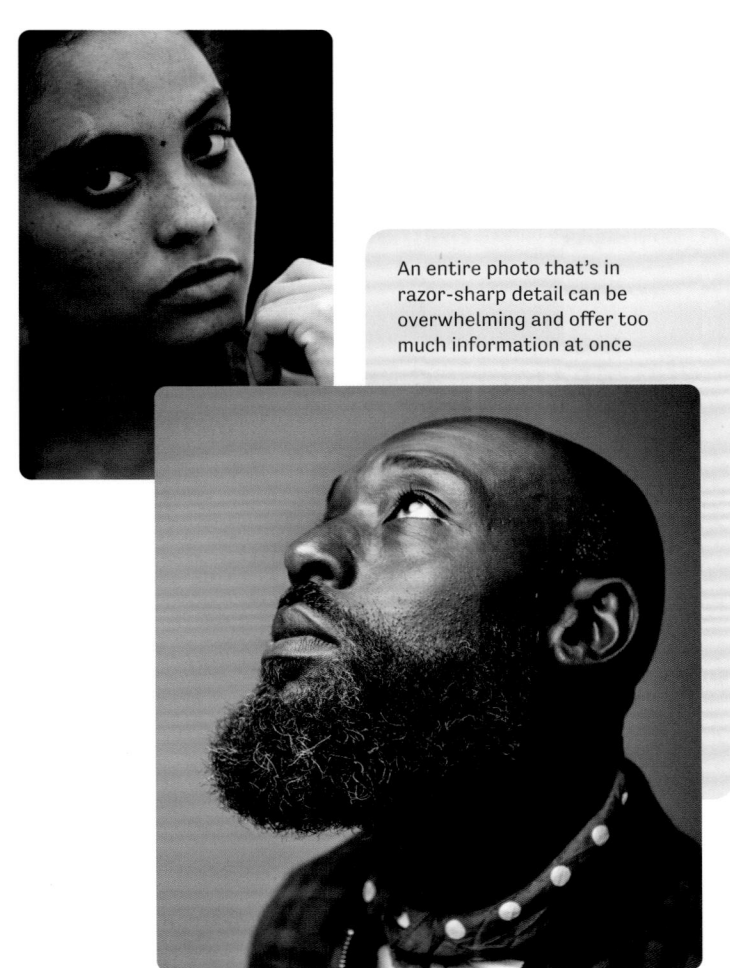

An entire photo that's in razor-sharp detail can be overwhelming and offer too much information at once

Well-Defined Shadow and Light Shapes

Hard light produces clear shadow and light shapes, which ultimately make it easier for artists to draw and paint what they see.

The shapes clearly define the anatomy of the subject and make breaking down the head and face much more manageable.

To contrast this, soft lighting usually blends everything together. Edges are lost and forms are difficult to define. For now, it's better to avoid these kinds of photos and opt for ones that will make your portrait drawing experience easier.

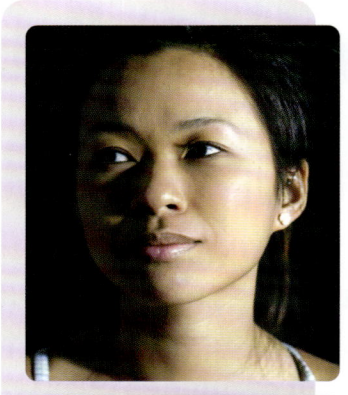
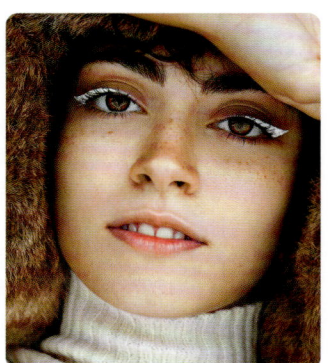
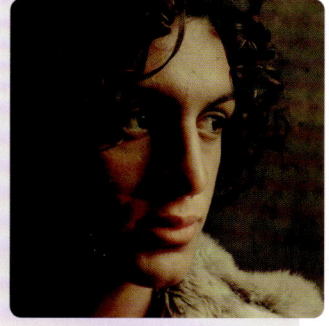
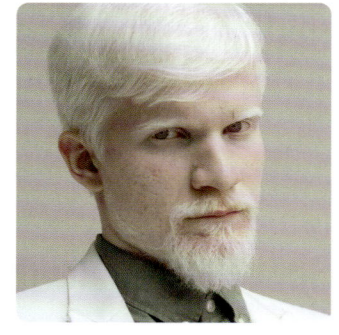

Clear shadow and light shapes help define the form

Forms aren't distinct when lighting is too soft

Simple Lighting Setup

Look for photos where the direction of the main source of light is obvious. Complex lighting scenarios may look cool, but they pose a lot of challenges for a beginner.

Take a look at the photos to the far right. The models are illuminated on both sides with different-colored lights. Can you tell what's actually in shadow?

The photos to the left have a clear light source. The top is in studio, lit from the left. The bottom is outdoors, lit from the sun above. These simple lighting scenarios are much easier to paint than the others.

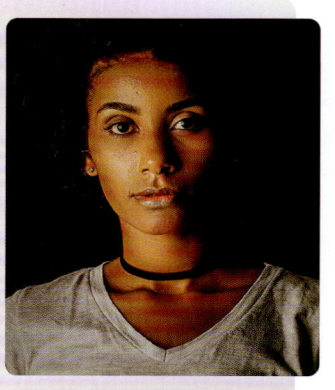
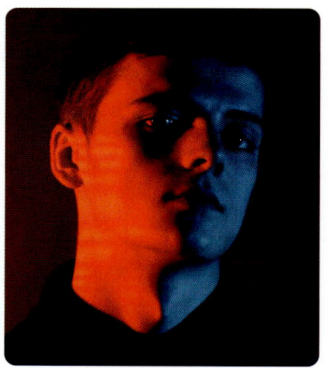
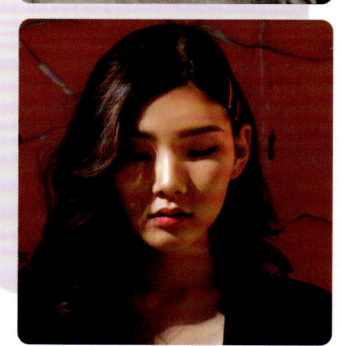
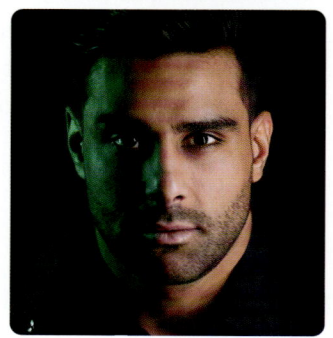

WHERE TO FIND IMAGES

The Internet

Maybe this one seems a little obvious, but bear with me! There are many websites that provide access to *free* stock photography that's been *cleared for commercial use*. That means if you ever want to sell your work or share the reference image itself (say, over social media), you won't run into copyright issues.

Two of the better stock sites are **pexels.com** and **unsplash.com**.

Pinterest can be a good resource, though I'd only recommend using it if it can be paired with a warning. While it's a great source for creative, high-quality photography, Pinterest's algorithm can ruin the overall experience.

You'll start to notice that after a while the models and their poses start to look alike. Social media has created an ideal "look," and pictures of models who are plastered with a ton of makeup, using multiple filters, and posing in a certain way are littered all over the platform.

Go ahead and use Pinterest for convenience, but be careful that *your* perception of what makes a beautiful and interesting human doesn't get skewed by what the algorithm is constantly trying to feed you.

Artist Reference Packs

There are a ton of photography packs that you can purchase (some are free!) that have been created exclusively for artists to use as reference. These packs are great because they're made specifically with artists in mind. You'll find that the photos are clear, have great lighting setups, and include models with a ton of variety in their facial features and body types. You can find various packs through a Google search or by browsing ArtStation's marketplace (look for vendors like **Obscura 29** and **Grafit Studio**).

SETTING UP REFERENCES

There are multiple ways to set up reference imagery using the iPad. Follow along with any of the three ways listed below, but keep in mind that your setup will really come down to personal preference.

Use the Reference Tool Built into the Procreate App

The reference tool is very handy, and I do recommend you give it a try. There's also more than one way to use it!

You can import a reference image from your photo library, or you can view your current canvas as a thumbnail.

Viewing your canvas as a thumbnail gives you a high-level overview of your painting so you can make sure the piece works even when you're really zoomed in and working on tiny details.

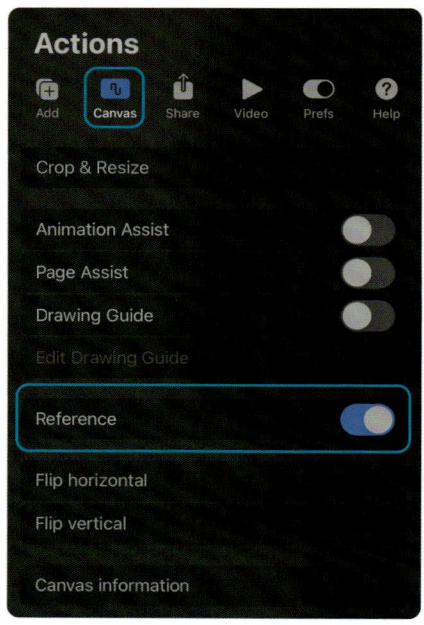

How to Set It Up

Actions > Canvas > Reference (toggle it on)

How It Works

1 Canvas
Allows you to view your artwork as a thumbnail. Pinch to zoom in and out of your artwork.

2 Image
Will import reference imagery from your photo library.

3 Face
Opens the iPad's camera so you can take a new picture.

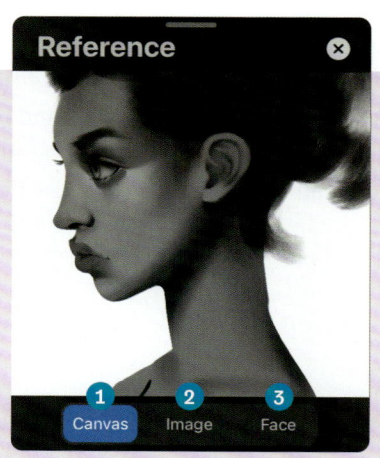

Place Your Reference Image Directly on the Canvas

This method requires you to have a large enough canvas to fit both your reference image and artwork on. The great thing about working in this manner is that you can draw rulers across the entire canvas to help you directly compare sizing, placement of features, and so on.

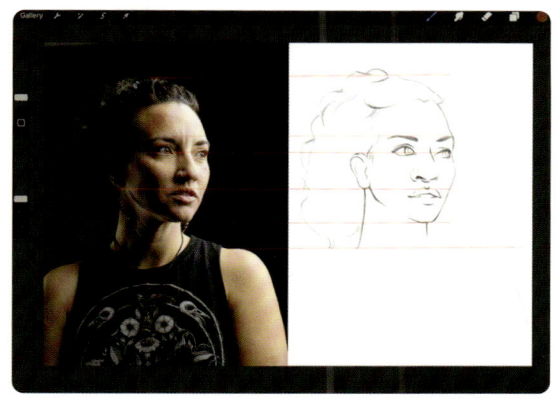

The downside is that you'll likely need to zoom in/out a lot while you work. You'll also need to hide/delete your reference and crop your canvas later to finish up your artwork.

How to Set It Up

Start with a wide canvas, then import your reference by going to:

Actions > Add > Insert a file/photo/Take a photo

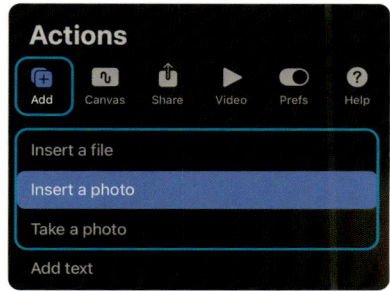

Use the iPad's Split View

The iPad allows you to open more than one app at a time. Using the multitasking feature, you can open up Procreate and your photo library (or another app like Pinterest) side by side.

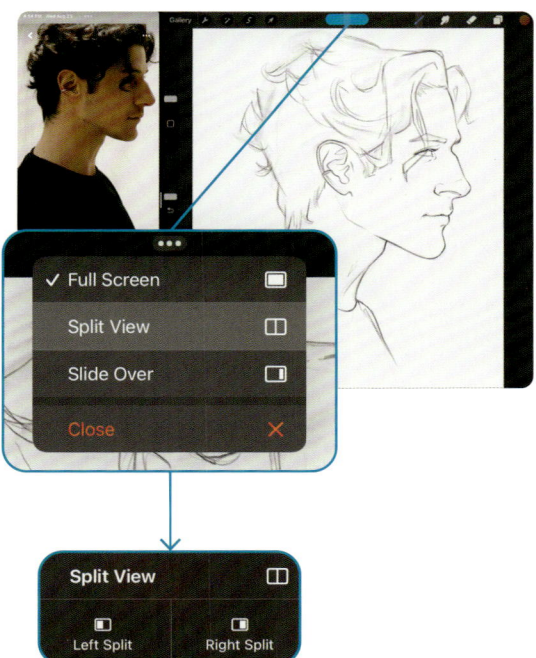

Bear in mind that while this feature is very useful, it also eats up a lot of screen real estate. The entire Procreate app will be squished, so your workspace may feel limited.

How to Set It Up

Tap on the multitasking button ••• at the top of the screen > Select Split View > Choose the second app you'd like to open.

To change the side of the screen that Procreate is on, tap ••• and select *Split View* once more. Now you can choose whether you want the app on the left or right side of the screen. Adjust the size of the apps by dragging the vertical app divider.

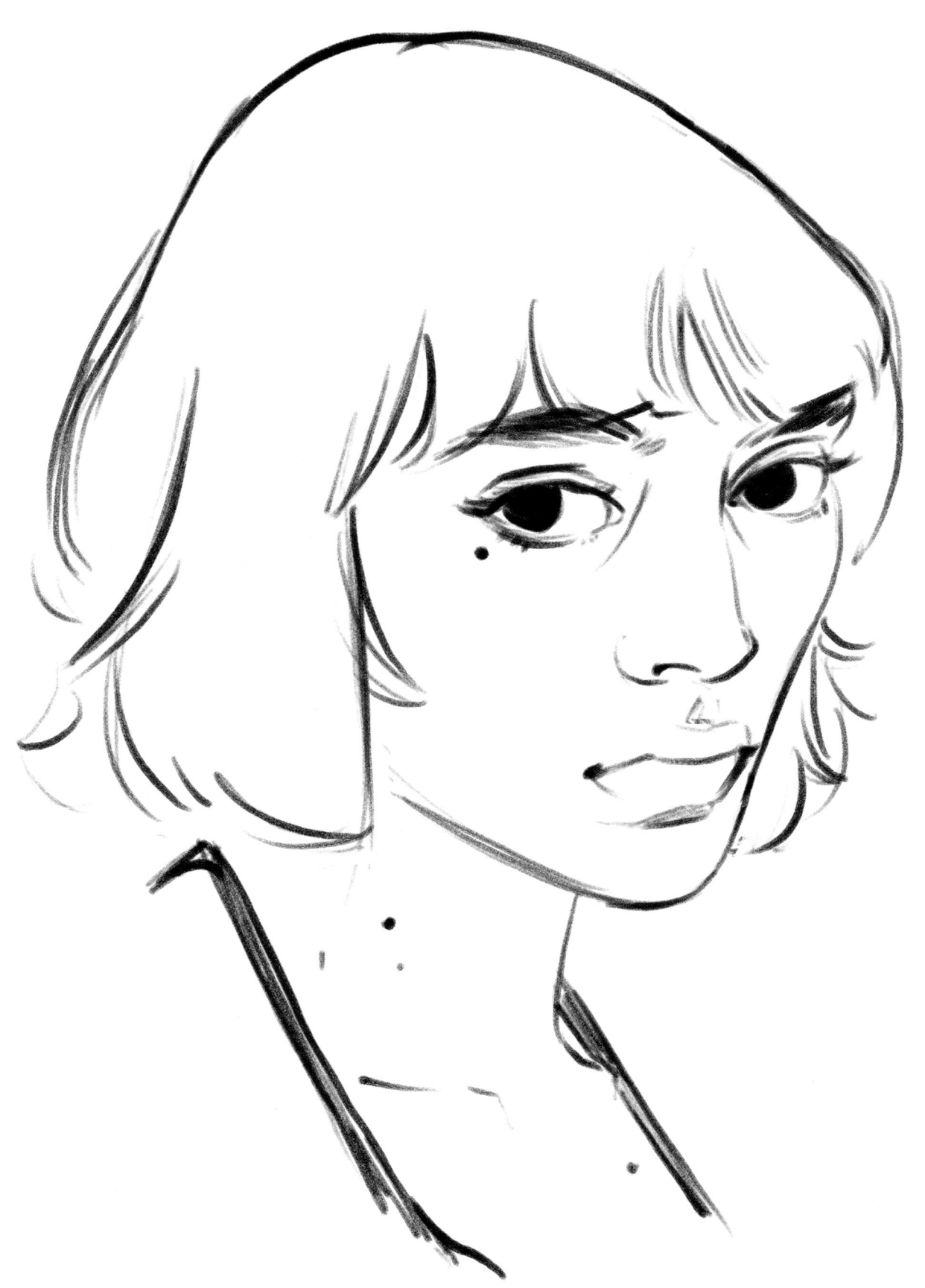

Portraiture
DRAWING

While it's true that a drawing can be a standalone piece of artwork, drawing can also serve as the foundation for a painting—it's a necessary first step in the process.

In this section you'll learn about the difference between drawing and underdrawing. You'll also learn two different methods for sketching your subject.

In the first method, I'll demo the use of a grid along with a technique called sight-size for accurate measurement.

In the second method, you'll get a walkthrough of a more gestural and freestyle approach while practicing what was covered in *Drawing the Head* in the anatomy chapter.

DRAWING VERSUS UNDERDRAWING

A drawing can be a finished piece of artwork, while an underdrawing is a preliminary step in a greater process.

If your intention is to create a portrait **drawing**, then you'll likely want the artwork itself to look refined and polished. This might mean that you focus more intensely on linework and shading.

If, instead, you want to **paint** a portrait, then the precursor to painting—the underdrawing— is essential for setting up a good foundation.

When underdrawing, you're not heavily focused on line quality, shading, or anything of the sort. What you're trying to do is set up a guide for yourself so that you don't get lost during the painting phase. The underdrawing will get covered up in the end, so by no means does it need to be perfect.

When I'm underdrawing I tend to focus on big shapes. I'll outline large shadow and light areas or make marks to indicate the planes of the head. When you're underdrawing, you might want to focus on similar things, or you might want to spend time drawing the areas that normally trip you up.

What's most important to remember is that an underdrawing should serve *you*. You only need to include the kind of information that will help you when painting; therefore, your underdrawings may look completely different from someone else's.

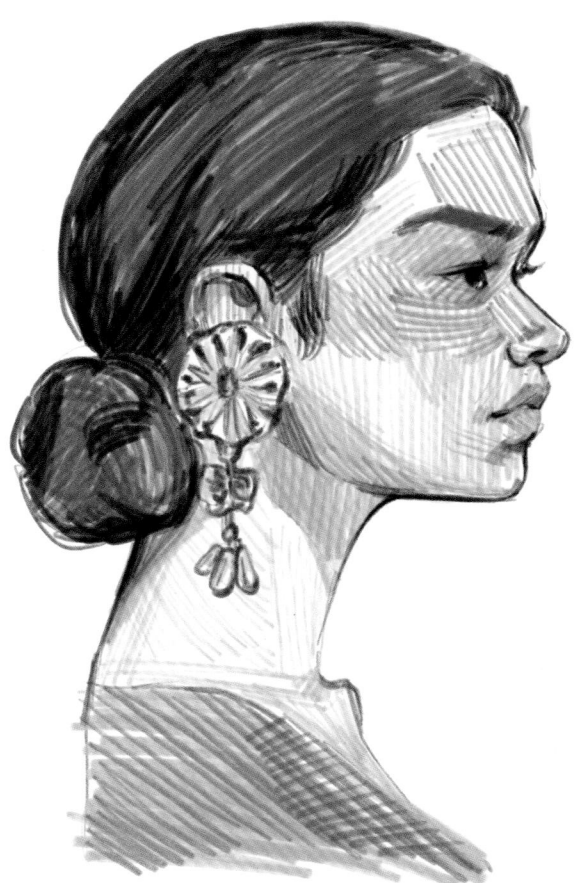

Left: An example of a finished drawing where linework was the main focus and tone was built up using hatching and crosshatching

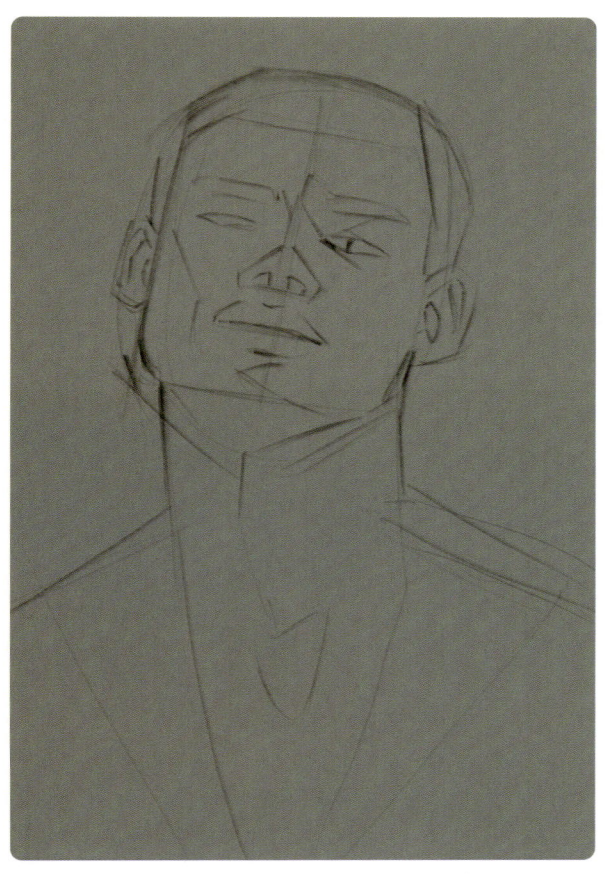

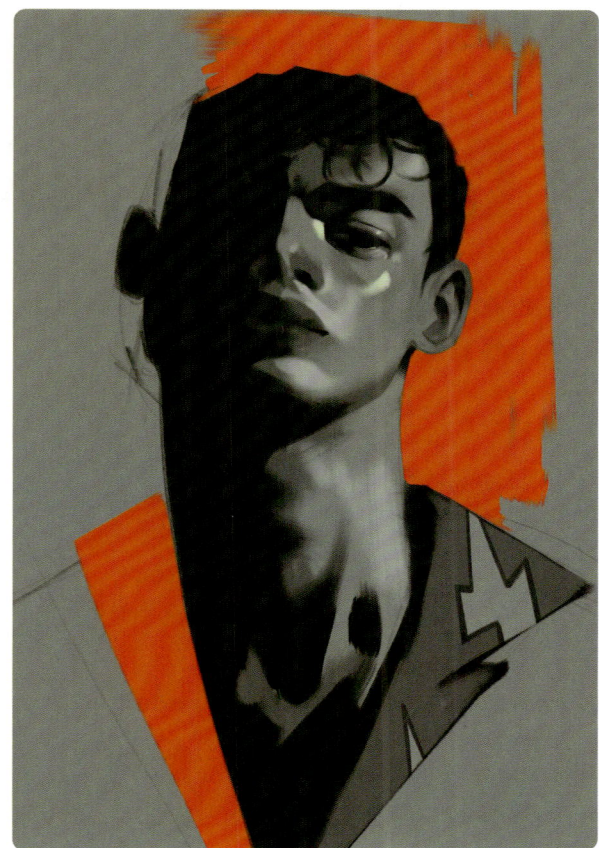

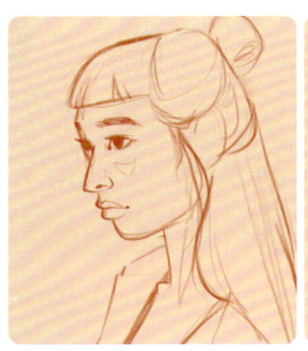

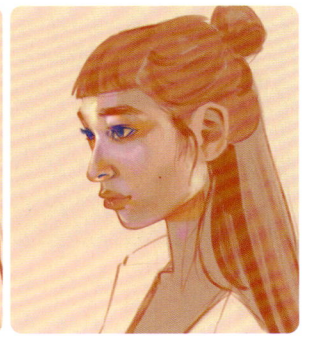

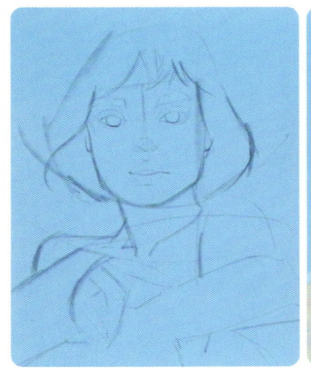

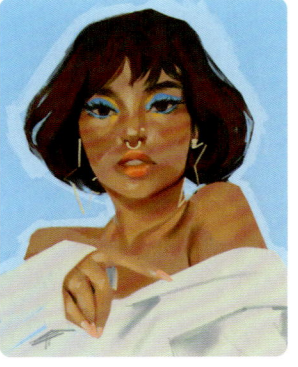

Here are examples of underdrawings that eventually turned into finished paintings. As you can see, they range from structural drawings to loose, gestural, and sketchy—either way, they're all far from polished.

As I mentioned earlier, the underdrawing phase is ideal for spending time with the features that normally cause you grief. If you're struggling to draw the planes of the nose, then you're sure to struggle painting them as well. This is the reason underdrawing is so important. Work out any issues in this phase because it's a thousand times easier to correct a simple drawing than it is to correct an entire painting!

OBSERVATION: A CRUCIAL FIRST STEP

Once you pick out a reference image, it's time to kick off the art-making process!

Before you start drawing, take a moment to observe your reference image while answering questions like these:

1. **What do I want the focal point to be?**
   Most of the time it's the eyes, but it doesn't always have to be.

2. **What are the big shapes I can see in this photo?**
   Look for large shapes created by shadow, light, or physical attributes like hair.

3. **Are there lots of little details I need to ignore early on?**
   This could be things like freckles, tight curls, or jewelry.

4. **Does the person in the photo have any quirks or interesting features I want to highlight?**

5. **What is it about the image that intrigues me? Is there a feature that I'm excited to draw?**

6. **How much of the body do I want to include?**

You don't have to write anything down or come up with lengthy answers. The time it takes to observe your image could be anywhere from a few seconds to a couple minutes. Just taking a bit of time with the image will help you form some semblance of a plan before drawing.

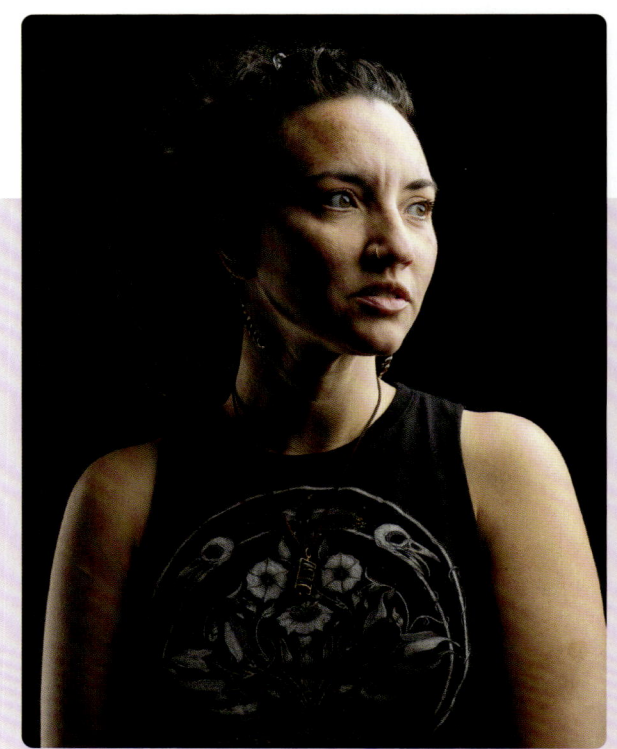

This is the reference image* I'll use during the method one demo. By answering the questions, I've determined that I want the model's eyes to be the focal point, and I'd especially like to explore rendering the volume of the hair.

There are large shadow shapes, particularly on the left side of the face. I can't see much of the earrings, so I'll ignore them.

* Reference image supplied by reference.pictures.

METHOD ONE
SETUP AND INITIAL SKETCH

Create a New Canvas

Create a new canvas and import your reference image directly onto the canvas. Refer to *Setting Up References* on page 86. The reference image and your drawing will be scaled 1:1, so now is the best time to crop your reference image if needed.

Turn on Procreate's *Drawing Guide* (outlined in the next step) as it will help you place your reference image correctly.

Right: Use the *Transform* tool to resize your image (shown) or the *Selection* tool to crop it.

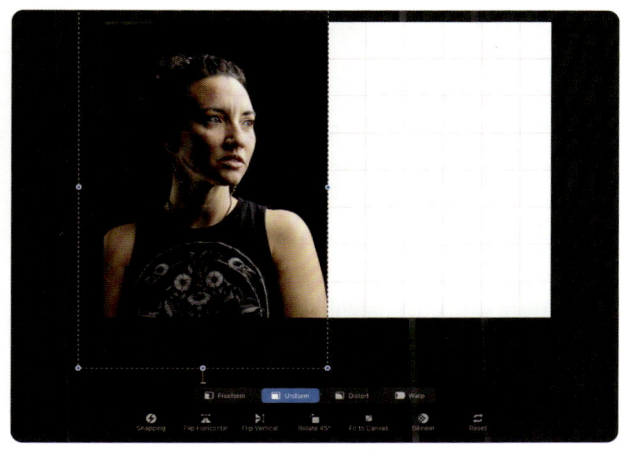

Turn the Drawing Guide On

Toggle the *Drawing Guide* on by going to:

Actions > Canvas > Drawing Guide

The option to *Edit Drawing Guide* will be enabled. Tap on it and adjust the size and number of blocks by using the *Grid Size* slider.

You can have as many blocks on there as you want, but I recommend sticking to a lower number. For example, my guide is approximately six blocks wide (three per side) by four blocks high. My canvas is split exactly down the middle so that my reference and the part of my canvas that I'll be drawing on are on opposite sides and are the same width and height as one another.

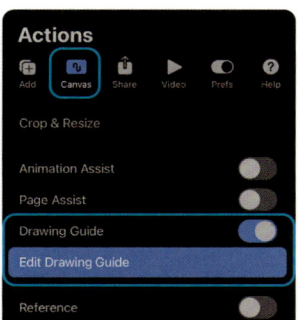

Left: *Edit Drawing Guide* is deactivated by default—the drawing guide must be turned on.

Below: Adjust the opacity, thickness of the guide lines, and the overall grid size using the bottom panel. Change the color of the guide by using the rainbow slider at the top.

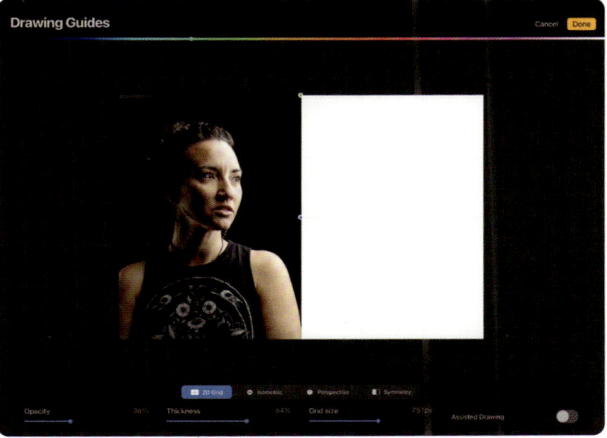

Start Sketching!

The grid helps break down complex subjects into bite-sized, manageable pieces, so try to focus less on drawing a "face" or a "person" and more on the **shapes you see within each block**.

Use both negative space and positive space to figure out placement.

Negative space is the part of an image that isn't occupied by the subject. It's typically the part of an image that you don't draw (like a blank background). It helps to look at the shapes that the negative space creates to help figure out if the sizing and placement of the positive spaces are correct.

Right: Draw the abstract shapes you see instead of trying to draw what you *know* the hair, or any other feature, should look like.

Below: The initial sketch. Notice how it's blocky and analytical—focus on getting the placement of features down accurately.

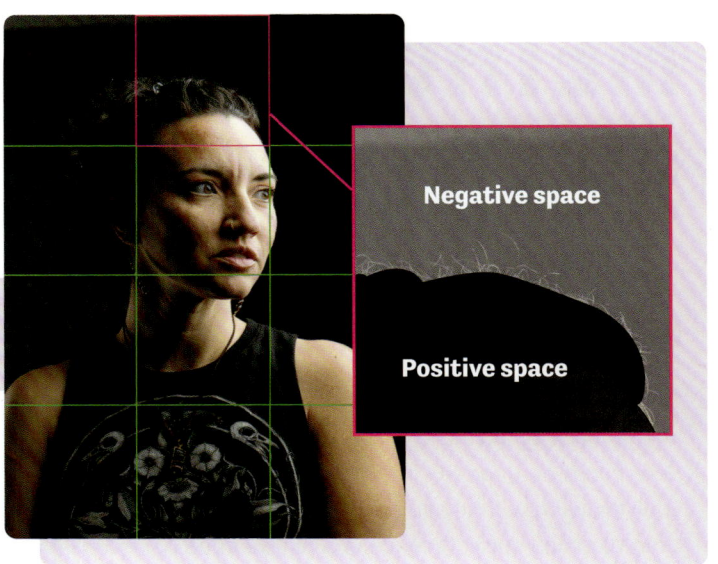

Negative space

Positive space

Abstract positive shape

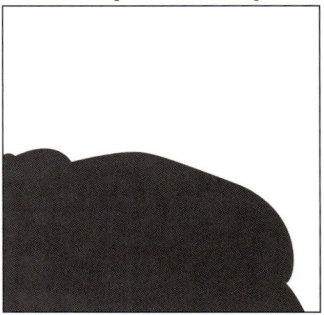

Abstract negative shape

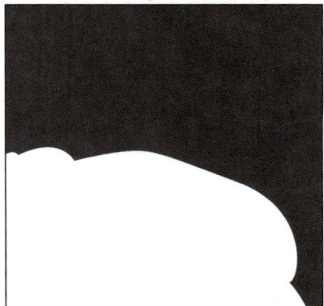

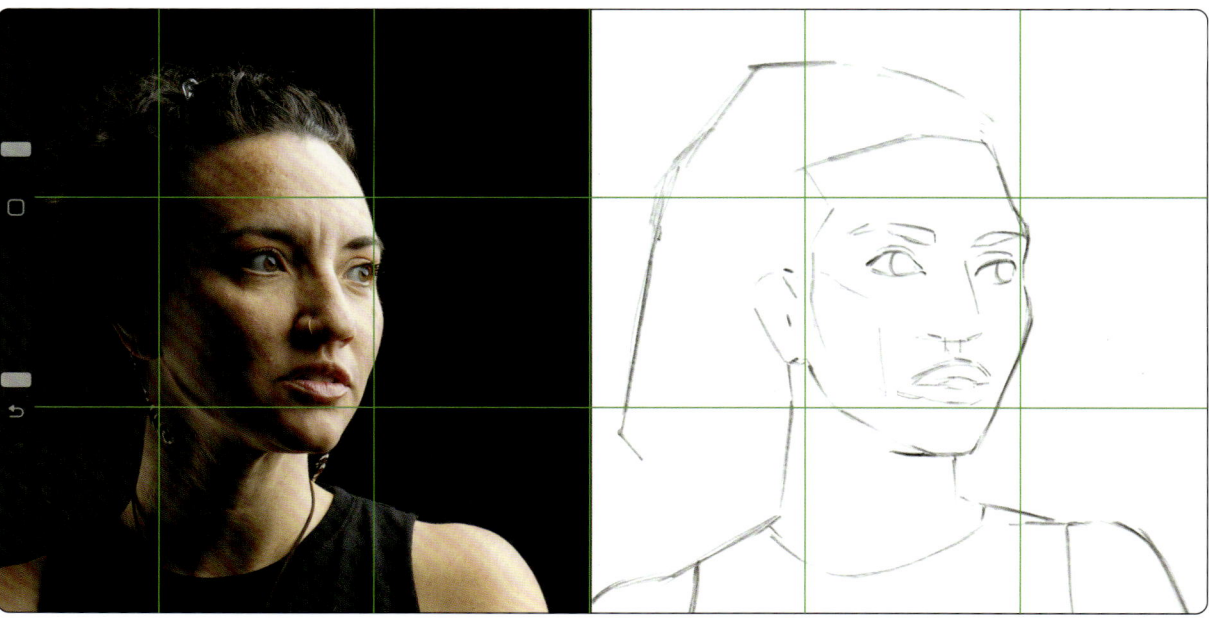

Check Your Work with Rulers

At some point in the drawing process, you'll either struggle with a feature or you'll have the urge to check your work.

Get over any hurdles by using the sight-size method. Since your reference image is exactly the same size as your drawing, you can use rulers to help you figure out if your alignment is off.

On a new layer, using a different color, draw straight horizontal lines from one point of your reference image across your entire canvas. Check to see if your drawing is aligned with the reference.

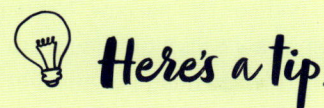

Here's a tip!

To make a perfectly straight line, trace over one of your grid lines and hold your Apple Pencil in place until the line snaps. Release, then switch to the *Transform* tool to move your new line anywhere on the canvas.

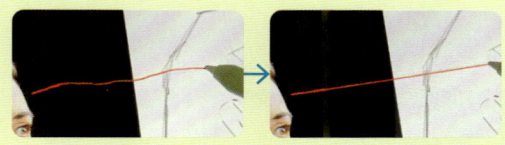

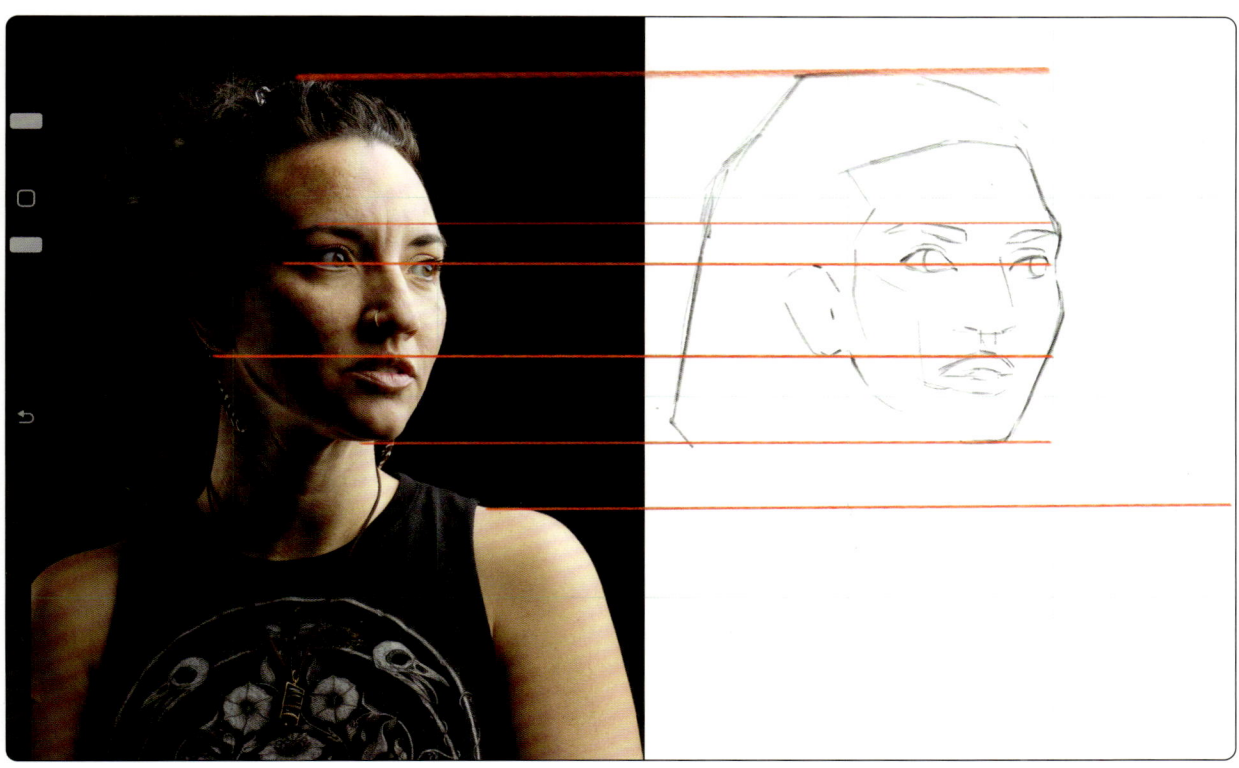

Horizontal lines won't help you catch parts of your drawing that are too wide or too narrow. To check the width of features, draw a straight line from a single point on your reference image to another (like the ear to the outside corner of the eye, as shown). Make sure this new guide is on a separate layer so that you can use it as a ruler.

Once you draw your guide, switch to the *Transform* tool to move it across the canvas. Turn on Snapping > Magnetics to move your ruler across the canvas seamlessly.

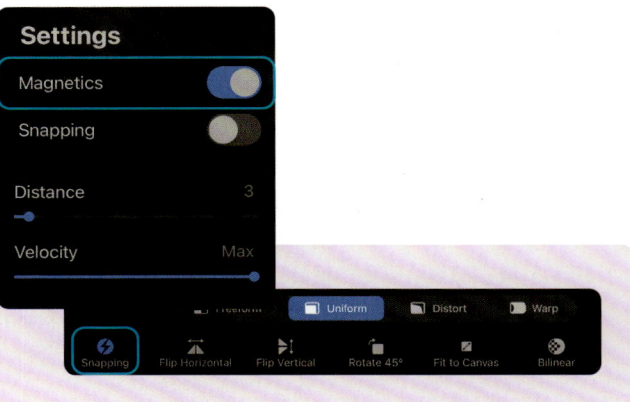

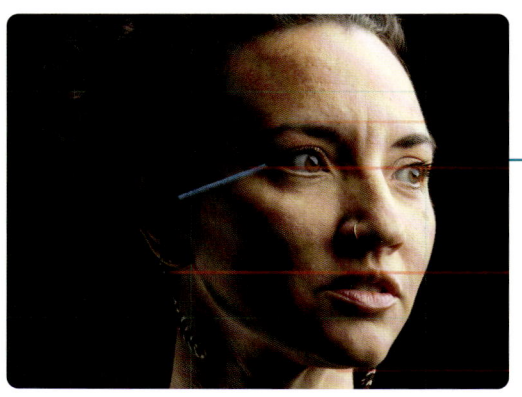

Move your ruler across the canvas to compare widths

Adjust Your Drawing with Tools

If you notice that something in your drawing is off, instead of erasing and redrawing that piece, you could use Procreate's *Selection* and *Transform* tools to make adjustments instead.

Here's an example: while I was happy with the shape of the ear that I drew, I noticed that the size and placement were slightly off.

To remedy this, I first used the *Selection* tool to isolate a part of the ear.

Then I switched to the *Transform* tool to move that part of the ear closer to the head, which alters both the size and placement of the ear at once.

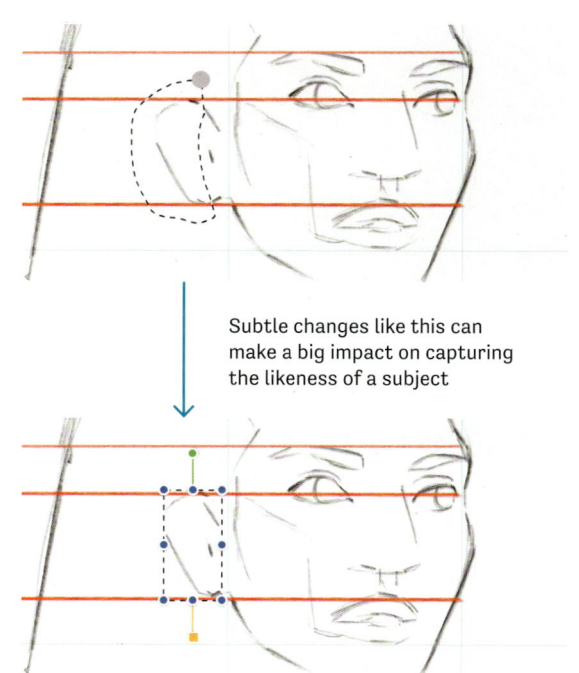

Subtle changes like this can make a big impact on capturing the likeness of a subject

Finish It!

Continue drawing, checking your work, and making adjustments until you're satisfied with your preliminary sketch.

Use as many layers as you feel comfortable with and capture the likeness of the model to the degree you're happy with. (If you want to create a stylized drawing, then you don't have to be hyper accurate.)

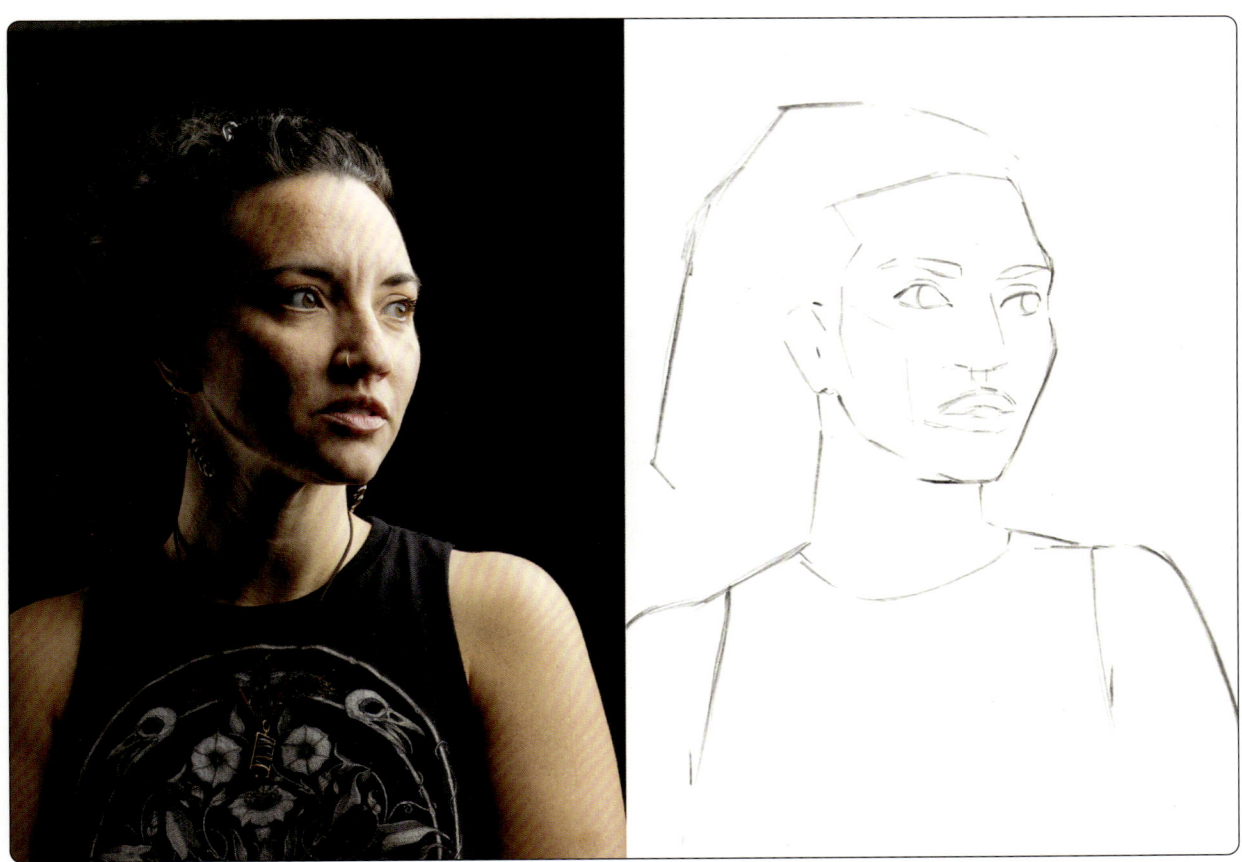

Believe it or not, you've just created a simple underdrawing!

That means from this point onward, you may be ready to start painting. If that's the case, skip ahead to *Portraiture Painting*, page 115.

If, however, you want to capture more information in your underdrawing (like shadow shapes), follow the steps outlined on the next few pages.

If you want to turn your preliminary sketch into a polished drawing, skip ahead to page 102.

UNDERDRAWING

You've got the bulk of the work done; now it's just a matter of adding in some extra markers that will help you during the painting phase.

Painting will really showcase the form of your subject, which means it's important for you to understand and communicate plane changes by rendering the shadow and light areas of your model.

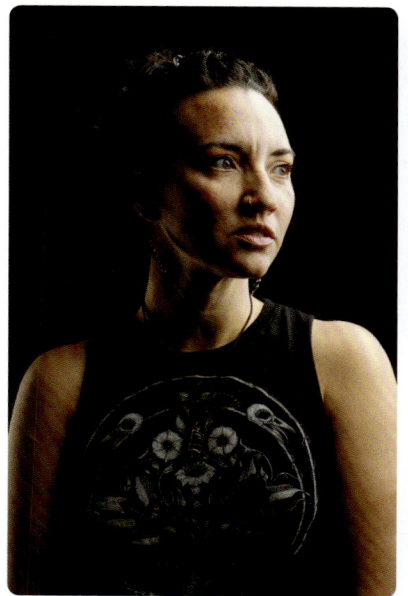
Original reference image

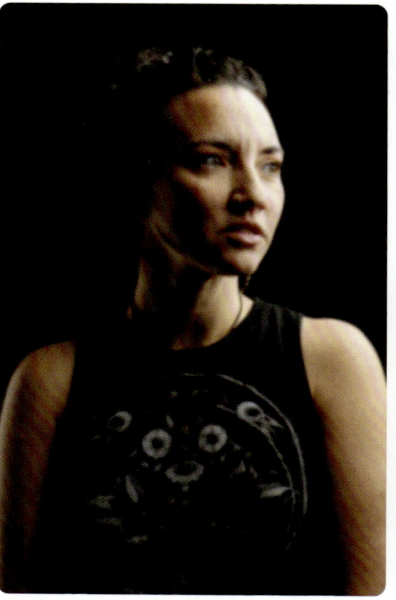
Blurred—similar to squinting

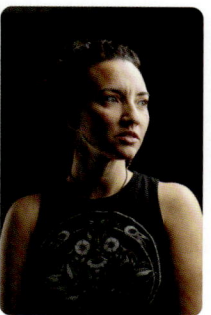
Zoomed out

To find the shadow and light shapes, it helps to squint at your reference or zoom out really far (or do both at the same time). In doing so, you're less likely to get caught up in the details of the image and seeing the larger picture will become easier.

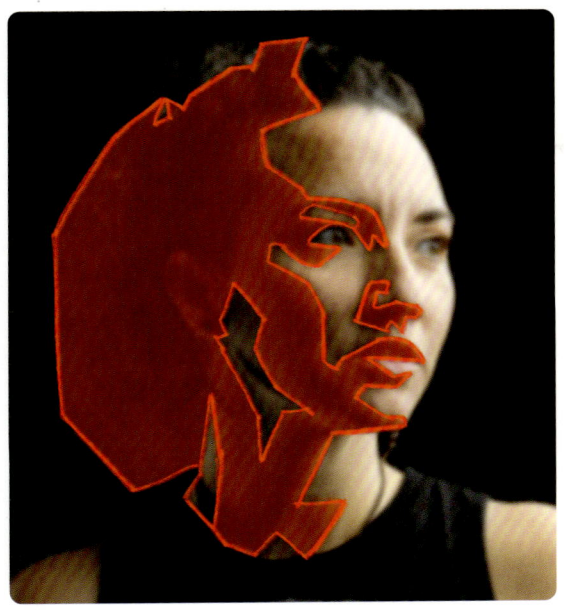

Outlined in red are some of the darkest shadow shapes. These will be some of the shapes you'll want to capture in the underdrawing.

Focus on finding the "edges" of shapes and block them in with simple hatching.

Don't hone in on subtle shifts in value or gradation because you can deal with blending edges when painting.

Also, don't worry if entire features disappear within each other. For example, the hair is a very large shape and mostly within shadow. The ear itself somewhat disappears within it—that's okay. You don't have to draw a feature just because you know it exists.

Create a New Layer

Lower the opacity of your initial sketch, then create a new layer.

Use this new layer block in the big shadow shapes or outline large highlights.

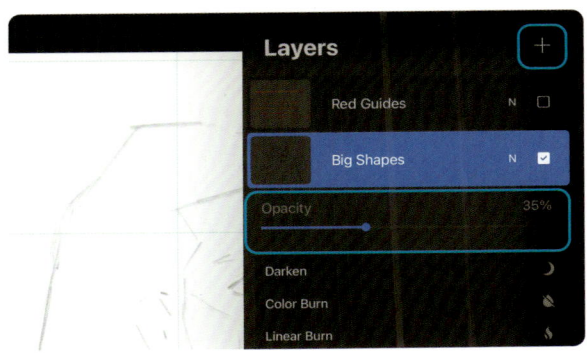

 Here's a tip!

Instead of changing the size of the image that's set up on your canvas or pinching constantly to zoom in and out, open *Reference* to pop up a small thumbnail of your image.

Actions > Canvas > Toggle Reference "on"

Change the size of the window by dragging the bottom-right corner.

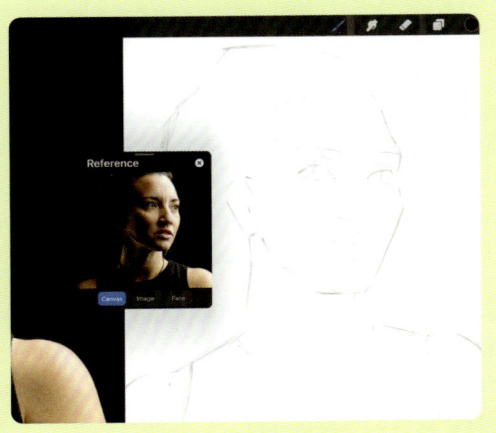

Fill In the Shapes

Once you draw the outline of the shapes, you can fill in the shadows with hatching, block everything out with a value, or simply leave it as is.

I personally tend to use outlines only, but it can get confusing depending on the amount of information you capture.

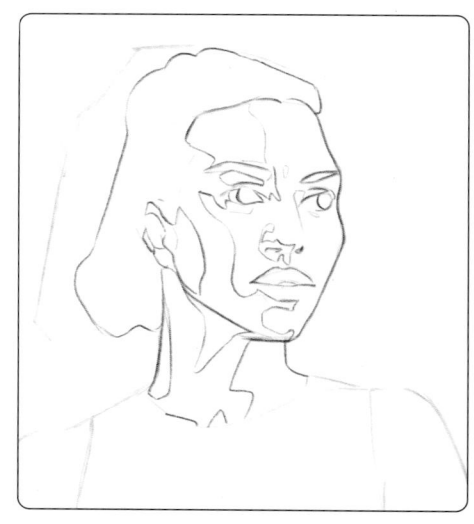

Right: The underdrawing with light and shadow outlined with a pencil brush

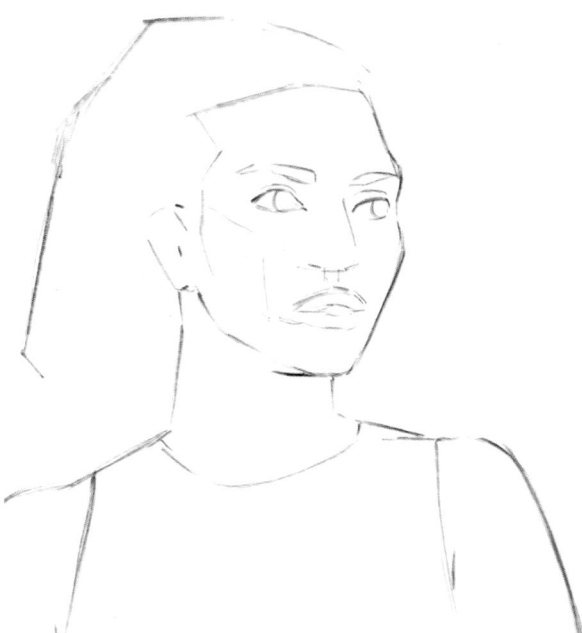

Underdrawing 1: Linework indicating the features and pose of the model

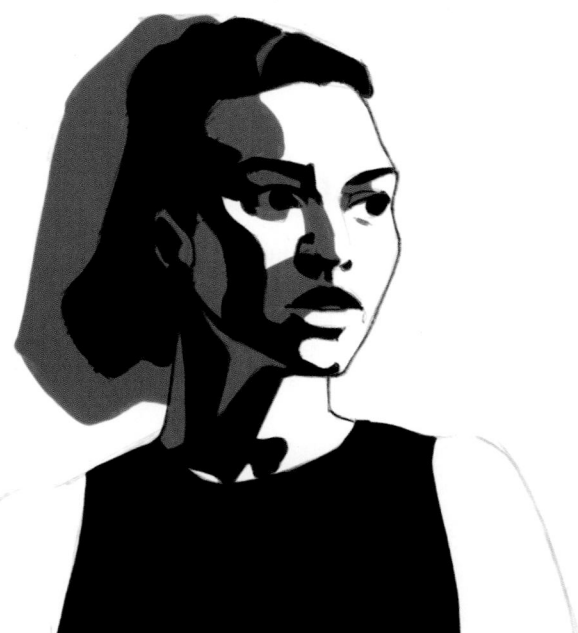

Underdrawing 2: Shadows have been blocked out to indicate the forms of the face and hair

Compare the underdrawings above. Notice how the first one provides a basic structure of the model in the photo but not much else.

The second version indicates plane changes through values and hard edges. Through a quick, simple process, you can get a much better idea of the shadow and light shapes you have to capture when painting in order to make a realistic image.

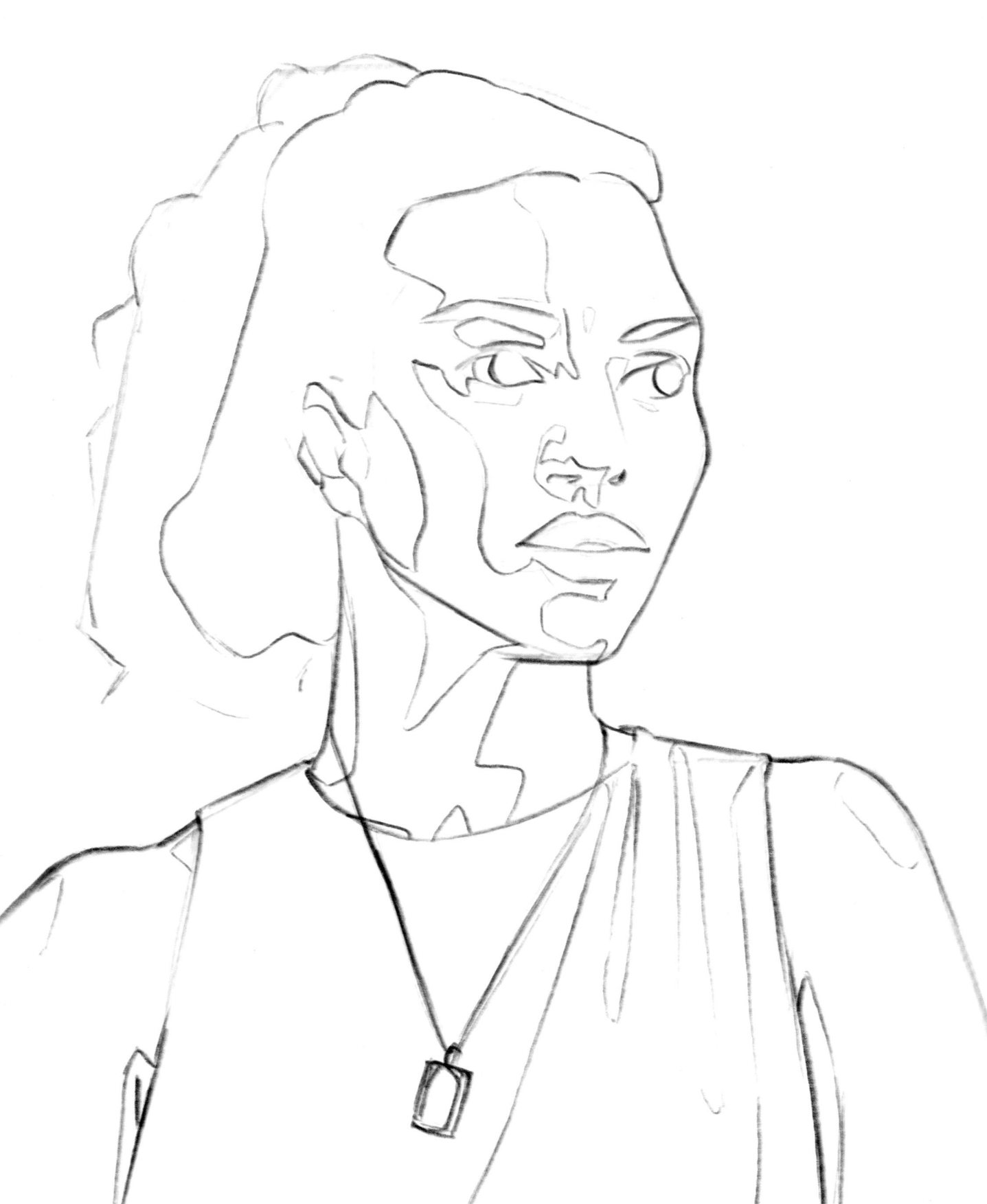

FINISHED DRAWING

With the initial sketch complete (pages 93–97), you can now start to render the final drawing.

Begin Rendering

On a new layer, choose a starting point and begin rendering the form through line, making sure that you don't obsess over a single feature for a prolonged period of time. Bounce around the canvas and build up your drawing all at once.

Working in this way has a couple advantages. First, it ensures that you don't spend hours, for example, working on the right eye only to realize when you move on to the left that the right is mishappen, too big, or too small.

Second, you give yourself a tiny mental break between features. If you're struggling with the nose, leave it alone and move on to another area of your drawing.

Flaws in your artwork are so much more noticeable after you've taken a moment to step away.

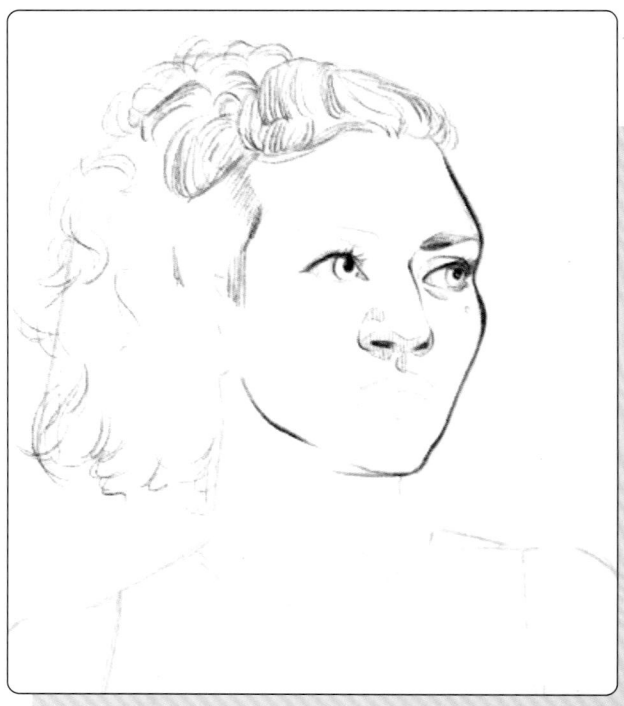

Build up your drawing all at once by bouncing around from feature to feature. The drawing may look incomplete, but that's just part of the process.

Build Up Tone

Where there are subtle shifts in forms or shadows, it's best not to use harsh, dark lines. You can use methods like hatching (short, light, repetitive marks) to build up tone and express these changes.

It's up to you how much tone you want to build up—you can be as excessive or minimalistic with hatching as you want.

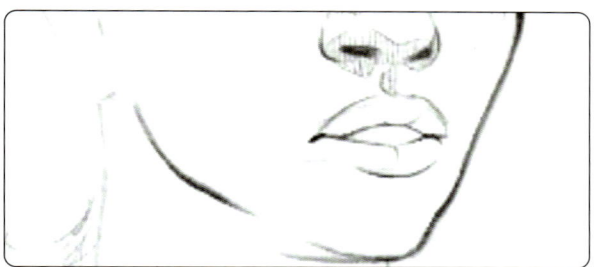

When drawing lips, it's ideal to use shading or minimal linework to describe the form. Using dark lines to outline the entirety of the lips results in a flattened and unrealistic look.

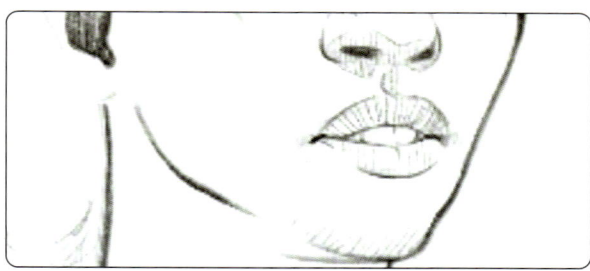

In this example, I've used vertical hatch marks to very simply describe the form of the lips

Save your darkest, thickest lines for areas that you want to pull away from the background.

In my example, I wanted my model to stand out from the background, so I darkened the lines around the contour of her face.

Here's a tip!

There are many ways to hatch. Your hatch marks can follow the directional form of the subject, or they can simply be used to build tone instead.

Below: In the first example, I've used very minimal hatching and the piece is mostly linework. In the second, I've built up tone and used hatching to help describe the form of the model. It's up to you how much of the face and body you want to describe in this way.

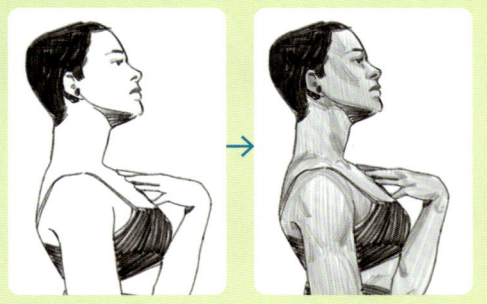

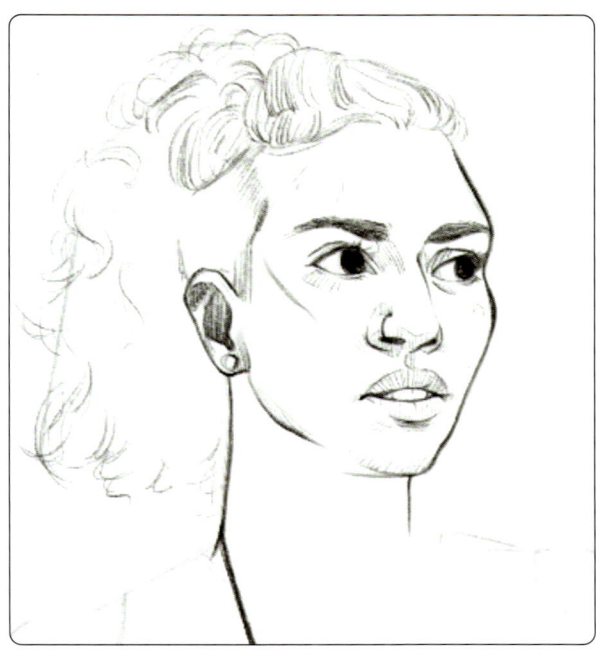

To soften harsh lines, try using the *smudge* tool.

Smudging will softly blend out the edges of your pencil lines. If you're using color, you can use smudge to blend them together.

Remember that turning down the opacity slider for the smudge tool will turn down its strength, allowing you to build up to the amount of softness you want.

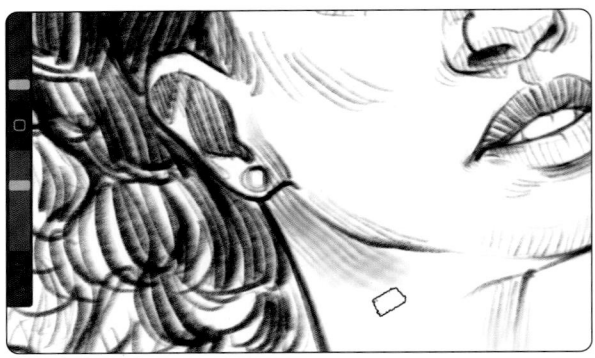

Draw the Hair

It's important when tackling hair that you don't draw every single little strand. It becomes visually overwhelming and can take away from the overall portrait.

Suggesting that the hair is curly or straight through use of just a few lines can have a great impact.

Right: Curly hair is handled in clumps or masses. There are only really a few lines in each clump that indicate direction. Near the edge of the hair, the lines get delicate and wispy. This gives a more lifelike feeling as opposed to boxing in the hair through use of an outline.

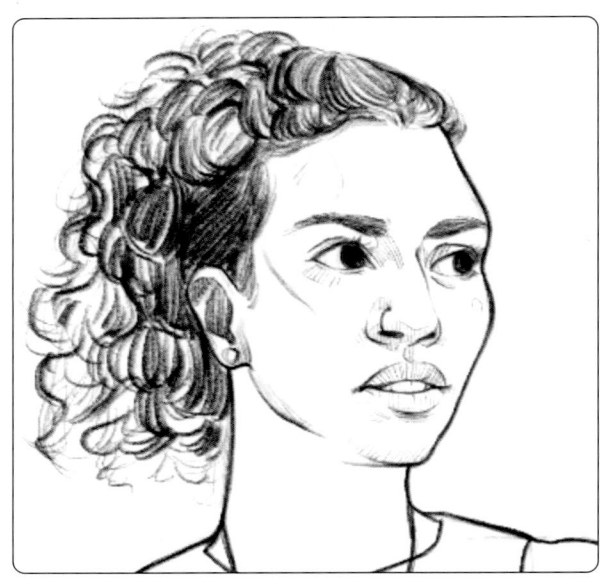

Finish It!

In addition to black, you also have white! Change the color of your pencil to tackle highlights or other details. I used white to add shine to the eyes, to rough in a pattern on the shirt, and to add a tiny bit of detail to the jewelry.

On a new layer, explore adding highlights using white. It's easier to change the opacity this way if it's too stark. This is a good alternative to making a destructive edit—like erasing parts of your drawing.

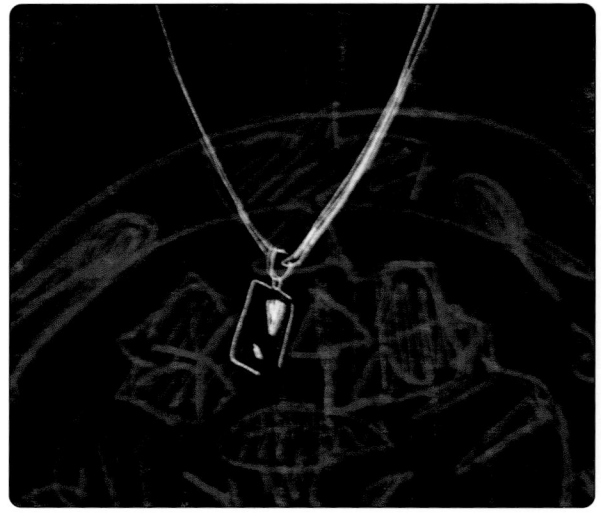

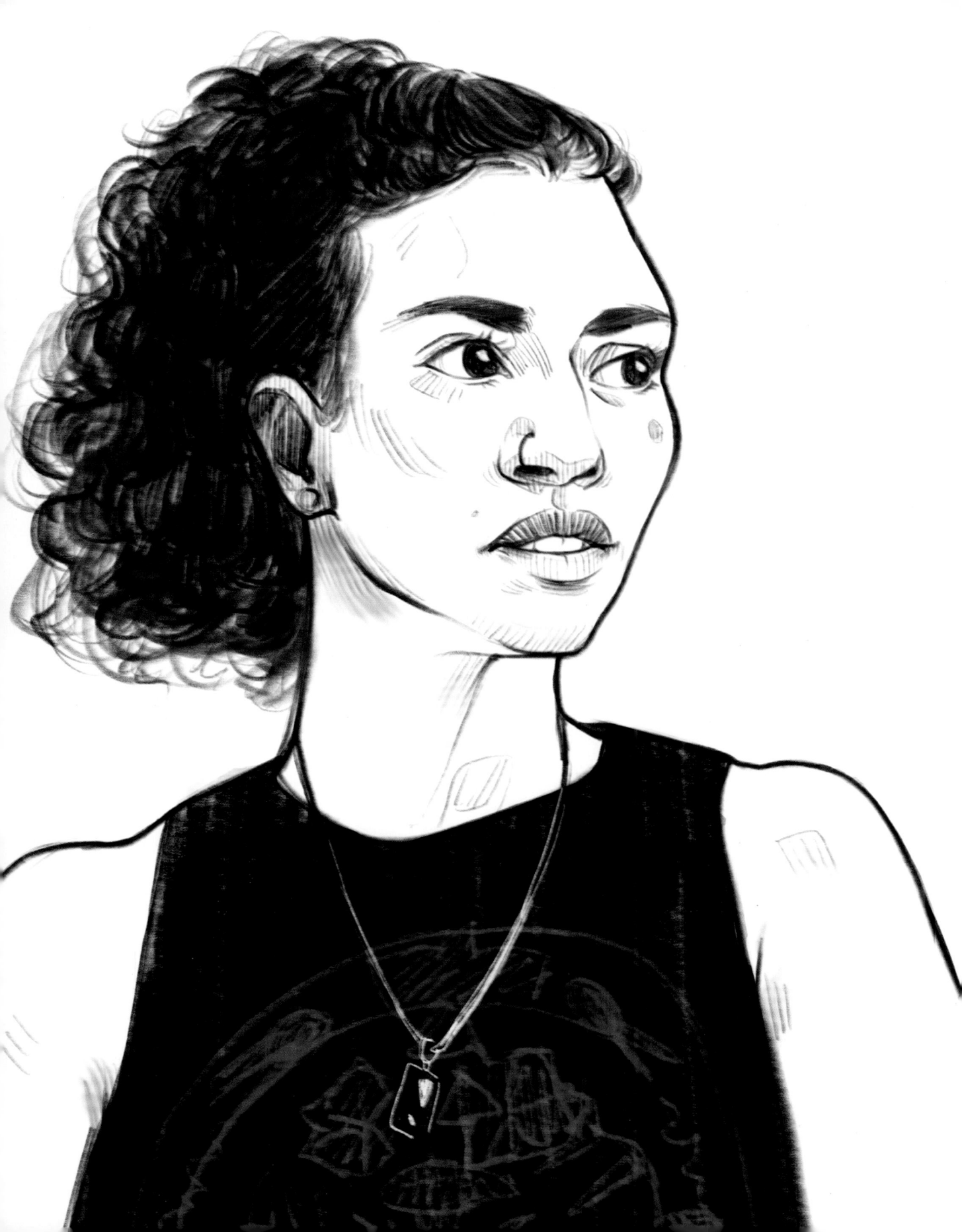

METHOD TWO
FREESTYLE

Using a different reference image, I'll demo a freestyle underdrawing using Loomis's method.

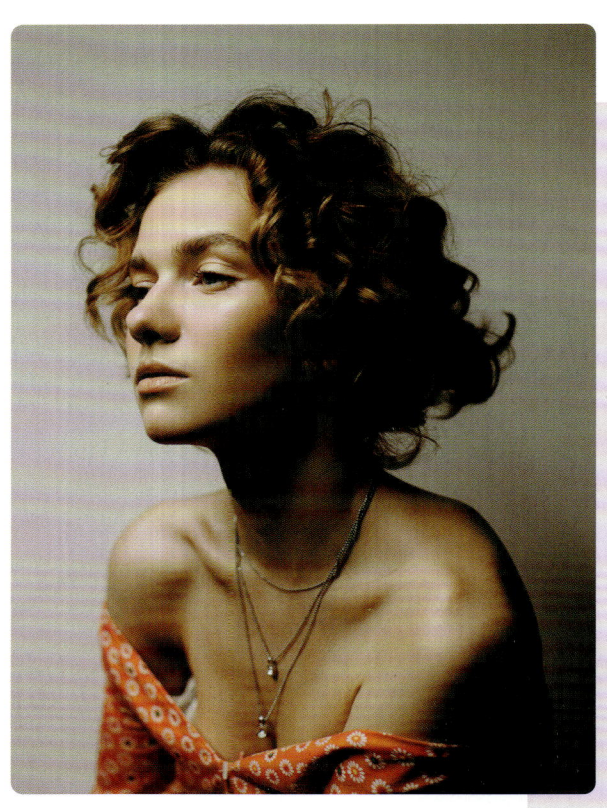

Observation

As mentioned previously, observation is a crucial step before you begin drawing.

Spend time getting to know your reference image and look for any sticky points that are likely to cause you trouble. You can start to brainstorm solutions to these problems now.

For example, if you think you're going to struggle drawing or painting the model's curly hair, you may opt to make the model's hair straight instead. If you decide you're up for the challenge, then you could decide to spend more time during this underdrawing phase to practice.

Start with a Sphere

Create a new canvas and set up your reference image (refer to pages 86–87).

Next, lay the foundation for the head by sketching a sphere.

Rough in a vertical guide that will serve to divide the center of the head. Mark off the brows, nose, and mouth.

Remember that Loomis's method is based off of the average head and your model may have unique measurements (like a long chin or more space between the nose and lips). Make sure that your guides are placed accurately to your reference photo and that you're not just following the formula blindly.

Refer to pages 58–59 in the anatomy chapter for a deeper walkthrough.

Setting Up Guides Properly

Determine the angle of the head in your reference image to figure out how to place guides for the different features. Draw over your reference if you're unsure or need clarification.

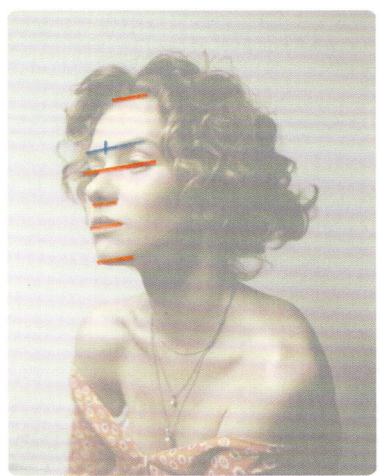

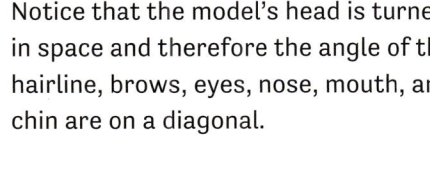

Notice that the model's head is turned in space and therefore the angle of the hairline, brows, eyes, nose, mouth, and chin are on a diagonal.

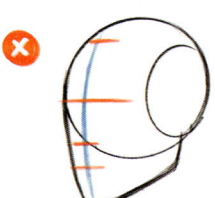

Drawing guides straight across a rounded form is a surefire way to get incorrect placement of features.

Add Features

With that complete, you can start adding in your features. I like to start with the nose as it's right in the middle of the head and serves as a great anchor point. Don't get caught up in adding tons of detail at this point, just get the structure of the features in place.

I sketched in the nose as a basic 3D shape. Things like nostrils and wings can be added later. It's most important to get the placement and perspective as accurate as possible.

While continuing with the process, you might notice that the features are very bland and that the head looks rather sterile—this is perfect!

Use your guides to help you with placement, but don't go on autopilot! Actively pay attention and compare the distances between features. This ensures you are indeed placing them correctly.

Cut and Correct

During the process, if you encounter an issue with placement or sizing, use the selection tool to cut and move pieces around. This can be faster than erasing and redrawing.

I did this myself—shrinking the nose when I realized it was too big and moving the mouth down because it was too close to the nose.

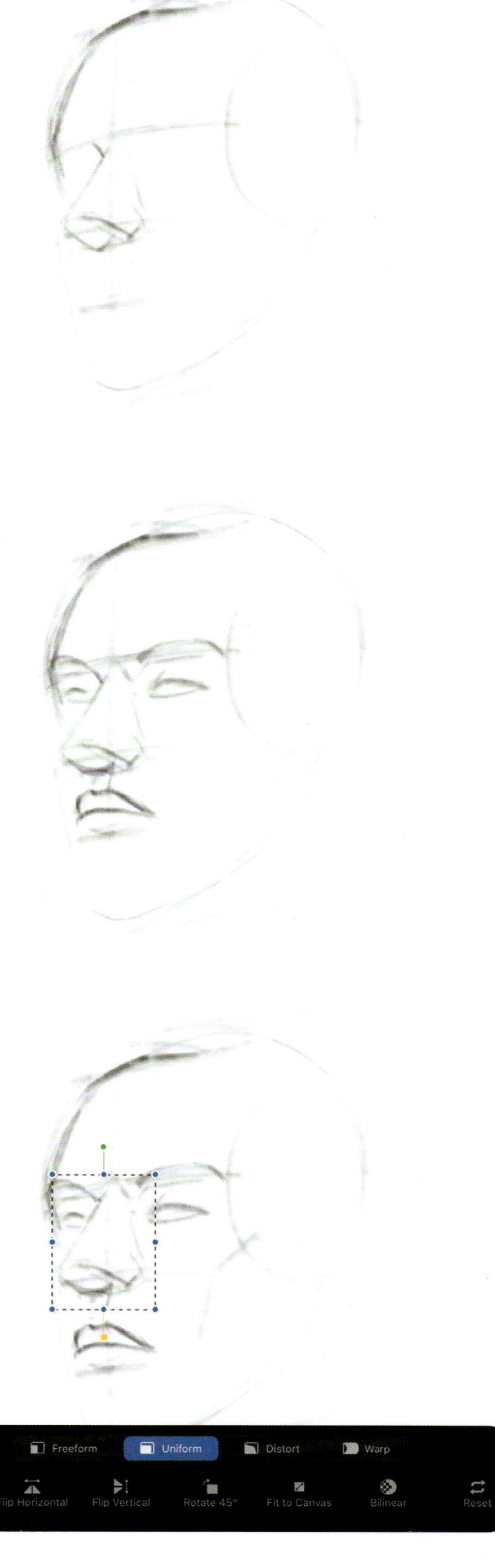

Block In the Hair

Squinting at your photo, look for the large shapes that are created by the hair. Draw in these shapes as opposed to individual strands. Don't worry about stray hairs, frizziness, or gaps; just try to get the general shape.

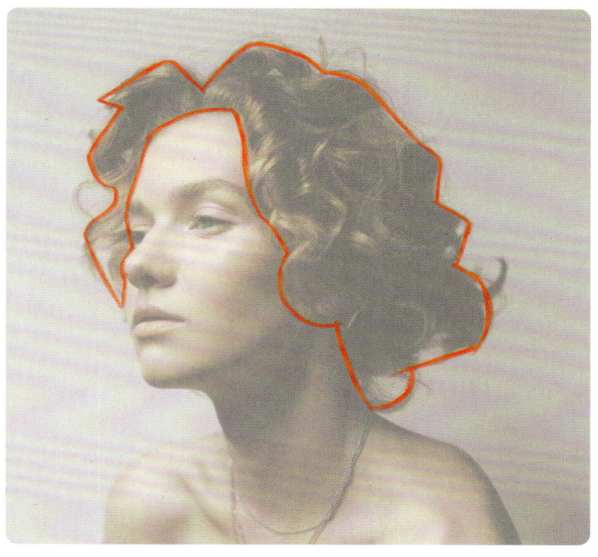 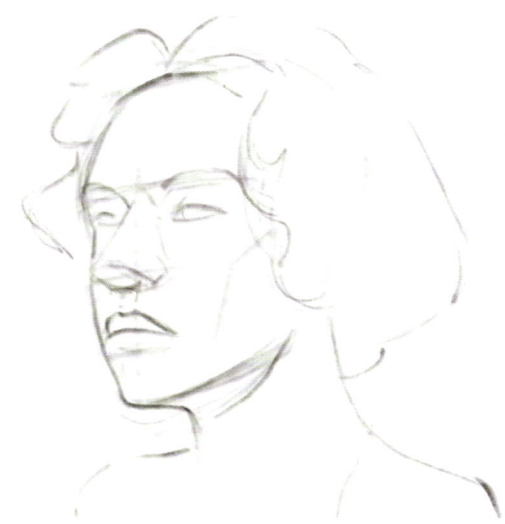

With the hair and shoulders done, your structural sketch is now complete! Lower the opacity of this layer and follow the next step.

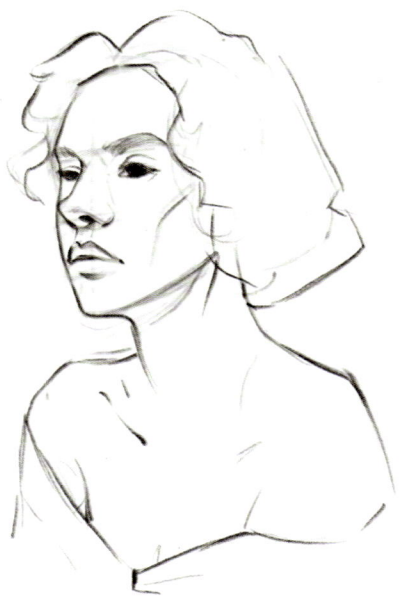

Refine Your Drawing

On a new layer, begin to hash out some of the detail that was purposely ignored earlier.

You can focus on defining the shape and character of the nose, working on the lips or teeth, and refining the shape of the eyes.

It's possible to spend a lot of time in this phase, and that's okay. If you're struggling with a feature, refer back to pages 60–75, where the technique for drawing each one is broken down into steps.

Ask Questions

If you're getting close to completing your drawing, but you're not yet satisfied with it, take a moment and ask yourself *why*.

Sometimes the artwork looks "off" but you may not know how to fix it. Answering questions like these may help you determine what's going on:

1. **Is my perspective off?**
2. **Are the features in proper alignment?**
3. **Is the drawing accurate to the reference?**

If your drawing looks off, then chances are there's an unfavorable answer to one of these questions—but hey! That's okay! It's all a part of learning and getting better. I'll show you how to address any changes that need to be made in the next step.

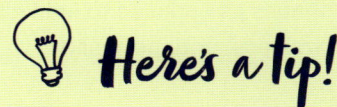

Here's a tip!

Take frequent breaks. It's important to step away from your artwork and give your eyes and brain enough time to reset.

After staring at something for so long (sometimes hours...), it's easy to miss mistakes, but taking even 10 minutes to step away from your work will allow a bit of clarity when you return.

Use Liquify

Using Liquify to manipulate your drawing is much faster than erasing and starting from scratch. Liquify is an adjustment; find it here:

Adjustments > Liquify

Liquify's menu will appear at the bottom of the screen. You can *Push*, *Pinch*, or *Expand* parts of your image. Use *Size* to adjust your brush size and *Pressure* to adjust the strength of the liquify effect when using your Apple Pencil.

You can experiment freely with liquify, expanding the eyes, pinching the nose and pushing the face. The alterations you make don't have to be drastic; sometimes subtle adjustments are all you need. If you're unhappy with a change you've made, you can tap *reset* to start over, or you can use *reconstruct* and paint over the areas that you want to go back into their original state.

To apply your changes, simply exit out of liquify by selecting another tool like the paintbrush.

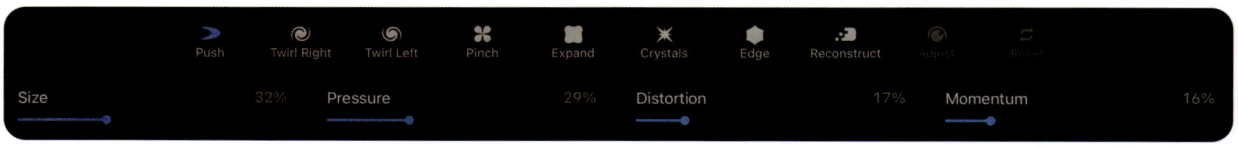

Here's a working example of how I used liquify:

After I had spent some time observing my work, I realized that I wasn't happy with the likeness I had lacked to captured.

The face and eyes that I had drawn were both much too narrow. The face was squished and elongated, and I needed to widen it.

I duplicated the layer that my drawing was on for good measure and so that I could compare my changes afterward. I then activated liquify on the duplicated layer.

I chose push, then dialed up the size of the brush so I could push a large area of the image at once. I lowered the pressure so that I had more control over the change I was about to make.

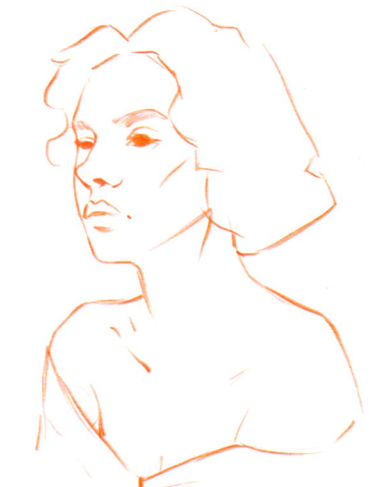

Original drawing

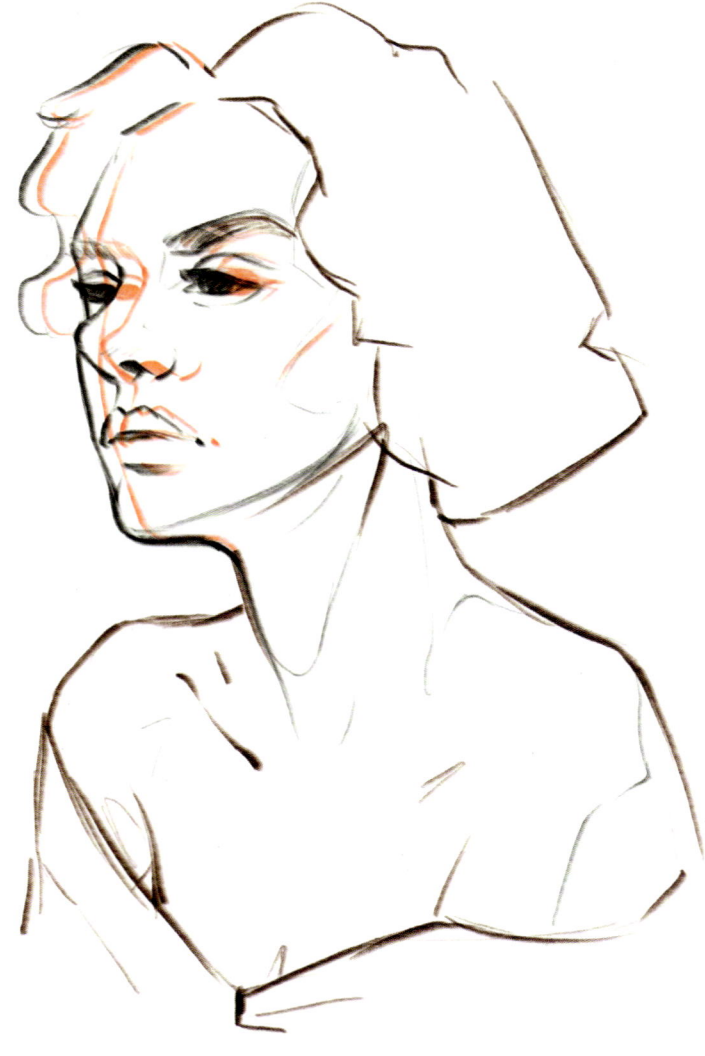

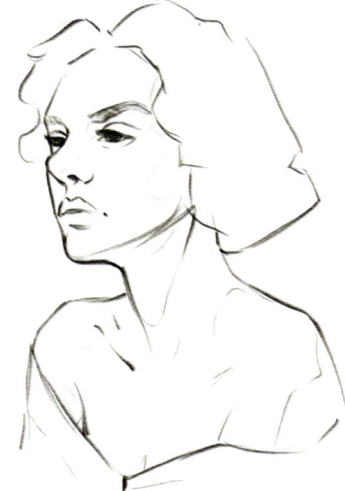

Liquified drawing

Comparison of the original in red versus the liquified layer in black

Redraw If Necessary

I have a personal habit of redrawing my portrait sketches over and over again until I'm happy with the final result. I find that each time I do this, the drawing, along with my familiarity with the reference image, improves.

To redraw over your sketch, lower the opacity. Create a new layer and do a combination of tracing and changing your sketch.

The number of times you redraw a portrait is totally up to you. In this case, I felt that it would benefit me personally to take one more stab at redrawing the portrait after making changes in liquify.

If you feel this step is unnecessary for you, that's okay—skip it. But if you feel like you could still improve your underdrawing, give it a try. How detailed and accurate you make an underdrawing (and the number of times your redraw something) is *always up to you*.

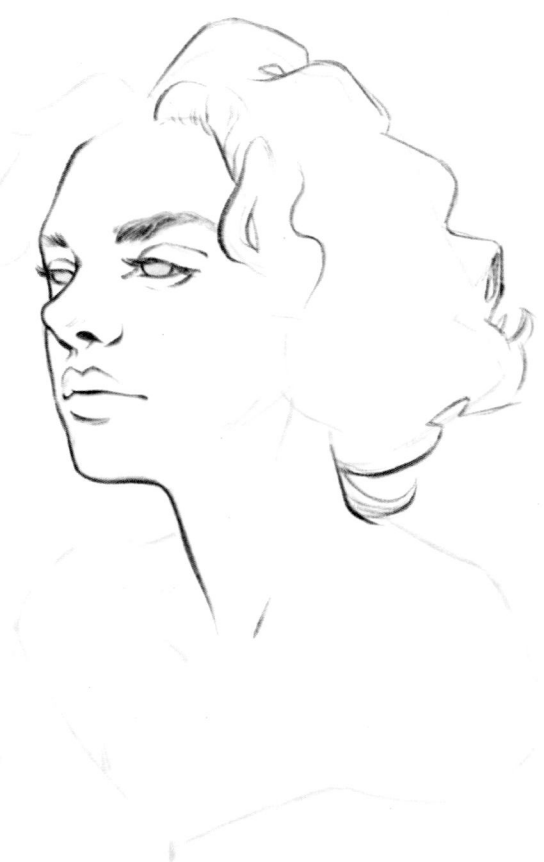

Right: Redrawing on a new layer. Some areas are traced, while others are improved upon. The hair begins to get more definition, while the eyes and lips are very subtly corrected.

Finalize Your Portrait

The final underdrawing is showcased on the next page. As you can see, I defined the shape of the hair (still in larger masses) and drew in large shadowed areas—this is to set myself up for painting. I also experimented with the eyebrows and the eyelashes, particularly practicing how I want the strands of hair to group together or to lie. Again, this is all for the sake of making the painting stage easier for myself.

If there's an area of your reference image that you suspect will give you a hard time when painting, spend more time experimenting with that area in your underdrawing phase. Make mistakes here, clean them up, then try again. It's much easier to make corrections in this phase than in the painting phase.

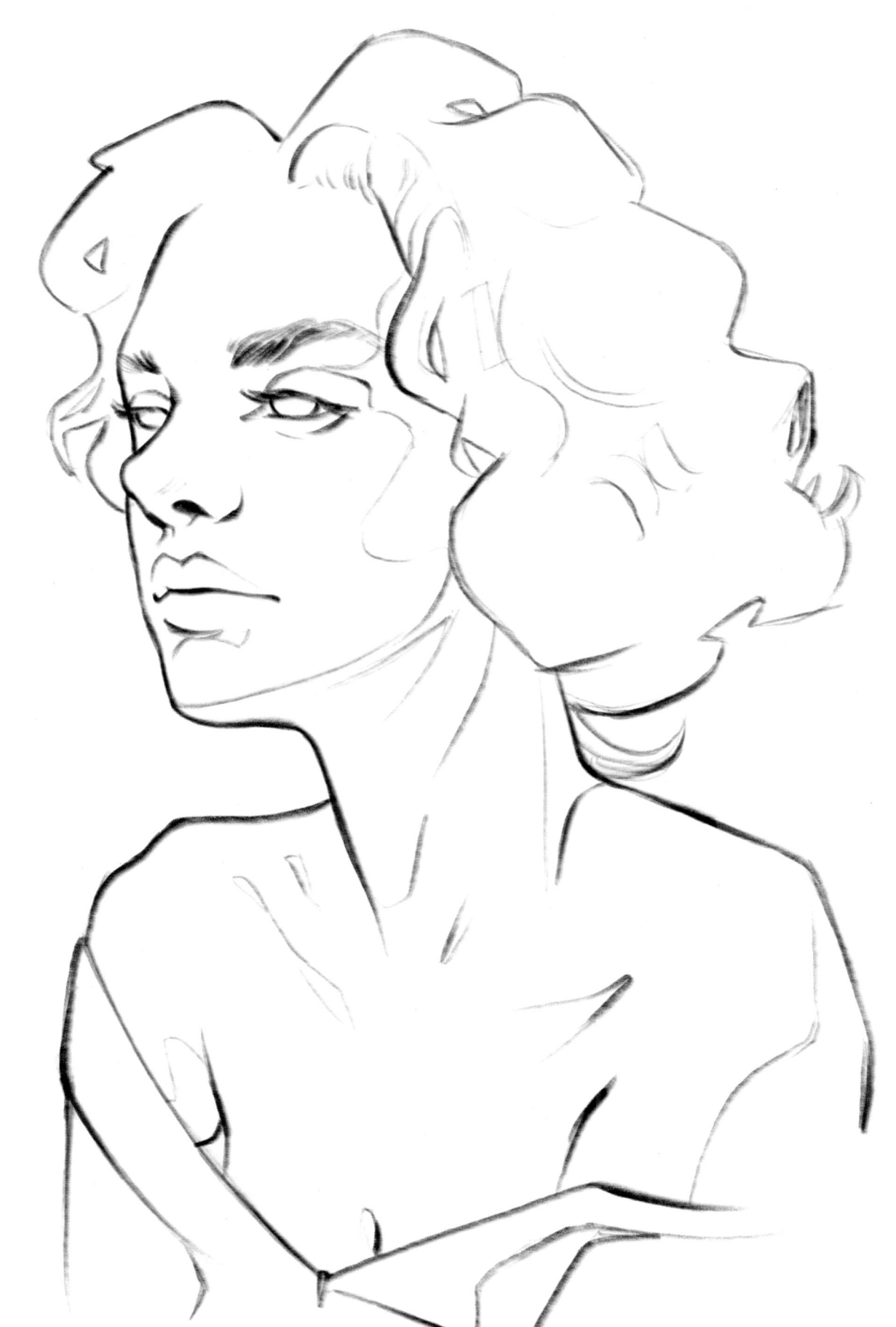

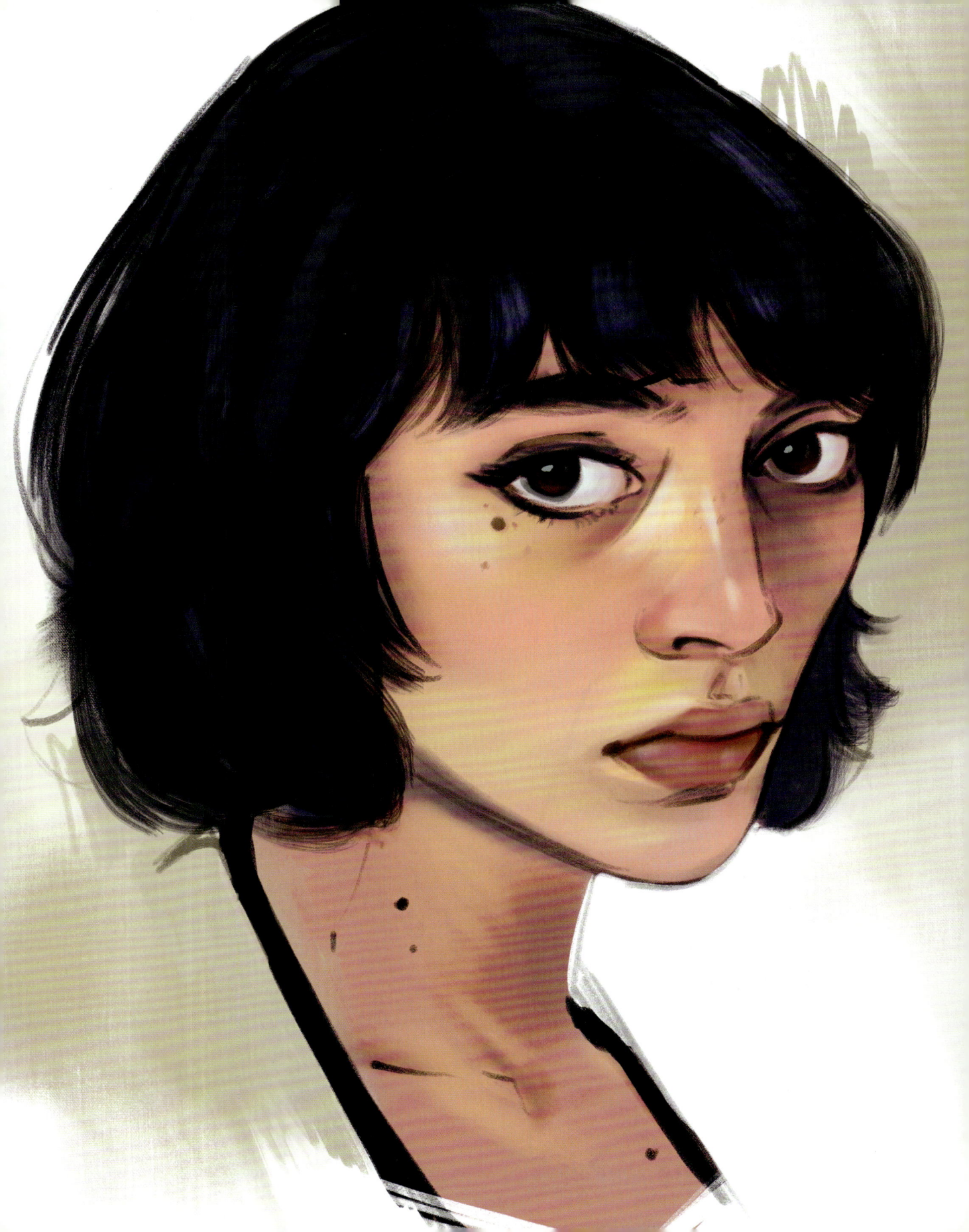

Portraiture
PAINTING

The painting process is broken down into two main phases. In the first phase, you'll create a value painting using only shades of grey. In the second phase, you'll add color to your value painting.

This method of painting is the easiest way for beginners to tackle the complexities of portrait painting. The two phases allow beginners to intensely focus on very important aspects of painting—value and color.

The entire process is actually an old-school technique that was used by oil painters. A traditional artist would create a monochromatic painting (typically done in shades of grey or burnt umber) called a grisaille. Once it was dry, they would add layers of transparent, colored paint on top, which would complete the look. This process is made a thousand times easier thanks to the digital medium.

PHASE ONE

VALUE PAINTING

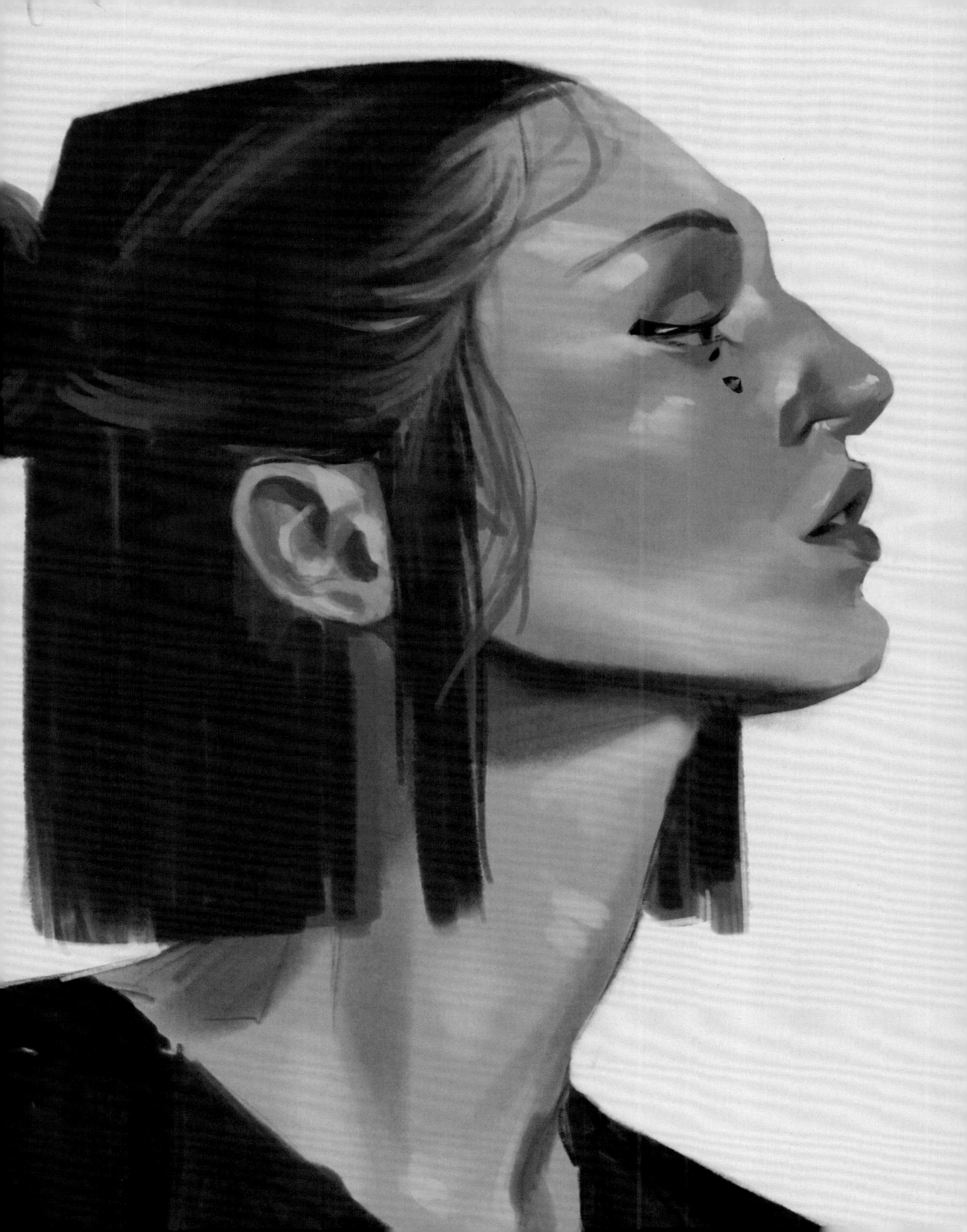

ALL ABOUT VALUES

What Are Values?

Value is the term used to describe how light or dark a hue is—hue being color. Take a look at the swatches below. The blue swatch on the left is **lighter in value** than the blue swatch on the right.

Light blue swatch   **Dark** blue swatch

Values are best understood when hue is completely removed and the swatches are placed in between black (the darkest value) and white (the lightest value). In this manner, it's easy for our brains to process light versus dark. Below are the same blue swatches, but with hue removed.

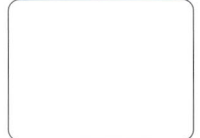   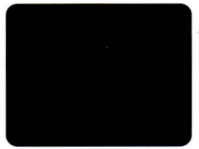

White   **Light** blue swatch   **Dark** blue swatch   Black

This method of knocking the hue out becomes even more valuable when comparing colors that are not the same or colors that have completely different saturation levels.

Sometimes colors look similar in value, like the green and orange swatches below. However, if you take a look at their equivalent greyscale swatches underneath, you'll see that the orange is actually darker.

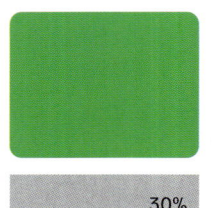 vs. 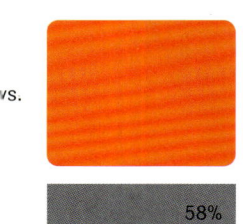   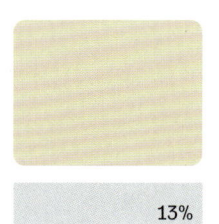 vs.

30%   58%   13%   8%

The percentage listed is the amount of black that's present in the swatch

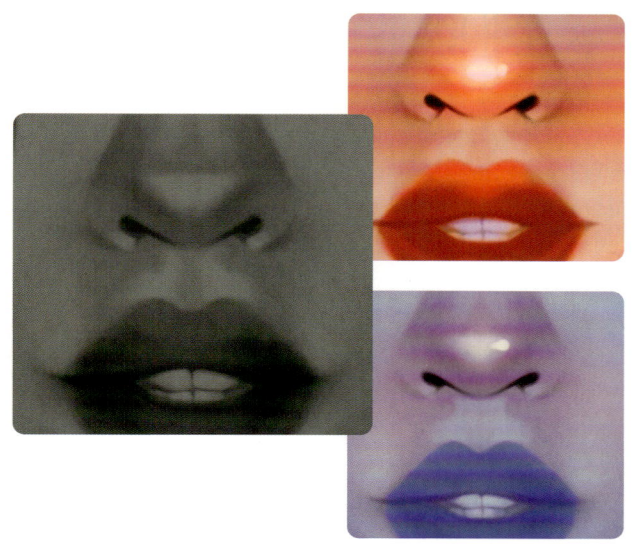

Why Are Values Important?

It's value, not color, that describes form and dimension. This is why it's so important for artists to practice drawing and painting in greyscale first before moving on to color.

The truth is, we all see colors differently— this is especially true for those of us who are color-blind. I'm of the opinion that color is irrelevant to a successful painting. As long as your values are accurate and realistic, you can use color expressively in your artwork without repercussions.

Why Paint in Greyscale First?

To put it simply, painting in greyscale really reduces the complexity of creating a painting. As shown on the previous page, when comparing colors against each other, it can be tricky to figure out the differences between values. When beginners paint in color, they tend to make incorrect value judgements, which will cause issues with the painting overall.

Another reason to paint in greyscale first is because it's difficult for beginners to create work that's enjoyable when there are so many different aspects of a painting that need to be focused on all at once. By painting exclusively in grey, an artist has the chance to reduce overwhelm and spend time honing in on one extremely important skill— value control.

In the end, ensuring that your values are accurate will yield a painting that is realistic and believable.

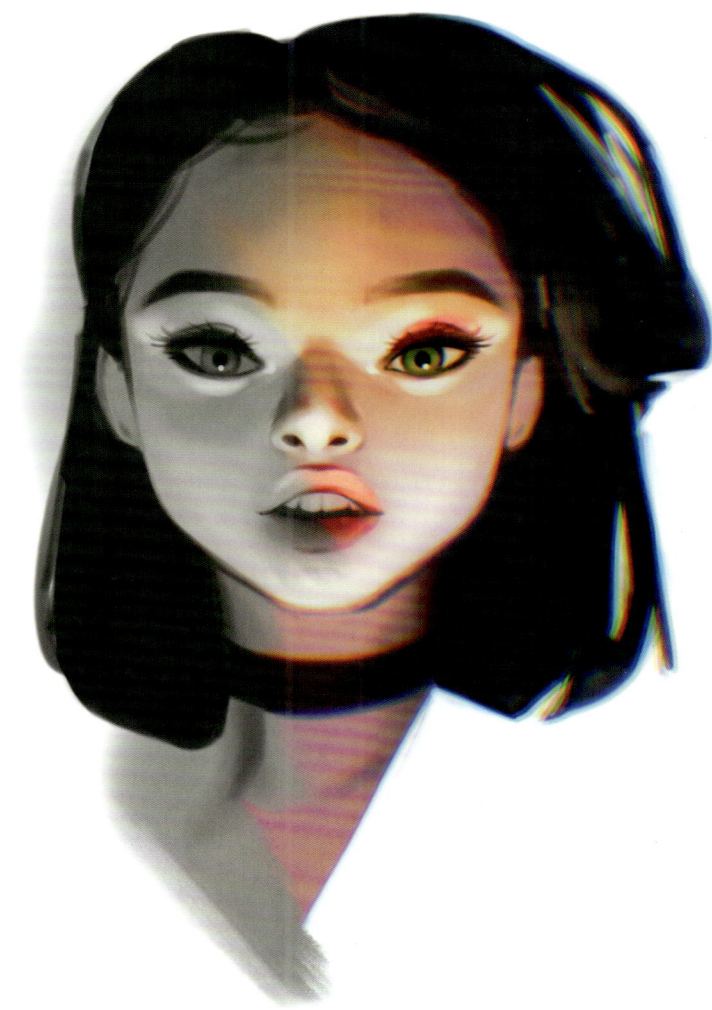

What Is a Value Scale?

It's simple! A value scale showcases a range of values from light to dark. The scale is used by painters as a kind of reference. You may hear "value scale" being used interchangeably with "greyscale"; however, a value scale can actually showcase colors, as well. Sometimes the scale is organized as a gradient, but most often it's a series of swatches that are neatly lined up together.

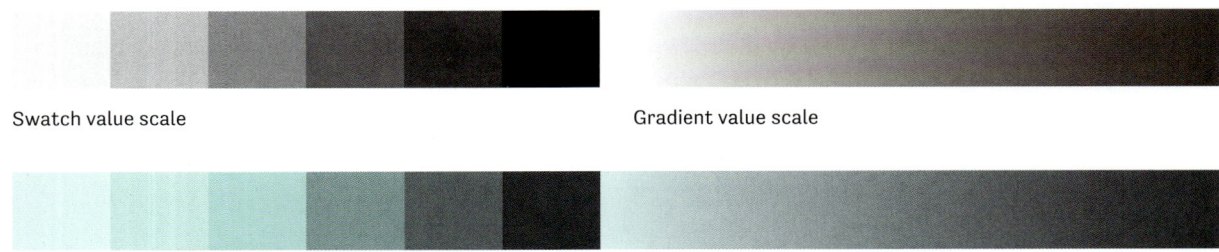

Swatch value scale

Gradient value scale

Swatch color value scale

Gradient color value scale

A value scale doesn't have to start with white and end with black, and a painter doesn't have to use every single swatch that's in the scale. An artist might choose to target a certain range within the scale to exclusively work from, resulting in what's called a high-value range scale or a low-value range scale.

High-value range: Can be created by targeting a few swatches on the lighter end of the value scale

Low-value range: Can be created by targeting a few swatches on the darker end of the value scale

For the sake of ease, I'll teach you how to paint using a greyscale and show you how to set it up as a palette in Procreate.

CREATE A GREYSCALE PALETTE

You only need to set this up once. Whenever you want to start a value painting, your palette will be ready to go!

Open the Palette

Open your color panel. Select *Palettes* from the menu bar at the bottom of the window.

Tap the + icon to create a new palette.

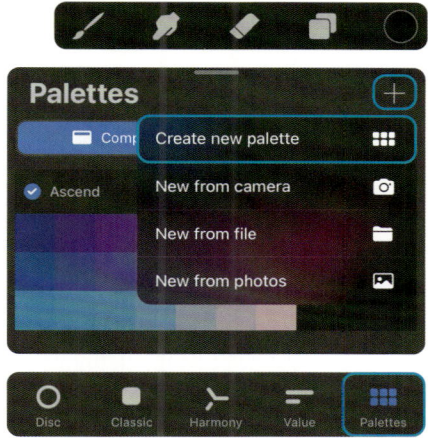

Name/Rename Your Palette

Tap on *Untitled* to change the name of your palette. I chose something simple and straightforward, like "Greyscale." The new palette will automatically be saved to your Palettes library.

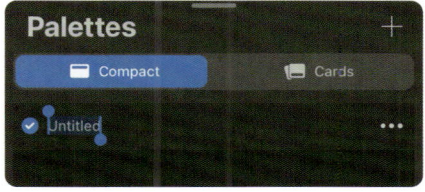

Set as Default

Make sure the little blue checkmark (the default palette) is set to your new palette. It should do this by default, but if for some reason it doesn't, use the three dotted icon • • • in the top right corner to *Set as Default*.

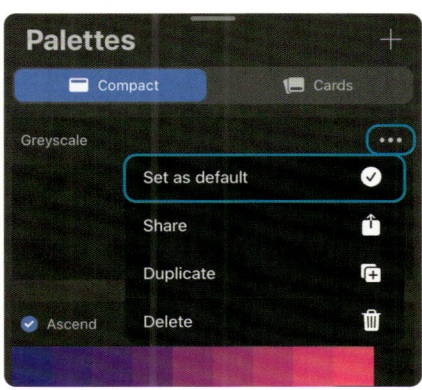

Create Swatches

Select *Value* on the color panel.

Notice that when you choose other color panel options like *Value*, your default color palette appears at the bottom of the window. Right now, it should be completely empty.

To add values, use the *B*, which is the brightness slider in HSB (hue, saturation, brightness).

Set B to 100% to get pure white. Add it to your palette by tapping an empty square within the palette window.

I like to decrease the brightness of my values by about 15% per swatch—give or take 5%.

In total, following this kind of thinking, you'll end up with seven swatches, including pure white and pure black. That means you'll have five grey swatches to paint with, since we never initially paint with pure white or pure black (more on this later).

Here's an example of my completed Greyscale palette:

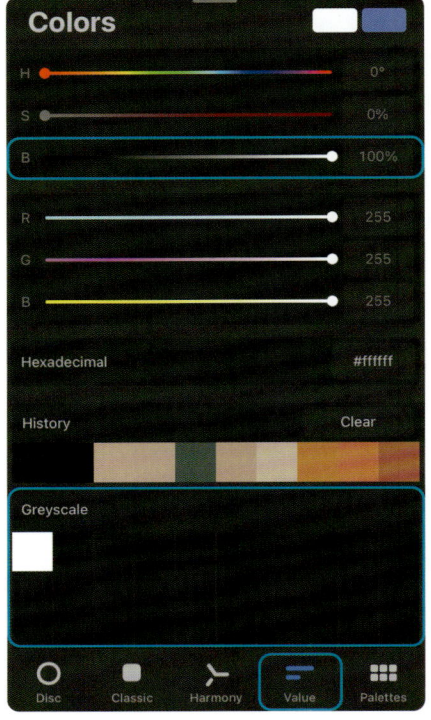

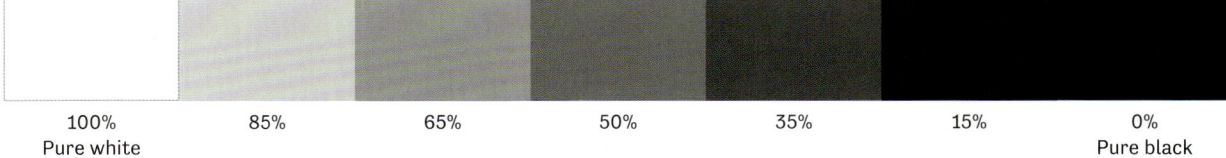

| 100% | 85% | 65% | 50% | 35% | 15% | 0% |
| Pure white | | | | | | Pure black |

Feel free to add or remove swatches as you see fit. Personally, I think that the seven-step scale is a great scale to start with. If you have too many swatches in between white and black, then you stand the risk of getting way too nuanced with the shades of grey—which can lead to confusion and overwhelm when painting.

SET UP YOUR BRUSHES

Selecting Brushes

The last thing I want you to do before you start painting is to choose which brushes you'd like to use. I typically paint with three brushes, and I use one additional brush just for smudging.

I recommend brushes like these:

1. A **soft brush** for general painting
2. A **hard brush** for adding sharp definition to the focal point, certain shapes, or edges
3. An **airbrush** for soft, subtle blending or laying down a ton of paint at once

If you're using Procreate's default brushes, you can find a version of each of these under *Airbrushing* in the library. I'll be painting with brushes I purchased from MaxPacks* as they're my personal favorites and my go-tos. I've used them for years and I really enjoy the way they feel when I paint.

Below is a comparison of the brushes I use versus default Procreate brushes you can find in the brush library.

My brushes (MaxPacks brushes)

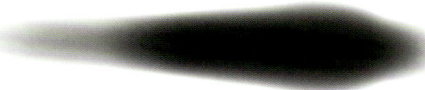

1 Shader soft round

2 Shader hard round

Big fat airbrush

Soft smudge

Procreate brush library

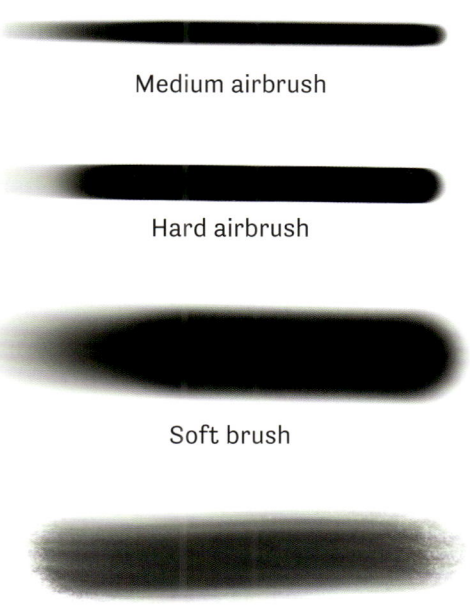

Medium airbrush

Hard airbrush

Soft brush

6B compressed

* *MaxPacks is a third-party Procreate brush maker. Brush packs can be purchased at https://maxpacks.com/. Please don't feel like you need to spend additional money to get good brushes—you don't. I just wanted to share a favorite resource with you.*

Adjusting Brush Pressure

You may have noticed that the brushes I use have a tapering effect whereas the default brushes that Procreate comes loaded with do not.

Tapering will give a more realistic sensation when painting or drawing on the iPad. As you press harder on the screen, your brush will create a darker, denser line.

You can change the settings of the default brushes so that they too can taper if this is an experience you'd prefer to have when painting.

Essentially you'll set the brush to become responsive to the amount of pressure you exert. When pressing down hard, the brush will get larger and put more paint onto the canvas. When you ease up, the opposite will happen.

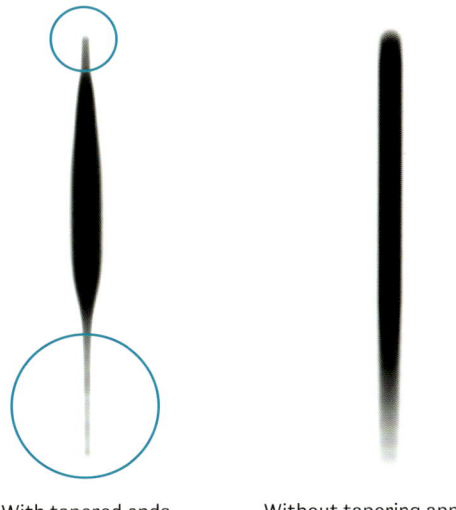

With tapered ends   Without tapering applied

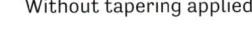

Enter Brush Studio

Tap on the brush you want to alter. When it's highlighted blue, tap once more. This will open up *Brush Studio* in Procreate and allow you to alter that specific brush's settings.

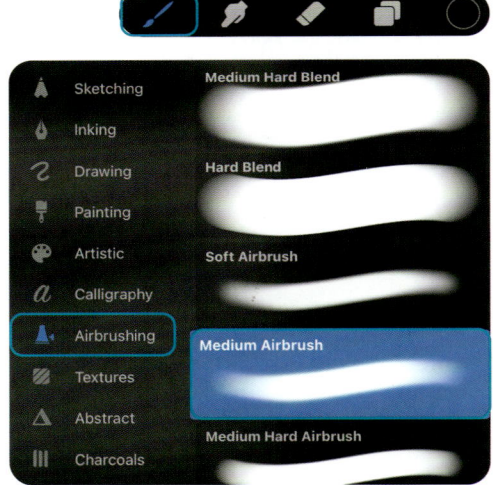

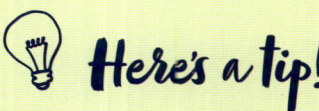

Here's a tip!

The preview of the brush will show whether or not pressure settings have been applied. Notice the difference between the two brushes shown here.

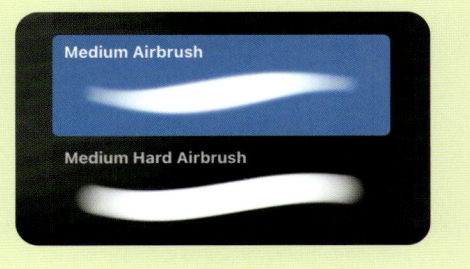

Make and Test Changes

Tap *Apple Pencil*. The first section is for *Pressure*. Under *Size*, move the slider to the right.

Try out any changes you make by drawing on the *Drawing Pad*. Keep experimenting by playing with the slider and then testing your changes.

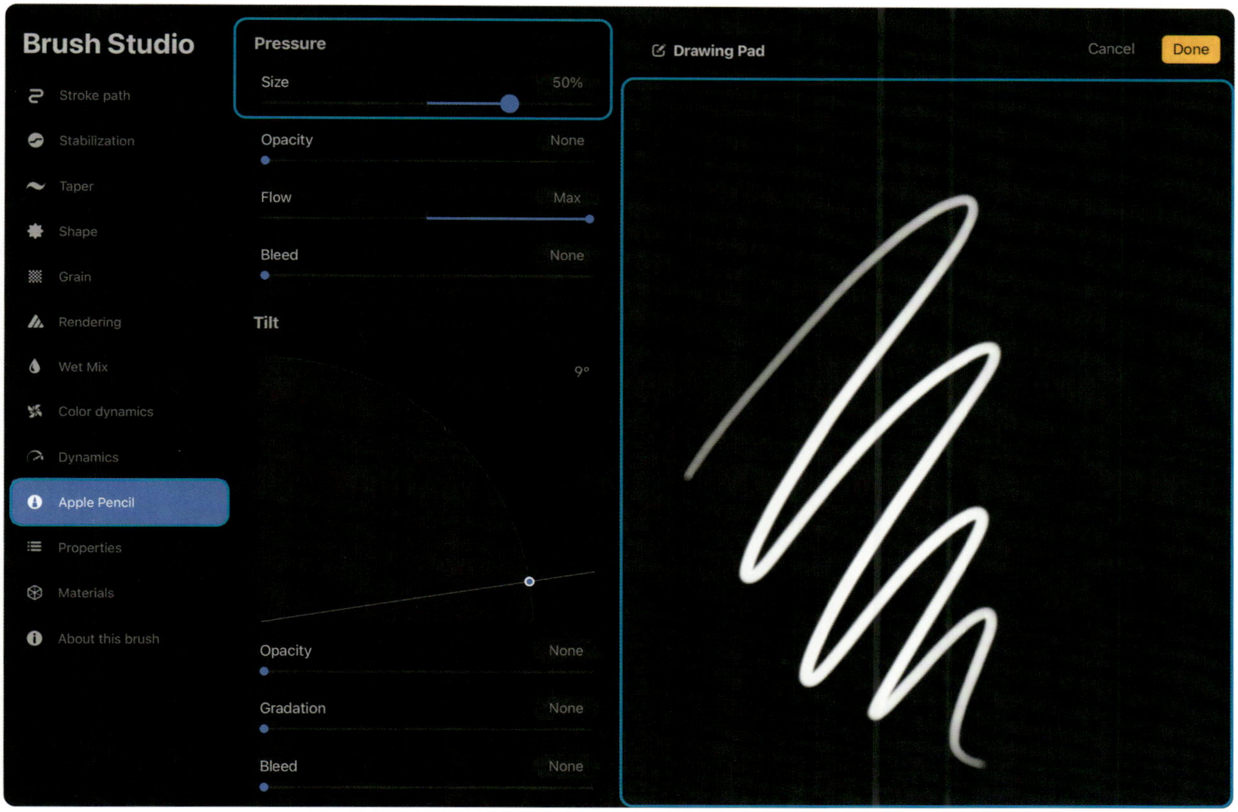

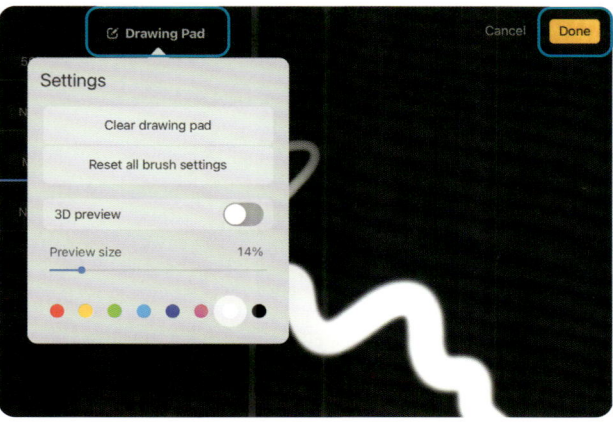

Reset or Apply Changes

To reset the settings of the brush or to clear the drawing pad, just tap on *Drawing Pad* to bring up these options.

Once you're happy with your results, tap *Done* to save your new settings.

CONVERT YOUR REFERENCE

This is very much an optional step. Painting in shades of grey will be a challenge when working from a colored reference image. Convert it to black and white if you're struggling.

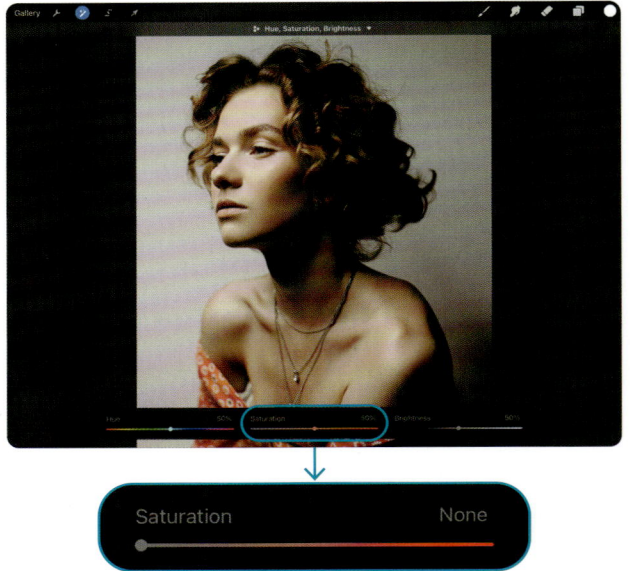

Open and Convert Your Image

From the *Gallery*, tap *Import* or *Photo*. Select your image to open it on a new canvas.

Use an adjustment to remove all instances of color. Go to:

Adjustment > Hue, Saturation, Brightness

Turn the *Saturation* slider all the way down to 0%.

Adjust Contrast (Optional)

If you want to make changes to the contrast in your photo, use *Curves*.

Adjustment > Curves

Save Your New Image

Save the image to your iPad:

Actions > Share > PNG > Save image

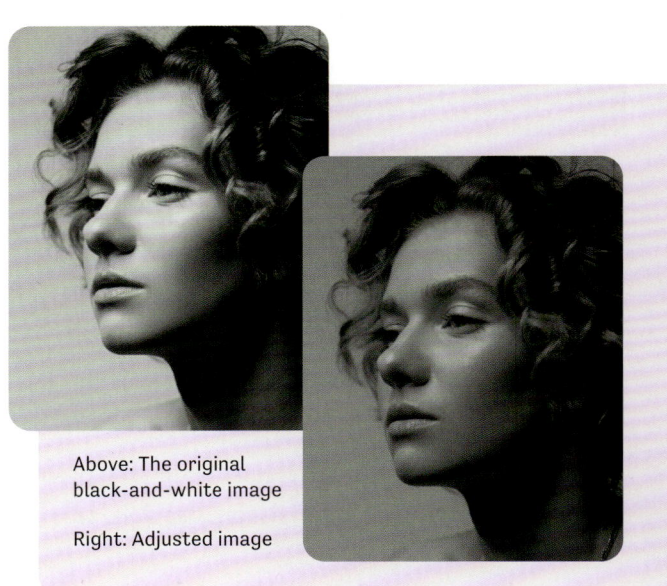

Above: The original black-and-white image

Right: Adjusted image

CREATE A VALUE PAINTING

When painting, always start from large to small. This means that you should start by blocking in very large masses of value while ignoring minute details at first.

Create a Base

To kick off the painting process, start by laying down base values.

To find base shades, squint at your reference photo and take a stab at guessing what the average values are for the large masses. Ignore any nuance within—think big picture!

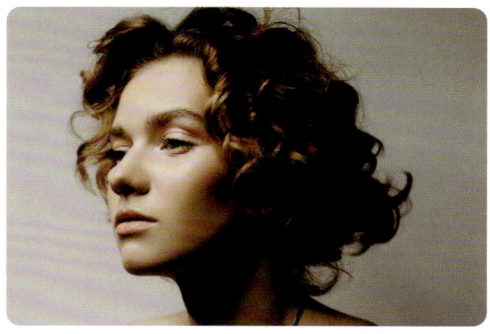

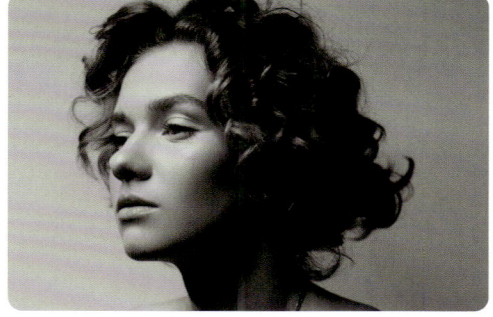

Try to guess the average color of the skin

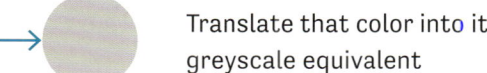

Translate that color into its greyscale equivalent

Above is the process that should be happening *in your brain*. Of course, it's tricky at first, but it gets easier with practice. This is why I mentioned previously that it's hard to paint in greyscale using a colored photo reference. If you're feeling frustrated or overwhelmed, convert your image into black and white. You can do this at any point, and you can use your colored image as reference and the black-and-white one to check your work.

Anyway, don't stress out about getting every value perfectly correct! Instead, I encourage you to try your best and check your work when you're feeling unsure.

In my example, the large masses I block in are the skin, hair, and clothing—that's it.

The hair is easily the darkest mass of the three, while the skin and clothing are quite similar in value. The skin is trickiest since it contains varying highlights and shadows, but at this stage, I feel that it's best to oversimplify what you see. As a result, I've made the skin a little lighter than the dress.

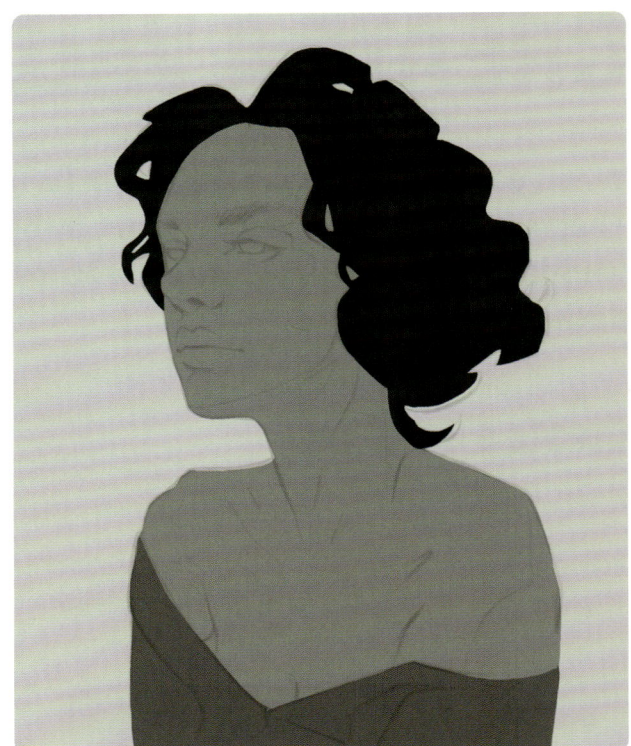

Fill In Values Quickly

To quickly fill in the base values, use the *Selection* tool as opposed to a brush.

Working in layers, trace around the perimeter of a mass, then drag and drop your active color in to fill the entire selection.

Make sure each mass is on its own layer.

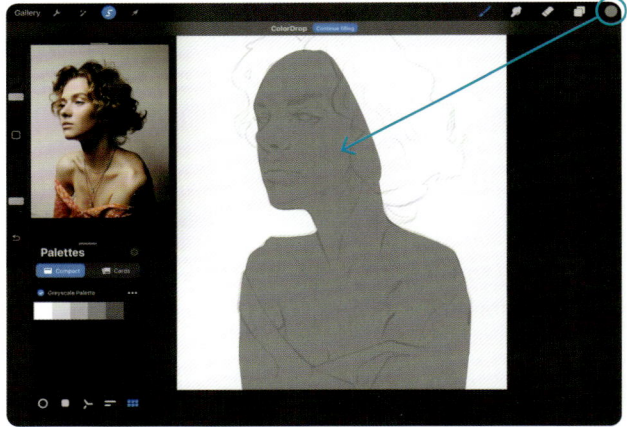

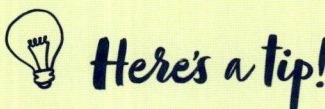 *Here's a tip!*

Avoid using pure black or pure white! Rarely ever in real life do we see absolute pure black or white, and using these pure values poses a real problem when working digitally. Later in the painting process, we'll add color to this value painting. When you use 100% black or white, you will struggle to add in hues, as they just won't take. Your resulting image will look over- or underexposed.

Work on Different Layers

I want you to create separate base layers so that you can activate Procreate's clipping mask later on (you'll see what I mean in the next step).

The number of layers you create is completely up to you—it's largely up to your comfort level.

In my example, I've used a total of four layers. I divided the hair into two separate layers because it looked to me like there was background hair (behind the model's face) and foreground hair (in front of and covering parts of her face).

The reasoning behind splitting the hair into two layers is based on my previous painting experience. I knew it would make things easier for me in the long run. But, of course, you don't have to do the same.

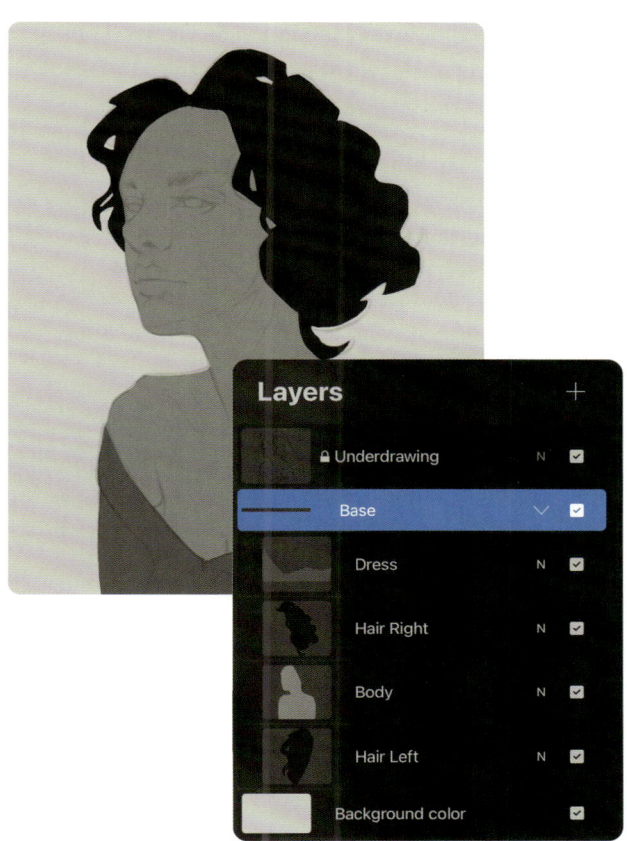

Add Shadows

Now that the big picture is laid down, you can start adding shadows in. Working only within the lower end of your value scale, squint at your reference to find the darkest shadows.

Create a new layer.

Tap on the thumbnail of that layer to bring up its options. Select *Clipping Mask*. If you recall from page 25, a layer that has the *Clipping Mask* property applied will allow you to paint on that layer instead of working off your original base layer. Your base layer will define the boundaries of the clipping mask, which means that anything you paint outside the lines will not show up so long as the mask is active.

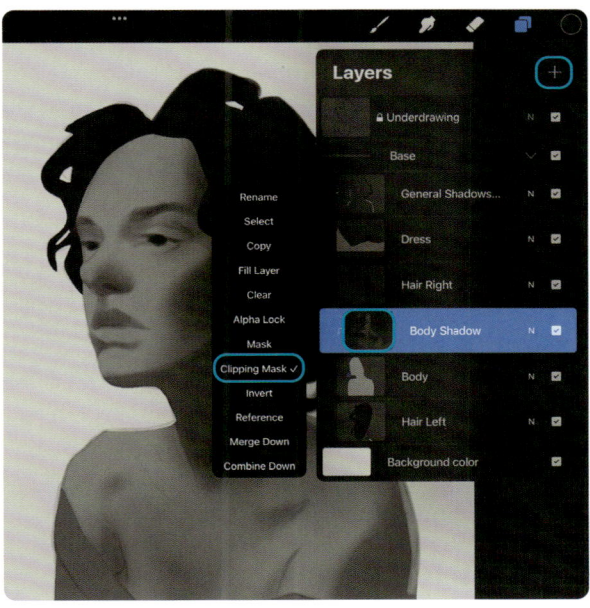

When adding shadows, you should be focused on building up the darks within your painting. Ignore the highlights for now as those will come later.

Since you've probably already mapped out some of the larger shadow shapes in your underdrawing, it's easy to fill them in during this stage.

I like to paint most of the shadows with my soft round brush or a very large airbrush if the shadow shape is large or diffused.

I recommend that you don't focus too much on blending everything perfectly right now. Focus on getting those shapes in, and then you can go back and properly blend your edges with an airbrush or the smudge tool.

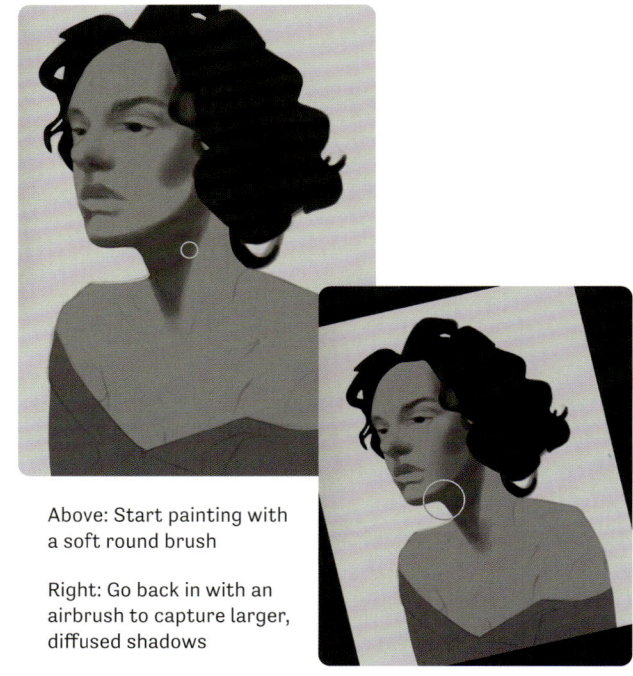

Above: Start painting with a soft round brush

Right: Go back in with an airbrush to capture larger, diffused shadows

Don't Perfect One Area of the Painting at a Time

It's a good idea to build up the painting all at once. That means you can't just focus on perfecting the shadows in the face while ignoring the hair and the dress.

The best way to build your painting is to bounce around the canvas. Don't worry if you haven't captured all the shadows of the face; move on to the dress, the body, or the hair anyway and come back to the face later.

Paint the Hair

If your model has light hair, then you can stick to painting in the shadows. My model's hair is dark—and since I've already used the darkest value on the greyscale (aside from black), I can't go any darker. If you're in a similar situation, then start painting in some of the light shapes.

Keep the lights of the hair very subtle and very diffused. Don't pull out highlights right now, just give the hair a bit of dimension.

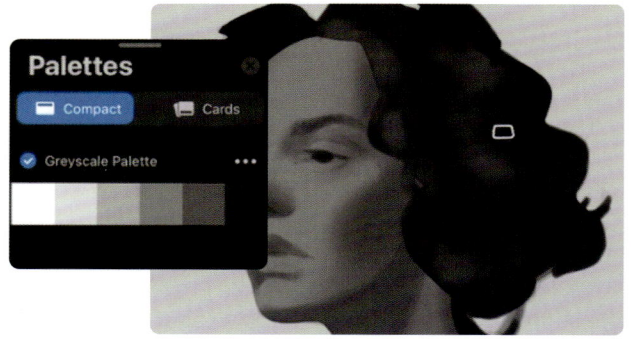

Above: The base layer for the hair is already the darkest value next to black. Choose a lighter value and start painting in light shapes.

Check Your Work!

After you've added your shadows, take another look and see if you've captured the **darkest darks** of the image. Squint at your reference, then at your painting. What differences do you see?

Make corrections to your values if necessary.

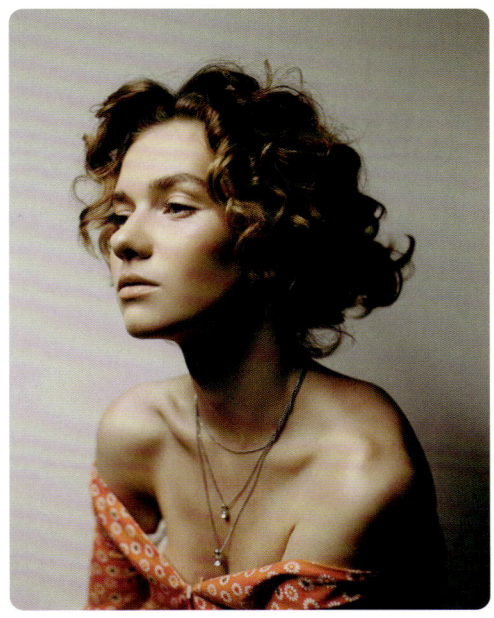

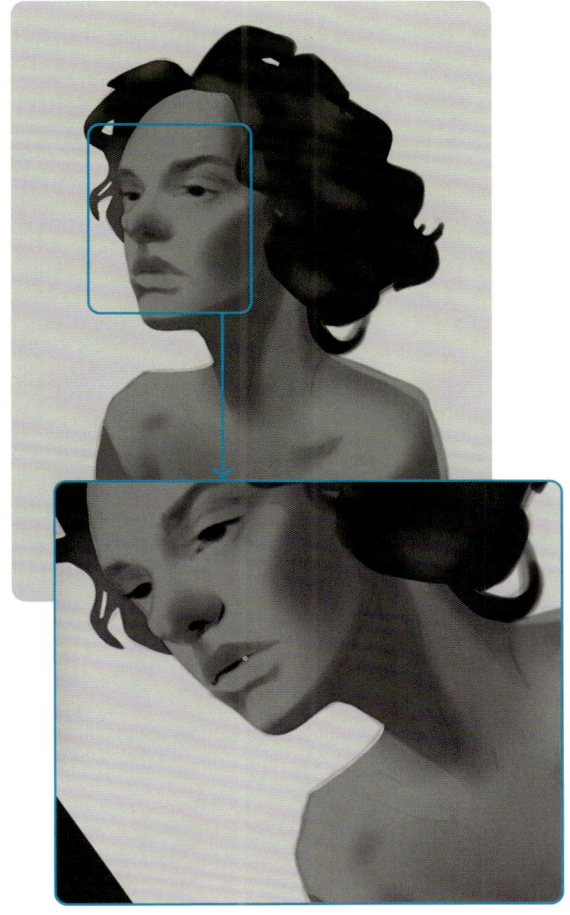

When I did this exercise, I noticed that the features of the face (which are so important in a portrait!) were not dark enough. The eyes, the bottom of the nose, and the lips needed to be much better defined.

I went back in with the soft round brush and my darkest value so that I could add definition to those features.

 Here's a tip!

Keep zooming in and out of your painting and keep flicking your eyes from your reference image to your painting. Problem areas will become more obvious this way. When you notice a problem area, you can go back in and fix it up—either making the area darker or lighter.

To reiterate, you're working from big to small. That means you just keep going back into an area and making tweaks. You can use as many clipping mask layers as you want if you're feeling a bit timid around making drastic value changes or erasing your work.

At this point, your painting will be missing highlights, which makes it look rather flat, but that's okay, as the highlights will be added during the coloring phase.

Once you've completed your greyscale painting, step away from your iPad! I mean it—go take a break. It's extremely important as artists that we remove ourselves from our work for at least 10–15 minutes every now and then. Doing so will reset your mind and you might find that once you come back to your final painting, you'll see glaring issues you were completely blind to before.

If you want to make any final adjustments, you can merge all the layers and then apply an adjustment using *Curves*. *Curves* gives you great control in adjusting the strength of the lights, darks, and midtones of your painting. Refer to page 159 for details on using *Curves*.

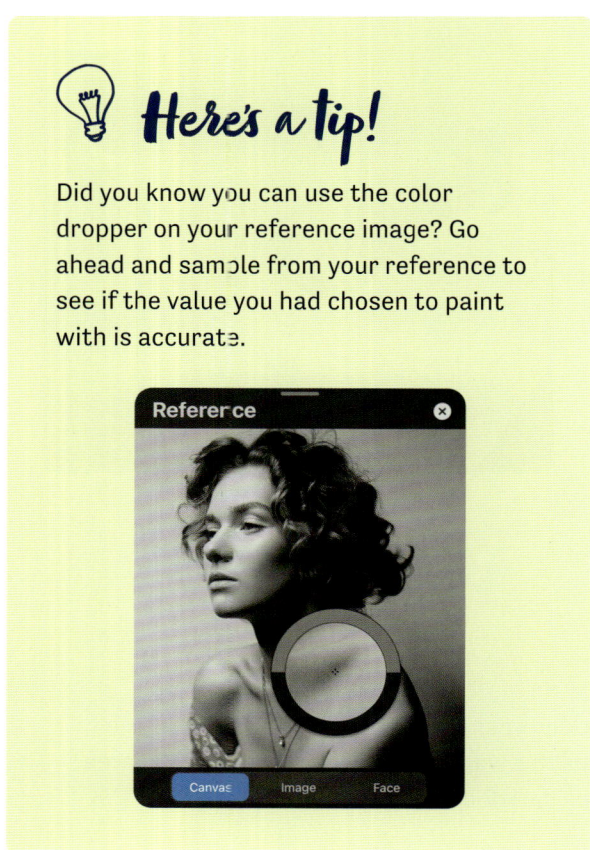

Here's a tip!

Did you know you can use the color dropper on your reference image? Go ahead and sample from your reference to see if the value you had chosen to paint with is accurate.

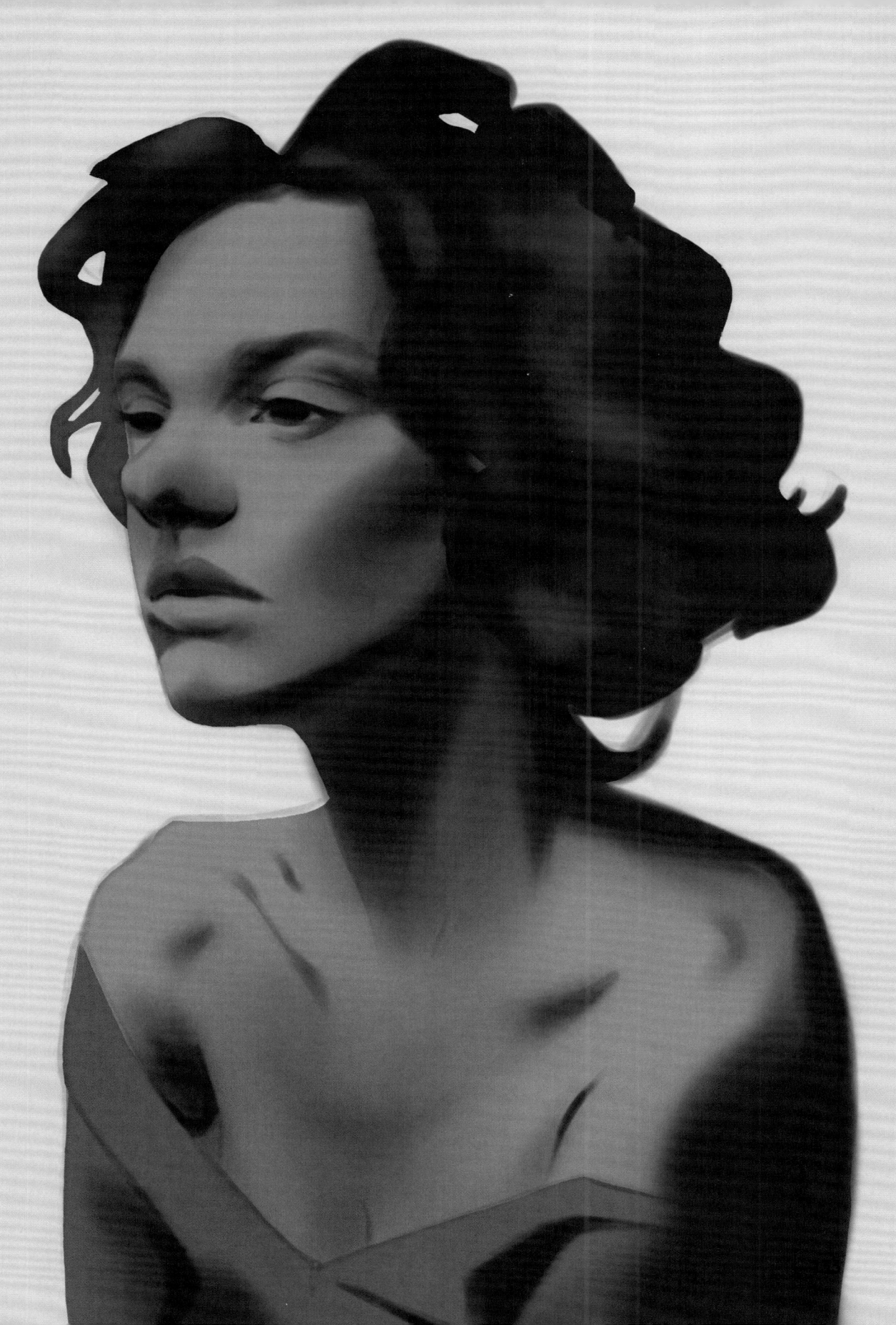

PHASE TWO

ADDING
Color

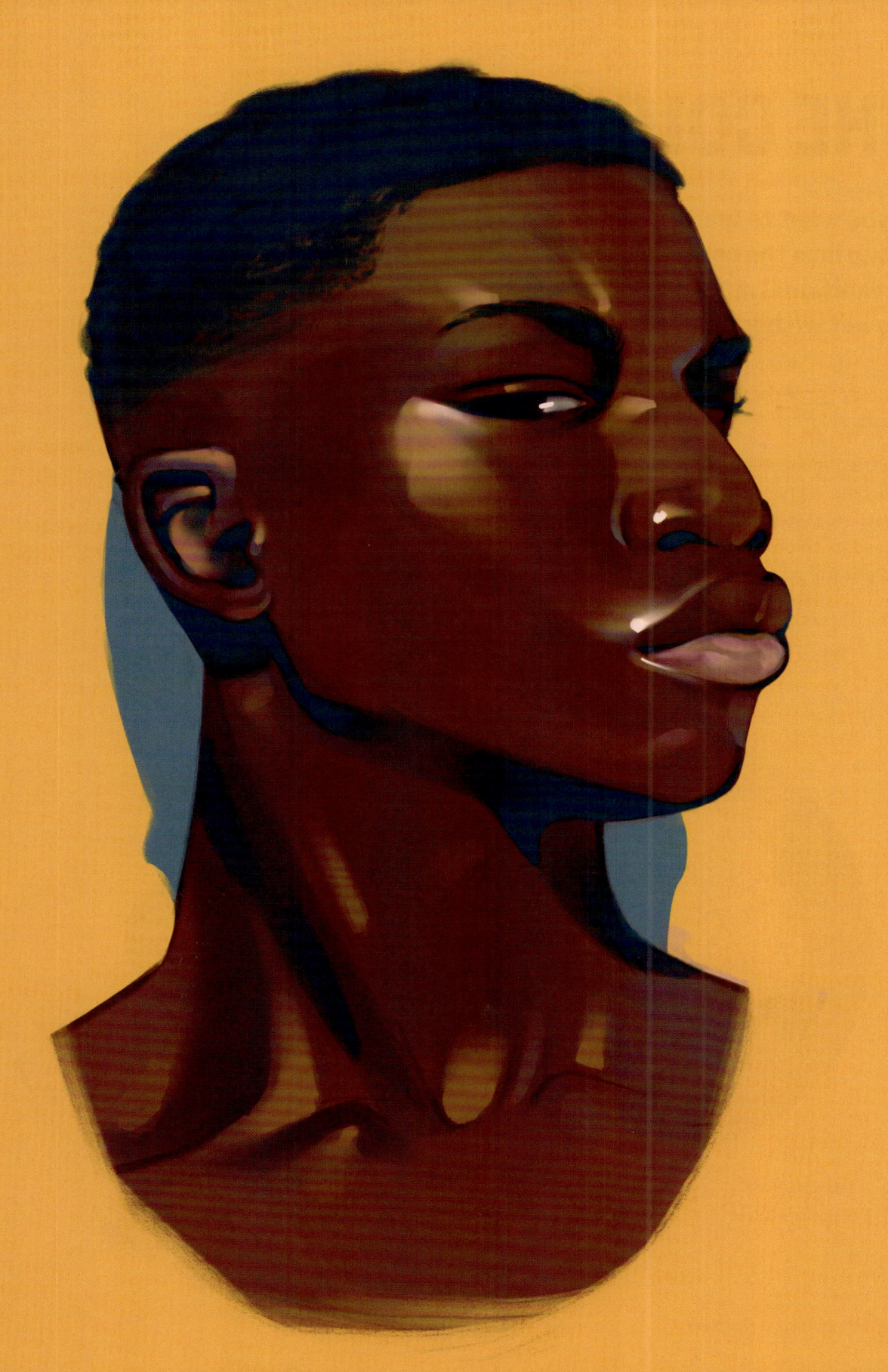

THE COLOR WHEEL

If you want to learn about color, you'll inevitably bump into the concept of the color wheel. It's quite a traditional method of teaching color theory, but it's not without flaws.

The purpose of the color wheel is to showcase relationships between colors.

The traditional wheel shown below was based on artists' paint. The primary colors are used to mix every other color on the wheel. The secondary colors are a 50/50 mix between two primary colors.

One of the most useful relationships that the wheel highlights is the one between complementary colors—colors that sit opposite each other on the wheel. When used sparingly, they can create interest and balance within artwork. When used overwhelmingly, they can be jarring or create a sense of discomfort for the viewer because of their high contrast.

The traditional color wheel, based on painters' pigments

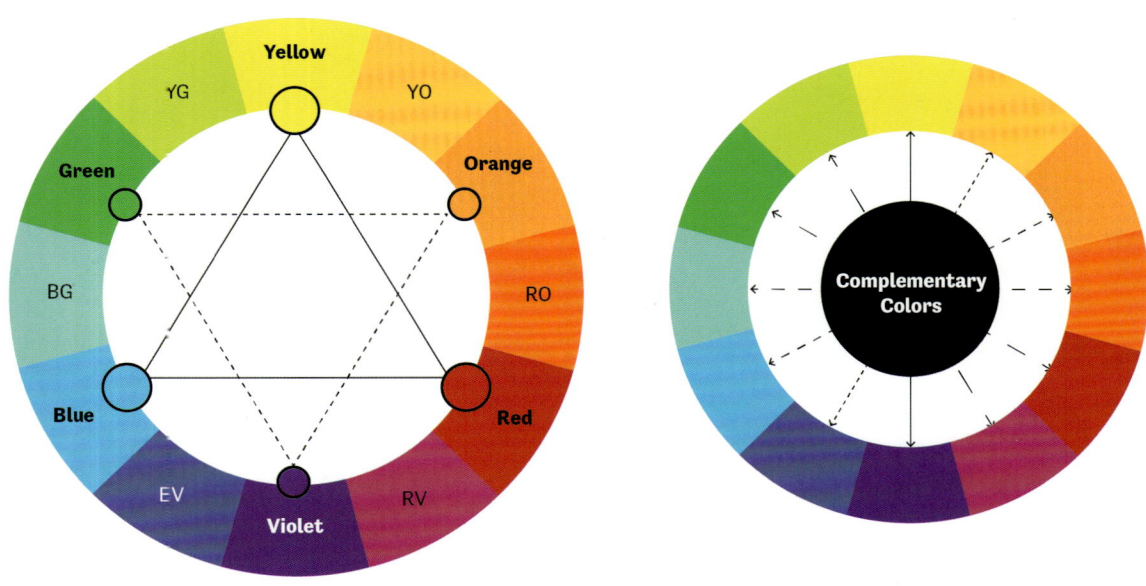

—— Primary Colors

----- Secondary Colors

PRIMARY COLORS

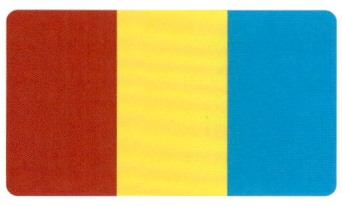

Traditional Primaries—RYB

The traditional color wheel was created based on physical paint pigments. The primary colors are red, yellow, and blue. The idea is that all of the colors on the wheel can be created by mixing these primary colors together but it's impossible to make a primary color from any other color. While this may be true when working specifically with paint, it's certainly not true when working with inks or light. This wheel is probably the one most of us are familiar with; however, please keep in mind that it's not ideal for a digital artist to use a wheel that was created originally for painters limited by pigments.

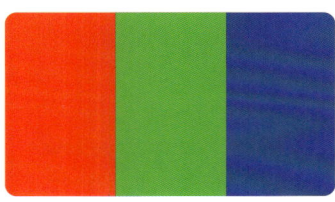

Digital Primaries—RGB

Red, green, and blue are the primaries of the digital world. These are based on the light spectrum and not pigments. When you mix the three primary lights together you will end up with white light. This color space offers an insanely wide range of possible colors, including neons and other vibrant colors that are hard, or even impossible, to replicate off a screen.

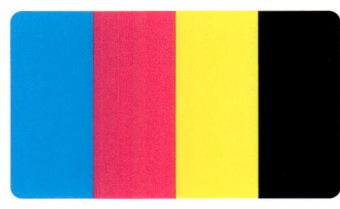

Printer's Primaries—CMYK

Cyan, magenta, yellow, and black (CMYK) are the primaries that are used for print. These inks can be laid on top of each other or mixed together to create many different colors. When working digitally, you'll often have to choose to work in either the RGB or CMYK color space. If your final piece is destined for print, then you'll want to work in CMYK as this color space is designed for print.

The colors available to print are limited when compared to RGB because the colors you choose in the CMYK space must be physically possible to mix using inks. Because of this, when you convert a file from RGB to CMYK, you may notice that your artwork appears dulled.

HELPFUL TERMS

Brightness

Typically another word for *value*. The two are used interchangeably.

Chroma

The purity of a color. To reduce a color's chroma, add a neutral color such as grey, white, or black (this will make it appear dulled).

Color Model

A system that describes color numerically, such as RGB or CMYK.

Color Space

A defined range of colors within a color model, such as sRGB or Display P3. (Both are based on the RGB color model, but Display P3 includes a wider range of colors.)

Color Profile

Software code that determines the specific colors that a device can input or output. It ensures consistent color management.

For example, you're on a desktop computer and its color profile is set to sRGB. You're painting on your iPad, whose profile is set to Display P3. When you view your artwork on your desktop computer, some of the colors look a little washed out. This happens because color profiles across devices can be different, and in this case, your iPad has a wider range of RGB colors available to display than your desktop computer.

Hue

Typically another word for *color*. *Hue* and *color* are often used interchangeably.

Primaries

Colors that cannot be mixed or made using any other color. Your primaries will change depending on the color space you're working in.

Saturation

The intensity of a color in relation to pure grey.

Shade

Adding black to a color.

Tint

Adding white to a color.

Tone

Adding grey to a color.

Value

How light or dark a color is. For example, yellow is lighter in value than a deep red. Value is best understood when working with greys because things like saturation can trick our eyes into believing that a color is lighter or darker in value than it actually is. See page 118 for visual examples.

CHOOSING COLORS

Knowing the final destination of your artwork will help you choose the appropriate color space (or profile) to work in. If your artwork is meant to be printed, then you may want to work in CMYK. If your work is going to be viewed on screen, then stick with RGB.

The Color Disc

One of my favorite palettes is the *Disc*. It's a simple and intuitive way of choosing colors. The disc is made up of an outer hue ring and an inner saturation circle. It works like this:

Step 1
Choose your hue (ex., orange, red, or green).

Step 2
Adjust the saturation and brightness of the hue. For intensity and vibrancy, stick to the right of the circle. For tints, shades, or tones, move the reticle to the left.

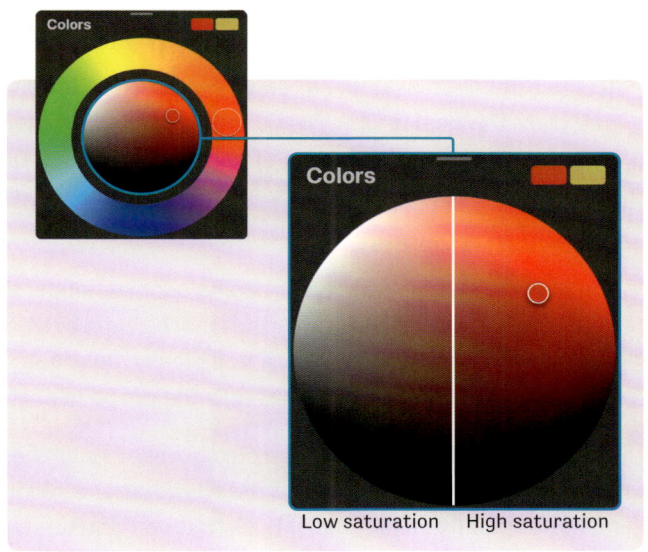

The Classic Palette

This palette may look a bit more complex than the *Disc*, but some people find it easier to use.

Step 1
Select your hue using the first slider.

Step 2
Change the hue's saturation with the second slider. To make it more saturated, move the slider to the right.

Step 3
Change the brightness of the hue. To make it brighter, move the reticle to the right. To make it darker, move the reticle to the left.

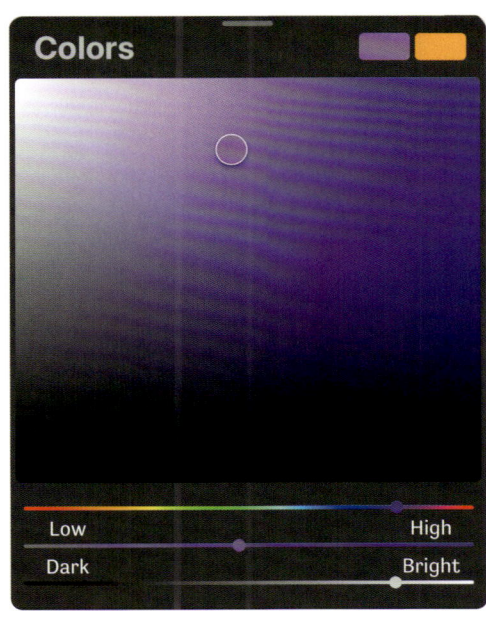

LIMITED PALETTES

Working with colors can easily get overwhelming. To avoid this problem, you can set up a limited color palette, which will reduce the range of colors you'll use and make painting much more manageable.

To the right is an example of color exploration that I've done with limited palettes. The goal is to try out a different combination of colors and to be able to see the **big picture** of your final painting. Don't worry about nuance and subtle color shifts; instead, try to paint in big shapes and avoid blending.

You can see swatches of color beside each attempt. If you take a closer look, you'll notice that there aren't more than seven colors per attempt. You can work with even fewer if you please. Just don't go crazy and have 20 different swatches! That defeats the purpose of the limited palette...

The colors that you pick can be purely based on preference or mood. You don't always have to paint exactly what you see in your reference image—actually it's probably best that you don't, since cameras have a tendency to flatten subtle shifts in color (especially in the skin of a subject) or bump up contrast in unrealistic ways.

Right: I shrank down my underdrawing so that I could quickly paint over it and create color thumbnails. These thumbnails will give me a good idea of the relationships between the colors I've chosen and whether or not they're effective.

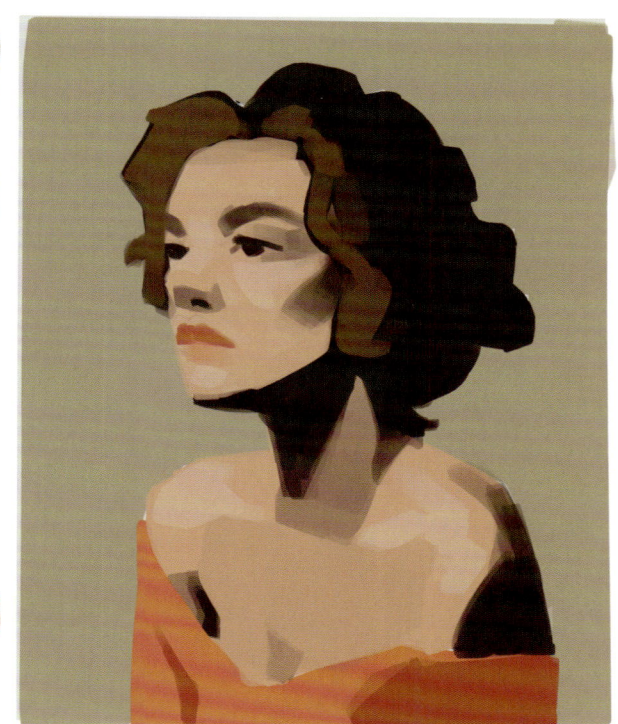

CLOSEST TO ORIGINAL

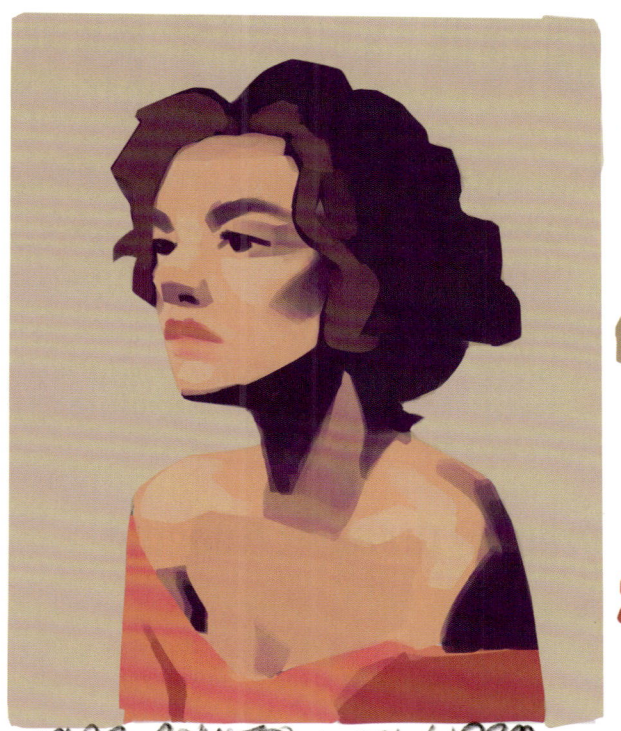

COLOR ADJUSTED - COOL/WARM

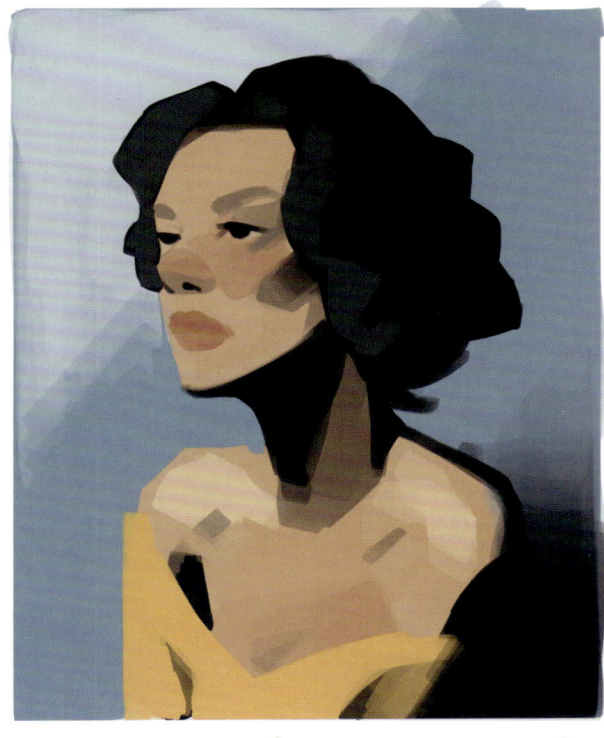

MOODY BLUES + COMPLEMENTARY

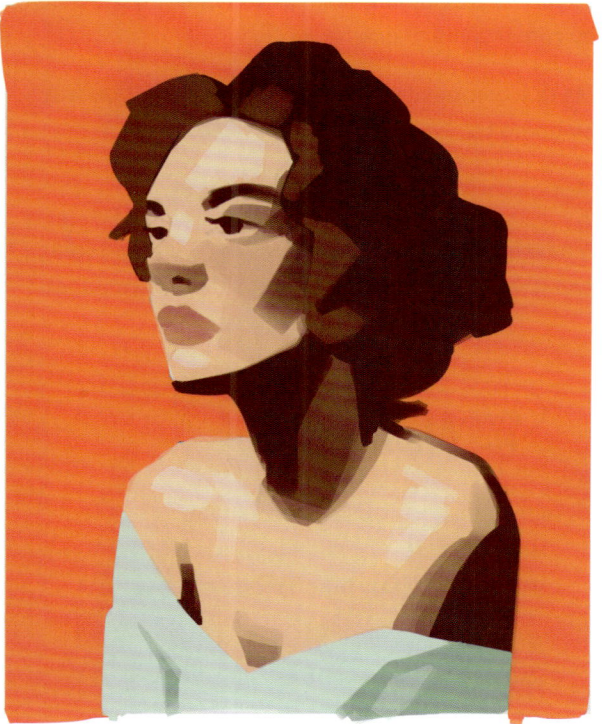

BRIGHTER/BOLDER COLOR

GRADIENT MAP

This optional step uses *Gradient Map* to knock out all instances of grey in your work.

It's a priming step that typically results in a richly colored final painting; however, I've made many paintings in which I've skipped this step entirely that have turned out just fine. The use of *Gradient Map* can help things come together quickly.

Prep for Gradient Mapping

To use *Gradient Map*, you'll need to have your entire painting on one single layer. But first, it's best to separate the background from the subject to make painting easier for yourself later.

In your layers panel, turn off the *Background Color* by tapping the checkmark.

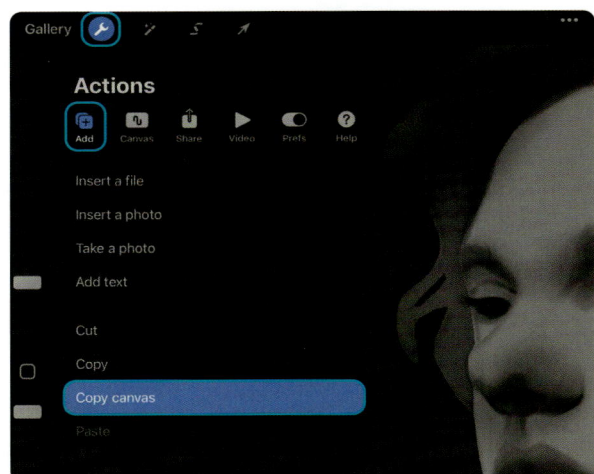

Make a composite layer in a non-destructive way by going to:

Actions > Add > Copy canvas > Paste

A new layer will be created called "Inserted Image," and it will show up at the top of the layers panel.

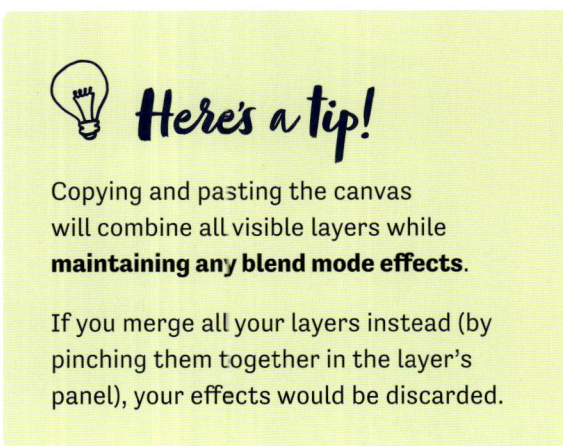

Here's a tip!

Copying and pasting the canvas will combine all visible layers while **maintaining any blend mode effects**.

If you merge all your layers instead (by pinching them together in the layer's panel), your effects would be discarded.

Now that you've got your painting on one layer, set up the workspace by turning your *Background Color*'s visibility back on. Open the *Reference* panel and import your chosen color thumbnail.

Actions > Canvas > Toggle Reference on

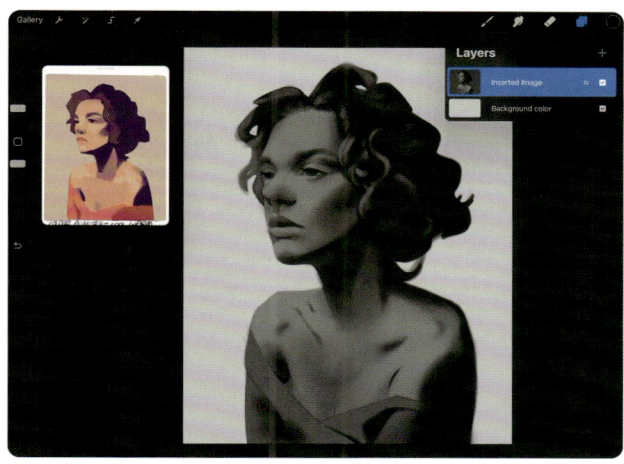

Under *Adjustments*, select *Gradient Map*. You can choose one of Procreate's default maps, like "Mystic," "Breeze," or "Instant," or you can create your own.

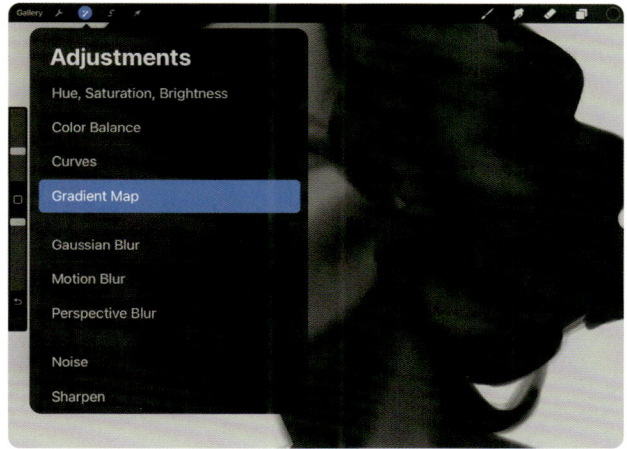

Create Your Own Gradient

To create your own gradient, tap on the + icon in the top-right corner of the *Gradient Library*.

The gradient that you create here will automatically save to your *Gradient Library*, so go ahead and give it a name.

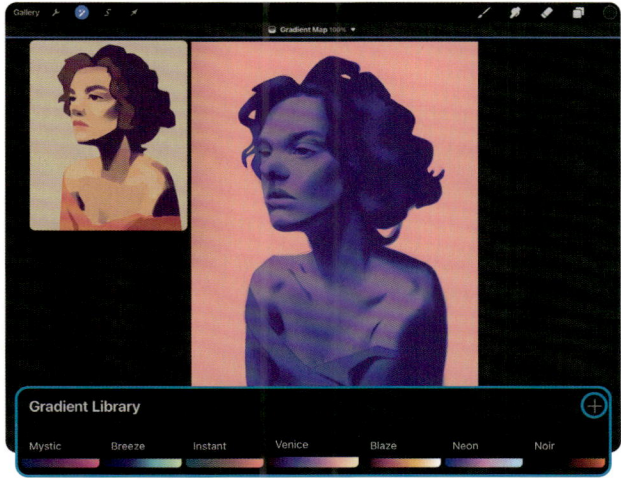

Gradient Map replaces all of the original grey tones in your artwork with colors that you choose. It will map the shadows, midtones, and highlights of your image to the colors in the gradient that you set.

Use your color thumbnail as a guide in choosing your colors.

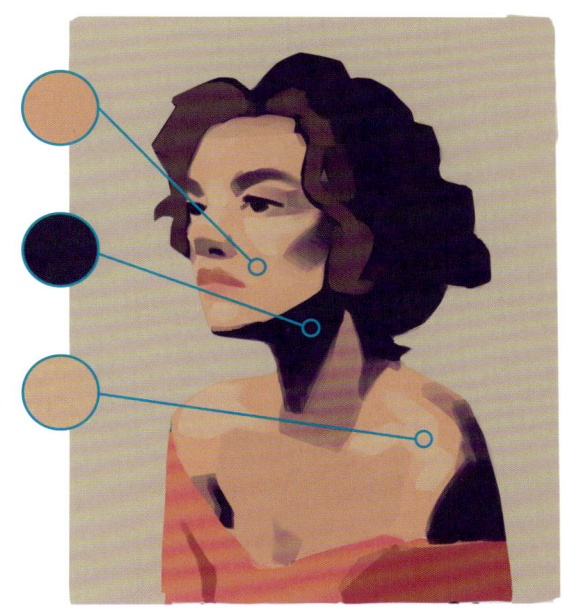

Set the Colors of the Gradient

The squares on the slider are called color points. Tap on one to bring up the *Color Picker* and set the color for that particular point. You can add new points by tapping anywhere on the slider. Delete a point by long pressing on the point.

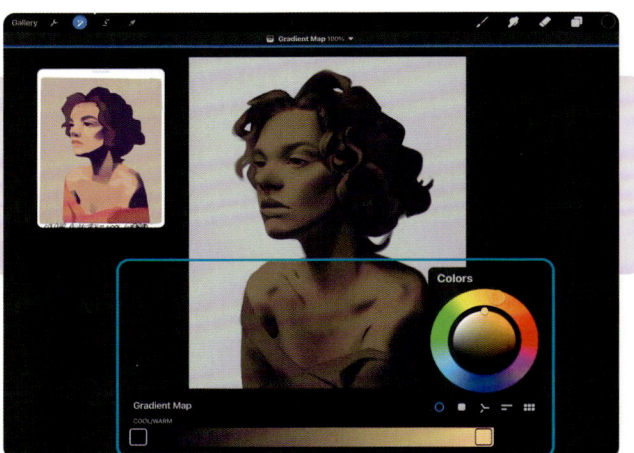

Tap *Done* to save the gradient map to your library and set the changes you made to your painting.

It can be a bit tricky to get the colors in your gradient to match with your color thumbnail. In my example, I've primarily focused on bringing purple into the shadows and yellow into the midtone (I want the warmth of the yellow for the undertone of the skin). I didn't bother fussing over the difference between the midtones and the highlights since my painting is missing highlights anyway.

To wrap up this step, change the background color to match your color thumbnail more closely.

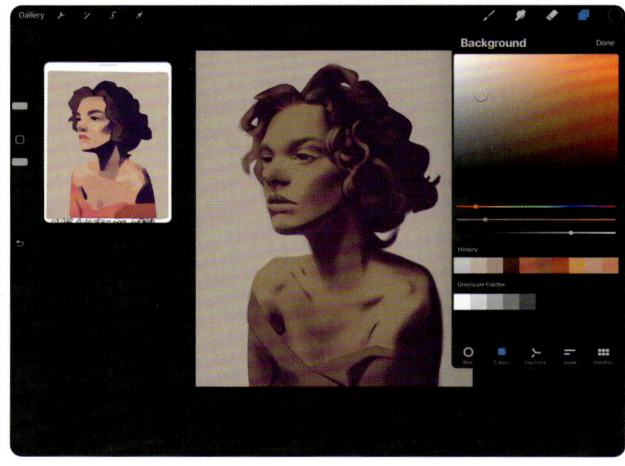

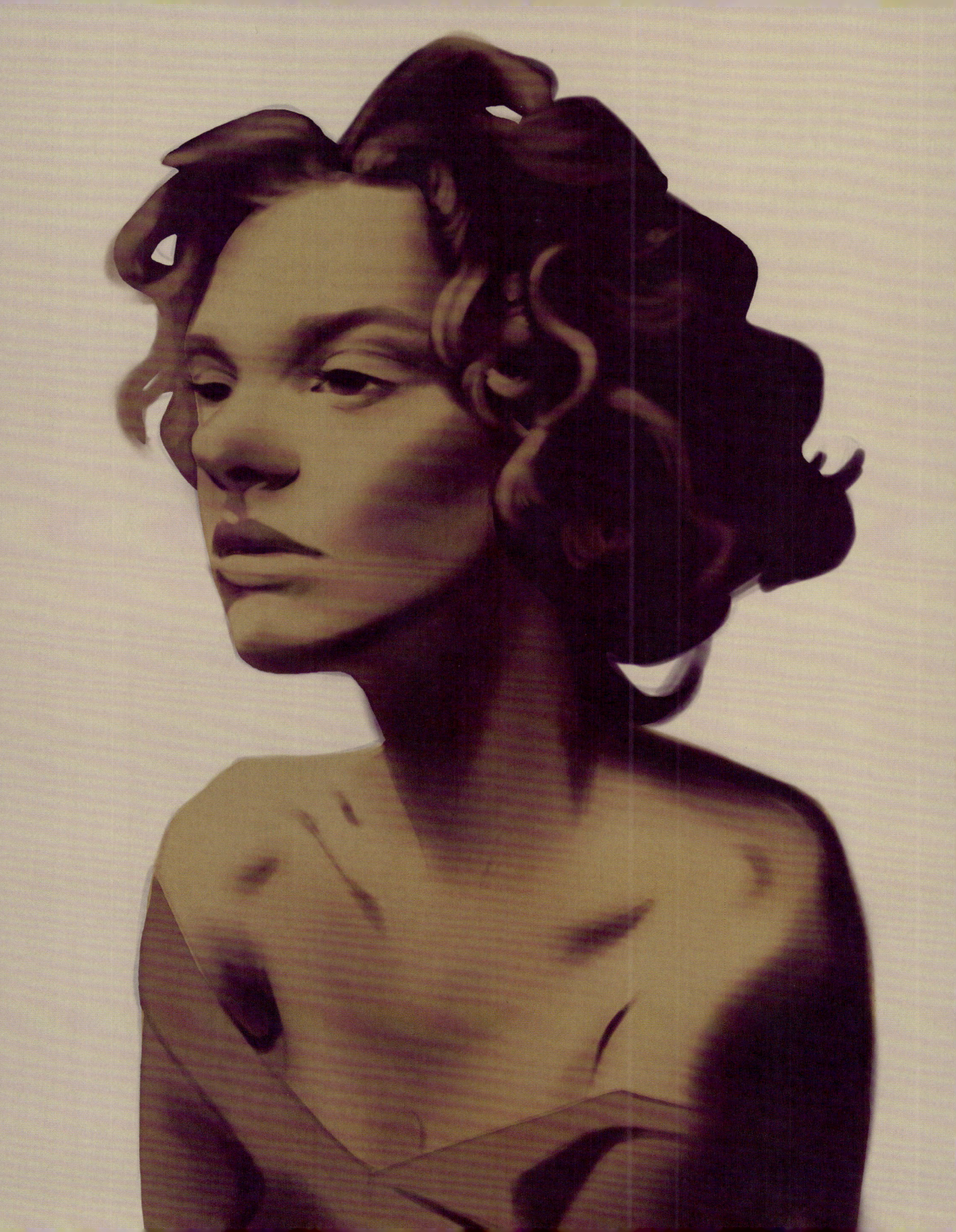

BASE COLORS

This phase is about slathering on large swaths of color! You're not rendering the painting yet; instead, you're laying down a foundation of color.

A base color is a starting point for your colored painting. It will be the average color that you see in your reference image (or that you choose to make up).

You can estimate a base color, just like you did for the value painting (page 127), by really squinting at your reference image and allowing the highlights, shadows, and midtones to blend together.

Another way to choose your base color is to use the eyedropper tool to sample colors directly from your color thumbnail.

Typically you'll have a base color on its own layer for each of these:

1. Skin
2. Hair
3. Clothing
4. Jewelry/props

In my example, the dress that's in the reference image has a pattern on it, but the majority of the dress is red. The base color would therefore be red, and the complex pattern would be dealt with during rendering.

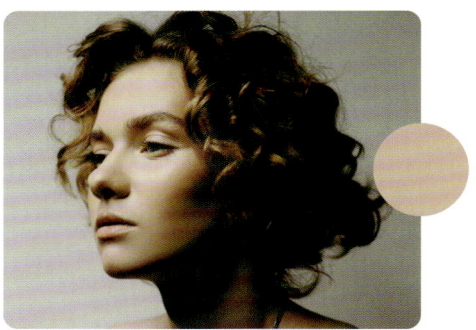

Try to guess the average color of the skin

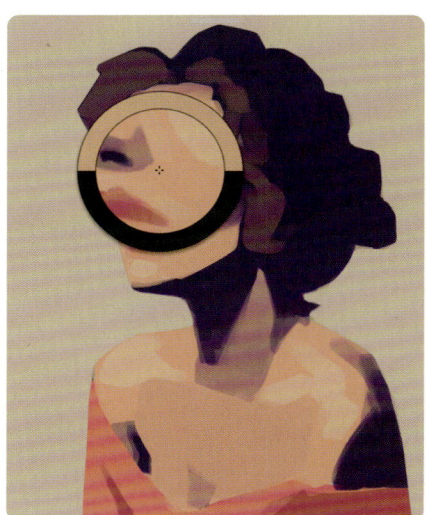

Use the eyedropper to sample from your color thumbnail

Apply the Base Colors

Create a new layer and set the blend mode to *color*. Paint in the base color of the skin. If the color you chose is very high in saturation, the base might look a little unrealistic. Adjust your color as needed.

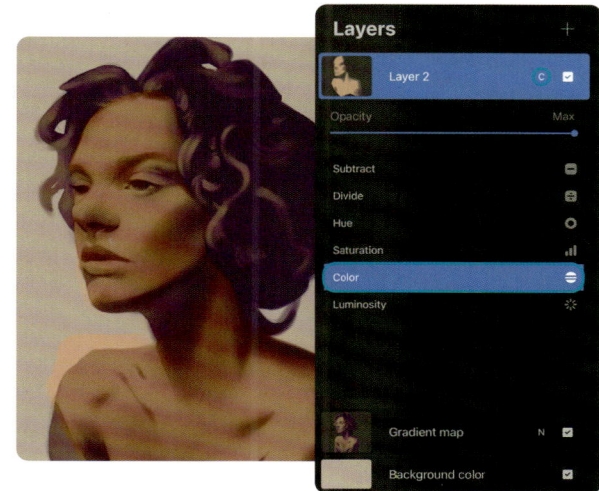

Clip Bases to Your Painting

Remember when you separated your value painting from the background during the *Gradient Map* phase (pages 142–145)? The reasoning behind this was so that you could utilize the *Clipping Mask* to apply your base colors to your value painting without worrying about coloring outside the lines.

Tap the thumbnail of the layer to bring up layer options, then choose *Clipping Mask*.

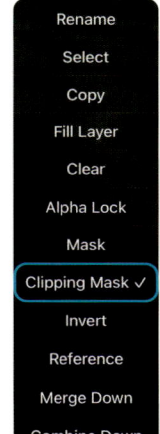

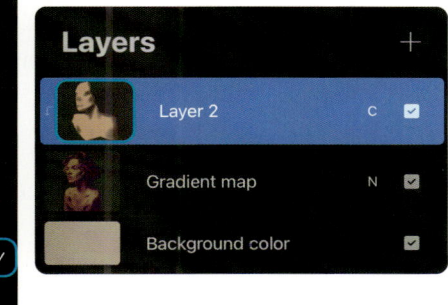

Finish Base Colors

Continue making base layers for things like the clothing and hair.

With the base colors applied, you might notice that something funky has happened: Those beautiful gradients you set up during the *Gradient Map* phase have all but disappeared! To fix this, go back in with an airbrush eraser and gently scrub away some of that paint.

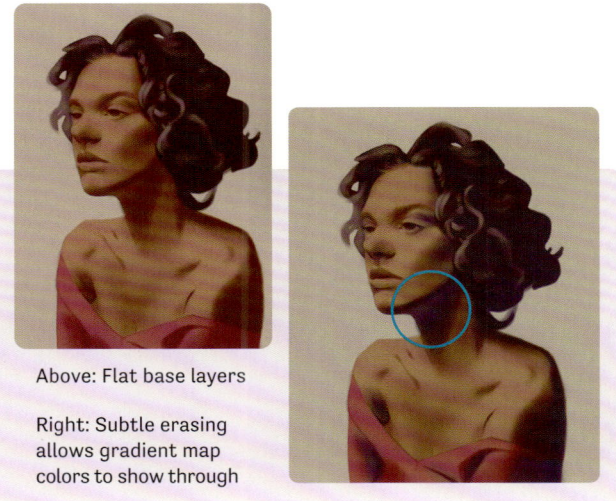

Above: Flat base layers

Right: Subtle erasing allows gradient map colors to show through

In my example, I used the airbrush eraser (with opacity lowered) to erase a bit of the color I had added to the skin, hair, and dress. This allows some of the purples from my gradient to show through in the shadows.

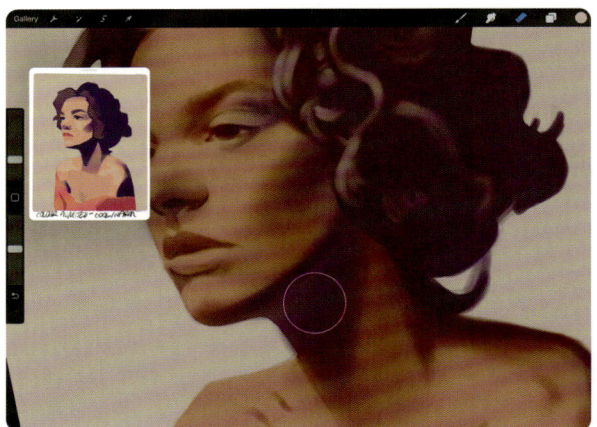

For your own reference, this is what my layers panel looks like. In total, I have:

- three base layers
- a value painting with *Gradient Map* applied
- the background color layer

Notice that all my base layers are clipped to the "Gradient map" layer. You will have something similar, give or take a base layer or two.

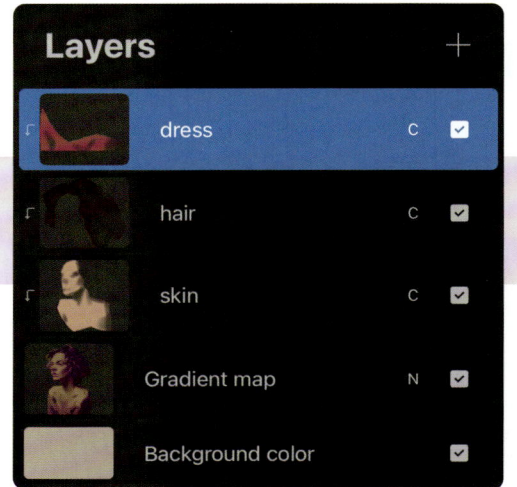

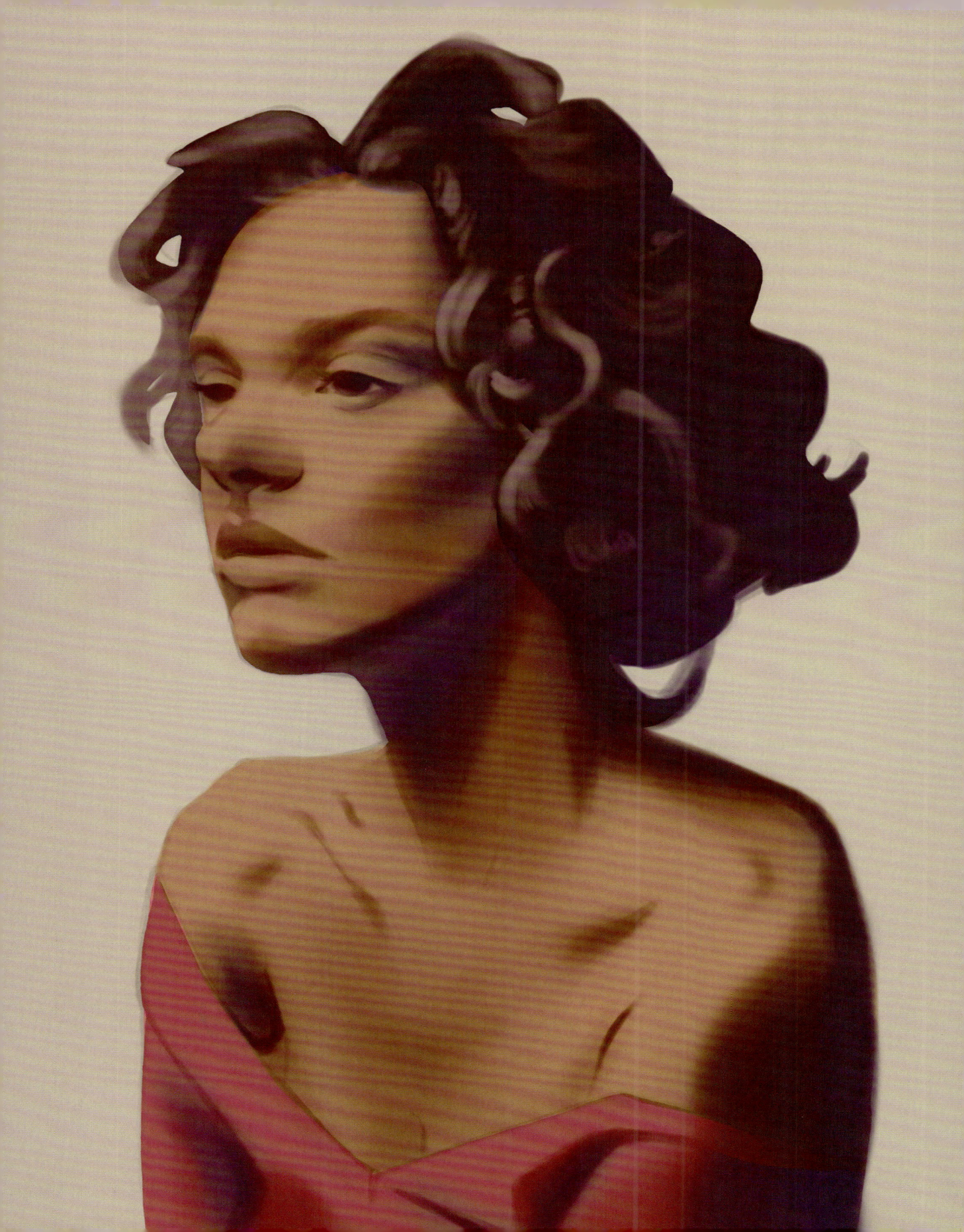

COLOR DIVERSITY

Now that you have a solid base, you can start adding interest to your painting by incorporating a variety of different colors.

In real life, both objects and people have a wide assortment of colors that show up on their surface—these colors could come from the subject itself (blue veins under the skin) or from the environment around it (red light reflected off shiny hair). Incorporating a mix of these colors into your work will help your paintings look much more realistic.

Color Zones of the Face

Since skin is a very complex and often tricky subject to paint, I'll take a moment to break down a common concept called the color zones of the face.

The face can be divided into three main color zones:

1. **The forehead**
   Yellow in color due to thinner skin and a lack of capillaries and muscles.
2. **The middle of the face**
   Reddish in color due to many capillaries close to the surface of the skin.
3. **The mouth and chin area**
   In males, blue due to stubble or hair follicles underneath the skin. In females, this zone may be more neutral or green in hue when compared to the middle zone.

Use the color zones of the face to identify and incorporate common colors that may show up on a subject. Please bear in mind, though, that these zones are extremely subtle in real life and that they're particularly useful only for painting fair-skinned subjects.

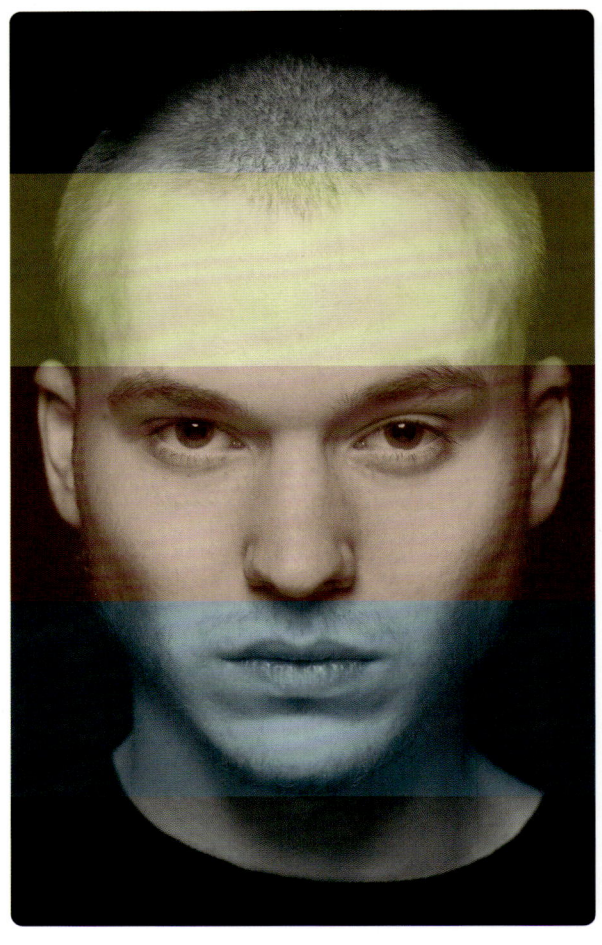

When it comes to adding color diversity to a painting, it's really up to you how obvious or subtle you want your colors to be. Some artists like to stick to subtle shifts in color, while others really like to bump up the contrast.

Ultimately, there's no right or wrong way to paint.

Dark Versus Light Skin

Painting dark skin is not like painting fair skin. You cannot simply take those peach or pink hues and make them darker.

When it comes to painting dark skin (ranging from brown to black), it's a good idea to bump up the reds in the skin to avoid creating an overall green complexion.

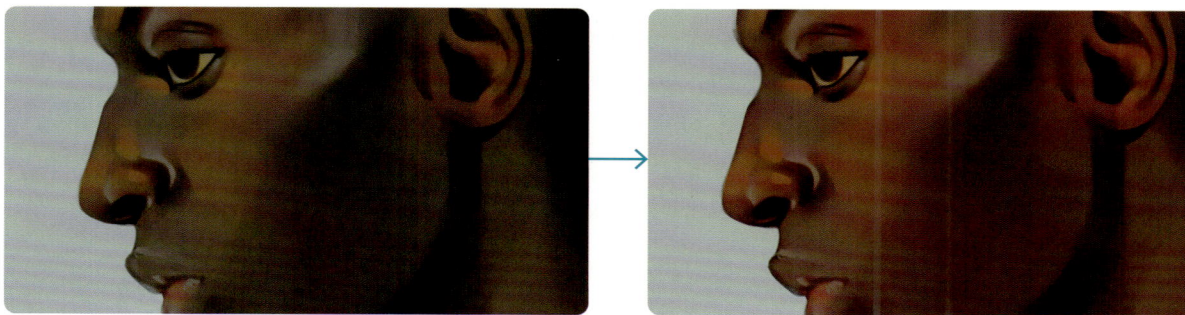

Painted normally, without enhancing the reds   Bump up the reds to make a more vibrant skin tone

Melanin in the skin will mask a lot of the colors that come from within— the purples or blues of the veins and the yellows or whites of the bones.

Instead, highly pigmented skin will reflect a lot of the environmental light around it and the highlights will be tighter. This means that the environment that your subject is in becomes very important to pay attention to. For example, if your subject is outdoors, your highlights are more likely to be blue (reflected from the sky). If your subject is indoors, then your highlights could be yellow or white depending on the warmth of the artificial light.

Add Color Diversity

On a new layer, use a soft brush to paint in a diverse range of colors. Switch the blend mode to *Soft Light* or *Color* and lower the opacity to gain more subtlety.

Bearing the zones of the face in mind, I added red into the nose and cheeks as well as the lips. I lightly painted a bit of yellow into the forehead. The chin was already looking much too blue, so instead of intensifying it or adding green, I used the same yellow of the forehead to brighten and neutralize this area.

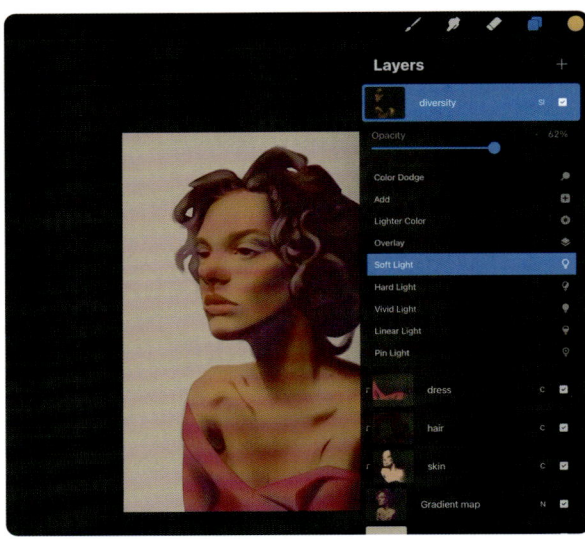

Method to the Madness

Don't forget to add diversity into the hair and clothing! Pay attention to what colors are showing up in your reference image and incorporate some of those.

My reference didn't give me much to work off, so I improvised. If you have to make it up, give it a good think—don't just throw random colors everywhere.

1. What is directly under the skin that can impact the surface color?
2. Is the environment casting colors on my model?
3. Can I add visual interest by adding complementary colors in?

As an example, I added yellow near the shoulders and collarbone since the bone is close to the surface of the skin. I added red near the top of the breasts since they're fleshy masses and likely to have lots of blood flow.

Since my model's hair is a warm golden brown, I added yellows and oranges into the highlighted areas, which I knew would also complement the blue I was using for the shadows.

At this stage, your painting might look quite strange and unrealistic. That's not a problem, though, as you'll begin to render the painting in the next step. Trust the process!

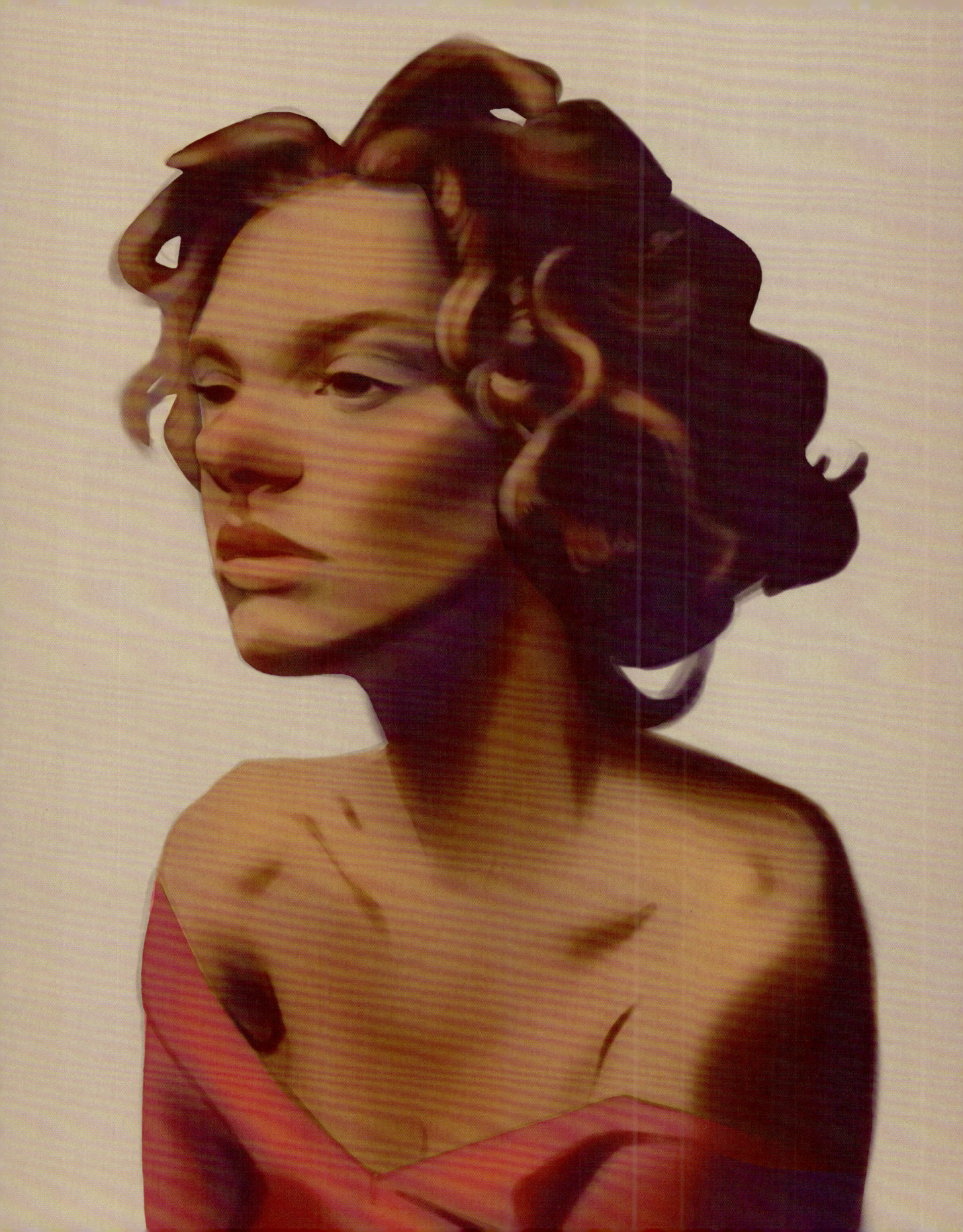

RENDERING

Now the true fun begins!

In this stage of painting you only have to focus on rendering the subject. You're going to add dimension to your piece primarily by introducing highlights. You'll sculpt the forms of the face, finesse your shadows, and add detail to the hair and clothing. Overall, the rendering process can take a very long time as you noodle away and fuss over tiny details—patience is key!

Start Wherever You Want

Now is a good time to pull up your original reference photo if you don't have it up already.

Start rendering wherever you please. For me, this is typically the nose, cheek, or eye area. For you, it could be the lips. It doesn't matter where you start since you'll eventually get to every feature.

I started with the highlights near the eyes. I wanted yellow/greenish highlights on my subject, so I color sampled close to the area I was about to paint, then adjusted the *hue ring* so that the sampled color leaned more toward yellow than red. I then adjusted the *saturation circle* so that the color was brighter.

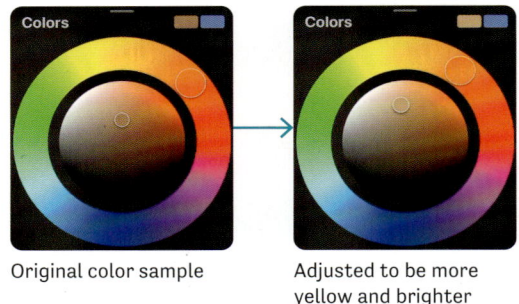

Original color sample   Adjusted to be more yellow and brighter

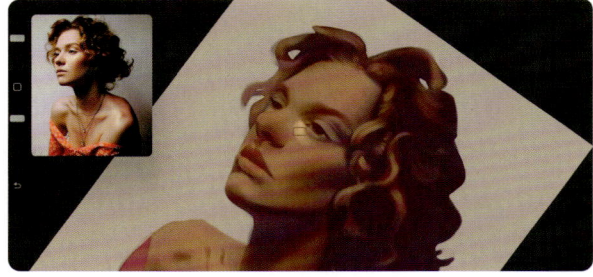

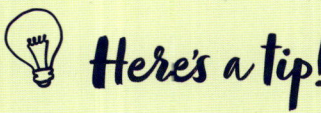 Here's a tip!

You can add color into your highlights; they don't always have to be stark white. White is best saved for **specular highlights**, which are bright spots that are concentrated and small. Highlights can be much larger areas, so painting with white isn't recommended as you'll end up with very dull and lifeless colors.

When rendering, I recommend using a hard brush to lay down a bit of paint first, then going back in with the smudge tool to soften and blend out some of the edges. This ensures you get both hard and soft edges in your work—achieving visual interest in your painting.

To ensure accuracy, pay close attention to the different levels of brightness in your reference and compare them against each other. For example, the chin and forehead of my subject are bright, but they aren't as bright as the tip of the nose, cheek, or eyelid. When rendering, I should make sure I don't make them the same brightness as or brighter than those areas, otherwise I'll break the illusion of reality and my painting will look off.

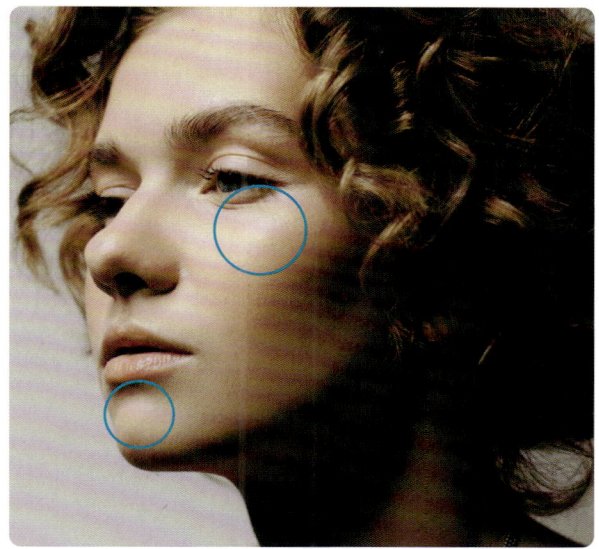

Compare brightnesses against each other and ensure you don't make all highlights the same intensity

Layers Can Help You Work Confidently

You can work with multiple layers if that makes you feel comfortable. Sometimes, when approaching an area of the face that I'm not as confident in painting, I'll make a new layer and give it a go. This way, if I completely muck it up, I can just clear the layer. Other times, I can use the eraser tool on my new layer to soften harsh edges without destroying other parts of my painting that I'm happy with.

Just like the greyscale painting, don't forget to jump around the canvas. Don't stay in one spot for too long and render it out completely. Add some of those highlights to the body and jump back to the face. It's so important that you build up your painting in a holistic way so that you don't end up with areas that are overly rendered.

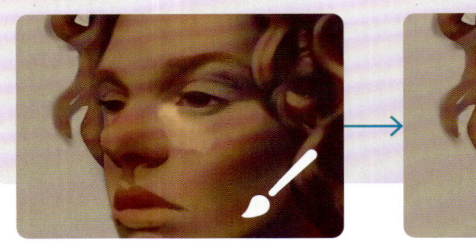 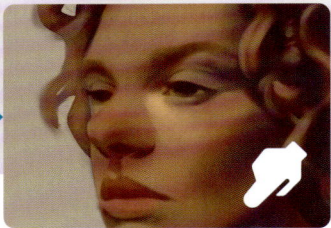

I used a square brush with a hard edge to lay down paint, then switched to the smudge tool to soften and blend the edges near the cheek and under the eye.

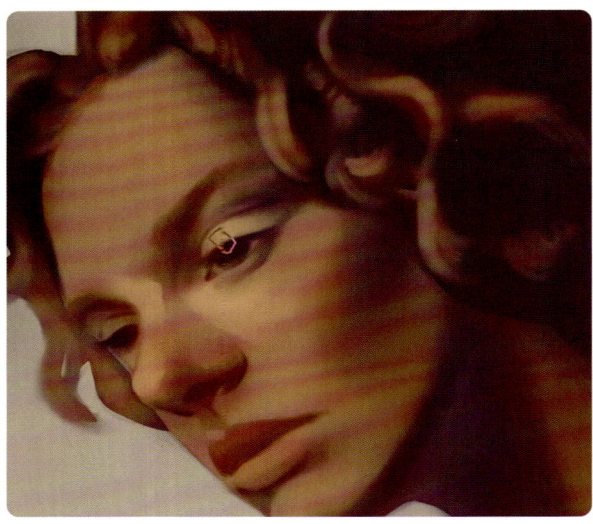

Continuing the process, I brought highlights to the nose and eyelids.

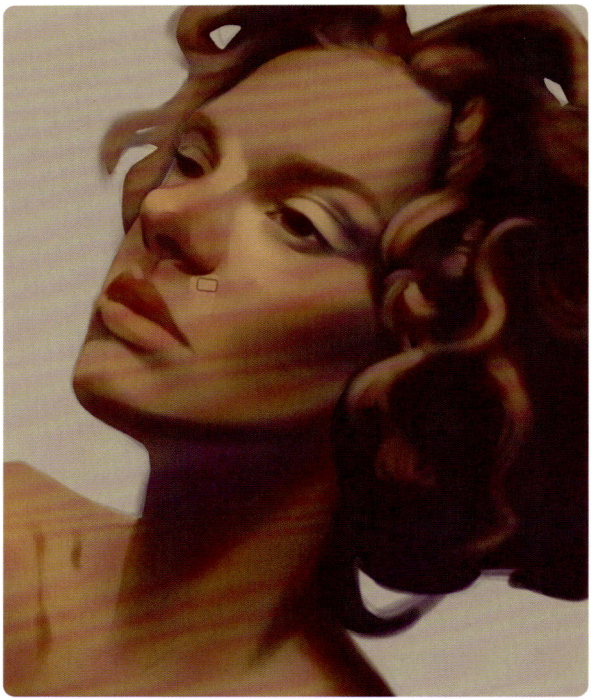

Remember to pay attention to the brightness of the highlights. The area near the nasolabial furrow is bright, but it's certainly not as bright as the eyelid. If I paint this part in too harshly, it'll age my subject.

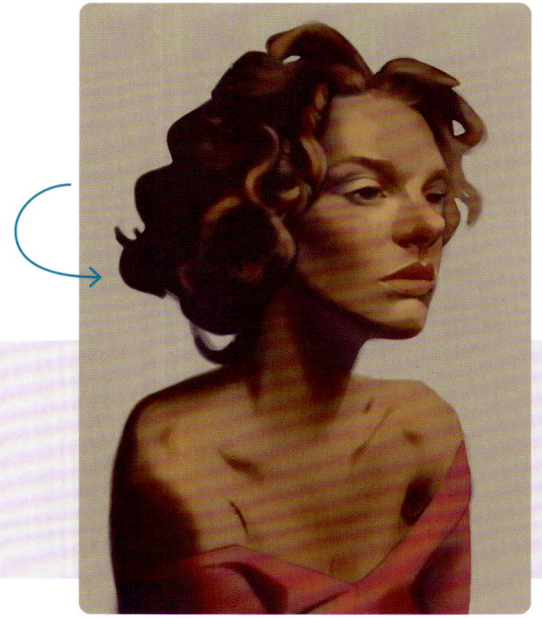

Flipping your canvas from time to time is a great way to spot errors. In a way, it works similarly to taking breaks. It gives your brain a different perspective of your art after staring at it one way for many minutes (or hours).

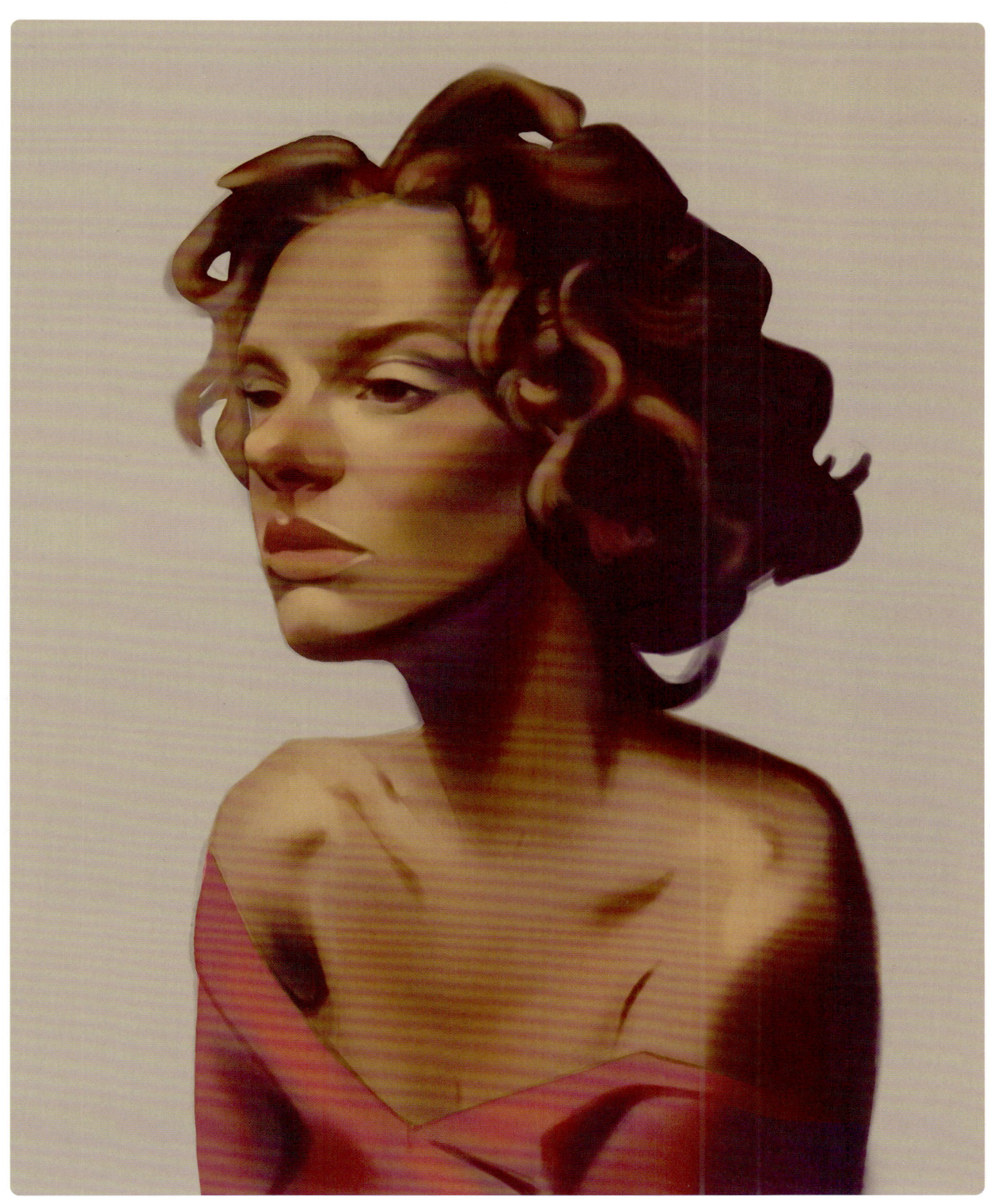

This part of the rendering process is complete for the time being. The only thing I focused on was adding highlights to the face and body.

Troubleshooting

Sometimes when painting, you'll notice that something is drastically off and want to correct it.

Instead of repainting and re-rendering everything (what a pain!), you can remedy sweeping issues with adjustments.

To make an adjustment, follow these steps:

1. Create a composite layer. Turn off your background color first and then go to Actions > Add > Copy Canvas > Paste.
2. Apply your desired adjustment on the layer called "Inserted Image."

You can do this at any point in time during the painting the process. If you're adjusting for brightness, you could opt to use the *Curves* adjustment to do so.

If you're troubleshooting for color, you could try playing around with the individual red, green, or blue channels of *Curves*, or you could opt for the *Color Balance* adjustment instead.

To fix up placement or sizing issues, try using *Liquify* to alter specific parts of your art.

You can also use more than one adjustment on a single layer. Refer to pages 39–41 for a deeper walkthrough of *Adjustments*.

Once you're happy with your adjustments, apply them and create a new layer to continue rendering.

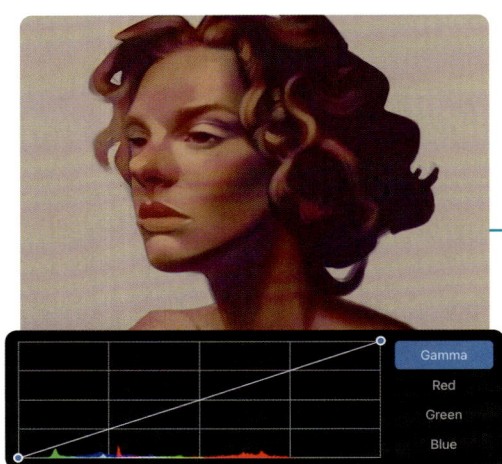

My painting was too dark and the colors were muted

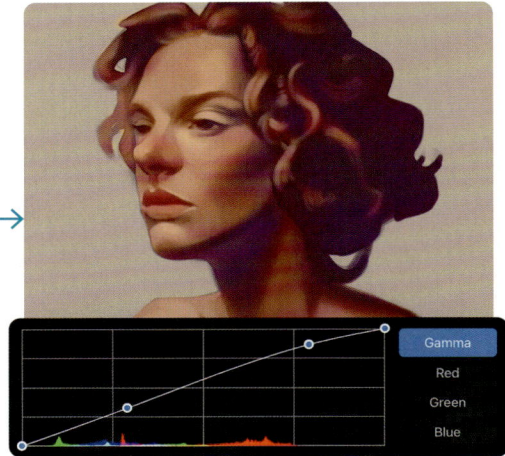

I added two nodes on the histogram to adjust the brightness and contrast

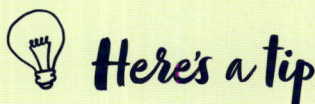 *Here's a tip!*

While using *Adjustment*, tap anywhere on your canvas to invoke *Adjustment Actions*—a helpful hidden menu! Tap on *Preview* to switch between the before and after of the adjustment you're making before you commit to applying it.

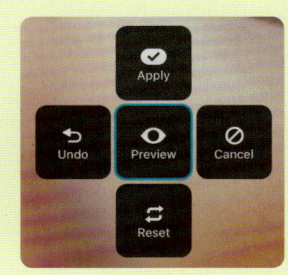

Using Curves

A lot of Procreate's adjustments and filters are pretty straightforward; however, anyone can benefit from an introduction to *Curves* as it can take a bit of getting used to.

With *Curves*, you're adjusting the color and tonal value (how light or dark a color or shade is) using a graph called a histogram.

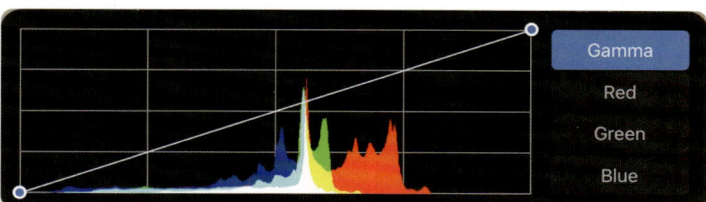

The histogram is a visual representation of the colors on your layer, not the entire painting. There are three different channels: *Red*, *Green*, and *Blue*. You can think of these color channels as your primaries. When these colors intersect, they are indicating that other colors, such as purple, are present on your layer.

The *Gamma* channel is like a master of the separate channels. By altering the histogram on *Gamma*, you're adjusting all three channels at once. When you work on a single channel, such as *Blue*, you're only adjusting the amount of blue on the layer (increasing it or decreasing it).

Working with Nodes

Tap the diagonal line to place a node. Move nodes along the diagonal line to manipulate your image.

Brightness is controlled vertically. Move a node up to lighten and down to darken.

Contrast is controlled horizontally. Move a node left to decrease contrast and right to increase it.

Tap on an existing node to bring up the option to delete it.

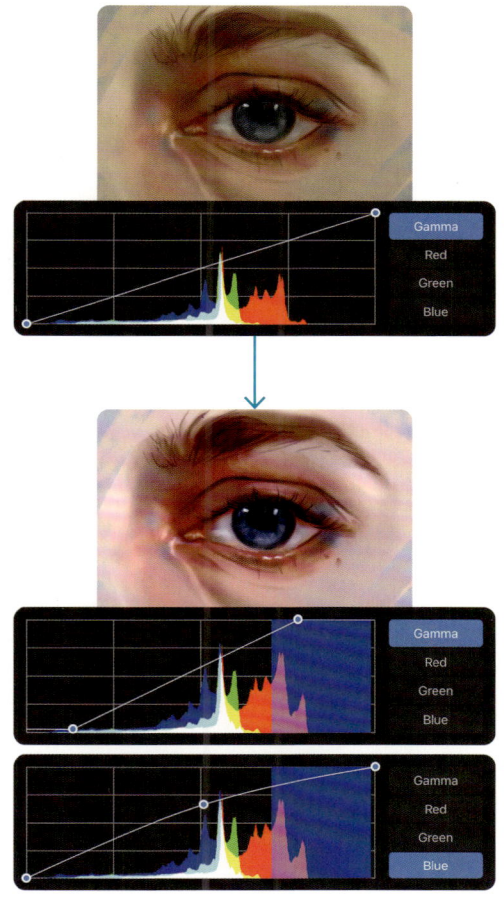

Overall contrast was adjusted using *Gamma*. The amount of blue present in the image was increased using the *Blue* channel.

Bump Up the Contrast

Due to the absence of pure black and white in the original value painting and the way I used the adjustment tools when troubleshooting, my painting was lacking in contrast.

If this is the same issue for you, then you can reintroduce lightness or darkness into the highlights or shadows respectively (depending on which one has washed out).

For example, your darks may not be as punchy as you want them to be. Instead of using another adjustment layer, I would recommend painting (or repainting) some of the shadows instead to ensure you maintain tight control over your work.

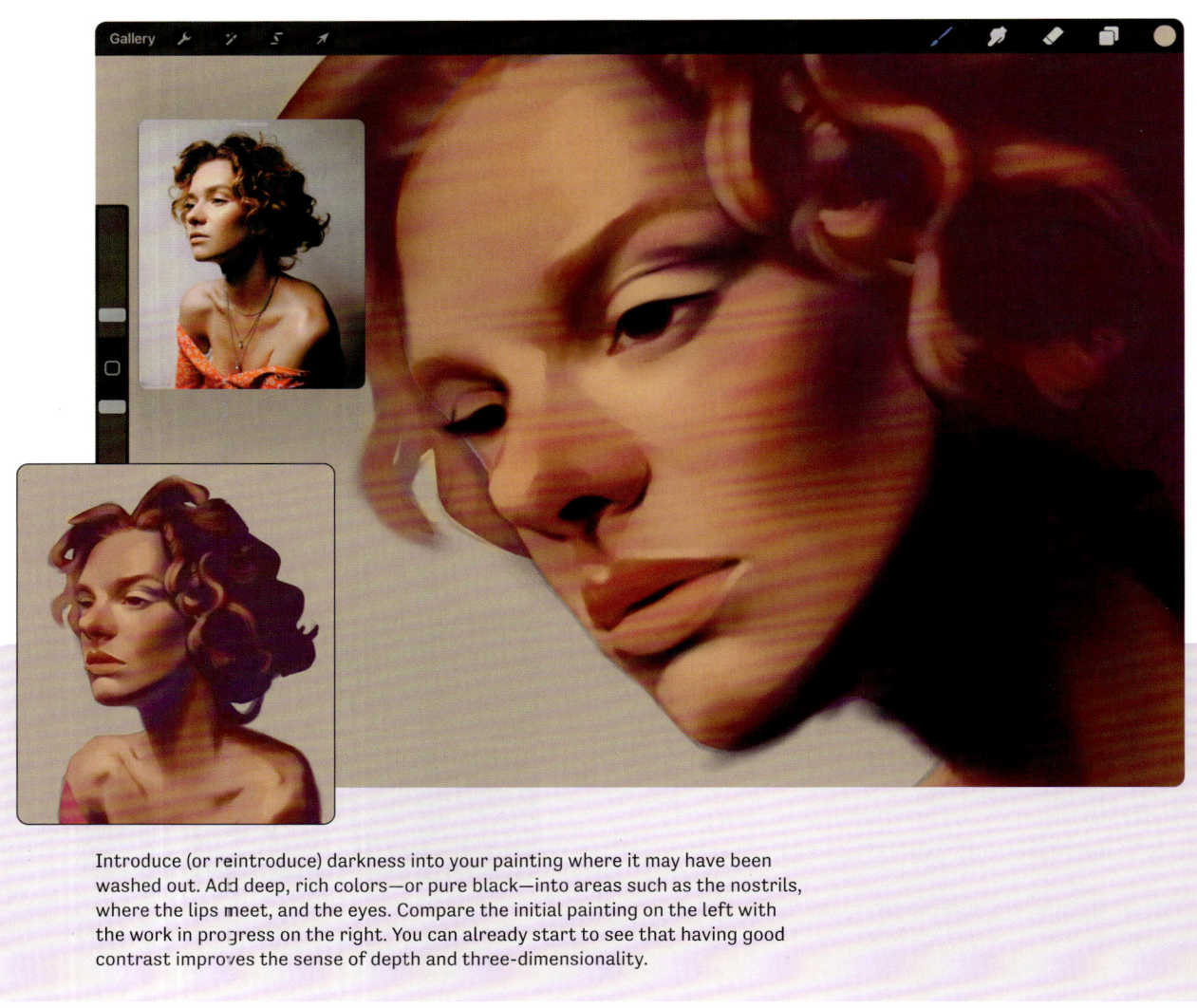

Introduce (or reintroduce) darkness into your painting where it may have been washed out. Add deep, rich colors—or pure black—into areas such as the nostrils, where the lips meet, and the eyes. Compare the initial painting on the left with the work in progress on the right. You can already start to see that having good contrast improves the sense of depth and three-dimensionality.

Start, but Don't Finish, the Hair

Hair can be a very tricky subject. If you paint every individual strand, you'll end up with a very busy, visually distracting mess. The best way to paint hair is by **suggesting** volume without painting in extensive detail.

Since this is a portrait and the face is the focal point, I would recommend painting the hair that's right around the face in detail while leaving the rest quite impressionistic and loose.

At this point, you may not have done much with the hair. Bring in some of the same dark color you had used for the nostrils and other shadowed areas to increase contrast. You can also start to add in some brighter highlights.

As you do this, zoom out to get a good look at your work. Does your painting look cohesive? Are you using the same colors for the shadows in the face as you are for the ones in the hair and clothing?

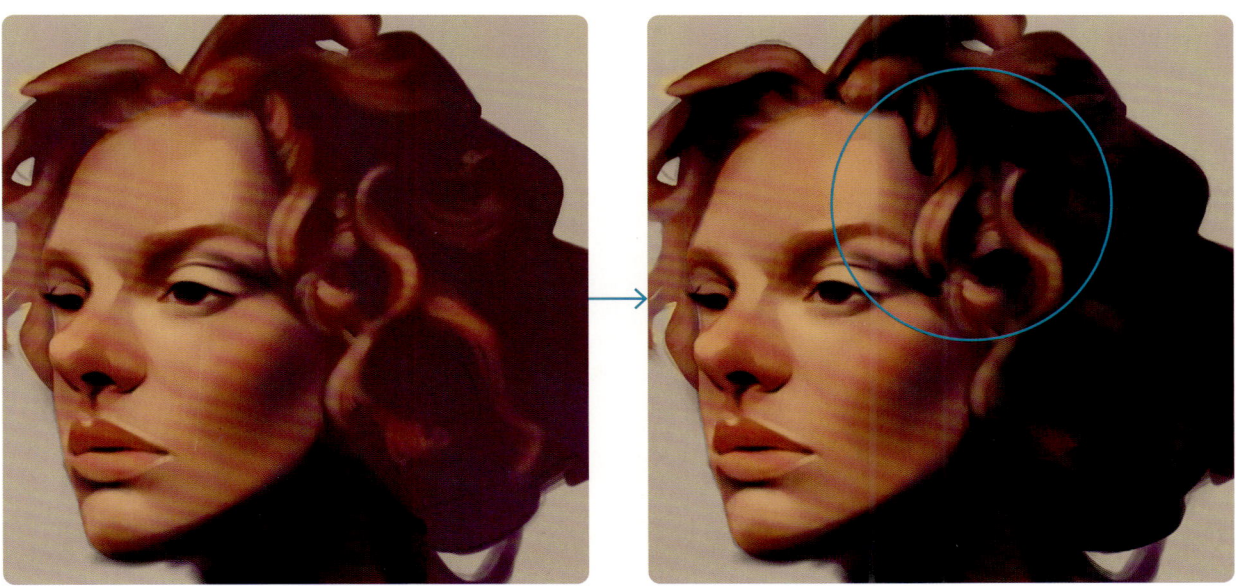

Notice that the hair near the face is rendered more tightly than the rest of it. I used a soft round brush to capture a bit more detail in that area, then used a big airbrush to add sweeping, loose shadows elsewhere.

I've also not bothered covering everything with black. I find the purple in the shadows quite pleasant, so I want it to show through here and there.

Layer Panel Peek

A lot of newer digital artists struggle with knowing how many layers to use in a painting. I've said this before, but there really is no right or wrong answer—it depends on your comfort with the program and how you paint.

Here's a peek at the number of layers I've used up until this point. You'll recognize the gradient map layer, base color layers, and color diversity layer. From there I've got multiple layers for highlights and shadows. I tend to make a new layer when I tackle a big part of the painting. (Layer 9, for example, is just for the shadows of the hair.) Again, this is my personal preference and not a rule.

I find that the more comfortable you get with the program and with digital painting in general, the fewer layers you're likely to use. But really, don't sweat it!

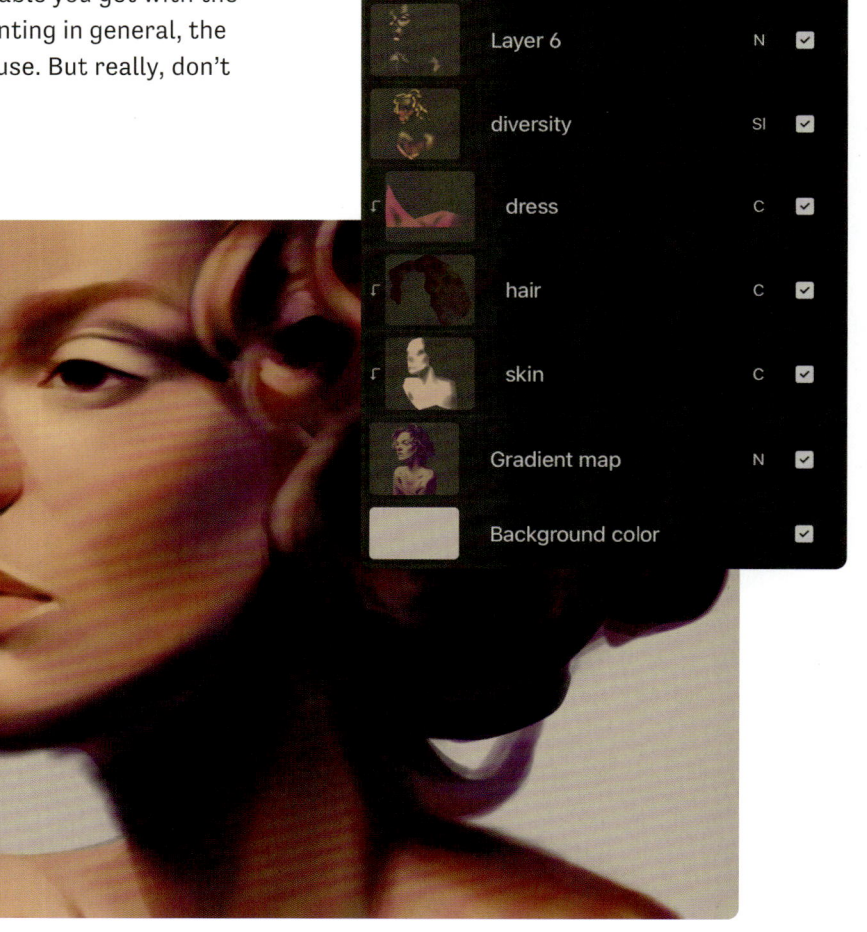

Add Specular Highlights

You're getting to the end of the rendering process. There are just a few more things to do. First, make sure you've captured the specular highlights (the very brightest spots) on your model.

I always leave these for the very end. Adding them in makes a huge difference. Not only do the specular highlights add to that sense of three-dimensionality, but they also give information to the viewer regarding the whereabouts of your light source and the texture of the surface you've painted.

Generally speaking, wet, shiny, or oily surfaces will be more reflective, and their specular highlights will be very bright and tight. Materials that diffuse light or are matte in nature (like a cotton shirt) may not have these kinds of highlights at all.

You'll usually find specular highlights on the T-zone of the face (it's oilier than the rest, making it much more reflective). The T-zone includes the forehead, nose, and chin. The eyes and lips, often being wet, may also have these intense bright spots.

Makeup will also impact where specular highlights appear, as some forms of makeup (like lip gloss or highlighter—typically applied on the cheekbones, under the brows, down the length of the nose, and at the inner corners of the eyes) are made to be highly reflective.

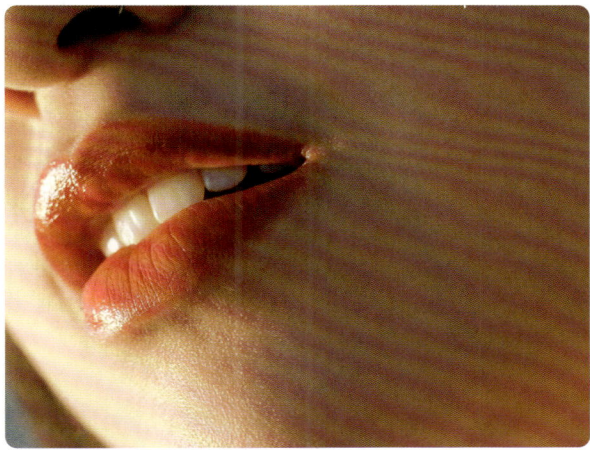

The way light is reflected off of a surface is what tells our brain whether a surface is shiny or not. If you fail to capture the highlights accurately, the texture of your surface will not be communicated well—you could end up with a matte lip instead of a glossy one.

The skin, lacking in the same kind of specular highlights that the lips have, appears much more matte in comparison.

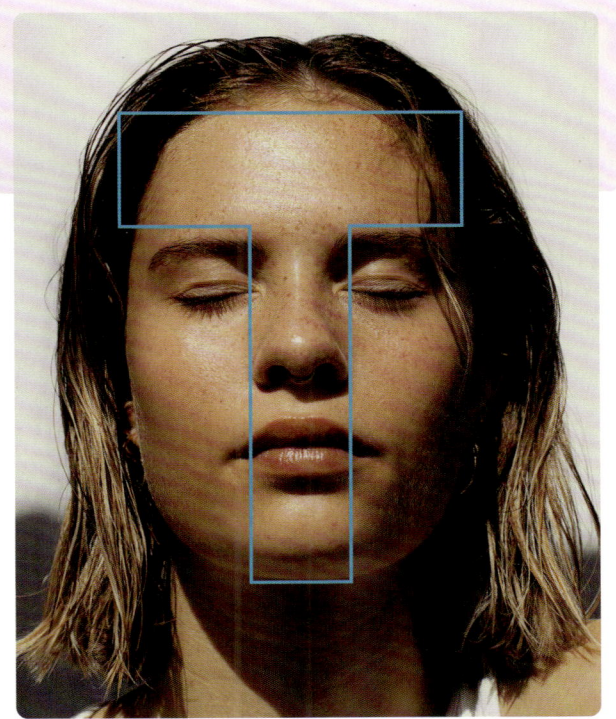

Tight specular highlights on the bridge and tip of the nose. In contrast, the highlights on the chin and cheeks are much more diffused.

One of the reasons I save specular highlights for the very end is to ensure that my brights stay bright. If you add these highlights into your work too soon, you may start color sampling from them and bringing that brightness into other areas of the painting (where it shouldn't be). It's extremely hard to undo this process once it's started. You can always build up the brightness of a painting slowly over time, but undoing it once it's overexposed is a tougher feat.

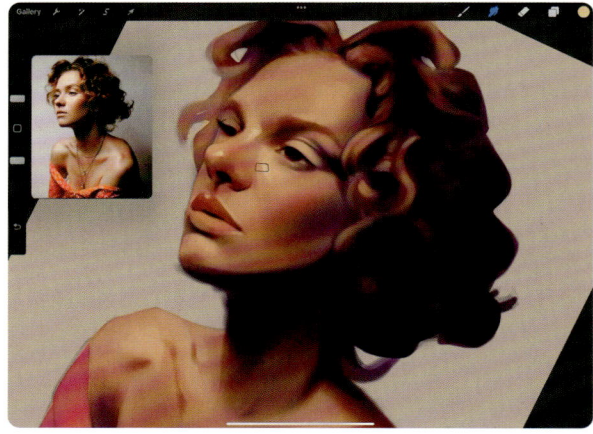

Referring to my reference image, I add in the most obvious bright spots—on the bridge and tip of the nose

Continue to add specular highlights in other areas of the face or body.

In my example, you'll notice that I'm keeping them pretty rough and not blending them out. This makes them punchier and adds texture to the work.

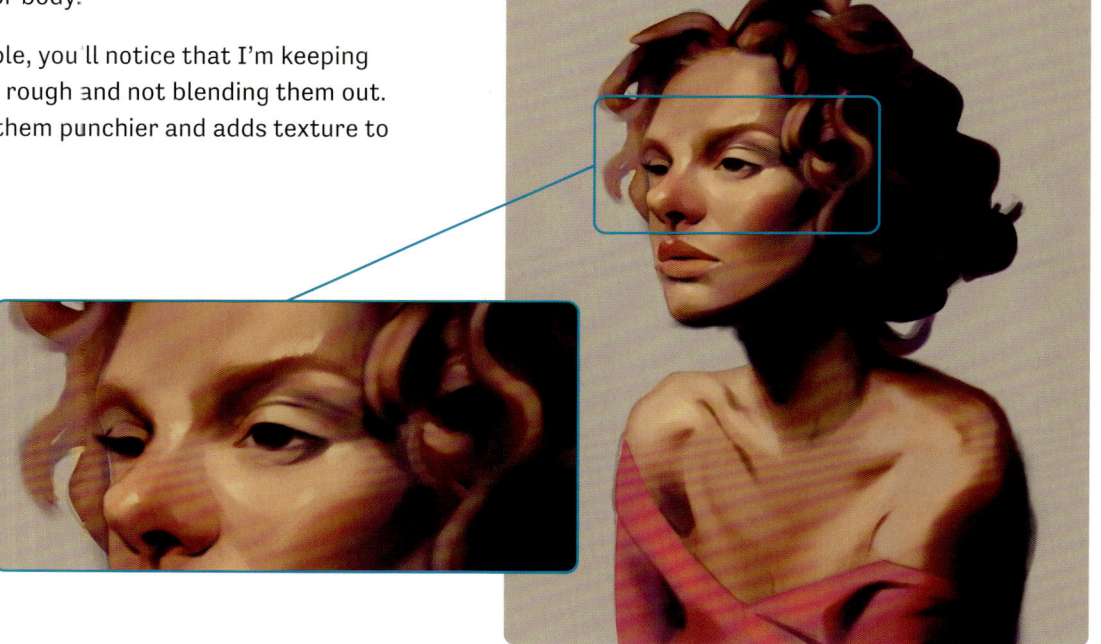

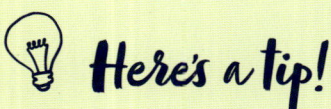 **Here's a tip!**

Don't go overboard with your specular highlights! Adding too much of them can destroy your hard work. As the famous artist James Gurney says, "Highlights are like salt. A little makes the food tasty, but too much ruins it."

Create a Pattern for the Clothing

Here's a quick and easy way to add patterns, or repetitive detail, to clothing or objects.

1. Create a new layer and draw your pattern.
2. Change the blend mode to whatever suits your needs—if your pattern is darker than the material, you can use *Multiply* or *Linear Burn*. *Screen* and *Soft light* are great if you want your pattern to remain relatively light. There are also other blend modes that can give you cool, iridescent results like *Overlay* or *Color Dodge*.

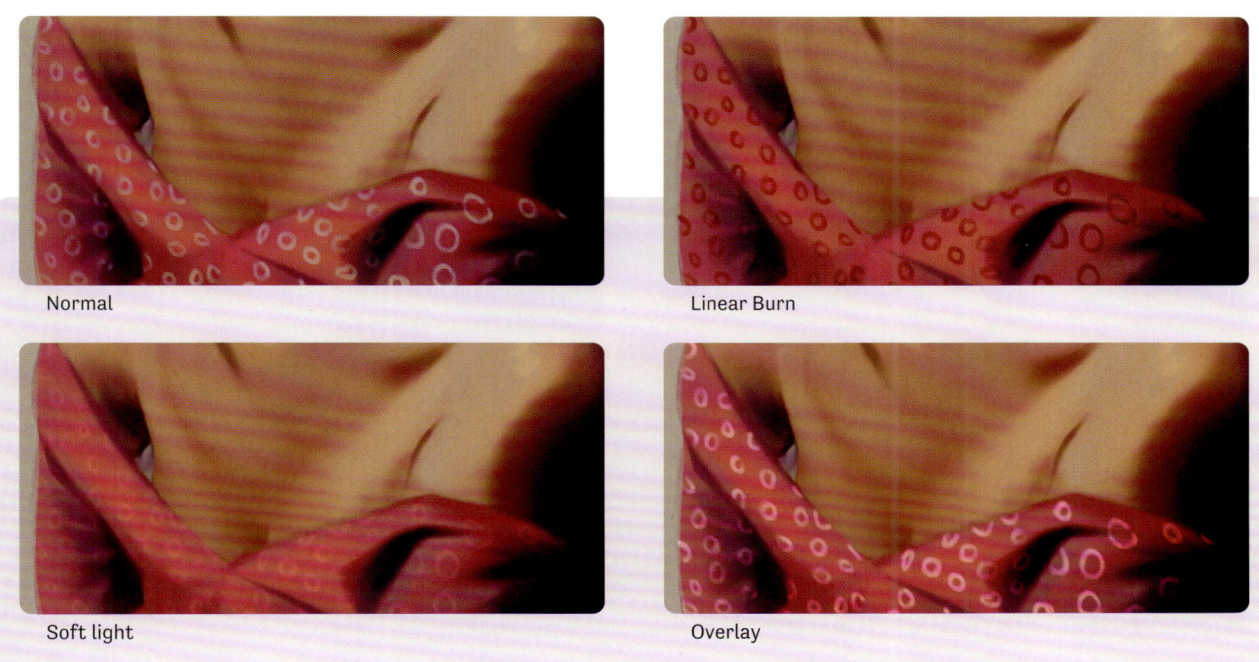

Normal

Linear Burn

Soft light

Overlay

3. Apply a layer *Mask* to your pattern and use black to conceal parts of the pattern that are too visible.

   Layers > Tap thumbnail > Mask

Use the opacity slider to reduce the transparency if the pattern is too strong.

Right: I concealed parts of the pattern that were in shadow to ensure the pattern itself wasn't unrealistically glowing in the dark.

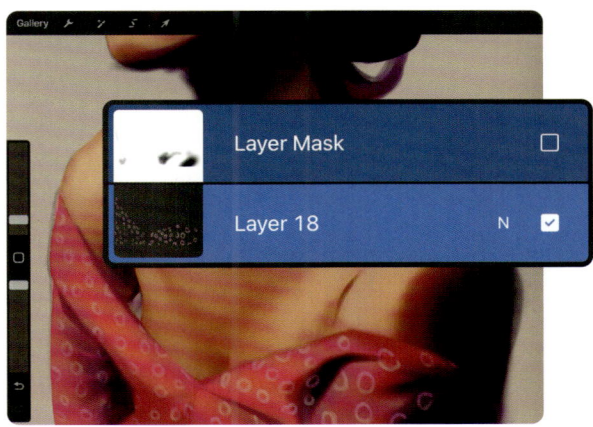

Finish the Hair

At this point in the painting process, your hair might look like a wig perched atop your model's head...but that's not a problem! All you have to do is mend your lovely wig to the head.

To do this, you're going to blend the hair and the skin together using tiny brush strokes. If it helps, think of it this way: instead of using the smudge tool to blend one color into another, you're using tiny brush strokes instead.

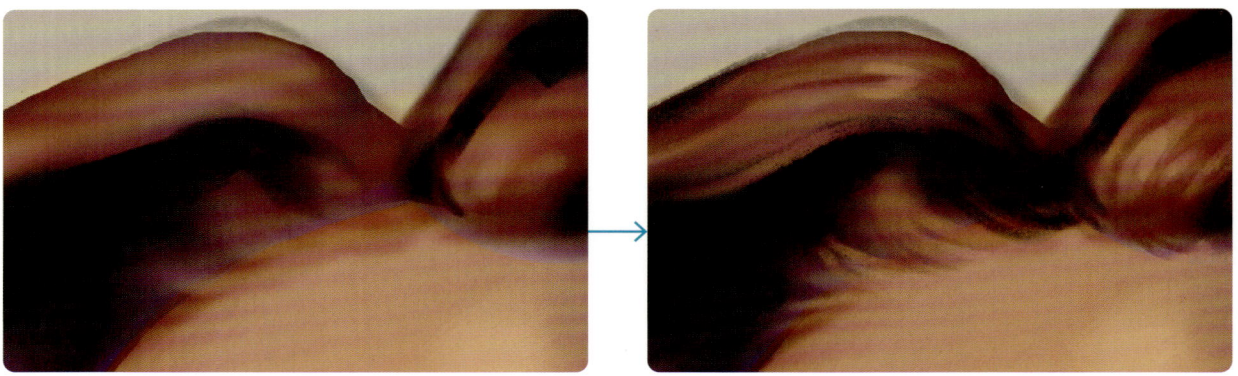

1. Turn the size of your brush way down.
2. Use the eyedropper to color sample the hair that's right up against the forehead.
3. Use light strokes to paint the hair into the forehead.
4. Now do the reverse—color sample the skin of the forehead and paint light strokes into the hair.

Much of the rest of the hair is actually painted in the same way. You're going to color sample from the area you want to add detail to and then use a small/thin brush to paint a few strands in. Continue to color sample and paint back and forth between light and shadow areas.

This process can be very tedious so please be patient with it! Some artists like to switch to a rake brush, which is a type of brush that creates multiple strokes at once, to help speed up the process. Feel free to experiment with these types of brushes.

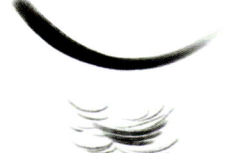

Textured brush single stroke

Textured brush 20+ strokes

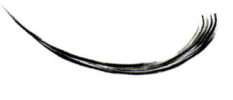

Rake brush single stroke

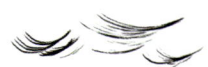

Rake brush 7 strokes

Add Details

To make sure your painting doesn't end up looking too dull, you can switch to a brush with texture to paint in details like the eyelashes and wrinkles of the lips.

Texture adds visual interest to a piece. If you use a very textured brush while painting in the details, you can help pull the viewer's attention to these specific spots—because they'll stand out from the rest of your work.

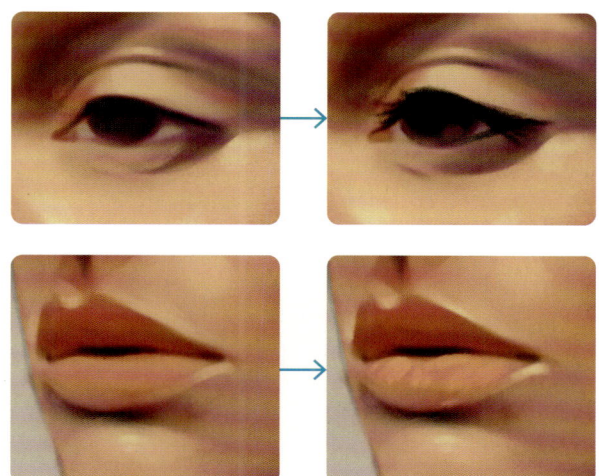

Clean Up Your Edges

There are multiple ways to clean up your painting. Here are two:

Method I

1. Create a composite layer, making sure you turn off the background first.

   Actions > Add > Copy Canvas > Paste

2. Group all of your working layers together and turn the visibility off.

   Swipe right on layers > Tap Group

3. Apply a *Mask* to the layer.

   Layers > Tap layer thumbnail > Mask

4. Paint with black on the "Layer Mask." This will clean up your edges in a non-destructive way. If you want to "erase" anything on the mask, switch to painting with white instead.

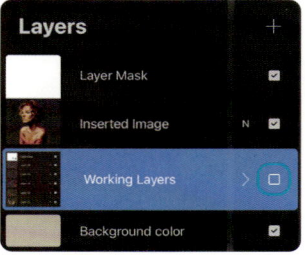

After grouping layers together, turn the visibility of the group off. If you don't do this, you won't be able to properly see the cleanup you're doing.

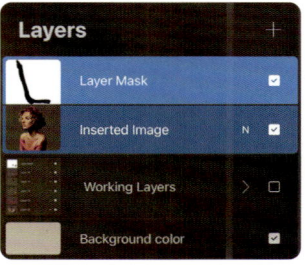

Only paint on the "Layer Mask" layer. See how it's highlighted in a brighter blue, which lets you know that it's the active layer.

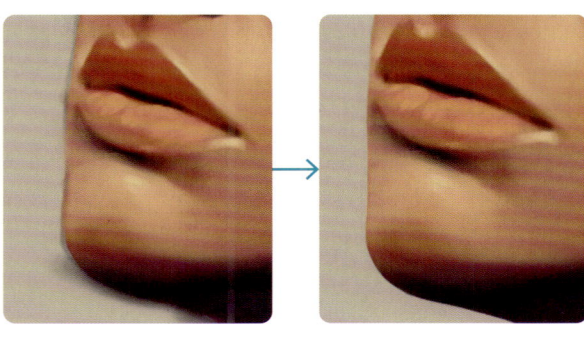

Before cleanup   After cleanup

Method 2

1. Create a new layer.
2. Use the eyedropper tool to color sample your background.
3. Paint the edges in on your new layer.

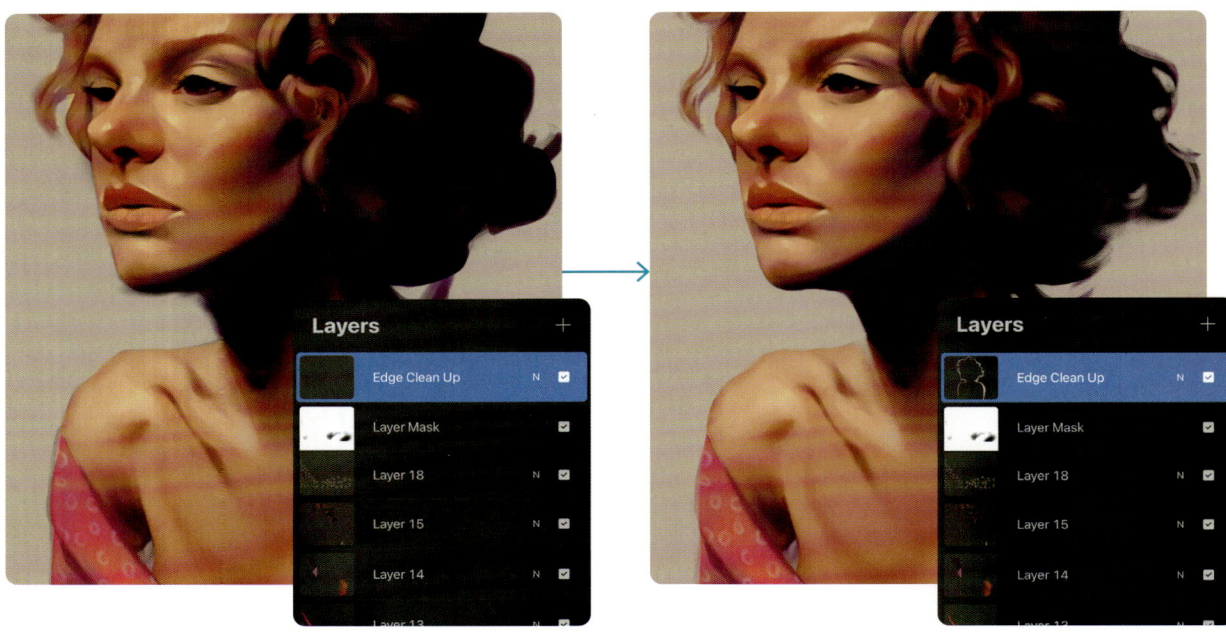

Create a new layer and paint the edges on that layer

While doing the edges, you can also refine the hair by creating gaps of space between clumps of hair and softening the edges

A Note on Clean Edges

Not all of your edges have to be hard. In real life, some edges seem to blend into the background, usually as a result of lighting.

In particular, when cleaning up the edges around the hair, you want to do so gently. Hair and fur don't have such hard, defined edges, and they often appear wispy in real life.

Turn the opacity of your brush down so that it takes a few strokes to clean up the edges. You can also switch to an airbrush or use the smudge tool to soften areas that are too sharp. This will give you a much more realistic result.

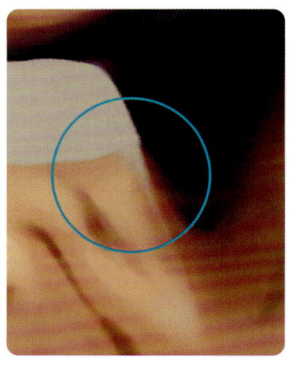

Soft edges help tie the subject into the background, avoiding the look of two completely separate components

Finish the Painting!

Once the edges are complete, you're practically done. At this point, you should step back from your work and assess it.

1. Is there anything missing?
2. Could you make further refinements or add details or texture?
3. Does it need an overall color correction?
4. Do you want to add snazzy effects?

Once I was done with the edges, I realized that the hair could still use a bit of work. I made a last-minute decision to add in the necklace that was originally in the reference image. Making choices like this at the end of a painting can cause a bit of grief, but it's also totally okay to change your mind and take a stab at trying something!

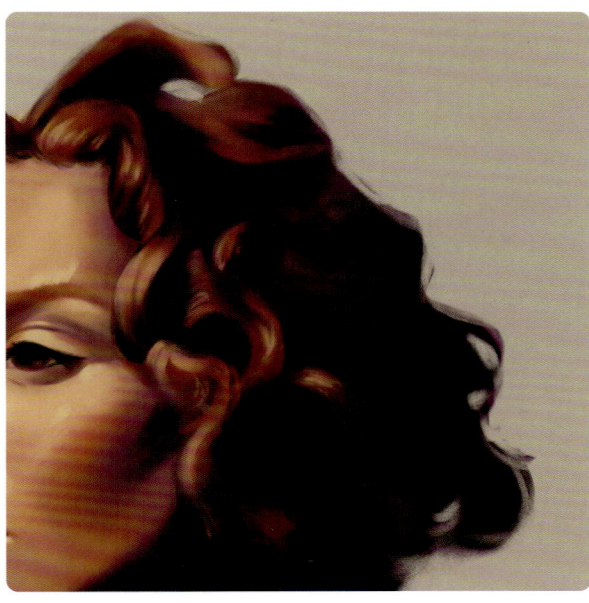 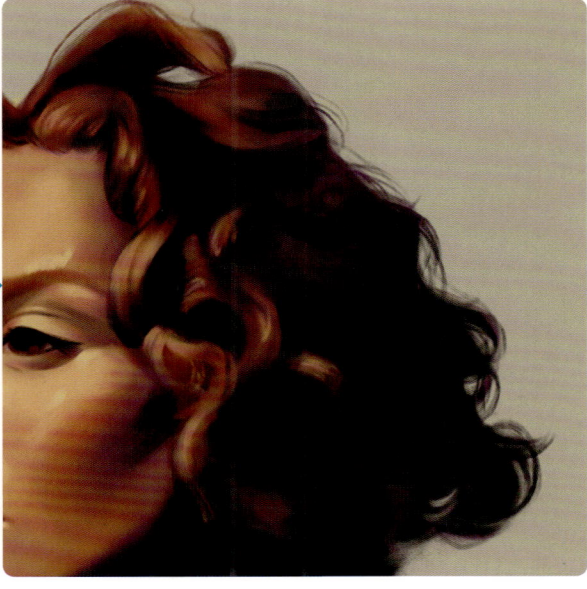

This is the hair after edge cleanup. It's not terrible, but it's missing some life and a bit of realism

On a new layer, on top of the edge cleanup layer, I took a tiny textured brush and added individual strands here and there

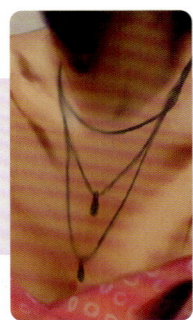 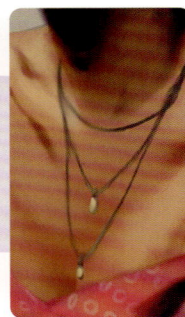 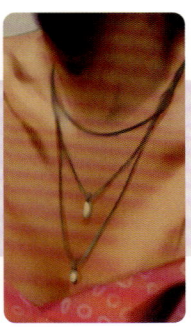

The necklace came together quickly. I sketched it in on a new layer, then added some pearls and a bit of highlights to the chain. Lastly, I color sampled a shadow on the skin and painted that in underneath the necklace to make it look like the necklace was actually draped on the model.

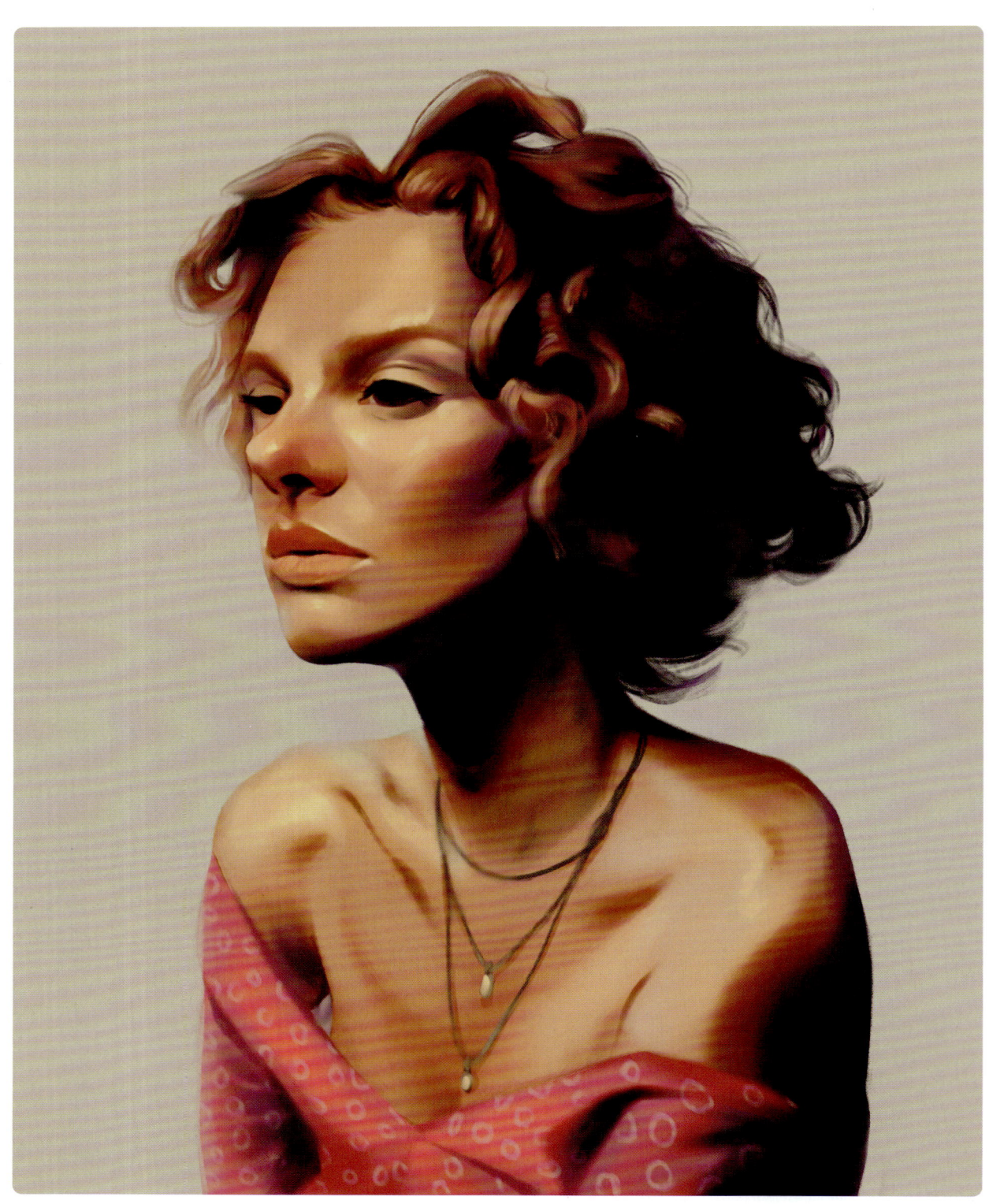

This is the completed painting. It's been color corrected but doesn't have any effects applied...yet.

ADD EFFECTS

Now that the painting is complete, a fun way to wrap up your portrait is with effects!

Create a composite layer of your entire final piece (this time you can totally include the background):

Actions > Add > Copy Canvas > Paste

Under *Adjustments*, choose whatever floats your boat! Try playing around with some interesting effects like *Blur* or *Chromatic Aberration*.

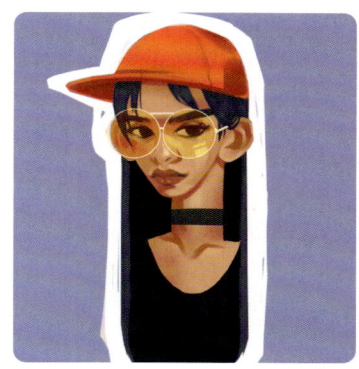

Original painting

Using Blur

Blurring softens your work and makes it look out of focus. It's a great way to enhance the focal point of your painting.

Gaussian Blur

This is a fairly neutral yet powerful blur. Slide your finger right to increase the blurring effect or left to reduce it.

Tap the top slider to open the Pencil option. Now instead of blurring the entire layer, you can select what parts of your image to blur by painting with a brush.

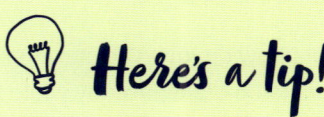

Gaussian blur set using the pencil. Paint the areas you want blurred with your paintbrush. Switch to the eraser tool if you make a mistake—they both work in this filter interface.

Motion Blur

This blurring effect is kind of streaky, giving the impression that there's movement in your work.

Perspective Blur

This creates a radial blur.

Positional blur radiates out in all directions from the focal point.

Directional blur will only blur from one side of the focal point.

💡 *Here's a tip!*

Use blur to help set your focal point. For example, if the eyes are your focal point, they should remain sharp while the rest of your image could be subtly blurred.

Using Chromatic Aberration

Chromatic Aberration will shift the red and blue planes in the painting (creating a halo effect in certain areas). It's one of my favorite filters as it creates really cool effects in a flash that would've taken forever to paint.

Perspective

Using *Perspective*, set a focal point from which the chromatic aberration will occur.

Transition controls the amount of blur applied to the chromatic aberration; 0% will give you a soft edge and 100% will make it hard.

Fall off controls where the aberration begins in relation to the focal point; 0% means it starts right at the edge of the focal point and as you move the slider up, the aberration will start farther and farther away.

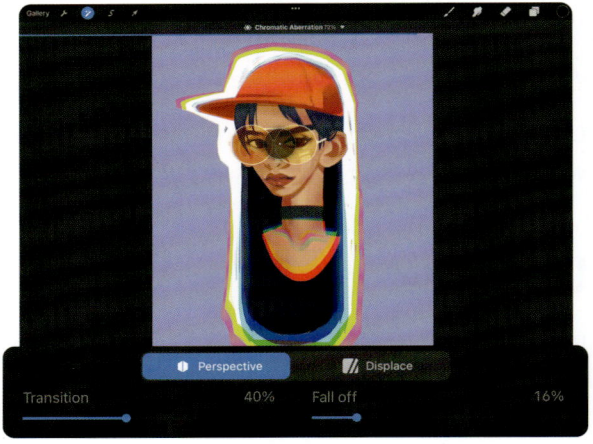

Chromatic aberration applied at 72% strength (top slider), transition at 40%, and fall off at 16%. Focal point is set on the eyes so that no blurring occurs there.

Displace

Displace will allow you to use your finger to shift the aberration horizontally or vertically.

Blur controls the amount of blur applied to the chromatic aberration from 0–100%.

Transparency controls how opaque the chromatic aberration is; 0% means no transparency while 100% means fully transparent.

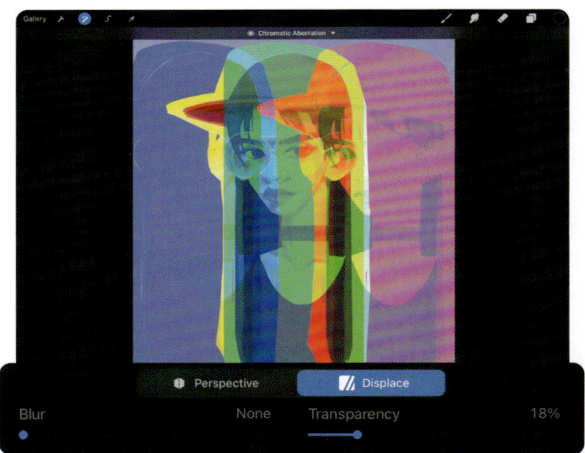

Chromatic aberration applied with blur set to 0% and transparency at 18%.

Layering Effects

You can apply more than one effect to a single layer. You can also apply effects to multiple layers and use masks to hide or reveal certain parts of the effect.

For example, I've used a total of three effects on my painting.

1. I created three composite layers.
2. On one I applied Noise, another Gaussian Blur, and on the last layer I applied Chromatic Aberration.
3. The Noise layer was my new base layer. I only applied a *Mask* to Gaussian Blur and Chromatic Aberration. I painted with black on the masks to conceal the effects near the face.

This is just one example of layering effects. Play around and experiment with different ones to find out what you like!

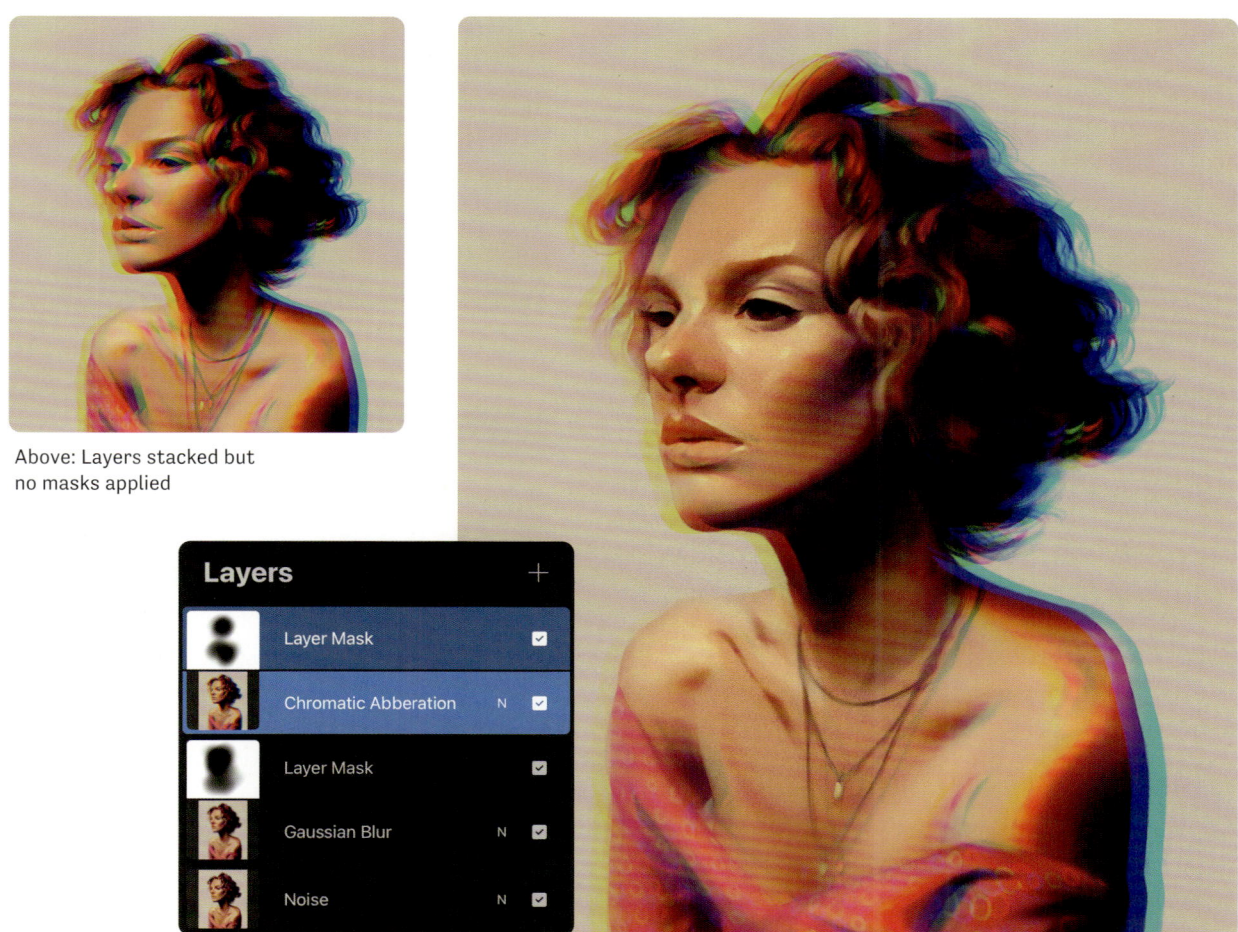

Above: Layers stacked but no masks applied

SHARE YOUR WORK

Congrats, you're officially done! To share your work in any capacity, you'll have to export it and save it outside the Procreate app.

Share an Image

Actions > Share > Choose your file type (JPEG, PNG, etc.) > Choose where you would like to send your file*

* I recommend *Save Image*, which will download your artwork to the Photos app on your iPad. If Photos syncs with iCloud, then you'll be able to access your artwork on your other Apple devices as well.

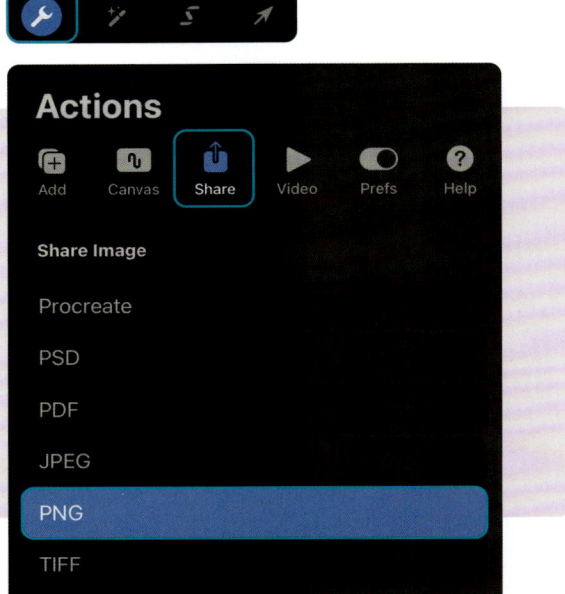

Share a Video

Preview Your Time-Lapse

To preview your video before you export it, go to:

Actions > Video > Time-lapse Replay

Use your finger to scrub the timeline. Slide right to fast-forward through the video and left to rewind.

Save the Video

To export the video of your painting from start to finish:

Actions > Video > Export time-lapse video > Choose the length you want to export, wait a moment for the video to render, and then choose where you would like to send your file

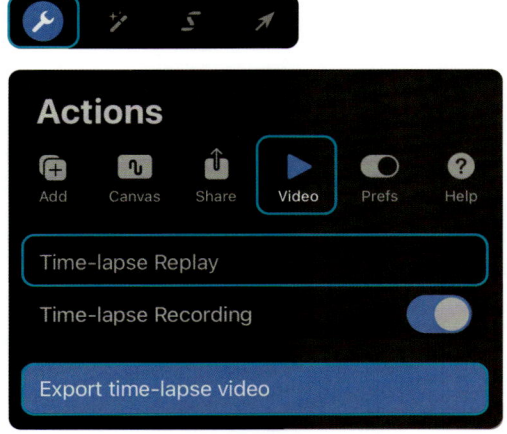

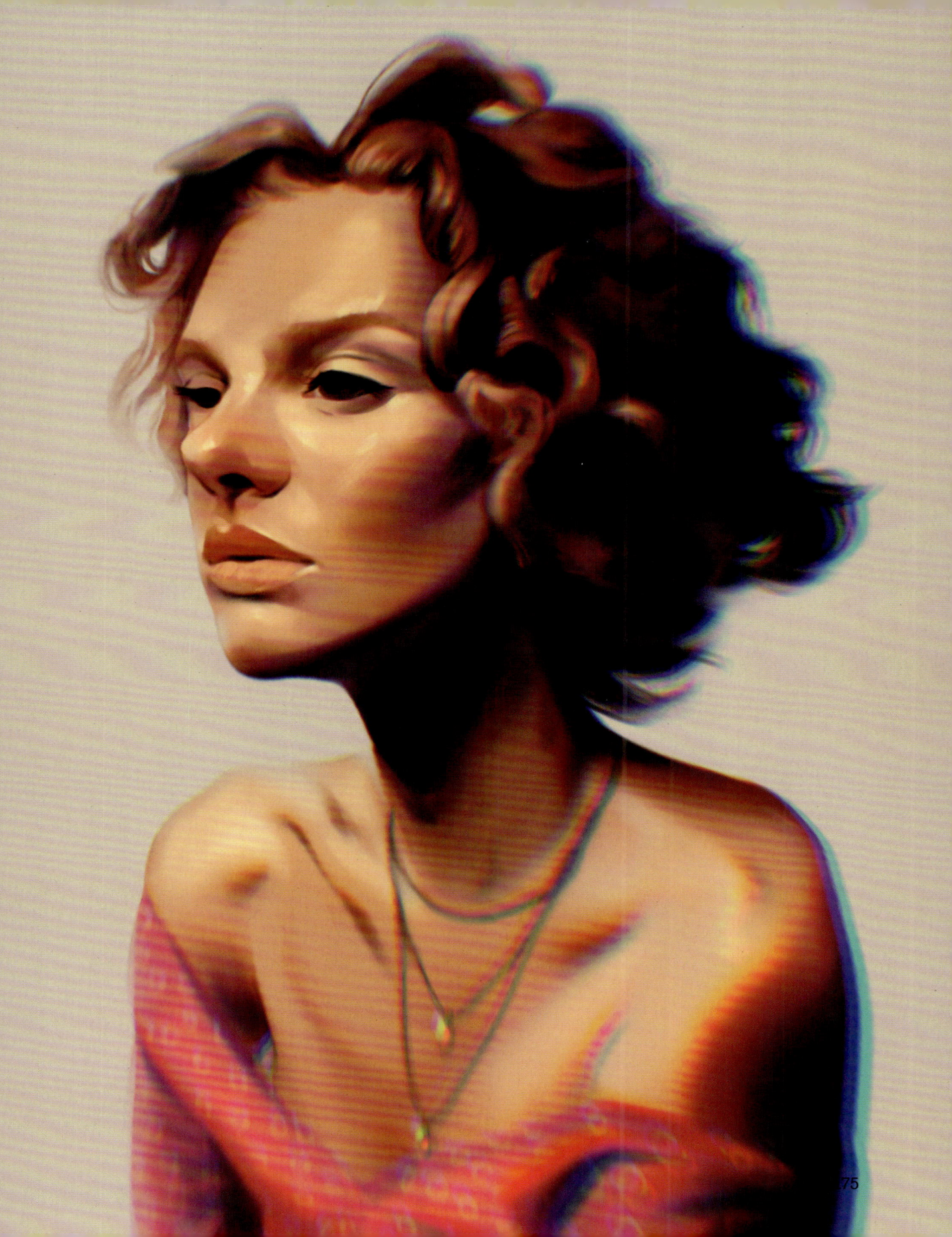

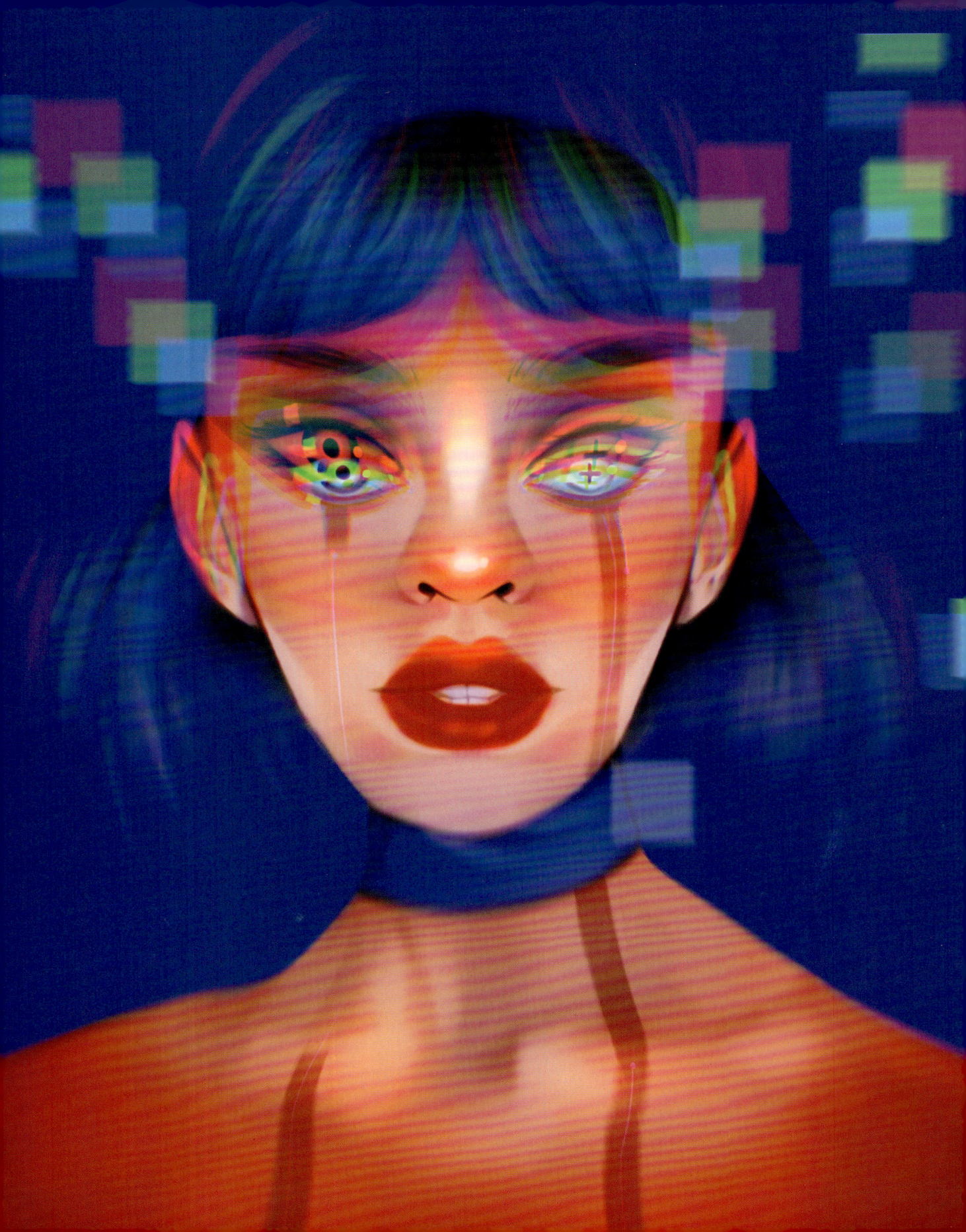

Artwork
BREAKDOWN

A collection of various artwork broken down step-by-step.

I mentioned earlier that there are a million different ways to approach a painting. Some people sketch first while others jump straight into it. For this gallery, I've chosen a variety of pieces that I hope will show you that there's no right or wrong way to approach making artwork. Although there are beginner-friendly methods to painting a picture, you don't have to adhere so strictly to a single process—and it's probably best if you don't.

One of the best things you can do for yourself as an artist is to spend some time discovering your own process.

By jumping straight into a painting (and creating a mess), you may discover that it really benefits you to sketch your subject first.

Don't be afraid to fail.

Each piece will teach you something new that you can apply to another creation.

SYMMETRY

Turn on the *Drawing Guide* to quickly and easily make a full face portrait.

There's something quite enjoyable about using Procreate's *Symmetry Drawing Guide*. When using it, you only need to focus on drawing half of the portrait!

Something to bear in mind when creating these types of portraits is that they can become stale. Perfect symmetry doesn't give our brains much stimulation—there's no special little detail to catch our eye and hold our attention.

To make my portraits more interesting, I turn off the guide sometime after my initial sketch. I continue to turn it on and off during the entire painting process—*on* when I want things like the eyes to be aligned and symmetrical, and *off* when I want to add small details like highlights, beauty marks, or reflections. The subtle asymmetry that this creates is already a lot more interesting.

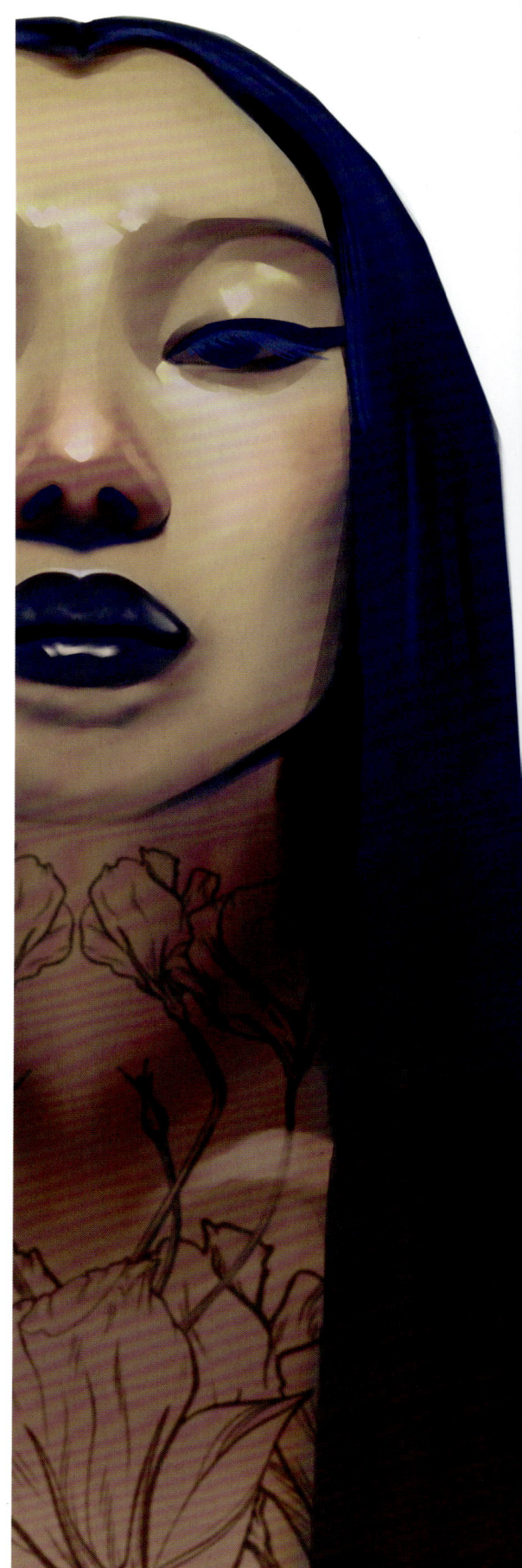

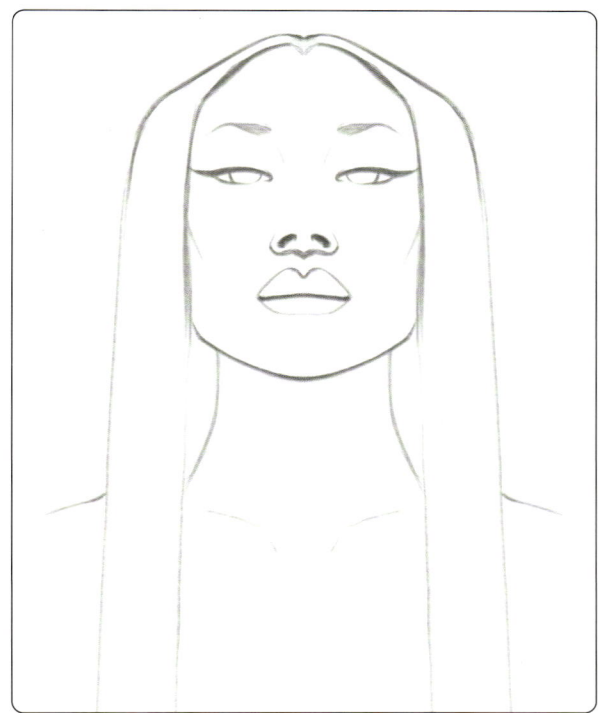

Initial sketch

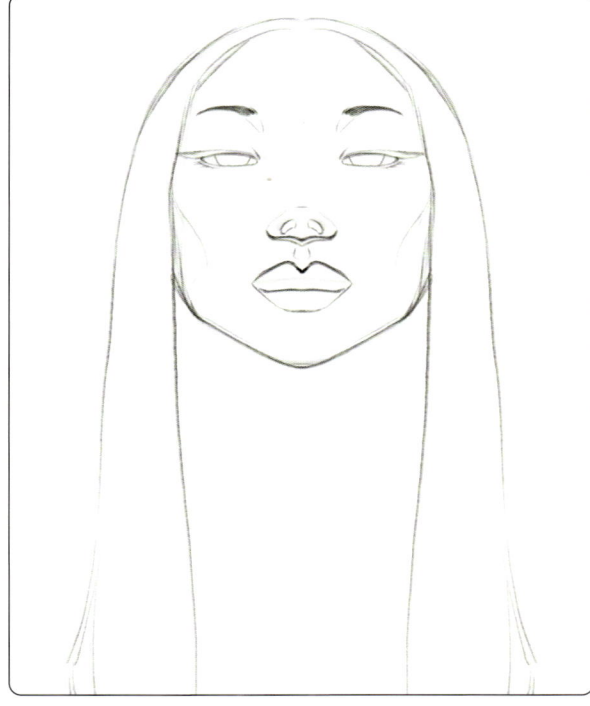

Initial sketch at 10% opacity with new sketch layer on top

Sketching

I turned on the Symmetry Drawing Guide by going to:

Actions > Canvas > Toggle Drawing Guide On >
Edit Drawing Guide > Symmetry

After setting the color and thickness of my guide, I did two different sketches. By default, a new layer will not have the guide applied. Whenever I sketched on a new layer, I would have to manually apply it:

Tap the layer thumbnail > Select "Drawing Assist" from the menu

It usually takes me a couple of sketches to feel comfortable before proceeding to painting. My first sketch is usually the messiest, ugliest, or most rigid version. After I get the first one out of the way, I try not to look at my reference photo so much and instead play around with exaggeration, stylization, or accuracy.

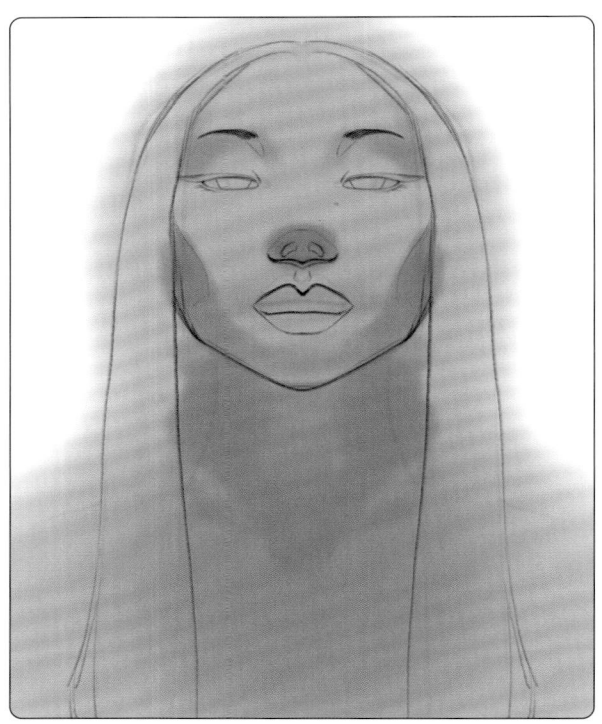

Creating a Base and Value Painting

I created another guided layer underneath my sketches and filled it with very light base values.

I then created another layer on top of my sketches and began painting in the darker values. Everything is symmetrical at this point—I'm leaning heavily on the guides and I haven't turned them off yet.

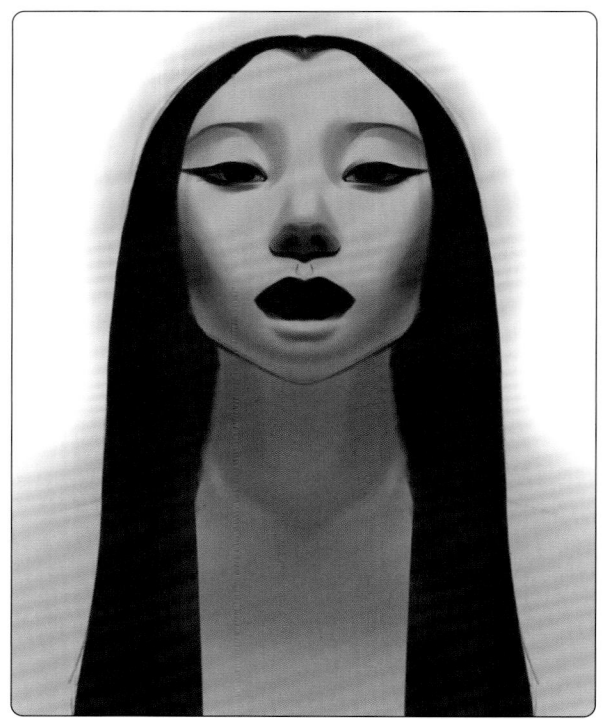

First pass of darker values

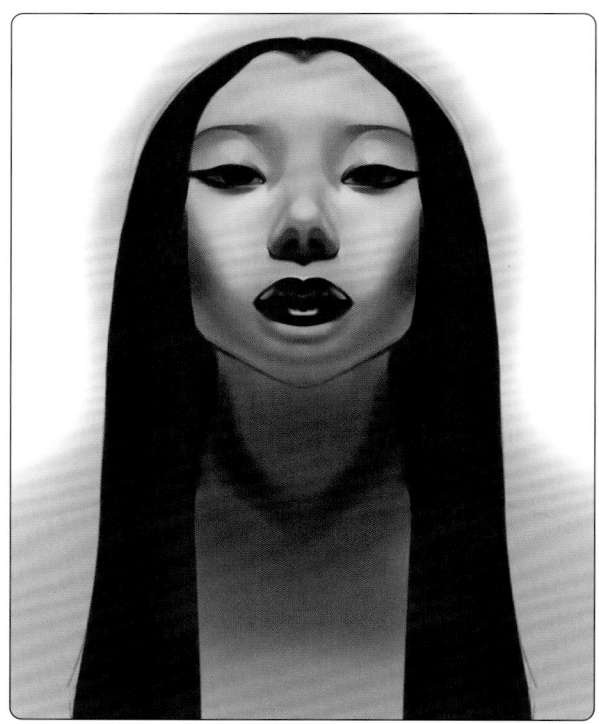

Adding highlights and beginning to render the face a bit

Adding Color

Once I had a decent value painting, I switched into color mode. The body is practically missing at this point but I was confident I'd be able to render that in color anyway, so I moved on with choosing my hues.

I used *Gradient Map* to apply a greenish color to the entirety of the value painting. Honestly, this isn't typically a hue I'd choose for a base, but I wanted to see if I could make it work.

My reference image was in black and white and in my mind, I wanted to work with deep blues and purples wherever there was black. To add life into the portrait and make sure it didn't end up looking too ghostly with all the cool tones, I made the skin nice and peachy. This complements the blues in the hair nicely. I used both *Color* and *Soft Light* to apply those colors.

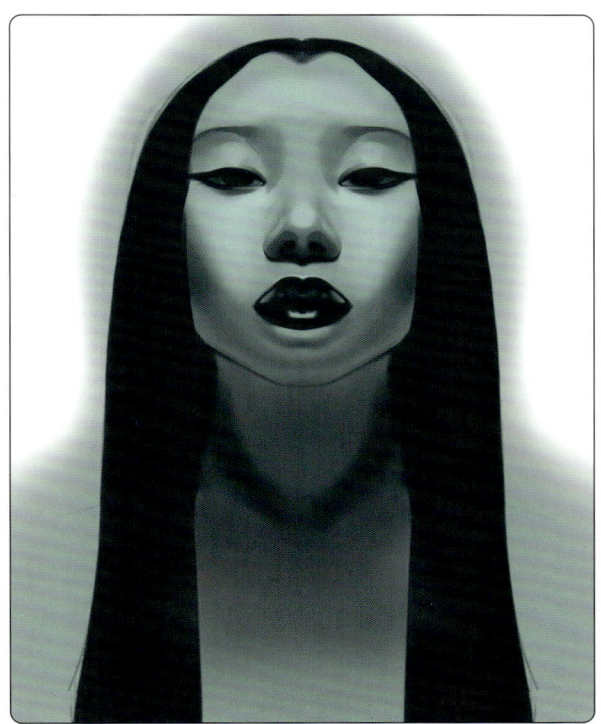

Gradient Map replaces all instances of grey with a green color

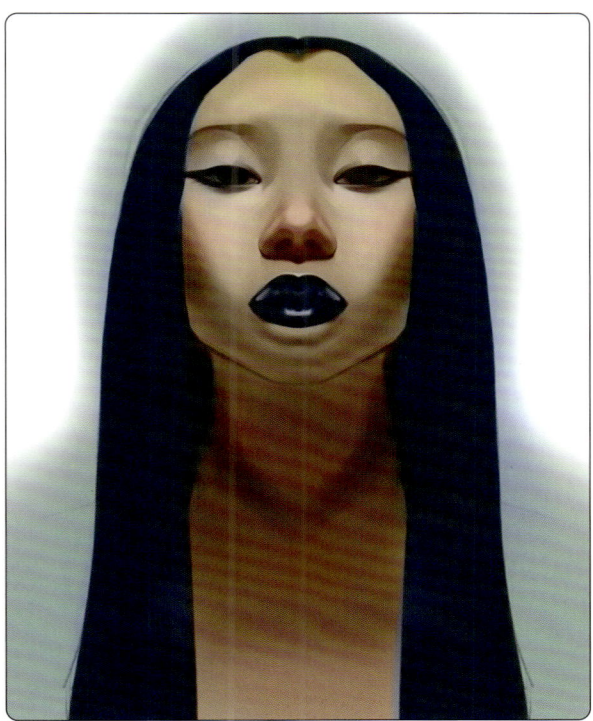

Color and *Soft Light* are used to apply the colors over the top of the value painting

Testing Asymmetry

This is the point at which I turned off *Drawing Assist*. The first thing
I tested was eyelashes on the model. I then started adding brighter
highlights. Notice that the highlights on the eyelids are different shapes.
Even the one in the middle of the brow ridge varies. I brought some of
this asymmetry into the highlights on the glossy lips and in the blush of
the cheeks. I really just started painting here and there, fixing things I
thought looked too perfect.

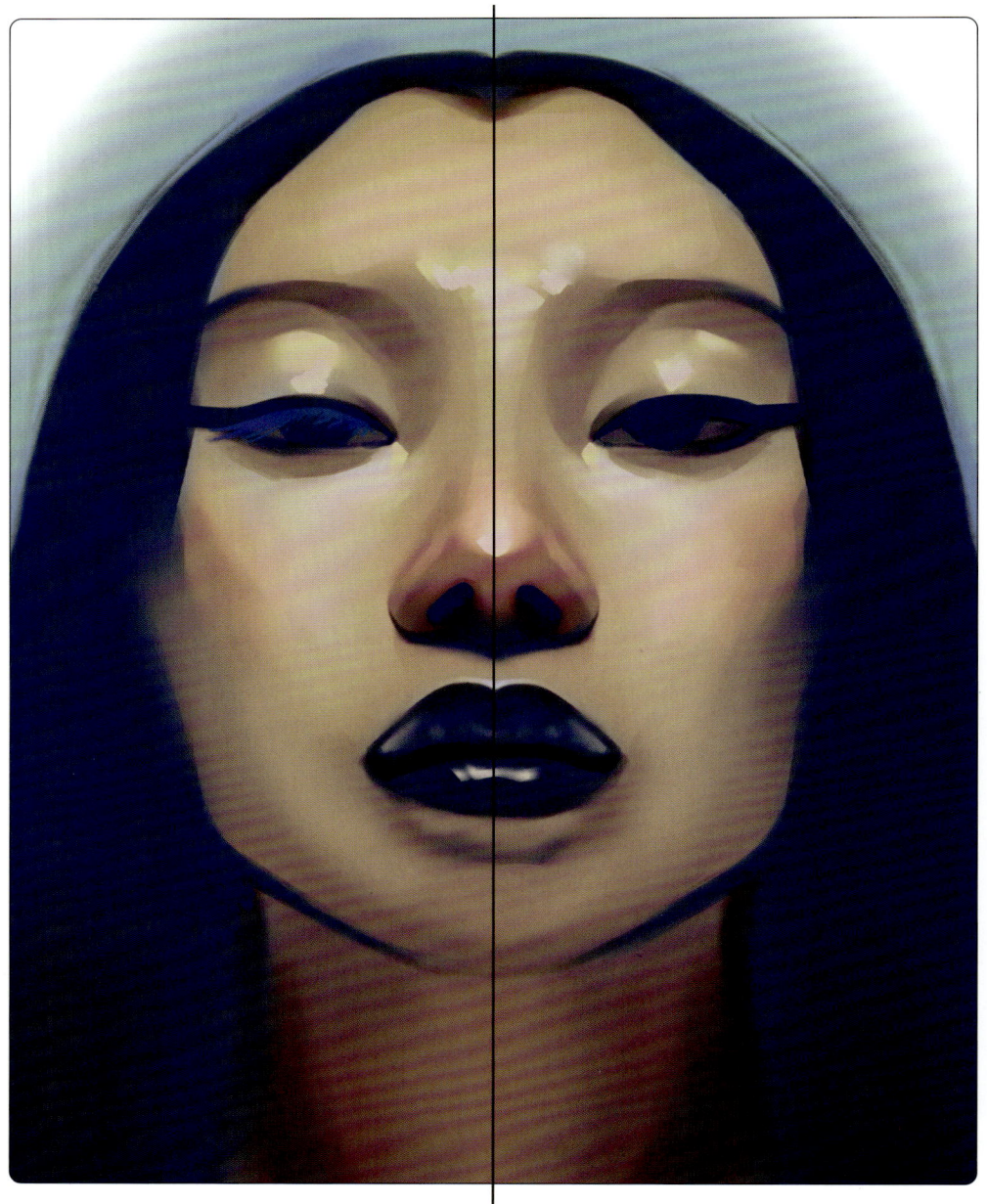

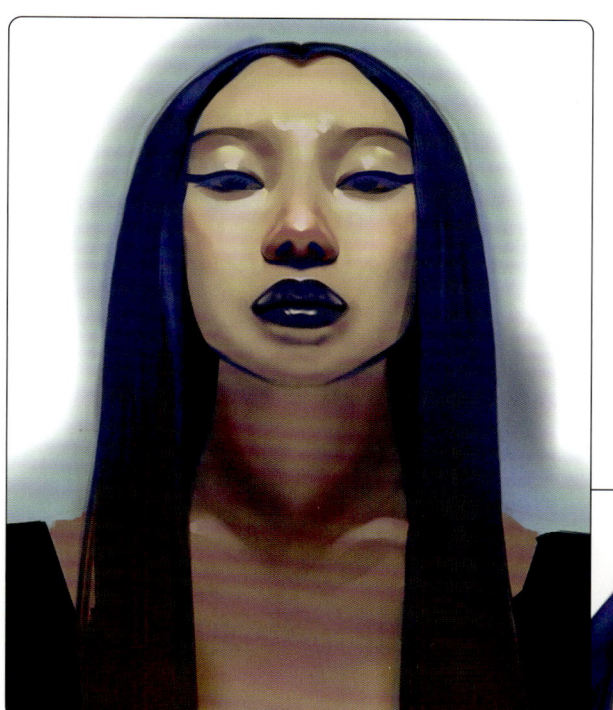

Happy with the way things were going, I continued rendering. I refined the hair, gave her eyelashes on both eyes, and cleaned up the halo of color around her head.

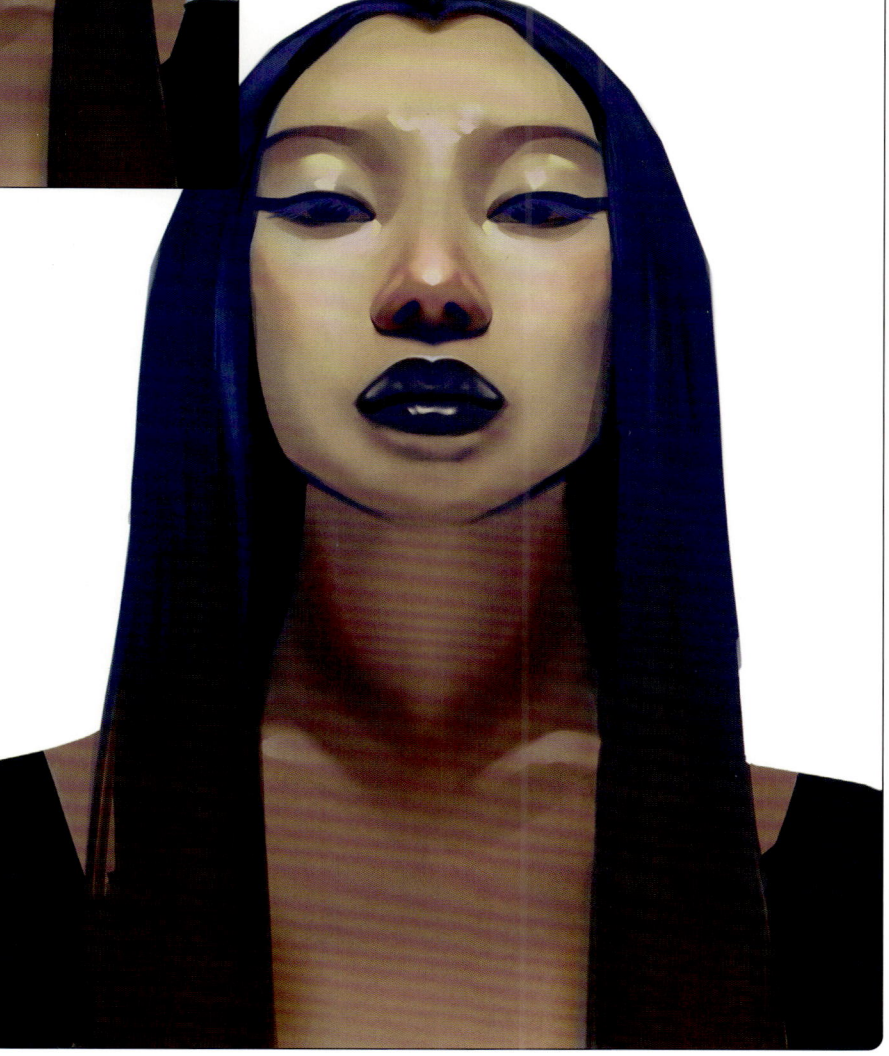

Adding Tattoos

Although my reference didn't have any tattoos, I wanted to add them in for fun. The neck and chest were so prominent, I couldn't let them go to waste!

To create the tattoo, I loosely mocked up where I wanted it to go on her neck. From there, I drew the floral pattern on a new layer, pretending that my painting underneath didn't exist. I wasn't trying to draw the tattoo onto the body because I knew I was going to use *Warp* to properly place the tattoo or her instead.

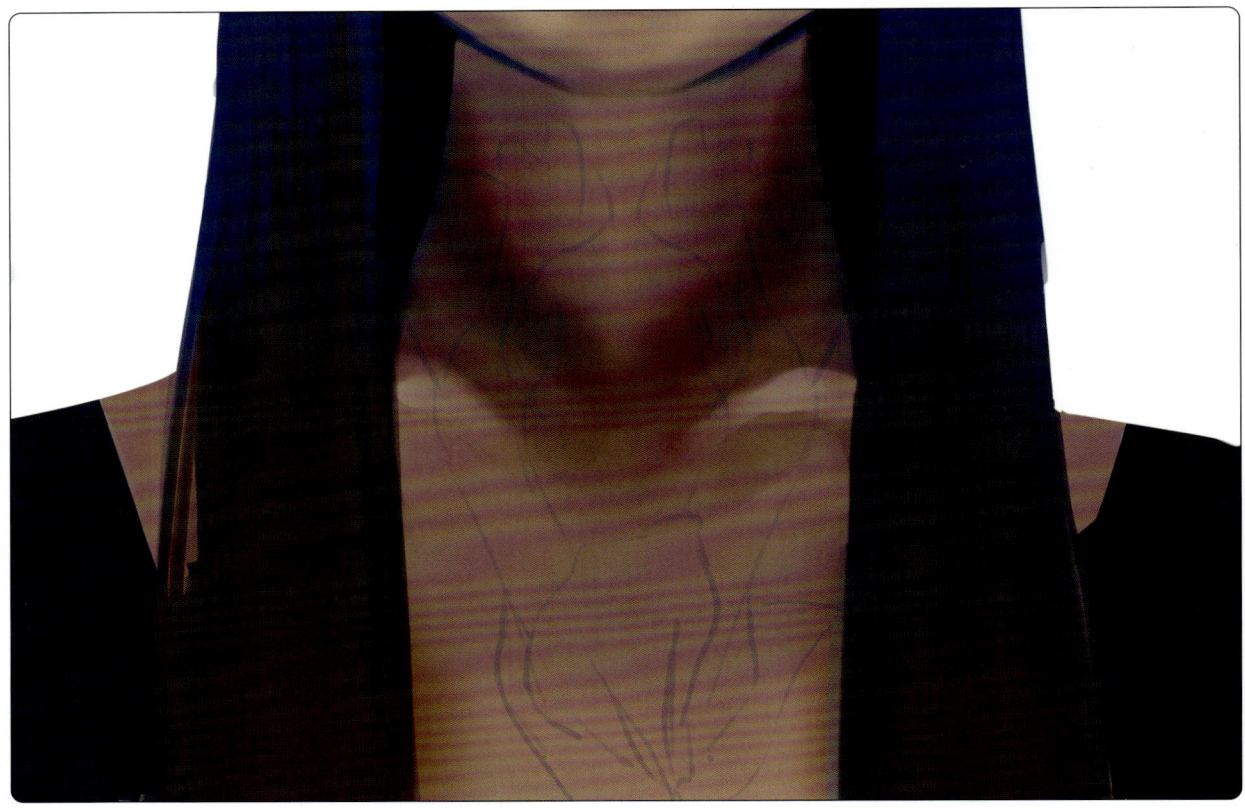

I focused on drawing the tattoo. To make sure my lines were clean, I turned on *Stabilization*.

<mark>Actions > Prefs > Pressure and Smoothing</mark>

On a new layer, I drew the floral pattern in black. I didn't worry about perspective or wrapping the tattoo around her neck. I just focused on the tattoo itself.

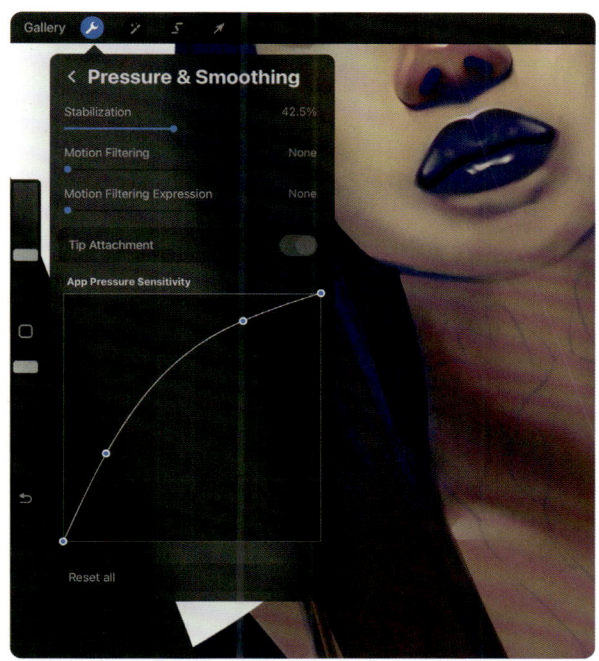

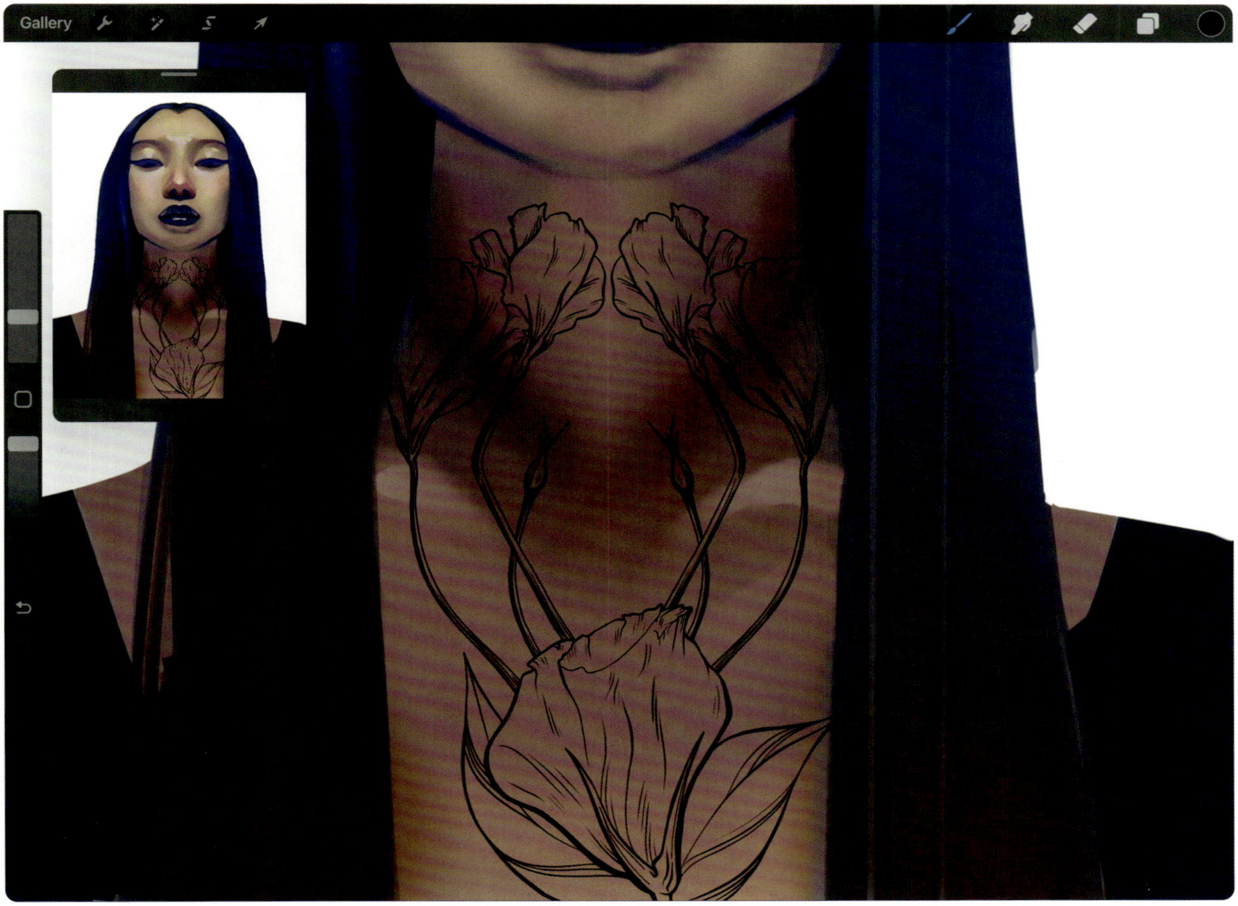

Once I was happy with my tattoo, I used the transform tool to wrap the tattoo around her neck.

Transform > Warp

Pull the nodes in the corners to manipulate the shape of the tattoo. You can also grab any of the grid lines and move them around (horizontally or vertically) to bend the tattoo.

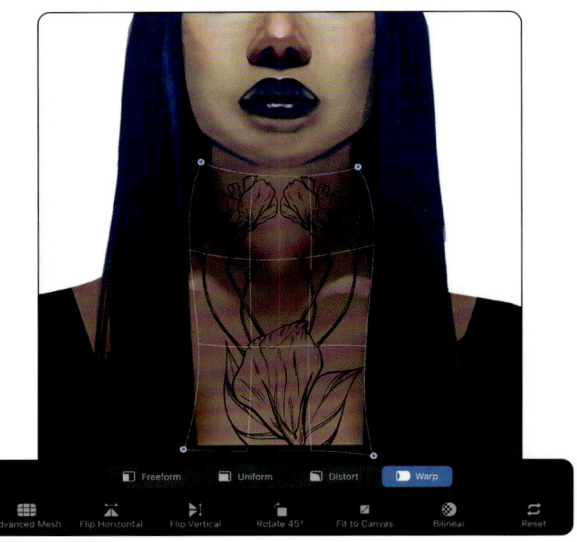

After the manipulation, my tattoo extended beyond the skin. I used a mask to hide the parts of the tattoo that went into the hair. I also turned the tattoo's blend mode to *Multiply* and applied a bit of *Gaussian Blur* so that it wasn't so crisp.

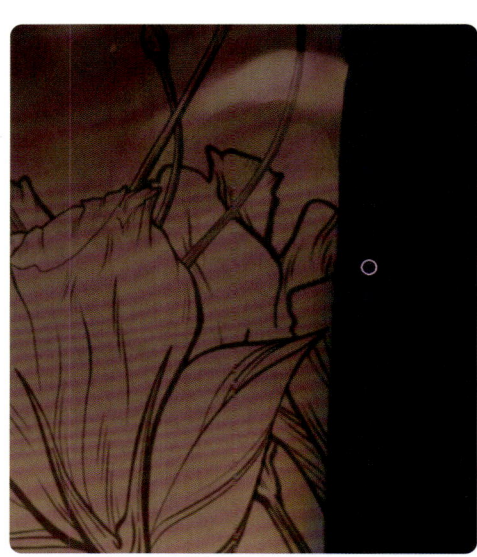

Before applying a mask

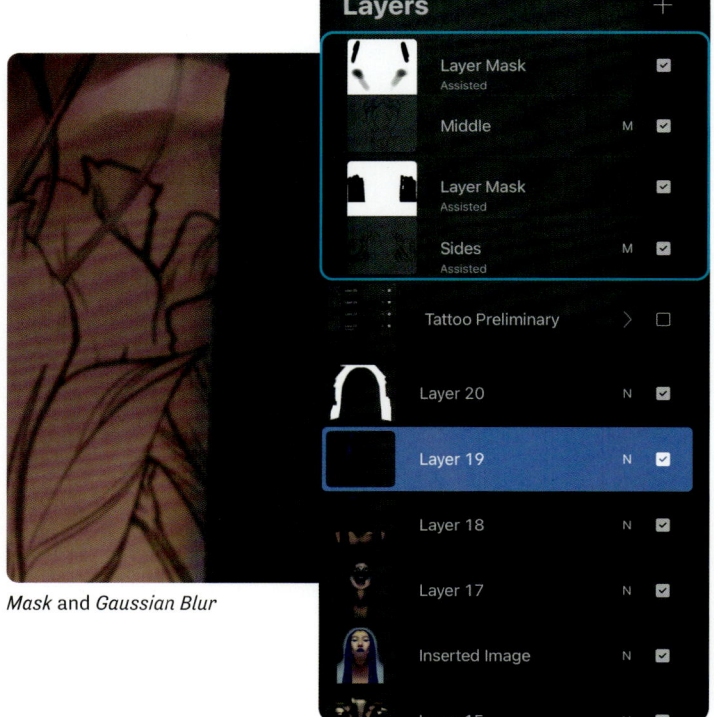

Mask and *Gaussian Blur*

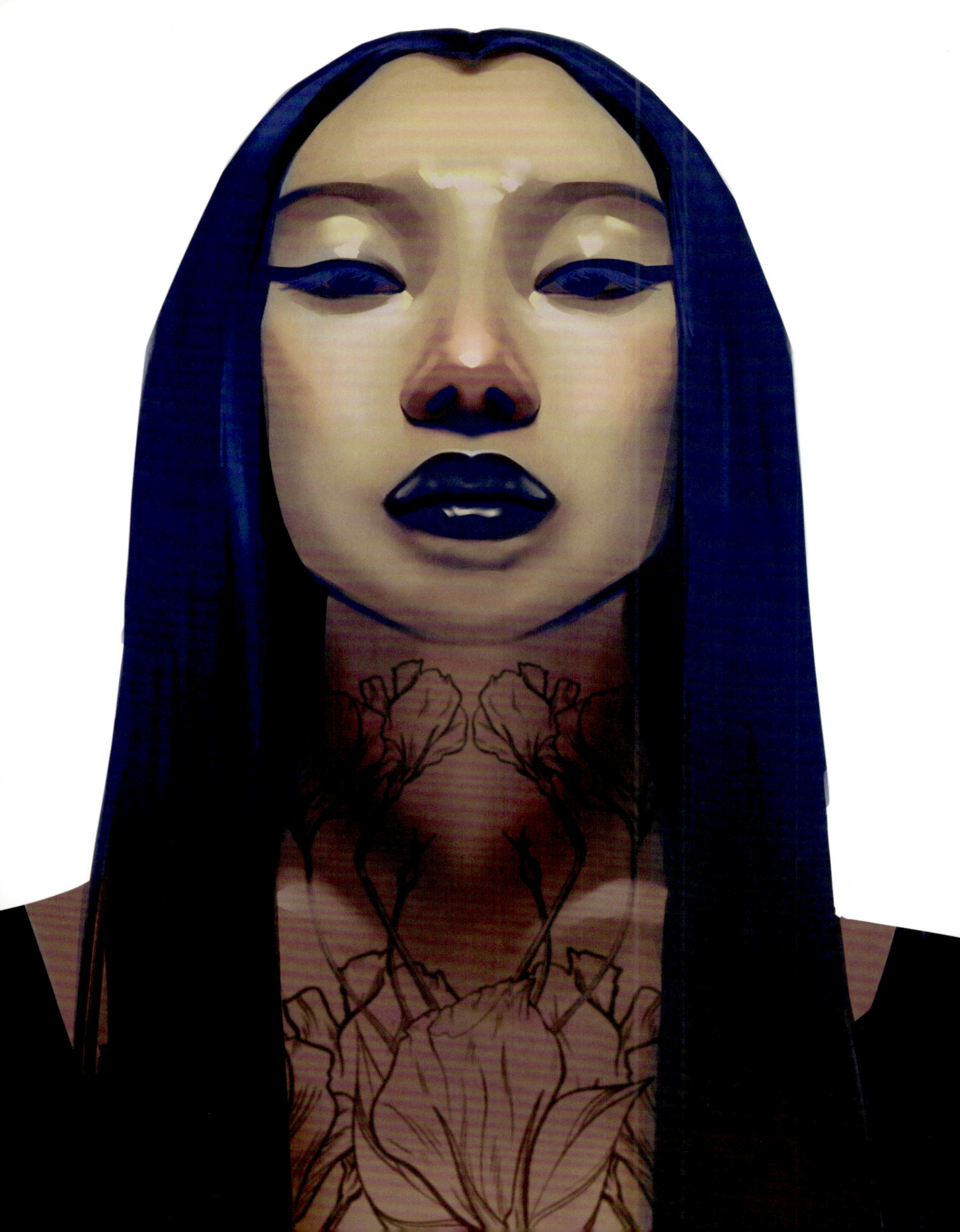

DRAWING IN A DIGITAL SKETCHBOOK

Turn your iPad into a portable sketchbook by adding a background paper texture and sticking to pencil and pen brushes.

I basically used just one brush for this piece—the Mechanical Pencil from The Comics MaxPack (a third-party brush maker). If you don't want to buy any brushes, you can certainly find an assortment of pencil brushes in Procreate's Brush Library. Try the Sketching brush set or the Charcoal set!

When I used to sketch in an actual sketchbook (this rarely happens anymore), I would use mechanical pencils, HB, or red animation pencils. Using brushes like these, limiting the number of layers I use, and adding a paper texture really make it feel like the good old days.

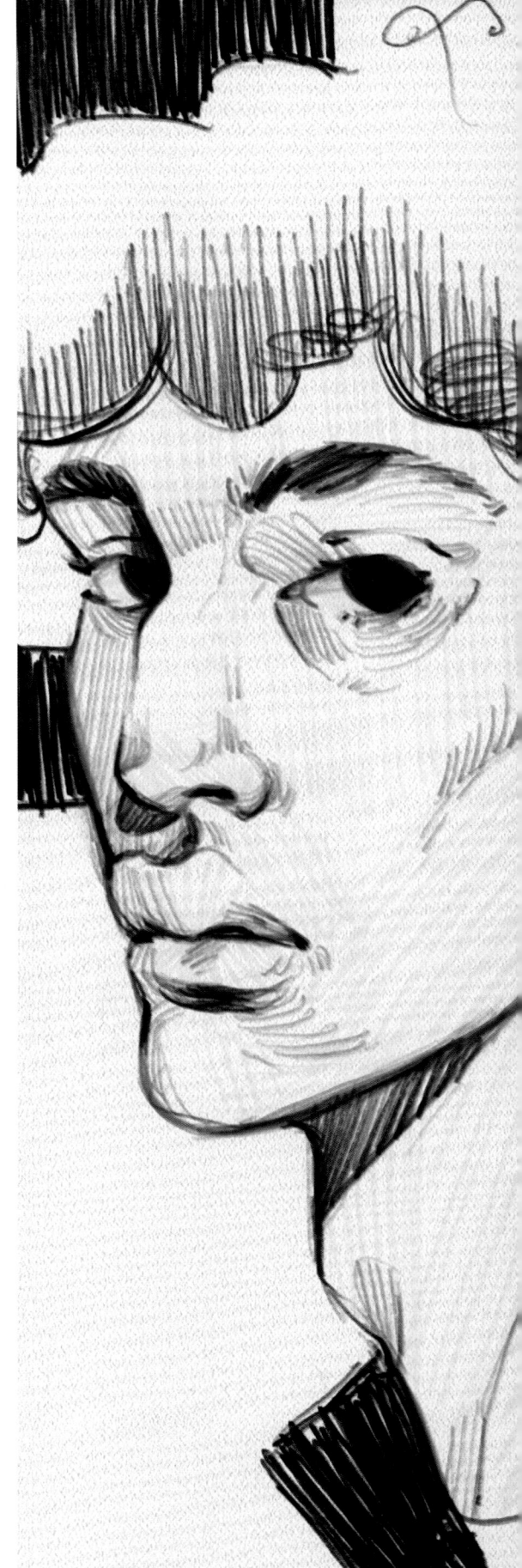

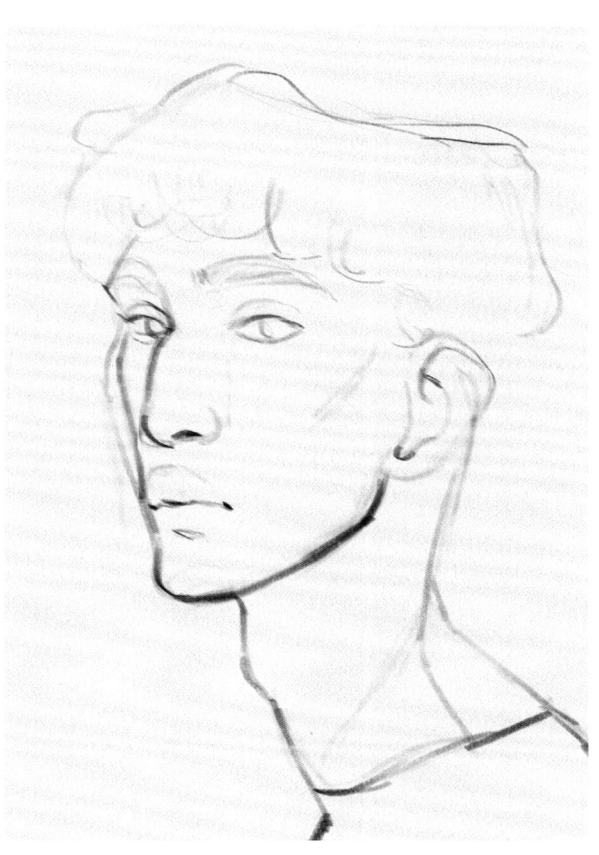

Initial Sketches

I started with a loose, gestural sketch. All I wanted to do here was map out the head, features, and neck so that I could get to the tonal work.

I used the Selection tool quite a bit to move pieces into place as my first stab at sketching the model was a bit inaccurate—I had to shift the brow and eye, move the nose up, and shrink the ear a bit.

Once I was happy with the sketch, I turned down the opacity, created a new layer, and sketched the model again using my previous drawing as a guide.

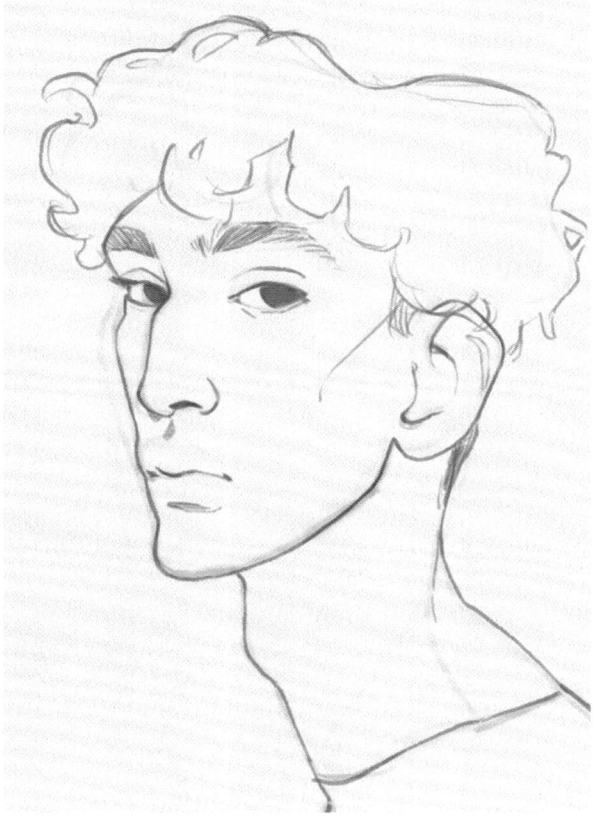

Building Tone

I chose a mid-grey color and began filling in the
shadowed side of the face. I continued this way,
building up the tone while knowing that I would
add in black later.

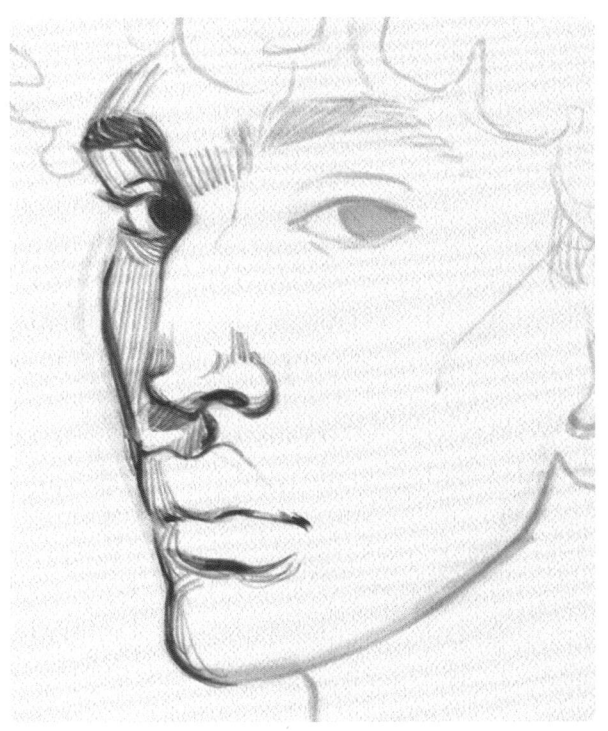

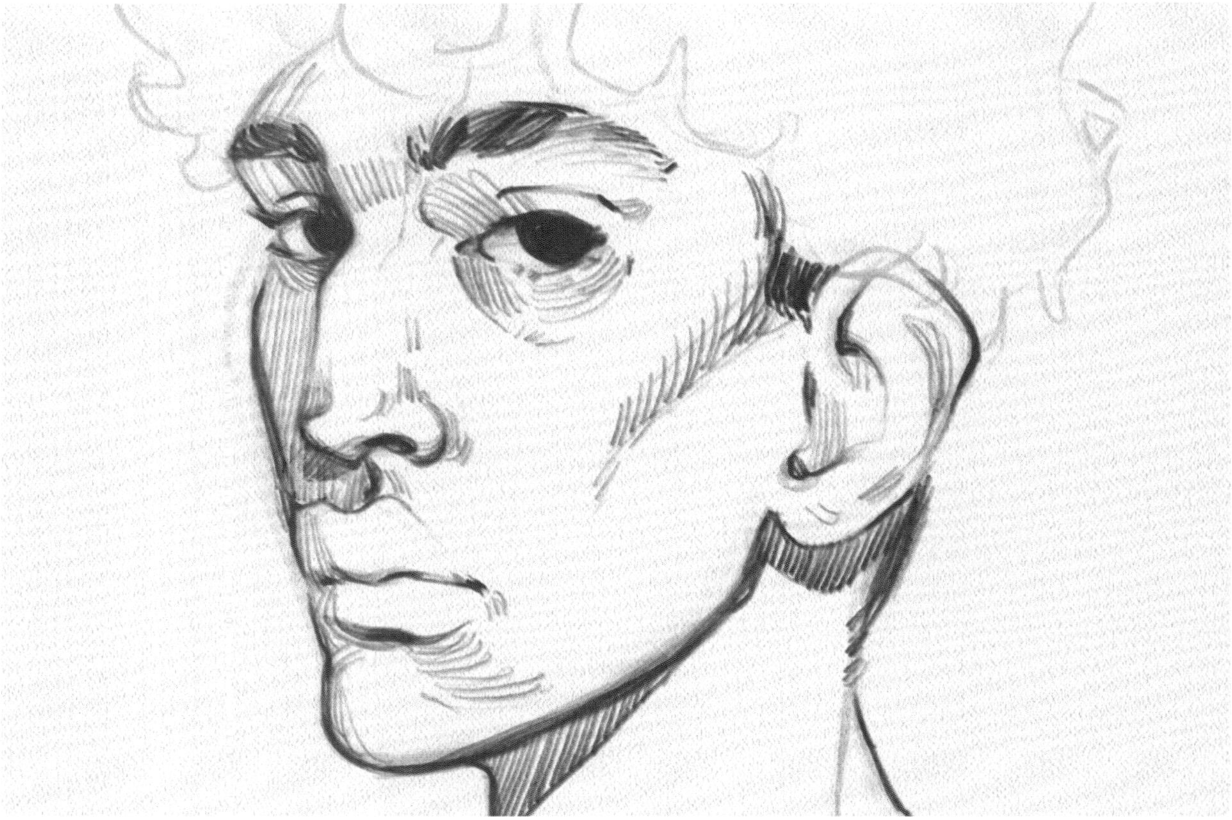

When making my marks, I bounced between following the form of the structure and using straight or parallel lines. This is purely personal preference. When I wanted the drawing to feel more dimensional, I used curved lines to showcase the form. Otherwise, I stuck to straight lines.

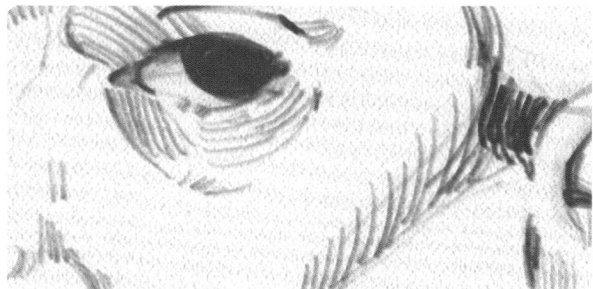

Curved lines around the eyes and cheek

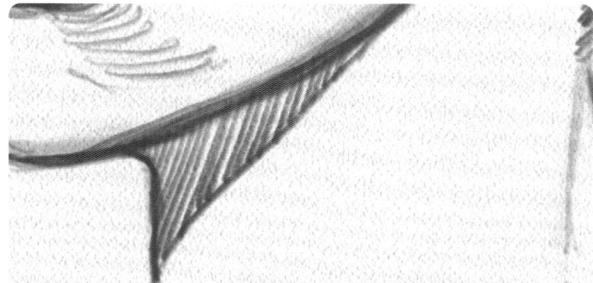

Straight, diagonal lines for the shadow on the neck

Next, I switched to pure black and went over the areas I thought could use more of a punch. That included the eyes, the brows, the nostril, and all of the shadows.

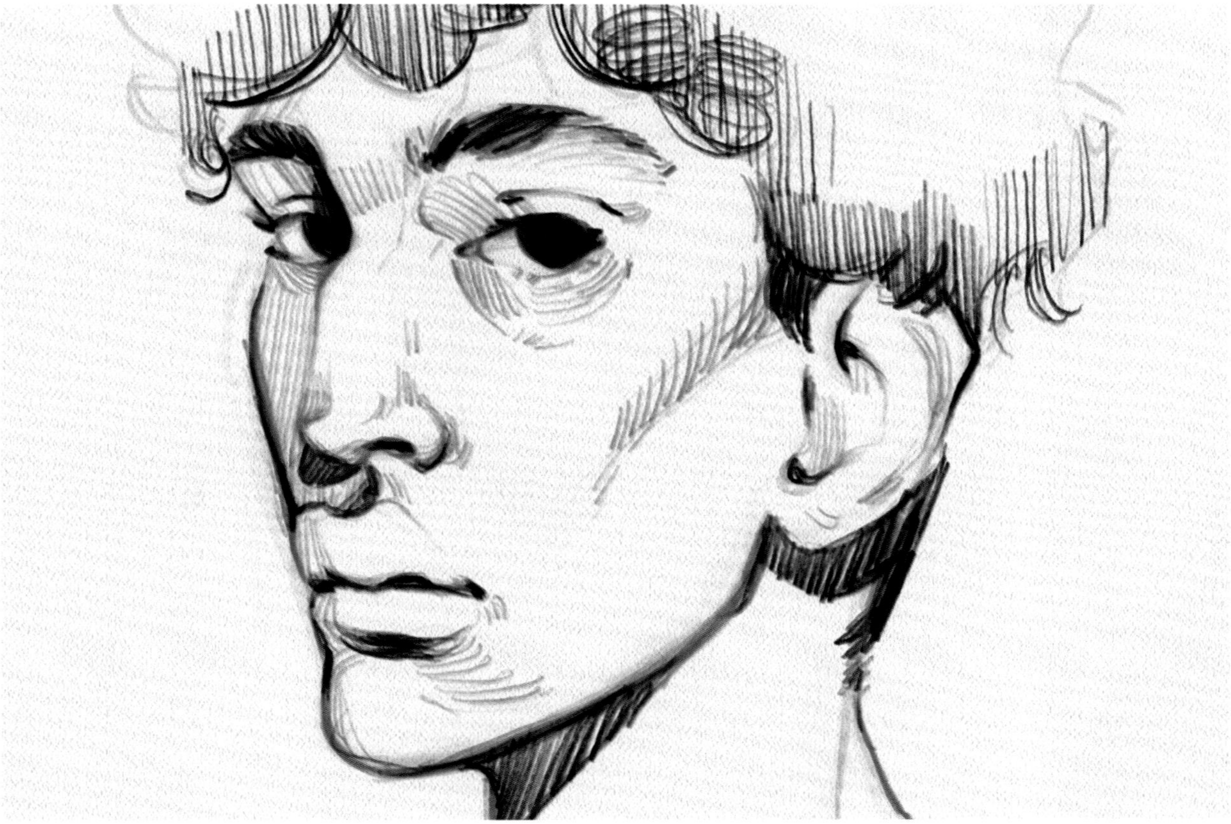

Finishing Touches

I thought the drawing itself looked pretty plain and I wanted to add something in that could help my subject stand out from the background.

I decided to play around with geometric shapes and at this point, I really was just playing around.

Because I was using black, which is so high in contrast against the paper, there was the potential for the shapes to take focus away from the subject. I experimented for a while with the placement and size of the shapes until I felt the image looked balanced.

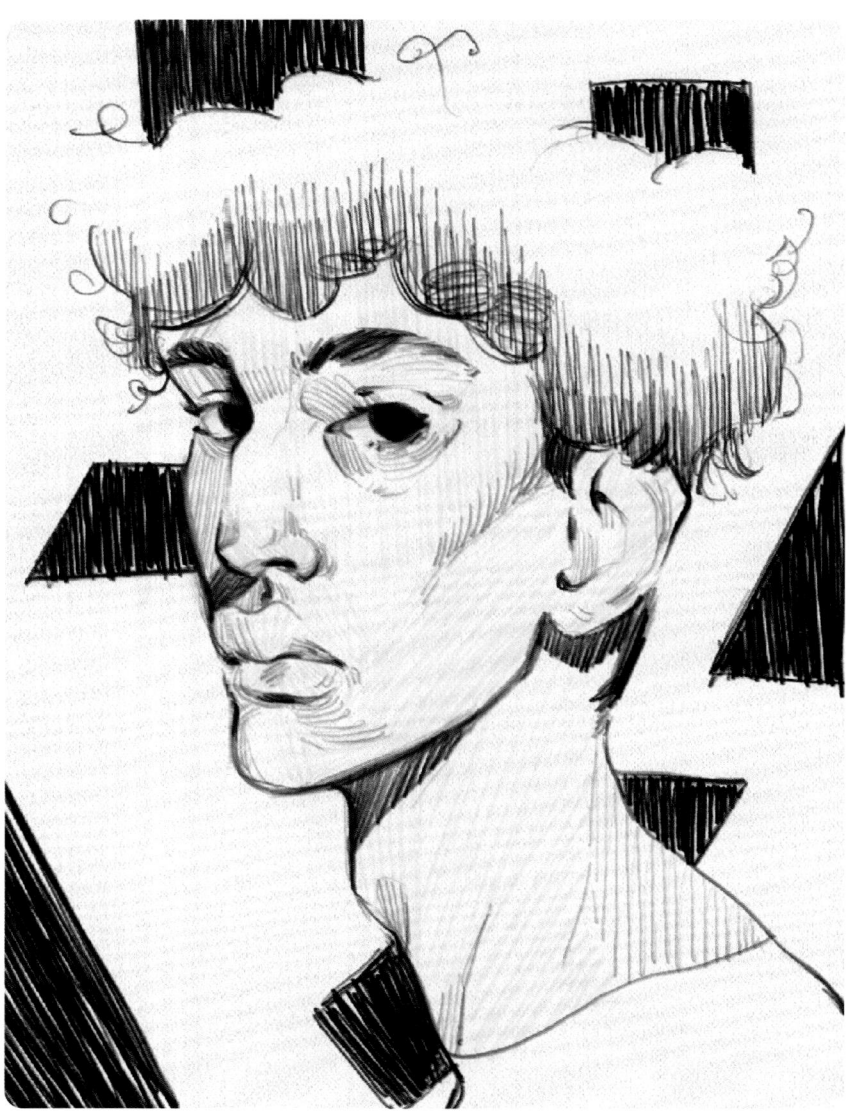

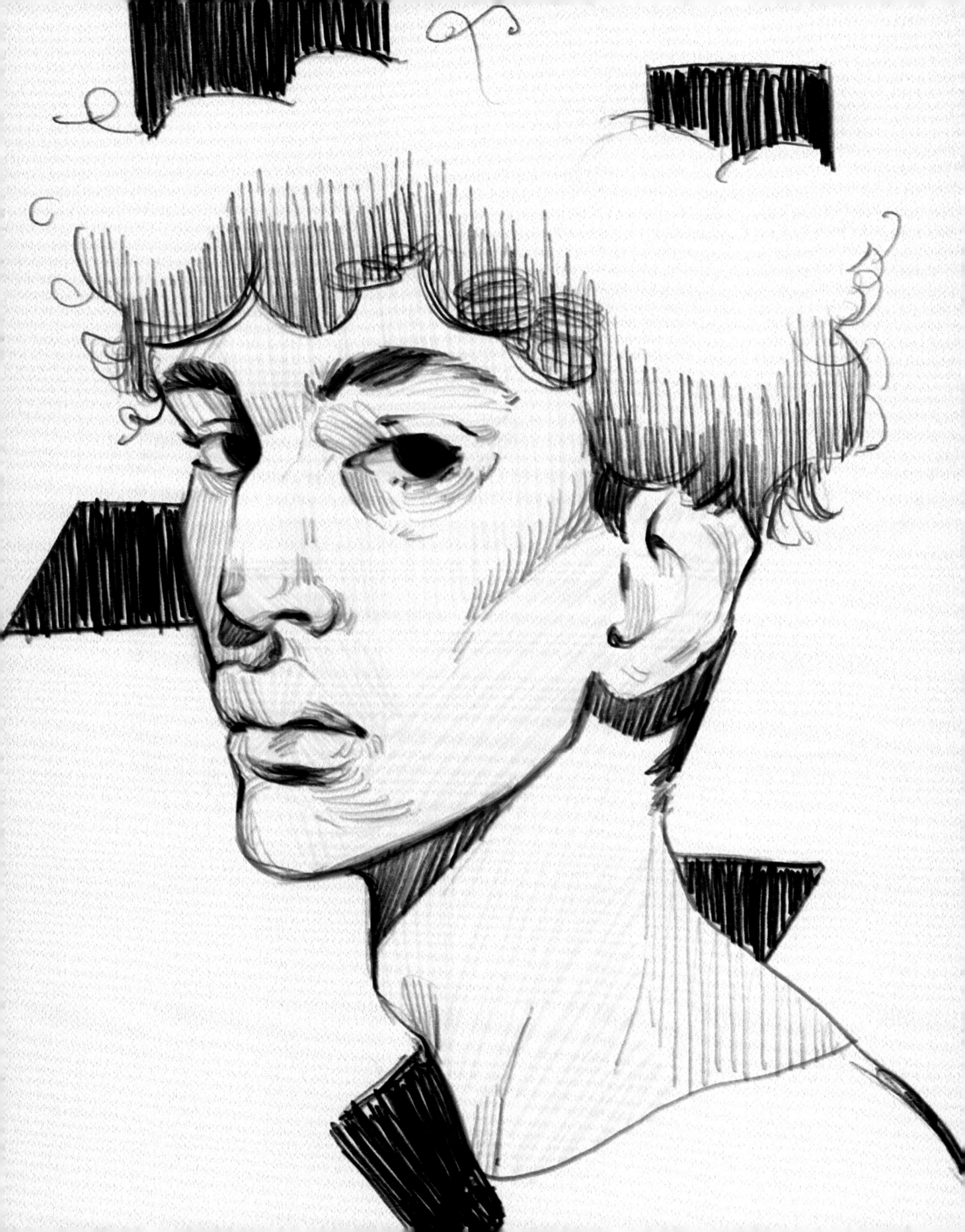

BLACK AND WHITE

Contrast becomes extremely important when painting in just black and white. The use of values will dictate how successful a painting is.

Admittedly, I didn't go into this painting with a plan. I was in one of those moods where all I wanted to do was slosh some digital paint around on the canvas. I felt impatient and stubborn, and I was low-key worried this portrait was going to be a total bust.

As time went on and the painting started to take shape, I gained confidence. I started to loosen up a bit and have fun—the impatience subsided and I began taking my time.

Sometimes we artists can show up to a painting charged with emotion or a state of being that isn't really helpful to the creative process. It's not the best way to start any kind of work, but sometimes showing up anyway is all you need to do, and the rest will kind of work itself out.

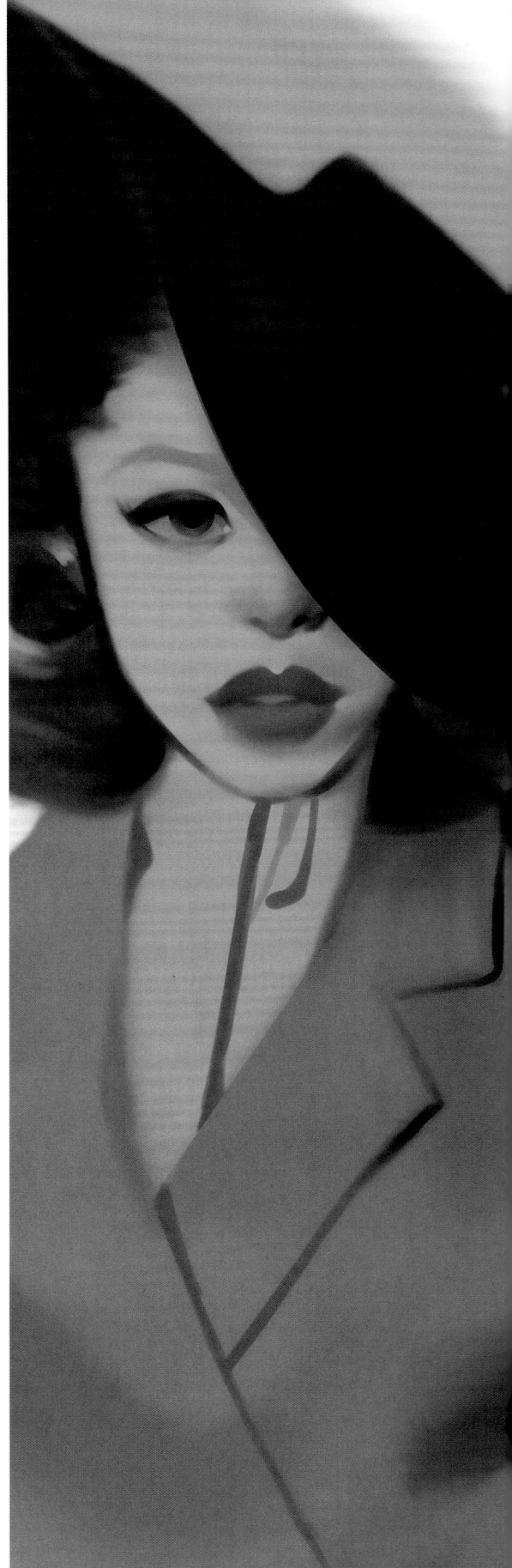

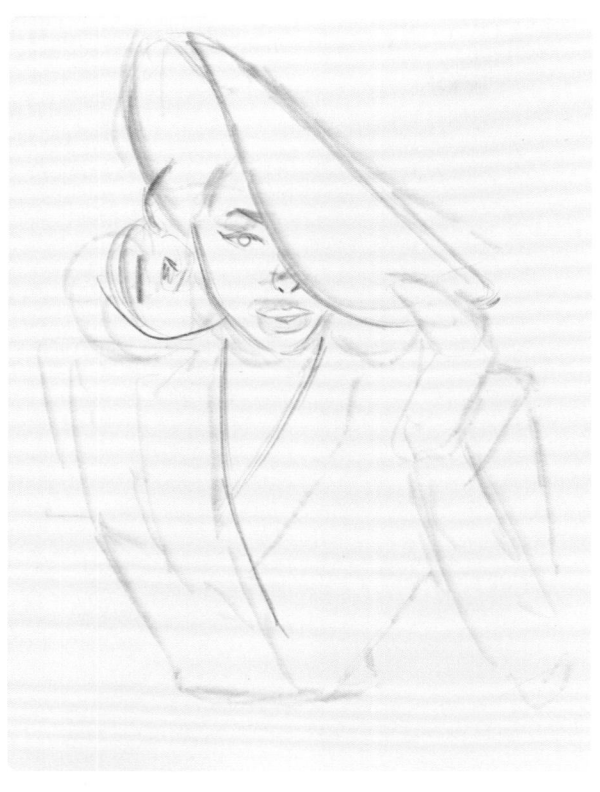

Sketching and Exploration

I took a couple minutes to come up with a very loose sketch. So loose, in fact, that the placement of the nose and mouth were quite a bit off. Although the purpose of sketching is usually to come up with a good foundation, I really just wanted to skip this part, and I decided that having a chance to warm up a bit was enough—I'd do the real work and worry about accuracy when I actually started painting.

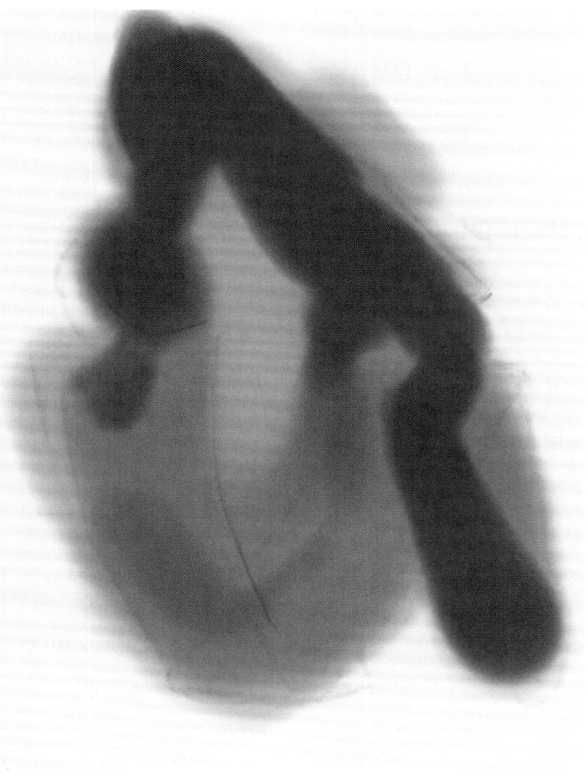

Anxious to lay down some pigment, I switched to my big fat airbrush and started painting in some base values. I painted right over my sketch, with no worries at all because I was never precious about it to begin with!

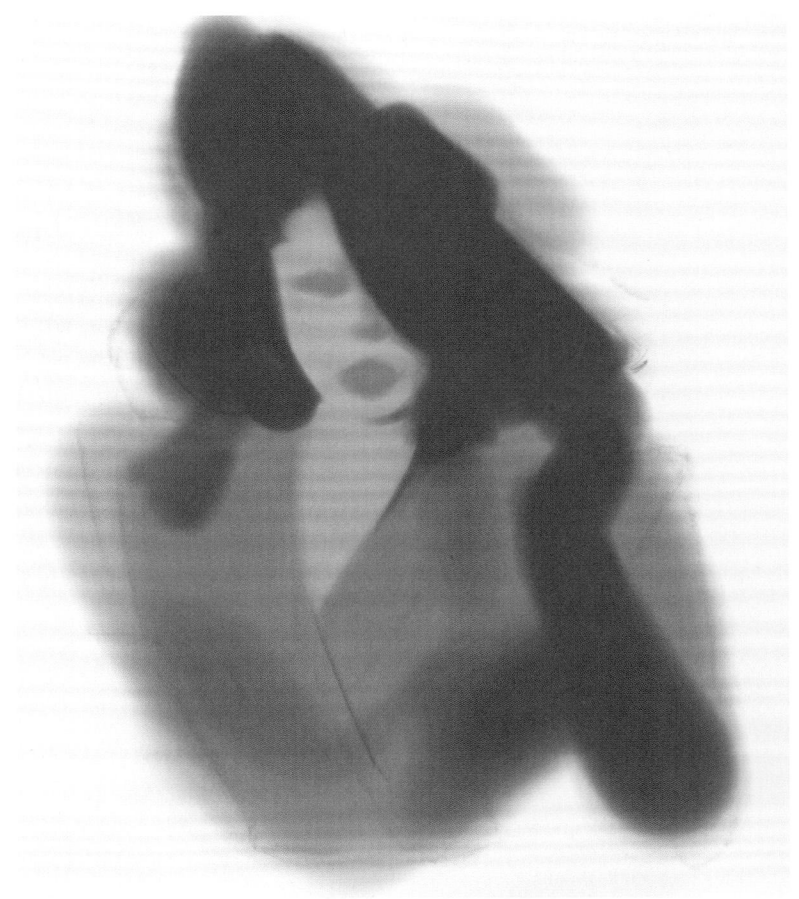

I then went in with my soft round brush to block in the placement of the model's facial features. I didn't draw anything in using outlines, but instead I blocked in the shapes that I saw—an upside-down triangle for the nose, a teardrop shape for the eye, and a pinched oval where the lips would be. This technique is a lot more akin to sculpting than to drawing.

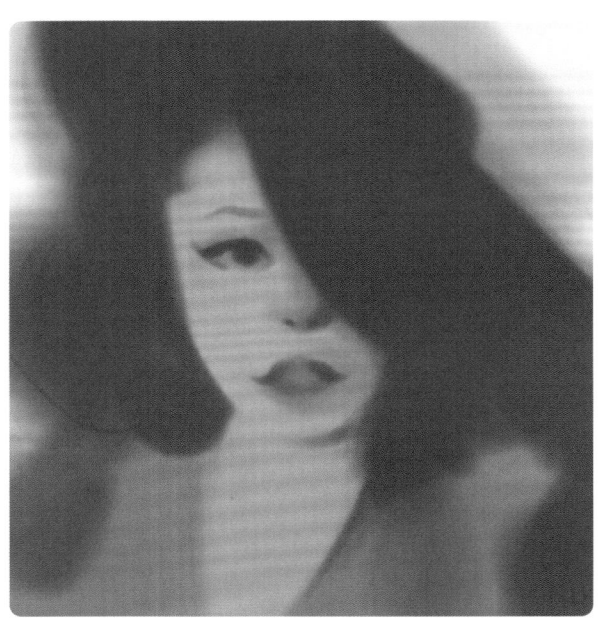

Finding My Way

Once I was happy with the placement and shapes of the facial features, I shrunk my brush down, changed the value to something a bit darker, and started to work in details like the eyebrows and nostrils.

I hadn't picked a super dark value at this point because I was "finding" my way through the painting. When I was happy with what I was seeing, I knew I could go in and pump up the contrast. Until then, I wanted to keep things light so that they'd be easier to wipe out and redo as needed.

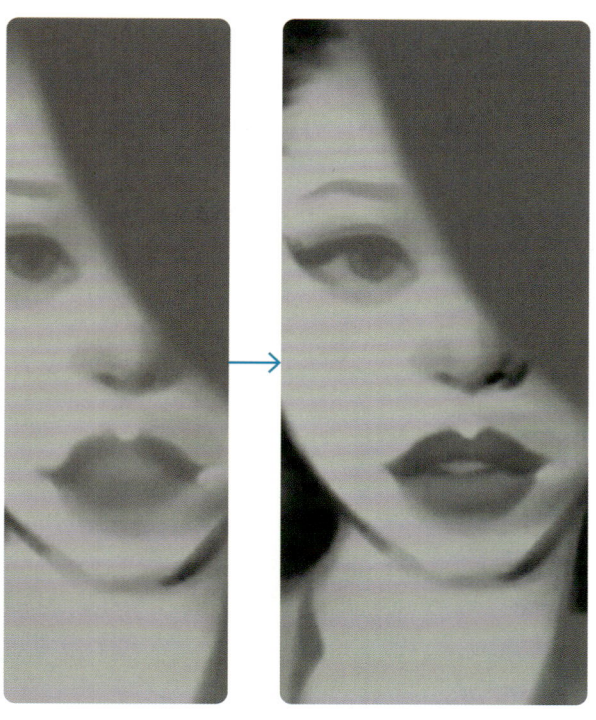

Fleshing Out Details

I zoomed way into my painting so I could get to work rendering key features. I really focused on sculpting the nose and mouth. This was the point in the painting where I started to slow down and enjoy myself. I introduced darker darks so that my painting wouldn't look so flat. As I continued in this way, I gained more and more confidence with the painting.

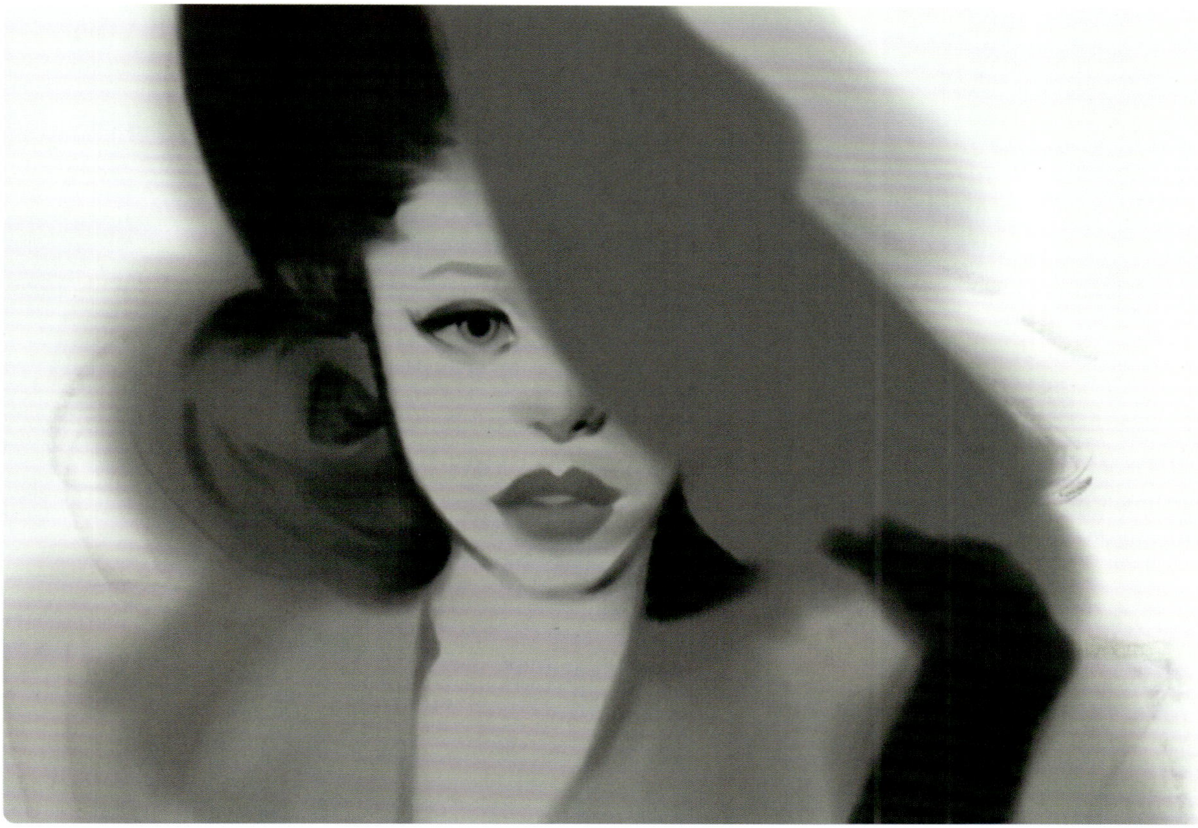

Establishing Contrast

Moving on from the facial features, I knew I needed to add those dark values into the rest of the painting to make it feel cohesive. I darkened the hair and the hat as well as the glove.

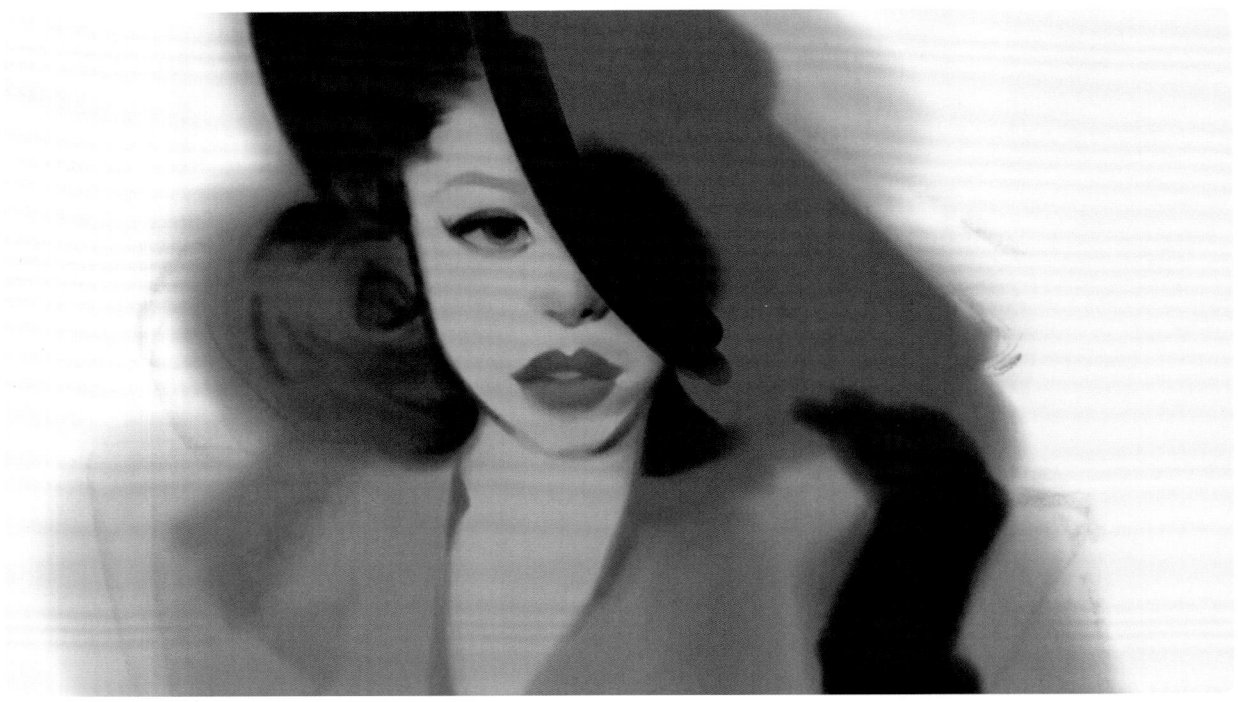

I also used those darker values to sketch in some of the details of the clothing.

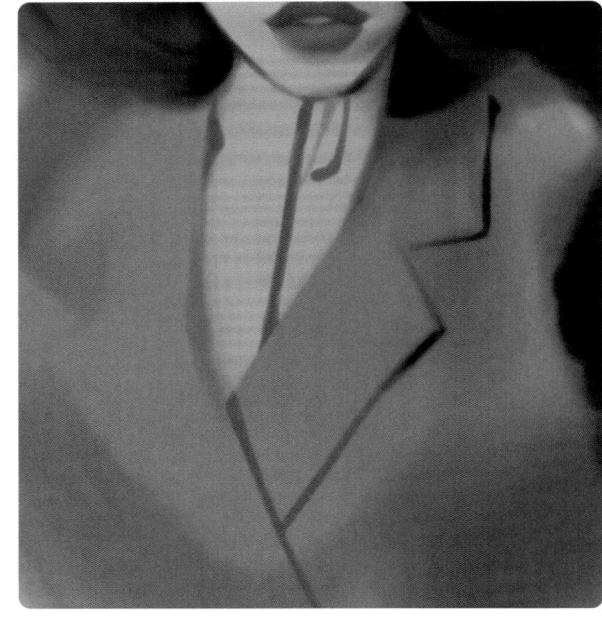

After that, I turned my attention to rendering the hair. I wanted it to feel three-dimensional but not too overdone. I really liked how the face turned out, and I wanted to keep that as the focal point. To me, that meant that the gloved hand, the clothing, and her hair would all need to be rendered simply and maybe even feel somewhat incomplete.

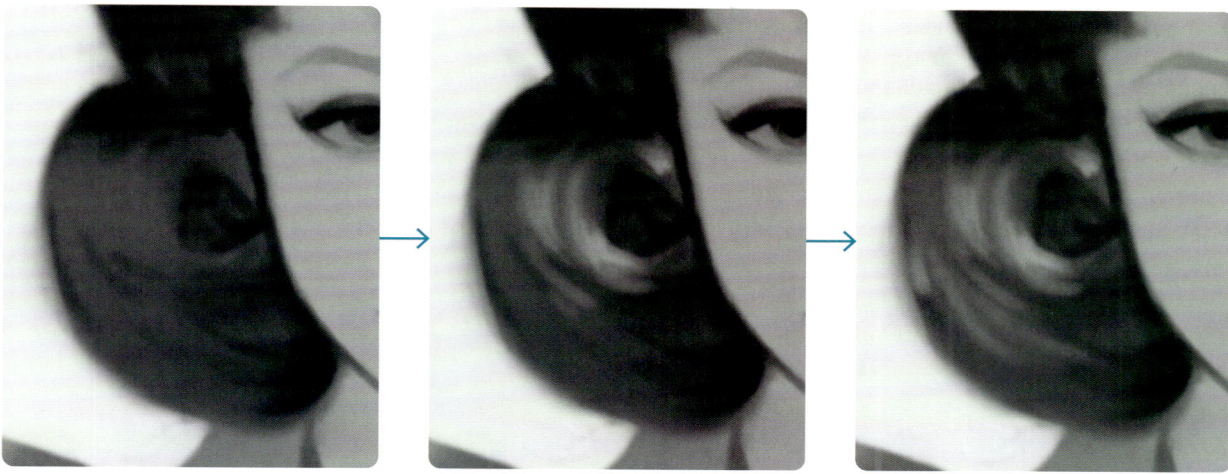

Cleaning Up

The painting was nearly complete, so my last steps were to clean up the edges. Since I used the big fat airbrush to establish my base values at the very start, I had a lot of soft edges I needed to get rid of. On a new layer, I used my soft round brush to carve out the figure and her shadow using a dirty white.

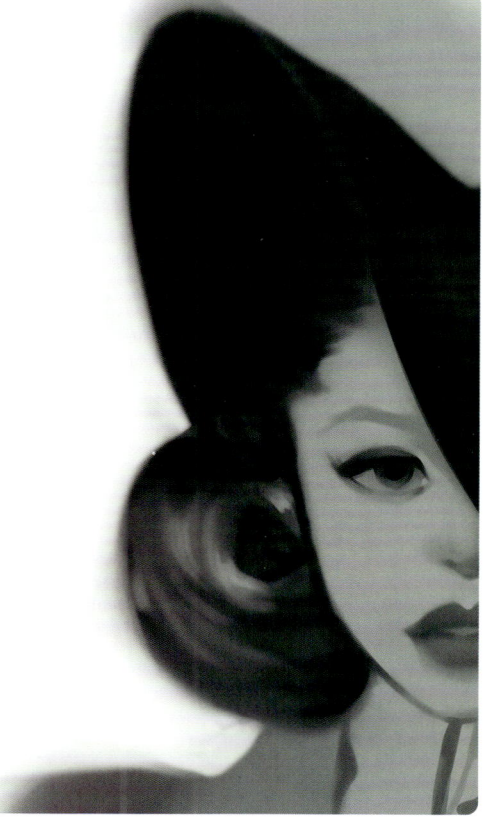

Last-Ditch Experimentation

I have a habit of changing my mind about a painting the moment it's "done." In this case, I started off wanting to paint a simple black-and-white portrait, and by the end of it, I wanted to see her in color!

I duplicated my canvas in case things went horribly wrong, then I grabbed some random purples, pinks, and blues, and gave it a try.

I used all sorts of blend modes, from soft light to divide to multiply. Once I got some colors I was happy with, I used a combination of the eyedropper and color tools to sample and manipulate colors I could then paint with. I used many layers and basically ended up painting over what I had already done in black and white (a very inefficient process that I do not recommend).

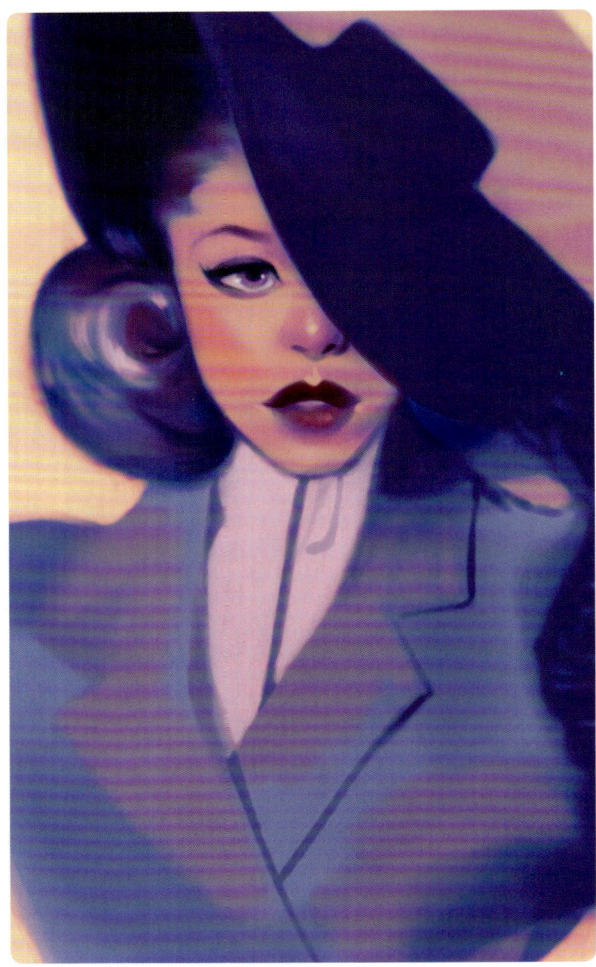

First color attempt

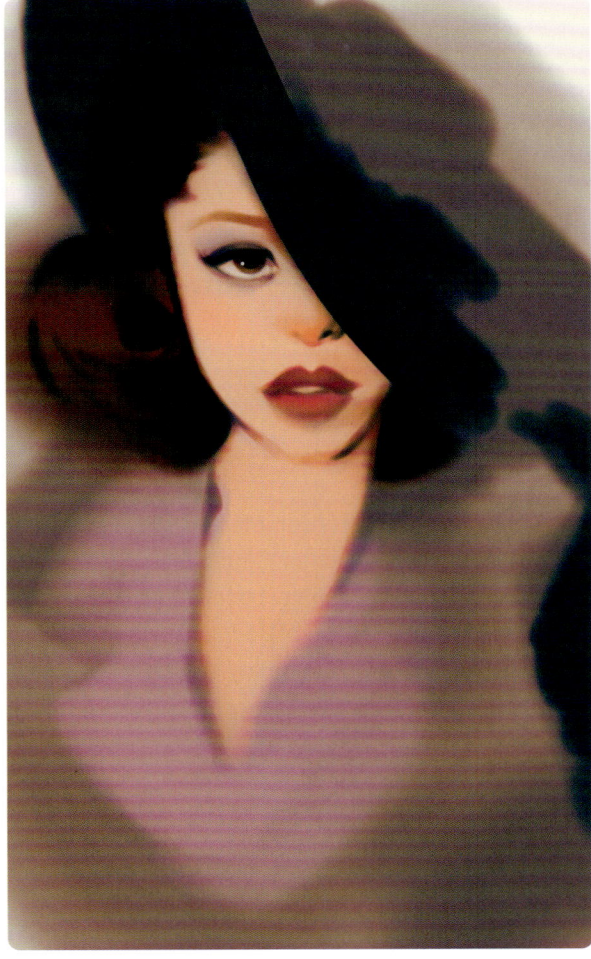

Second color attempt

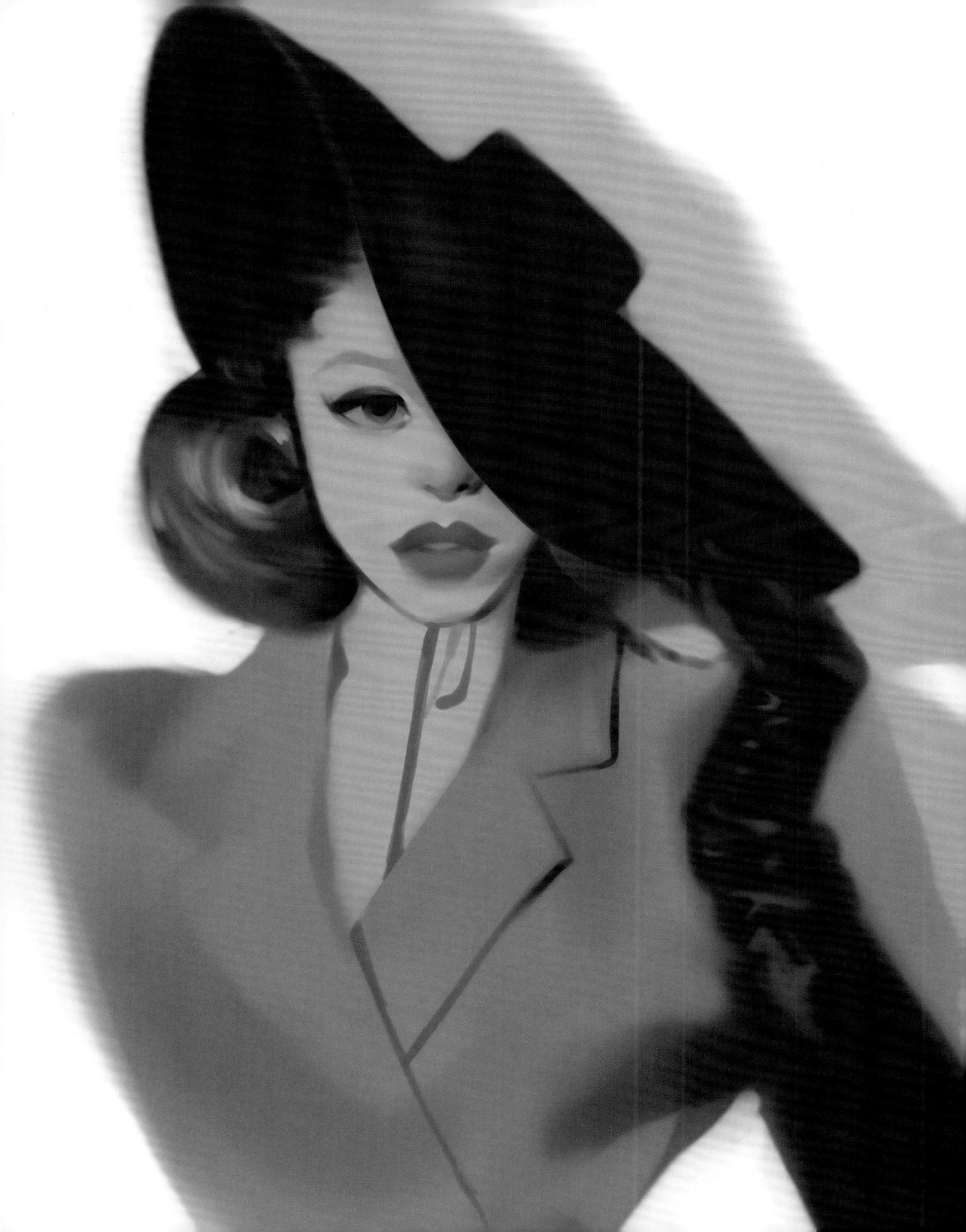

DIRECT TO COLOR

With enough practice, you will be able to paint directly in color.

Painting directly in color is a tougher process and involves a good understanding of color and color relationships. The more you practice color matching, the better you'll become.

When starting to paint in color, I recommend studying bite-sized subject matter. For example, this painting that I did was a simple study. I wanted to paint in color but I didn't want to use the eyedropper tool to sample from my reference. I wanted to practice and hone my own color matching ability. For this reason, I painted just an eye. If I had attempted an entire portrait, I think I would've been easily overwhelmed.

Set yourself up for success by choosing a subject you're interested in and that doesn't feel daunting.

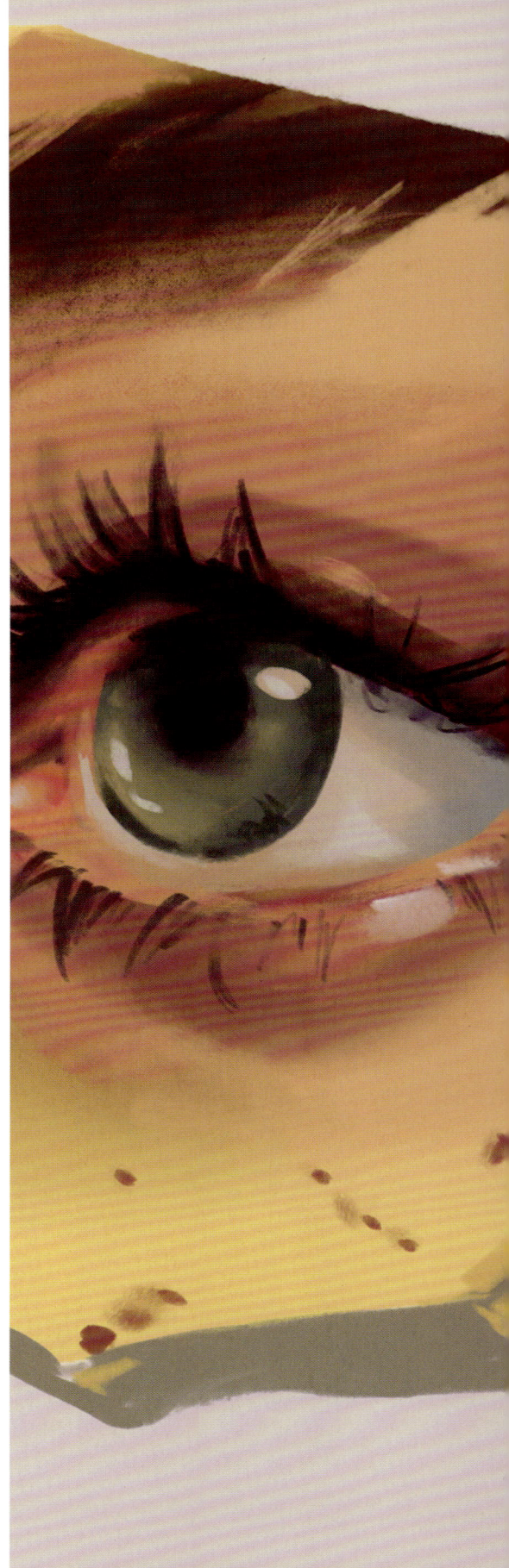

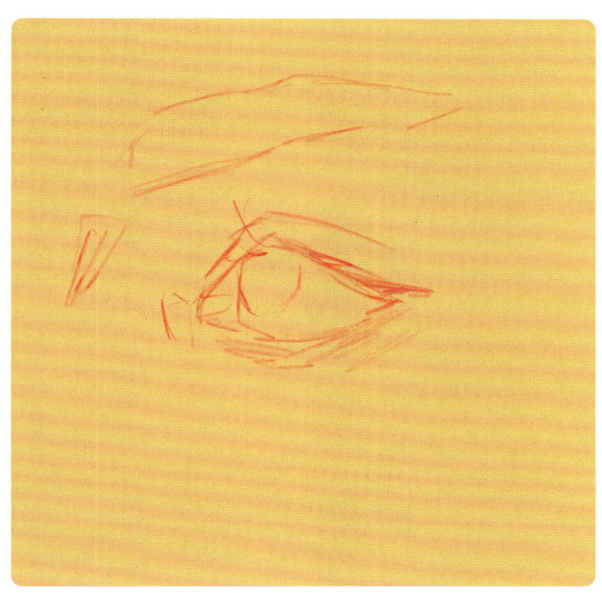

Underdrawing

I created a very simple underdrawing, just enough to get the shape of the eye and placement of the brow in relation. Since I knew I'd be painting directly in color, I figured I'd steer clear of black and white from the get-go. I changed the Background color layer to yellow and sketched using red.

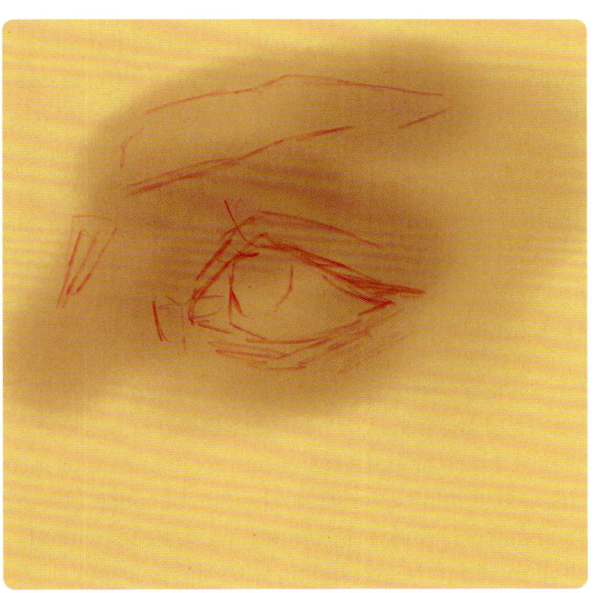

Laying a Foundation of Color

I started to establish a base of colors. On a new layer placed underneath my sketch, I used a large airbrush to loosely add in the average skin tone. I'm following the same process I would use to create a value painting, but this time I'm trying to color match my reference photo instead of painting in grey.

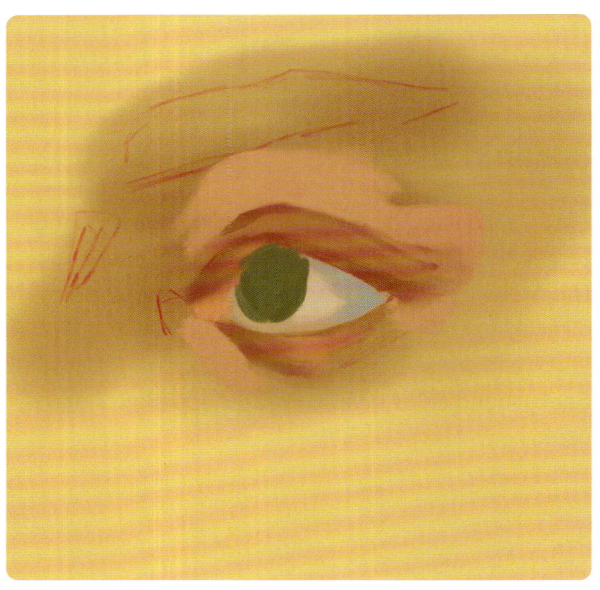 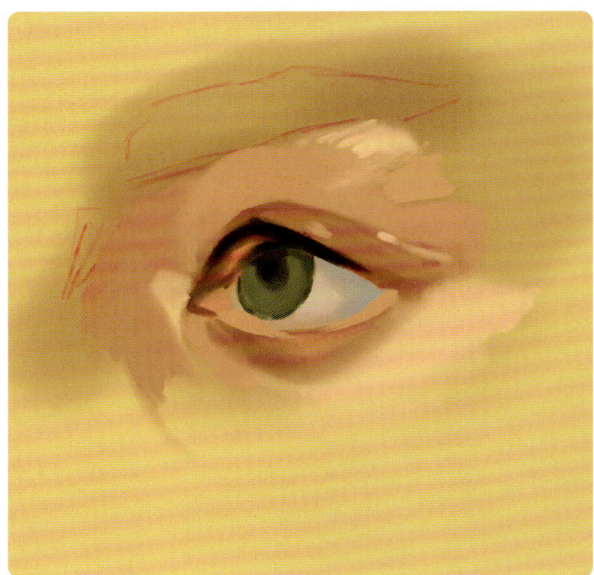

Painting What You See

I created a new layer and started to paint on top of my sketch. Again, I'm trying to color match my reference, which means that I need to paint what I see and stay away from the trap of painting what I know. For example, the whites of our eyes are not usually white due to lighting. The eyelid and eyelashes can cast shadows on the eyeball itself. If you paint the white of the eye using pure white simply because you think it should be white, it'll look strange and inaccurate. Notice that the "white" that I'm using here is actually more of a yellow and I've also introduced a bit of a cool blue for the shadow.

I continue to sculpt the eye with both highlights and shadows. I find that one of the big differences between painting in black and white versus color is that when painting in color, you need to bounce back and forth between the darkest darks and lightest lights of your image. Unlike value painting, it's hard to save the highlights for last because you need to constantly compare your colors against each other for accuracy.

I'm using a textured oil brush for this painting. By nature of the brush, it's hard to blend edges and create a nice smooth transition from one color into the next. I don't mind this, though, because I like the painterly feel. It is something to keep in mind, though; if you're struggling with the painting, maybe switching your brush will help!

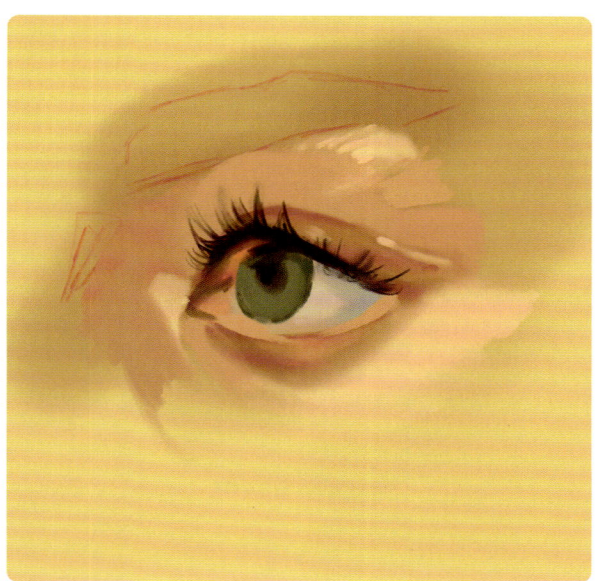

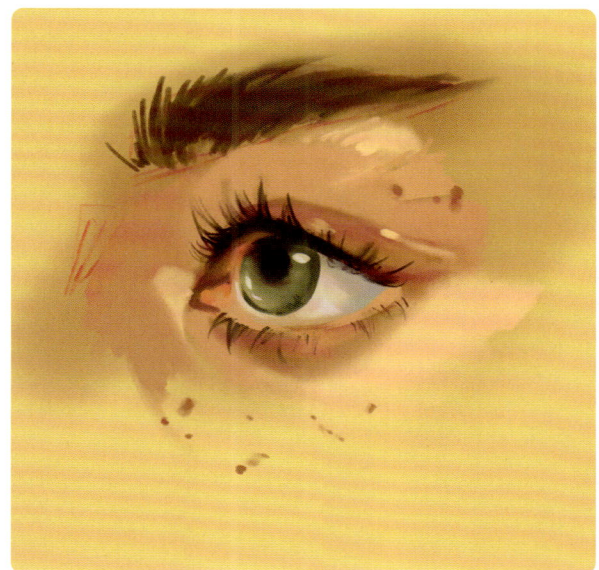

Normally I'd save the small details for the last step, but this time I decided to add them in before I felt anywhere near complete with the painting. The eyeline was looking a bit strange to me, and I wanted to see if it was really just the eyelashes that would make the difference.

When working on a study, don't be afraid to break your own process or try something new. If you can't experiment when studying, when can you? Now is the time to mess around and make new discoveries!

Sometimes the jump from one step to the next looks significant. But in this case, all I've done is add in some freckles, sketched in the eyebrow, and refined the pupil by adding highlights and specular highlights. Not much has actually happened, but the painting is looking like it's much further along now.

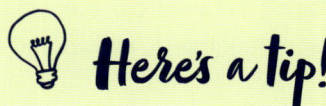 Here's a tip!

Replacing black with a highly saturated dark color (like a very deep blue or red) can be much more interesting than true black in a painting. These deep colors create a richness and vibrancy that black alone can lack.

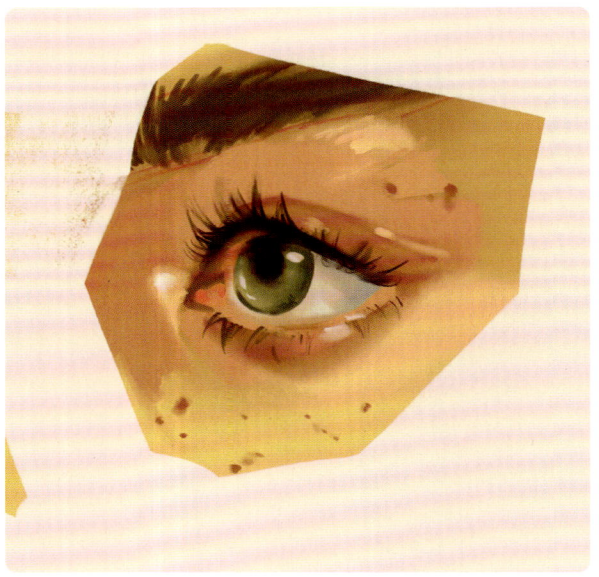

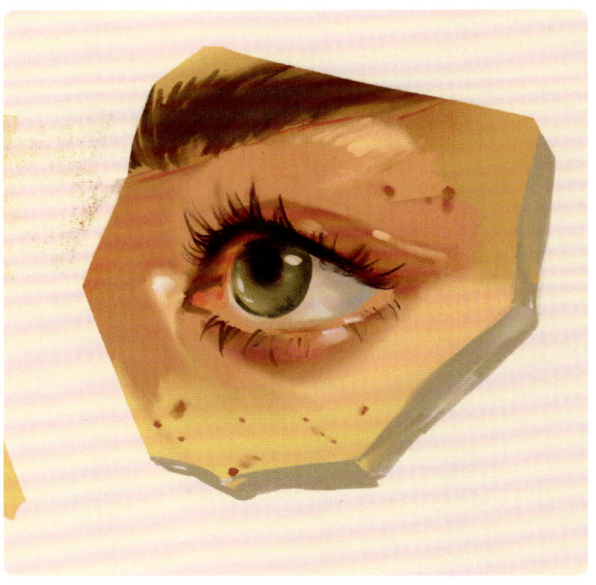

I decided that I didn't like all the space around the eye. It's just a lot of yellow, unpainted canvas. To change it up a bit and make the painting look more intentional, I created a new layer, took a large brush, and blocked out whatever I didn't want to see with light pink.

I then took a desaturated, earthy color and used it to paint in an edge. This edge makes it look as though the eye was part of a statue that was shattered.

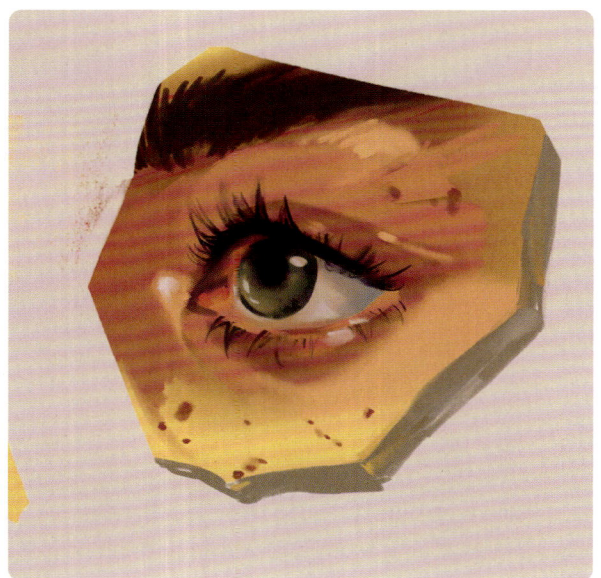

After taking a moment to observe my own work, I figure that overall, the painting is too yellow and it lacks contrast. I used *Color Balance* to subtly alter the highlights, midtones, and shadows so that they skewed a bit more in the direction of red and blue.

After making that final color adjustment, I went back in with my paintbrush for last touch-ups. These included softening the eyebrow, blending out some of the harsher highlights, and adding a bit of eyeliner.

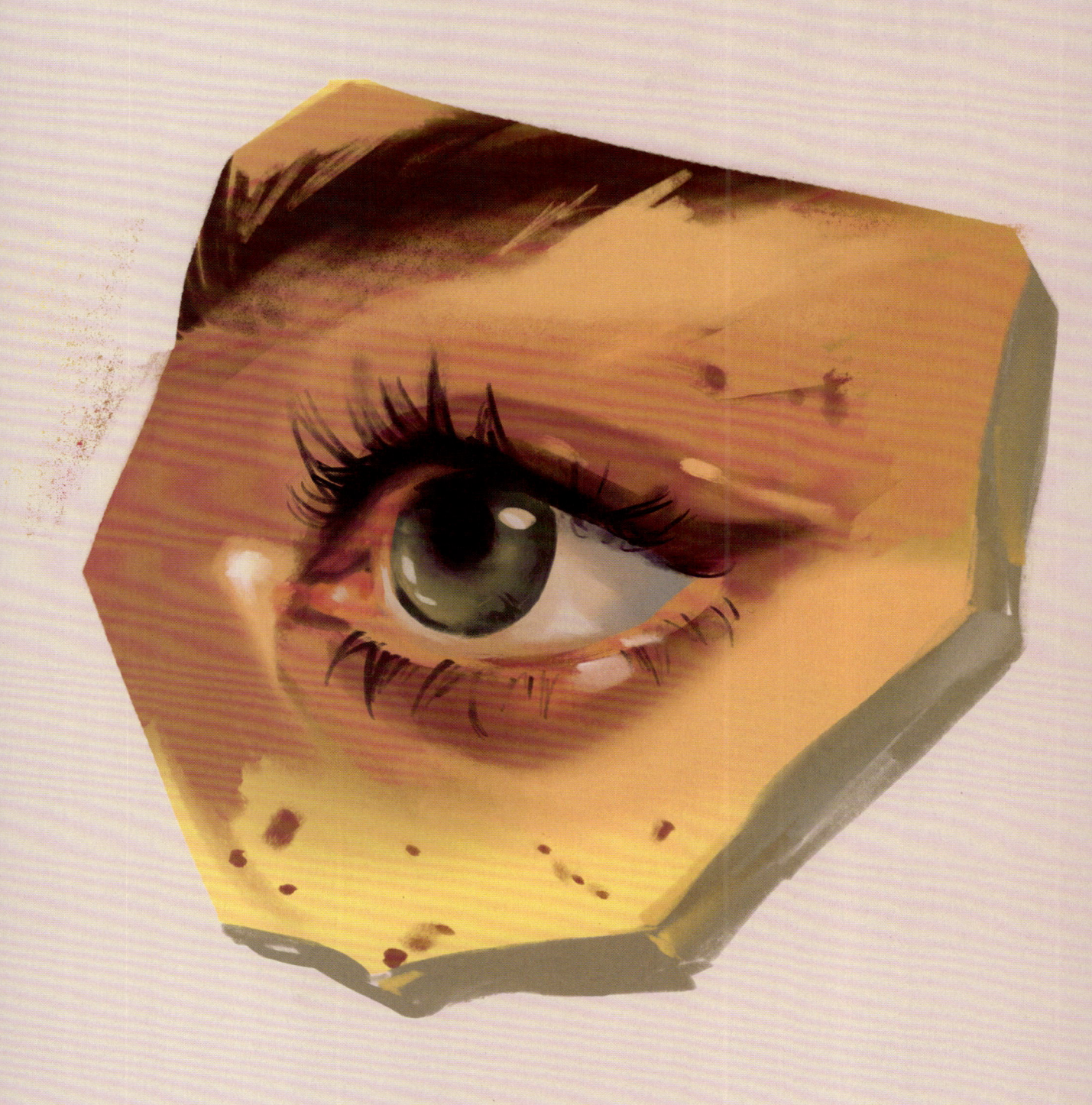

INDEX

About the Author

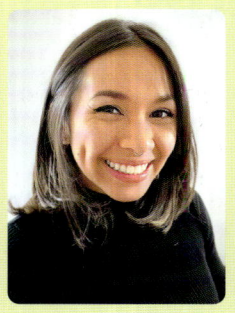

Illustrator, designer, and author Melissa de Nobrega has helped over 20,000 students improve their artwork through her online art classes. Her new book, *Portraits with Procreate: A Beginner's Guide to Drawing and Painting Faces*, delivers her gentle teaching style in a non-digital format.

Melissa works from her home in Toronto, Ontario, and is the creator of makebetter.art, an online resource for budding and amateur artists who want to...well, make better art. Access classes and other resources at makebetter.art or by following her on instagram @melissadn.art.